SOCIAL THEORY FOR BEGINNERS

Paul Ransome

'Bear in mind, Sir Henry, one of the phrases in that queer old legend which Dr Mortimer read to us and avoid the moor in those hours of darkness when the powers of evil are exalted.'

(Sir Arthur Conan Doyle, *The Hound of the Baskervilles*, London: George Newnes, 1902)

This edition published in Great Britain in 2010 by

The Policy Press
University of Bristol
Fourth Floor
Beacon House
Queen's Road
Bristol BS8 1QU
UK

t: +44 (0)117 331 4054
f: +44 (0)117 331 4093
e: tpp-info@bristol.ac.uk
www.policypress.co.uk

North American office:
The Policy Press
c/o International Specialized Books Services
920 NE 58th Avenue, Suite 300
Portland, OR 97213-3786, USA
t: +1 503 287 3093
f: +1 503 280 8832
e: info@isbs.com

British Library Cataloguing in Publication Data
A catalogue record for this book is available from the British Library.

Library of Congress Cataloging-in-Publication Data
A catalog record for this book has been requested.

ISBN 978 1 84742 674 1 paperback
ISBN 978 1 84742 675 8 hardcover

Cover design by The Policy Press
Front cover: image kindly supplied by www.alamy.com
Printed and bound in Great Britain by Hobbs, Southampton

OUTLINE CONTENTS

DETAILED CONTENTS

LIST OF FIGURES

PREFACE AND ACKNOWLEDGEMENTS

Social theory and sociological theory attempt to provide coherent explanations of human social action as it takes place in the context of other social actors and their actions and with the help or hindrance of the social practices and institutions that surround them. This book is about trying to explain those explanations to social actors who, despite being active social theorists in their own daily lives, have an interest in knowing more about the kinds of explanations offered by social theorists.

If you already have a working knowledge of social theory this book is not written for you. If you are reviewing the book to see if it is suitable for the students you teach then why not buy a copy or two and ask them what they think about it? As an anonymous philosopher once said, 'Those who have knowledge forfeit the capacity for ignorance.'

I would like to acknowledge the help of Karen Bowler and her colleagues at The Policy Press who have supported what is an ambitious project both in the writing and in the production. Most of all I thank my wife, Harriet, and children, Alfred and Willow, who tolerated my need to write this book. In answer to their refrain 'Haven't you finished that bloody book yet?', I can finally answer 'Almost!'

PER, January 2010

INTRODUCTION

Who is this book for and how do I use it?

This book has been written for people who need to know more about social theory and sociological theory but who have not yet had a chance to develop that knowledge. If you do already have a detailed knowledge of the subject then, for the same reason that Pelé and Ronaldo don't need books about 'perfect ball control', you don't need to read this book.

> **This introduction describes:**
>
> Practical organisation of the material.
>
> Intellectual organisation of the material.

Practical organisation of the material

The information in this book is divided into a number of different chapters. Each chapter is divided again into shorter sections. Throughout each chapter information boxes and headings are provided that are designed to help you find your way around, to highlight the key points and to practise what we have been preaching.

To find the general location of the information you need, you should first look at the *Contents* page at the front of the book and possibly at the *Index* of names and subjects at the end of the book. Having found the right chapter you should turn to the *information box* at the start of that chapter. Here you will find a more specific summary of what that chapter contains. Each chapter begins with a contents box (just like the one above) to show you what the chapter contains. At the end of each chapter there is a *key points box* itemising the most essential information covered in that chapter. This box will help you *review* the material you have just been reading.

In order to help you understand what part the authors, concepts and ideas described in that chapter have played in the development of social theory, there are also a number of *practice boxes*. These are simple suggestions about how you could practise some of the ideas for yourself. For example, in Chapter Three, *Émile Durkheim and the coming of industrial society*, one of the practice suggestions is to imagine how your daily routine differs from that of your great-grandparents in terms of the technology you use. Thinking about the answer to this question requires you to reflect on just how much we now depend on technology. It is difficult to imagine what our lives would now be like *without* technology. To put it the other way around, contemporary society is quite different from society a hundred years ago *because of* the levels of technology it contains.

Two other kinds of help – Glossary and links

Social theory often contains words and phrases that have a specialist meaning for social theorists. To help you 'crack the code' of social theory, a list of important definitions is provided in the Glossary at the end of the book. To illustrate, we have just been talking about functionalist approaches to social theory. Chapter Seven contains a full definition of **functionalism** but for quick reference you can look up the short definition of the word in the Glossary: **Functionalism.** An **abstract** approach in **social theory** that describes the various institutions and practices of society in terms of how they function to the benefit of society or the *social system* as a whole'.

It is also worth checking the Glossary for words that, although they have a common usage, have a specialist usage as well. For example, we have just used the word 'practice' in the phrase 'practices of society'. This word generally means the way something is usually done as in 'it is normal practice to read the book before writing the essay'. **Social practice** also has a specialist meaning in social theory to describe routines of behaviour that have become characteristic of that particular society. Social practices are inscribed into people's behaviour a bit like well-trodden footpaths in the countryside. Social practices become the normal or expected way of doing things.

The second kind of practical help reflects the fact that although authors, ideas and concepts can be grouped together reasonably neatly, often there are important *linkages* between one topic or issue in one part of the book and other topics and issues in other parts of it. When a particular concept or idea is discussed in another part of the book, or when it would be especially useful to know about related ideas and concepts, a brief cross-referencing note '*see also*' is provided to help you follow these links.

Intellectual organisation of the material

The other crucial dimension is how the material is organised in an intellectual sense. Getting the information you need about social theory is a necessary first step but on its own is not sufficient if you really want to understand something about social theory. We know, for example, that modern industrial societies today are characterised by the use of information technology, but how do we *explain* the circumstances by which this situation came about? What are the likely *consequences* of living in an information–intensive society? Who *benefits* from it and who does not? In addition, then, to having things organised properly around the various chapters and sections of the book, we also need a way of combining authors, ideas and concepts so that we actually understand something about social theory and not just gather up a few of its ingredients.

In this book we have organised things so that the content of each chapter not only describes the basic subject matter, but presents the information with clear reference to the particular *contexts* in which social theory has been developing. The three main types of context we will be referring to are:

- the *historical* context;
- the *intellectual* context of key authors, ideas and concepts;
- how concepts and ideas are played out in the context of social theory *as a whole*.

Sometimes the historical context is most important if, for example, a piece of theory develops directly in response to practical developments or innovations in society (was there such a thing as globalisation before the invention of the internet?). Sometimes it is the intellectual context that matters most because very often new ideas and concepts come directly from the individual work of particular authors (was there such a thing as the subconscious before Sigmund Freud?). Sometimes it is the position of an idea or concept in the context of social theory as a whole that is most important and especially so if a piece of theory results in a general change in intellectual trends (what is the difference between structuralism and post-structuralism?).

Practice box:

➲ Try looking up the subject 'discourse' in the index and contents page.

➲ Turn to the chapter that is mostly about 'discourse' and then find the section on Michel Foucault.

➲ What is the first key definition in that section? Check the short definition of **discourse** and of **épistème** in the Glossary.

We are now ready to look a little more deeply into the *subject matter* of social theory. In order to do this we must first think about what social theory is all about. Fortunately, this is the topic of the next chapter.

CHAPTER ONE

WHAT IS SOCIAL THEORY?

In this chapter we will be looking at:

The main *elements* of social theory

The *subject matter* of social theory

The *main themes* of social theory

The main *purposes* of social theory

Straight away we should note that although we will generally refer in this book to social theory rather than to sociological theory (and to **social theorists** rather than to **sociologists**) the two have a great deal in common. There is no need to impose a firm distinction between them. This issue is discussed in more detail in the final section of this chapter.

The main elements of social theory

At its simplest, and taking the words literally, **social theory** is the name given to theories about the human social world. Social theory is the body of knowledge about the nature of **social action** and the various contexts in which it takes place. Although social theory could be about any kind of society it is generally taken as referring to society in the *modern industrialised Western world*. Although social theory is not just a theory of **capitalist society**, because all of the societies in the industrialised West are characterised by the capitalist economic system in which goods and services are produced and exchanged for the purpose of generating profit, social theory always develops in relation to this key aspect of the social and historical context. The processes of **industrialisation, rationalisation** and capitalism are the key themes that modern social theorists have sought to explain. Clearly we need some explanation of these specific terms.

What is modern *society?*

The term **modern society** is used chronologically to distinguish societies that have formed more recently and continue to exist, from earlier kinds of ancient or pre-modern societies, which no longer exist. It is generally agreed by people working in the social sciences that the modern period began during the last decades of the 18th century around 1760. This is the period when mechanised forms of production emerged starting a process that became known as the Industrial Revolution.

The designation 'modern' is not just about chronology, but about differences between one *type* of society and another. Modern society is not just modern because it is the most recent kind (and we will be discussing the possibility of an even more recent form called postmodern society in Chapter Thirteen) but because it has features and characteristics *that make it modern.* A society that does not have these features would not be described by social theorists as modern no matter when it occurred in history, and even if it is still current today.

A further important aspect of the notion of modern society is that it refers to the kind of *intellectual outlook*, the world view, **beliefs** and expectations of the social actors living in it. To be a modern person means having ideas and expectations that are of the present day or which keep up with current notions and beliefs. In the same way that different aspects of technology and production come to be associated with particular kinds of society (or modes of economic production as Karl Marx puts it), so societies also come to be associated with particular ideas, outlooks and expectations. One society can be distinguished from another in terms of the different outlooks of the social actors living there.

What is industrial *society?*

The most important criterion used by social theorists in designating a society as modern is that they are **industrial societies**, that is, societies in which a significant proportion of the commodities that social actors consume are produced using machines. In industrial society, the wheels of industry are literally no longer turned by humans or by animals but by mechanical sources of power. The *types* of motive power (waterwheel, steam, internal combustion engine, nuclear power), the *scale* of industry (local workshops, medium- then large-scale factory production, globally organised production) and the *level* of technology (machines that assist manual production, machines that substitute for manual production, fully-automated production) are all constituent elements of industrial working.

Industrialisation is a process that moves forward as technical knowledge increases and as private investors or governments are able to supply sufficient capital to apply new innovations to the actual processes of work. Industrialisation began with the mechanisation of spinning and weaving tasks from around 1750 (hence the popular choice of 1760 as the start of the modern period), it moved on as more and more workers were concentrated into larger workshops and factories during the 19th century, and on again with the introduction of mass production techniques in the early 20th century. A second industrial revolution took place during the 1970s and 1980s as industrial working changed again to take advantage of the development of powerful and flexible computer-based technologies. A leading slogan of the time 'smaller, faster, cheaper, better' neatly captures the revolutionary potential of these new information and communications technologies (ICTs).

Today, the phrase **post-industrial society** is often used to emphasise that, for many people living in the West (see later), work has shifted away from heavy industrial tasks and manufacture towards personal, social and financial services. The heavy industrial tasks still need to be done, but in the age of globally organised production (*see* **globalisation**), they have been taken over by people in the developing world. We are still enthusiastic consumers of commodities produced industrially, often in other parts of the world, but the cutting edge of post-industrial work in the affluent West is dominated by communication and information technologies.

Industrialisation is not just about the different techniques used to produce things it is also about the general impact of ways of working, types and arrangements of employment on the nature of society as a whole. We will be exploring these issues more thoroughly when we look at theories of industrial society in Chapter Three, and especially Karl Marx's analysis of capitalist society in Chapter Four, but we can note here that one society can be distinguished from another not just in terms of different types of production, but in terms of the *way of life* that goes along with each type. Following Marx, many social theorists distinguish modern capitalist society from feudal society not just because things were produced differently in feudal society, but because the whole way of life was different. Why was it different? Because techniques of production required changes in the way that paid work was organised. For example, modern industrial society is characteristically urban rather than rural because factory-based systems of production require highly concentrated centres of population that are not found in the sparsely populated countryside. The introduction of factory production caused a shifting of the population away from the countryside and into new industrial towns and cities. Correspondingly, feudal society is characterised by a more widely dispersed rural population and has relatively few large towns or cities.

Also significant, especially for Marx, are the property relations that accompany the process of technological innovation. Capitalist society is different from feudal society because, within capitalism, the ownership of capital critically divides the population between those who own and control the **means of production** and those who, having no capital of their own, are obliged to work for them often under very poor working conditions. Technological innovation is thus not just about new kinds of machines and the style of working they require but also about wider social **relations of production**.

What is Western *society?*

For social theorists 'Western' means especially the geographical region occupied by Northern Europe and North America. Invoking the criterion that modern society is always industrial society, 'Western' also includes Central and Eastern Europe (countries that developed during the 20th century under the influence of the Soviet Union), Canada, Australia and New Zealand.

In addition to these regions, and emphasising the intellectual and cultural characteristics of modern society, 'Western' is also taken to include societies, even if they might be located in the geographical East, which have or are developing under the industrial and cultural influence of the industrialised West. Many societies around the Pacific Rim, whether they are newly industrialised (such as Malaysia, Thailand or Indonesia), or whether they have been industrialised for some time (like Japan, South Korea, Taiwan and Singapore), are categorised by social theorists as 'Western societies' in the sense that many of the people who live there aspire to, or have adopted, a Western outlook rather than the eastern outlook that is characteristic of their geographical region.

▸▸ Although we must leave this interesting topic for the time being, there are a number of very important questions here about whether global society as a whole is converging towards the Western model, and how and why the Western culture and outlook has become globally dominant. Some societies geographically located in the Middle-East (for example Syria or Kuwait) could be categorised as 'modern' or 'modernising' on the grounds of being at least partly industrialised. Other ambiguities arise if a society remains largely rural despite having some large urban, industrial centres (for example Argentina or Nigeria). These questions are addressed in Chapter Fourteen where we look at what social theorists have to say about the global dimensions of modern society.

The subject matter of social theory

The essential subject matter of social theory is human **society** and the social activities that go on there. Social theorists are not particularly interested in animal behaviour (this is what zoologists do), nor are they specifically interested in the environmental and atmospheric conditions in which human social action takes place (that would be called geography). They might not be terribly interested in the clinical aspects of the human mind and individual features of personality (this is the terrain of psychiatry and **psychology**). For social theorists, the challenge is to develop coherent knowledge of human social action as it takes place in the context of other social actors and their actions, and with the help or hindrance of the social practices and institutions that surround them.

For social theorists and sociologists it is the social context of action that matters not the predispositions of any particular individual. It is patterns of social interaction between social actors and how these are affected by social contexts that is the focus of their attention. Social theory is all about identifying and describing the elements that make up social interaction (social actors, contexts, practices), and developing sensible propositions about the dynamic processes that take place between them.

ILLUSTRATION

We can illustrate this way of defining social theory by using the example of people attending a football match. While there might be passing interest in the condition of the pitch and the weather, the real interest for the social theorist and sociologist is in describing and accounting for the complex patterns of behaviour that can be observed between people in the stadium. Each spectator remains an individual and has a slightly different perception of the match, but this experience cannot be separated from the *collective event* they have been participating in. Equally, although in one sense there can be no collective social interaction without individuals, the game on the pitch, the reaction of the crowd and the interventions of officials each contribute to an event that is *far greater than* the sum of its individual parts. The event spills over beyond the capacity of any particular individual's understanding of it. Similarly the actions performed by players, officials and spectators follow routines and convey meanings and emotions that are not controlled by any of those individual participants; they are features of the social situation itself. It is the nature of these beyond-the-individual phenomena, and especially the patterns and regularities that characterise them, which social theorists and sociologists are interested in.

The main themes of social theory

When we talk about the main themes of social theory or sociological theory we are referring to the main lines of enquiry, the principal issues and arguments that social theorists use in order to understand the social subject matter. They provide an intellectual map or set of problems that social theorists use in doing their work. Although there are overlaps between the themes of social theory and the themes of other academic territories such as philosophy, psychology or history it is the selection of particular core issues, and the central debates associated with them, which give social theory and sociological theory their distinct role and character.

The *order* in which social theorists might list the central themes of social theory (and indeed which items they might choose to include) is itself another area of debate among social theorists. In looking at the list as we have constructed it here, it would be useful to keep an open mind and think of each theme as no more or less important than any of the others. One of the easiest ways of distinguishing one social theorist from another is to identify which themes they concentrate on in *their* work. How would *they* construct a list of the central themes of social theory? This is one of the strategies we will be using in comparing and contrasting the various schools of thought in social theory in the following chapters. The themes we want to include in our list initially are:

- The struggle for necessary resources
- Power
- Ideas, beliefs and values
- Action and structure
- Micro versus macro analysis
- Models of social change (conflict and continuity)

The struggle for necessary resources

As we noted in the previous chapter the struggle for necessary resources is a feature of all kinds of society. Attempts to organise this struggle in a more cooperative way (people working together rather than separately to manage their survival) is one way of accounting for the emergence of society in the first place. It is quite common to describe society in terms of the prevailing form of cooperative productive activity that takes place within it. We conveniently describe many societies today as industrial societies because most necessary production takes the form of one or other kind of industrial process. Even modern agriculture is described as 'industrial' on account of the large-scale prairie farming techniques and highly streamlined rearing of livestock commonly used. Other kinds of society can be described as 'hunter-gatherer', 'pastoralist' or 'agrarian' because of the kind of cooperative productive activity used there.

Whatever the type, however, the bottom line is that people seek out ways to survive and, depending on how successfully they are able to do this, to live comfortably within the limits set by the natural and social conditions where they live. The quality of productive cooperation provides an important measure of the extent to which social actors can gain access to the resources they need in order to survive and prosper. A major preoccupation for social theorists is to understand as much as they can about how the struggle for resources takes place within society, which factors have the greatest impact upon it, and who are the winners and who are the losers. Even in societies that have the highest levels of cooperative productive activity (perhaps because they are the most technologically advanced), and where significant parts of the population could be described as affluent, other parts remain relatively poor. What causes access to resources, and the distribution of resources within a society, to become unequal?

Power

Although it is notoriously difficult to define, many social theorists would agree that **power** is closely tied to the struggle for resources. The more there is at stake in a particular situation the greater will be the quantity of the phenomenon we are calling 'power' potentially involved. If there is little at stake then the issue of power might not arise at all. A strong notion of power equates it with the idea of force. In this definition power is defined as the capacity to cause somebody to act (or to prevent them from acting) against their will. If force affects their ability to get access to necessary resources, than clearly this kind of power could ultimately jeopardise their survival. In capitalist society, for example, the majority of the population does not own the means of production and is therefore obliged to sell their capacity to work to an employer. The employer has power over the employees in the sense that they control access to work and the way that work is carried out. The only other sources of income available in capitalist society are private wealth, social benefits or criminal activity.

More subtle is the idea that power refers to a capacity to get other people to act differently by making them change their minds about something. In this definition power is more to do with persuasion rather than sheer force. Hegemony is an influential example of this version of the concept of power, which sees the exercise of power or authority operating through a combination of the threat of force supplemented by efforts to get the subject population to agree to act in particular ways.

▶▶ These and other ideas put forward by the Italian Marxist social theorist Antonio Gramsci are discussed in Chapter Eight.

The different forms of power found in society could be seen as manifestations of the different kinds of resources that social actors seek access to. Power takes different forms depending on the kinds of resources that are at stake. Economic resources and thus 'economic power' are certainly among the most important. Other resources, such as access to information, being able to contribute to the political process, being treated equally in society and, at a more individual level, the capacity to live as you want to live, all constitute different kinds of power. The kind of power that parents exercise over their children is not the same as the kind of power that governments exercise over the population but there might be interesting similarities between the two. For social theorists, society is itself a mechanism for the exercise of power since many forms of power can only be exercised in the context of social relationships.

Putting this the other way around, social theorists are especially interested in those social practices and institutions that give rise to different social contexts of power. For example, we might be particularly interested in the kinds of power associated with different kinds of political system. There are likely to be differences in the form of political power as it appears in a democratic system compared with forms found in a dictatorship. Moreover, political power in constitutional democracies, which have a written constitution (like France or the US), is likely to be different from political power in constitutional monarchies (like the UK), which have monarchies and no written constitution. We might want to ask what the characteristics of republican political systems are that give rise to this particular variant of political power.

Society also provides the context for the exercise of power in a further important sense, which is that it is in society that many of the different forms of power come together. For example, the struggle for individual autonomy, that is, the desire to act freely, is obviously bound up with access to economic resources (economic power), freedom of association (political power) and freedom from the beliefs of other people (ideological power). Each of these forms of power might be overlaid by another form that is uniquely found in human society, which is the power of the cultural milieu in which social action takes place. In many social contexts, access to and control over cultural resources is one of the most important forms of power and is highly valued.

Ideas, beliefs and values

This mention of cultural resources and cultural power brings us to a third important focus of debate in social theory and sociological theory, which is the impact of people's thoughts and ideas on how they act. There are a number of ways of looking at this issue and, because ideas and beliefs belong to society and not to individual social actors, social theorists are particularly interested in them.

The big picture

Looking at things philosophically, there is a fundamental question of whether social actors can make sense at all of the physical world around them unless they have an intellectual and conceptual vocabulary that allows them to do so. If social actors construct an understanding of those actions by means of thoughts and ideas, then clearly it is important to understand where these ideas have come from, how social actors become aware of them and how people incorporate them into their way of seeing the world. The very possibility of cooperative social action presupposes that social actors not only have the capacity to actively interpret the world around them but that they do so using the same ideas and beliefs as their fellow social actors. As noted earlier, society can be classified in a geographical and historical sense but it is also classifiable in terms of the set of ideas and beliefs that social actors living in it have in common.

▸▸   The importance of language and its involvement in how people understand and think about reality is widely acknowledged in social theory. This topic is discussed extensively in Chapter Nine.

Motivation

A second approach is to ask what is the role of ideas and beliefs as a source of motivation for social action? While much of social action is motivated by practical considerations necessary for survival it might also express needs and desires of a more abstract or esoteric kind. For example, the satisfaction a pianist gets from playing a piano is partly to do with the fact that he can later sell the performance and thus pay the bills, but it is also to do with more esoteric considerations like expressing creativity and individuality. These aspects of social action appear to express needs that originate from within the mind or personality of the social actor.

As we will be discussing in more detail in relation to the work of Max Weber in Chapter Five, it is not possible properly to understand social action without thinking about the **values** or **value system** that social actors are trying to express through their actions. Sometimes these values are based on religious beliefs (the idea of doing one's religious duty); sometimes they are based on political beliefs (perhaps the democratic ideals of freedom of expression and representation); and sometimes on general philosophical beliefs (perhaps the **humanist** belief in respect for others). Max Weber was especially interested in how the conduct of everyday matters such as business relationships and working practices are also shaped by the kinds of values that social actors seek to express. He suggested, for example, that what makes modern capitalism 'modern' (as distinct from earlier non-modern forms of profit making based on the exchange of commodities) is the way it was shaped by the adoption among the business and entrepreneurial classes of Northern Europe of a new form of **economic rationality**. This modern rationality fosters a belief in the virtue of making precise calculations about what actions are necessary to achieve particular ends. In business activity, being able to predict accurately what profits can be made depends on making precise assessments of the costs of production. Random factors such as fate and chance are discounted because they lie outside the new regime of calculation. The general attitude towards social activity thus becomes increasingly oriented around the values of calculation and instrumentality.

Society-wide beliefs

A third approach is to consider what kind of **belief system** characterises the whole of society. We noted in our definition of Western society earlier in this chapter, for example, that an important part of the Western world view is that it incorporates a Christian outlook. Although this does not mean that all social actors in the modern industrial West are practising Christians, or that all the ideas, values and beliefs of that society originated in Christianity, it does mean that many of the values that social actors living in those societies are most familiar with, and which they might refer to in making sense of their actions, can be associated more or less closely with a Christian outlook. The same social-theoretical principle of society-wide belief systems can be applied in examining the nature of social action in non-Western societies where the prevailing world view might draw on Islam, Buddhism, Hinduism, Confucianism and so on.

The prevailing value system of society as a whole provides social actors with sets of ideas for making sense of and legitimating many aspects of their motivation and behaviour. Differences between one kind of political system and another illustrate how general attitudes and expectations towards political organisation and representation also contribute to the world view of that society. One of the leading characteristics normally associated with modern society, is the presence of a **liberal** political outlook based on the principles of universal representation and freedom of political expression. This **pluralist** attitude ('plural' in the sense that a number of different views exist side by side) also underpins (at least in principle) a tolerant attitude towards diversity and difference. The general parameters within which social action takes place are significantly different in a society that has a liberal or open view of gender roles, of sexuality, of cultural and religious diversity, than they are in a society which does not. One of the most important points to grasp about value systems, and again something that Max Weber emphasises in his social theory, is that in and of themselves it is not possible to rank one value system 'above' or 'below' another. All one can do is consider the practical outcomes of those values as they are expressed in social action.

Action and structure

This and the next theme (the micro–macro debate) are really to do with the kinds of *strategies* that social theorists have come up with in trying to understand the nature of social action in social contexts and practices. They are part of the tool kit of social theory as much as they are part of its subject matter. The first of these strategies is to question the extent to which social actors are free to act according to their own goals and desires, and the extent to which the range of actions available to them is already determined by social practices and institutions. The action–structure debate is one of the longest running puzzles of social theory and we shall have a good deal to say about it in the following chapters.

The dilemma faced by social theorists here is that while there is a strong desire to believe that social actors really are able to act autonomously, to be individuals and to enjoy free expression (beliefs which are central to the liberal **humanist** value system just referred to), nearly all of the resources required to achieve these things come from outside the individual, that is, from society. We should not therefore underestimate the extent to which social context imposes itself on social actors as they seek out the resources they need and want. At the very least, social actors have to negotiate with others, and find ways of tackling the institutions and practices of society, in order to fulfil their aspirations. To the extent that social actors learn to frame their expectations within the limits of what can be achieved, this frame becomes a structure that limits their action. Some social theorists take this line even further and argue that the desires and expectations of social actors are entirely imposed upon them by the social structure; that social actors do little more than act out roles and behaviours that have already been set out for them by society.

Regarding the actual words 'action' and 'structure', although the notion of social action is relatively unproblematic since it obviously refers to people doing things and the results of these doings – action requires an actor and some kind of performative event – the notion of 'social structure' is more complicated and has been used extensively by social theorists and sociologists and in a number of different ways. We will be exploring these in subsequent chapters but to get started it is useful to think of social structures simply as those aspects of the social context over which individuals have no direct control. Some structures are relatively obvious, almost tangible, while others are less so. Most social structures combine both kinds of elements. For example, 'the economic structure', that is, the overall system of practical arrangements for producing things in a society, is structural in the sense that there are physical institutions and organisations, actual buildings and places of work, plus obvious patterns of activity and routines of work, many of which have developed into a legal framework of rules and regulations.

Less obvious, and yet just as necessary, the economic structure also includes patterns of ideas, beliefs and expectations about how the economic affairs of society should be run. The behaviour of everyone in that society is profoundly affected by the economic structure and yet no particular individual has control over it.

Social structures can sometimes be thought of as the habits and routines that social actors get into as they go about the business of organising their survival. It might be difficult to say exactly when a particular routine became established, or which social actor or group of social actors first started using it, but once established it tends to control behaviour to the extent that alternative routines do not develop. **Critical social theorists** argue that this benign conception is naive because social structures always benefit some social actors at the expense of others. The trick is to make it appear that a particular structure occurs naturally when in fact it has been deliberately introduced to confer an advantage. The capacity to impose or introduce new structural features in society is a very important form of power since it dramatically affects the conditions under which social actors act.

Micro versus macro analysis

The second strategy we should make ourselves familiar with early on is to do with the *scale* or *level of detail* that social theorists choose to concentrate on. This issue is closely linked to the action–structure dilemma, because, generally speaking, the more one concentrates on the structural causes of social action, the more one is likely to analyse things at a fairly general, large-scale or **macro** level. Correspondingly, those who are mainly interested in the fine detail of social action, have to look at things at a more precise, small-scale or **micro** level. Of course things are a little more complicated than this since it is perfectly reasonable to make observations about social phenomena at a fairly general level, and then to fill in some of the details by adopting a micro-level approach. Social action might very well be determined by large-scale structures like 'culture' or '**gender**' but it is debatable how aware social actors are of them. As with the action–structure dilemma, the difficult bit is to decide whereabouts between the various extremes the most realistic and accurate analysis can be made.

Returning to the football match illustration we made earlier in this chapter, at a micro level, a social theorist could produce a painstaking analysis of each and every move that was made on the pitch, or between each of the supporters in the crowd. Alternatively, a macro-level analysis could be made of the event in a very aggregated way a bit like taking a wide-angle photograph of the game from a helicopter passing overhead. Most would agree, however, that although in some sense both these alternatives provide an 'accurate' representation of what went on at the game, a more *realistic* representation needs to draw a little from both. In this example, the role of the match commentator is precisely to find such a compromise; to provide enough detail to allow spectators to make sense of the game, but also to capture the essence of the game in a much more general or panoramic sense.

Approaching these questions for the first time, the sensible thing is to accept that both micro and macro analysis have a role to play in social theory, and any final decision comes down as much as anything to personal preference on the part of the theorist. Some theorists, such as Karl Marx, Talcott Parsons and Anthony Giddens, prefer to develop their ideas at a macro, society-wide scale. Others, such as Max Weber, George Herbert Mead and Erving Goffman, develop their ideas very much at ground level. Like everyone else in modern Western industrial society, social theorists and sociologists have to become specialists and this usually means becoming an expert in one style, approach or strategy and less so in the others.

Models of social change (conflict and continuity)

Finally in this section we should say a little about what social theorists have to say about notions of social development and historical change. Until relatively recently, and following a view that had become very popular during the European **Enlightenment**, it was assumed that much like other kinds of organism, society develops in a linear fashion through historical time. Modern society emerged out of pre-modern society and sooner or later modern society will be replaced by something else. Notions of progressive forward motion, of becoming more mature, are among the most lasting motifs of the modern outlook. (This outlook contrasts quite sharply with the situation in pre-modern societies, which, being dominated by nature rather than by culture, rely on the idea of natural cycles and repetitions, not of forward motion.)

More recently the Enlightenment perspective has been questioned by theorists who challenge the rather complacent assumption that society progresses through historical time, let alone in accordance with some kind of grand historical plan. Although many unexpected and unpredictable events can be seen as helpful in terms of social progress, many others are not helpful and, depending on the criteria being used, can actually result in a reversal, a backward step in social development. The inability of social theory to predict the unpredictable always means that our understanding of social development and change is imperfect. Stuck as all of us are in the present, it is comforting to think that there is something called the future, and that this will be even better than the present. Trouble is, none of us can *prove* that it will be. The challenge here for social theory is to develop conceptions of how society develops and changes, of the mechanisms and processes involved, which keep an open mind about whether or how it will develop in the future. If we say that 'history' is to society what **'biography'** is to the individual, we can more easily grasp the notion that, like individuals, societies can, metaphorically, be knocked over by a bus.

Continuity and change

Despite the problems caused by unexpected events, natural disasters or just the unintended consequences of people's ordinary actions, social theorists continue to explore the mechanism of social and historical change. One popular approach is to try to understand where the balance lies between continuity and change, that is, to take a view on which bits of society will be carried over into the future and which will not. The degree to which society changes through historical time will significantly depend on how many or how few elements of the old are carried over into the new. It will also depend on how quickly the changes take place. Some theorists conclude that social change involves a rapid or **revolutionary** transformation of the whole of society, while others anticipate a much more gradual process of change in which quite a high proportion of the old survives into the new. One of the major tasks of social theory is to help us understand what kinds of things affect the scope and pace of social change.

Historical events

Speaking more generally, we should not underestimate the impact of actual historical events on the development of social theory itself. If it is only possible to understand social action by taking full account of the social context in which it takes place, then this will be especially so during times when the social context is in transition. Knowledge of how society is changing plays a very important part in accounting for the actions of individuals living under those conditions of change. Inevitably, therefore, social theorists are bound to be particularly interested in that period of Western history (the century after 1760) which saw the greatest concentration of forces for change that had ever been experienced. A concentration that had an almost universal impact on the social actions of the people who lived through it, and indeed of Western populations ever since. During the 1980s and 1990s, the emergence in social theory of new ideas about whether the modern period was coming to an end, and whether or how we could recognise new forms of 'postmodern society', also came at a moment in history when tremendous forces for change had resulted in major transformations in the nature of modern, industrial, Westernised society. We will be looking at these developments in postmodernist social theory in Chapters Twelve and Thirteen.

The main purposes of social theory

The quest for knowledge

The main purpose of social theory is to make intelligent propositions about social action, its contexts and social practices. These propositions provide frameworks into which the bits of concrete or real understanding we already have can be fitted. A bit like placing fragments of glass between the leaded divisions in a stained-glass window, the frameworks provided by social theory and sociological theory not only give us somewhere to put these bits and pieces of knowledge, they also help us make sense of 'the bigger picture'. Social theory is made up of knowledge about social action, but it is also a collection of *strategies* for carrying out the investigations that produce such knowledge about the social world in the first place.

Defining social order

A team effort

We have noted already that social theory and sociology are not the only games in town when it comes to developing new knowledge about social phenomena. **Anthropology**, media studies, gender and cultural studies, psychology, philosophy and history all draw on elements of social theory and sociological theory in their investigations. As we shall see in the following chapters, very often there are extremely fruitful interchanges of ideas across and between these disciplines in the development of new knowledge. In each case there is a spectrum of activity ranging from pure ideas and concepts at one end to the gathering of empirical data about social phenomena at the other. The pure and applied dimensions are always interlinked since general ideas and concepts provide the basis for research hypotheses. Equally, evidence gathered by empirical means stimulates the development of further ideas and concepts. Broadly speaking, the more general or abstract the conclusions being expressed the more purely theoretical they will be.

ILLUSTRATION

We can illustrate these points by using the example of putting a plug on a kettle. At a day-to-day level, we could all probably do this task without any very profound knowledge of electrics. It is simply a matter of following the instructions and connecting the correct wire to the correct pin. Manufacturers provide a diagram to help us do this. These bits of information, the instructions and recommended procedure for plug fitting, are, in theory terms, *basic conceptual tools* for completing a particular task.

Below this surface level, the professional electrician has greater knowledge of the domestic wiring system. She will know all about circuits and fuses, junction boxes and safety limits. She will have passed various training courses, and be regarded as proficient or qualified in her trade. The detailed knowledge required to be a professional electrician constitutes an altogether deeper and more fundamental theory of electricity. The concepts, language and terminology are still aimed at a practical application, but they are *qualitatively* different in the sense that they incorporate basic conclusions about electricity that arose as a result of previous investigations into the principles of electricity. This knowledge is also *much more general* than the simple theory-tools needed for plug fitting. Professional electricians have enough theory at their disposal to be able to do many different kinds of wiring jobs. For them, putting plugs on kettles is a stroll in the park.

At a still deeper level of generality, a professor of physics who specialises in the study of electricity will have an even more comprehensive knowledge of the principles that underlie the phenomenon we call 'electricity'. He will know about protons and neutrons, resistance and conductivity. This very general theoretical knowledge might bring him into contact with other aspects of theory and eventually into the pure realm of theoretical physics. The amateur knows that plugs make things work, the electrician knows what makes the system function, but the theorist knows how a fundamental knowledge of electricity carries over into knowledge of the physical universe itself.

Critical social theory

Having developed effective techniques of empirical investigation and theoretical reasoning the question then arises as to what we should do with the knowledge they generate? For many social theorists who are critical of the current state of society the answer is that better knowledge of society should be used to bring about positive social change. Knowing more about society gives us the capacity to change it. One could go a step further and argue that if social-theoretical reasoning is unable to contribute to social change then it really is a pointless undertaking (we will be discussing this critical approach in social theory in Chapter Eight). Also important is the **modernist** idea of 'the good society' as reflected in the liberal humanist philosophy of the European Enlightenment. Followers of this conception tend to assume that a superior and more civilised form of society can be attained and that this is something that humanity should strive to achieve. Knowledge of society, including crucially that developed by social theorists and sociologists, is seen as making a major contribution to this task. This topic is discussed in Chapter Two.

Reflexivity

Although we do not have time to discuss it adequately here, one of the unique features of sociological knowledge (as distinct from knowledge of the physical world for example) identified by Anthony Giddens is that it is 'reflexive' in that it feeds back upon, and in some measure is bound to affect, the social phenomenon under investigation. Whether or not the social theorist has a particular political or moral attitude about how society should be, the results of his investigation inevitably bring about change in society because social actors habitually modify their behaviour in light of new information about the social contexts in which they act. Logically, it is not possible to keep knowledge of social action separate from social action itself.

Key points box – In this chapter we have:

☑ Looked at how social theory has been defined.
☑ Described the main elements, subject matter and themes of social theory.
☑ Looked briefly at the purposes of social theory including social theory as a force for social change.

Practice box

⮕ Try writing a brief definition of 'social theory' using your own words.
⮕ From this chapter, select *one* part of the subject matter, and *one* theme of social theory that you think best describes what social theory is all about.
⮕ Look again at the *purposes* of social theory we discussed in the last section of this chapter and say which one *you* think is the most important.
⮕ Think of an example of a social phenomenon you are interested in. Make some theoretical propositions about it and list these in order of how *general* they are.

We are now ready to make a start with looking at the actual contents of social theory. Like all good investigations we should start with the question '*Where did social theory come from in the first place?*' To find out, turn to Chapter Two.

Further reading

Anthony Giddens, *Sociology* (5th edn) (Polity Press, 2006).

Mike Haralambos and Martin Holborn (2008) *Sociology: Themes and Perspectives* (7th edn) (Collins, 2000).

John Hughes, Peter Martin and Wes Sharrock, *Understanding Classical Sociology: Marx, Weber, Durkheim* (2nd edn) (Sage, 2003); and *Understanding Modern Sociology* (Sage, 2003).

John Parker, Len Mars, Paul Ransome and Hillary Stanworth, *Social Theory: A Basic Toolkit* (Palgrave, 2003).

Websites

For access to a vast range of material on sociology visit Sociology Online: www.sociologyonline.co.uk; and Sociological Research Online: www. socresonline.org.uk/home.html

Other useful sources can be found at the Dead Sociologists' Society: http://media.pfeiffer.edu/lridener/dss/DEADSOC.HTML

For a very extensive index of topics relating to society try: www.google. com/Top/Society/

In addition to the above most national newspapers and national organisations such as trade unions, campaigning organisations, charities, research institutes and government departments provide powerful web resources for locating information about society and social issues. Leading academic publishers also provide online access to the specialist journals they publish.

CHAPTER TWO

WHERE DID SOCIAL THEORY COME FROM?

The focus of this chapter is historical because we will be looking at some of the circumstances out of which social theory emerged during the 18th and 19th centuries. The background is important because although there has been much branching out during the 20th century, a better understanding of the more recent concepts, ideas and arguments of social theory can be had by setting these against debates that were already taking place. In order to understand the adolescent stage of social theory in the 20th century, we need to know something about its childhood in the 19th century, and identify the birthmarks of social theory in the centuries before that. It is interesting to note that although we are now very comfortable with the idea that there is such a thing as society, this is a relatively modern idea. Even as recently as in the publication between 1751 and 1765 of the famous *Encyclopedia* of the French **Enlightenment** there is no entry for the term 'society'.

> **The discussion in this chapter is divided into five parts:**
>
> Where did the idea of society come from?
>
> Auguste Comte and the 'positive science of society'
>
> John Stuart Mill's liberal positivism
>
> Herbert Spencer and the idea of social evolution
>
> The modern idea of society and how to study it

Where did the idea of society come from?

The discussion in the first part of this chapter is divided into the following historical periods:

- Classical and medieval ideas about 'society'
- The 17th century – the social contract
- The 18th century – the Age of Reason
- The Scottish Enlightenment
- The way forward

Classical and medieval ideas about 'society'

The earliest attempts at formulating a theory of society in the West are found in the works of Plato (427–347 BC) and Aristotle (384–322 BC). They saw society in a very **holistic** way, where everything was part of a larger whole. This was an **organic** conception of society as an essentially natural development and unfolding of basic human instincts, drives and passions. Their political philosophy was intended to understand how these forces and pressures worked themselves out in the world. This view of society, as being essentially determined by the rhythms and cycles of an underlying natural order, was carried over into the medieval period but with the important additional assumption that this natural order was determined by God. The medieval period was dominated by a highly scholastic interpretation in which religious texts were used to explain humanity and its place in the natural order or universe. The universe was completely subject to Divine Will and ruled by Divine Law. Most knowledge of the universe was outside human control and lay beyond human comprehension. All that one needed to know was that God was responsible for everything. The Bible and the Holy Scriptures derived from it were the only source of explanation, authority and instruction, and obedience to them was paramount.

The 17th century – the social contract

Through the work of Thomas Hobbes (1588–1679) and John Locke (1688–1774), a new idea emerged that although relations between humanity as a whole and God were entirely regulated by Divine Will, it was possible to reach some practical understanding of relationships between people. For Hobbes, all humans existed 'in a state of nature', by which he meant that they were dominated by their base instincts. Because basic human nature was essentially egoistic and self-centred, human relationships took the form of a 'war of all against all', of selfish and aggressive competition. Under these circumstances, Hobbes believed, 'the life of man' was likely to be 'solitary, poor, nasty, brutish and short'.

In order that social relations should not collapse into a state of total self-destruction, Hobbes developed the idea of a **social contract**, arguing that people are prepared to compromise a little by forfeiting some of their autonomy to a sovereign authority. In Hobbes' time, God still provided the ultimate form of authority but for more mundane earthly purposes, authority was vested in the monarch. The new social contract between individuals and each other, and between individuals and the sovereign authority, was embodied in Positive Human Law, which gradually displaced Medieval Divine Law. For Hobbes, society emerges at this time as a mechanism for achieving reconciliation and cooperation between people. Humanity needs society in order to move out of the state of nature. Society is recognised for the first time as providing the basis for social order.

John Locke was more optimistic than Hobbes, and argued that social relationships are in fact motivated by natural sympathy (rather than animosity) towards others. For him, the social contract was an expression of the natural sociability people felt towards each other. Locke also argued that obedience to a sovereign authority should not be based on coercion by an absolute monarch, but on a willingness among the population to surrender some of their rights to the community or 'commonwealth'. This was a much more democratic version of the social contract in which the authority of government depended on the consent of the population. People were only expected to surrender their rights on condition that this was necessary for the well-being of the community.

The 18th century – the Age of Reason

The idea that social actors could control their own destiny reached its adolescence during the 18th century. The dominant influences here were the thinkers and writers of the European Enlightenment and the Scottish Enlightenment who heralded the birth of the **Age of Reason**. These thinkers demanded that the human mind and human action had to be set free from superstition and fate. Within this **humanist** perspective (looking at things from the point of view of the human subject rather than seeing humans as subject to some form or authority beyond their control), the application of reason was the means by which this could be achieved. The model for this approach (and ultimately its methodology) was taken from the sphere of the **natural sciences**, which had also entered a period of rapid expansion. The credibility of its methods were epitomised in the work of Isaac Newton (1642–1727) whose description of The Laws of Motion in 1687 provided a new benchmark for what could be achieved by objective scientific investigation and reasoning. A number of individual contributions are important here.

The French philosopher Jean-Jacques Rousseau (1712–78) developed a third version of the idea of the social contract. He argued that the state of nature was essentially pure, simple and thus positive, while the state of civil society, as a human construction, was none of these things. Social disorder was the inevitable consequence of the opposition between the positive and the negative states of being. The solution, he thought, lay in the idea that individual will had to be subordinated to the general good. The sovereign authority, which was now embodied in the government and state rather than the monarch, is thus the only legitimate source of authority in society, and is always directed towards serving the general good. The object, then, was 'to find a form of association [society] which will defend and protect with the whole common force the person and goods of each associate, and in which each [individual], while uniting himself with all, may still obey himself alone, and remain as free as before' (quoted in Nisbet, 1967, p 49). As with previous ideas about the social contract Rousseau felt that it was society (as a form of association) that regulated social order.

Working in the field of the philosophy of knowledge, the Italian philosopher Giambattista Vico (1668–1774) challenged the idea that all knowledge had the same form as, and could be discovered by the same methods as, the empirical sciences like mathematics and physics. Adopting a **rationalist** perspective, he pointed out that even mathematical formulae are actually a creation of the human mind and cannot have an independent existence that was simply waiting to be 'discovered'. In saying this, Vico is suggesting that any understanding of reality, of society and of social order is a product of the creative human mind. Things might have a concrete, objective, tangible existence outside our minds (trees, cats, motorcycles clearly do exist as actual objects in the world), but our knowledge of them, the impression they make on our consciousness, is an internal not external phenomenon.

For Vico, this rationalist view of what knowledge is and where it comes from has at least two important consequences for how one might go about studying social phenomena. First, and even more than might be the case with knowledge of the physical universe, knowledge of the social universe only really comes into existence at the moment when social actors become conscious of it. Consciousness of what is going on during a particular piece of social action is part of that interaction. This dimension is entirely absent in the case of interaction between one kind of gas and another, or one chemical and another, because these elements do not have consciousness. Oxygen and hydrogen are not aware of their interaction and so cannot choose whether to become water or not. Second, Vico argued that it is highly improbable that social life is determined mechanistically in the same way that inanimate matter is governed by the laws of nature. However inspirational Newton's discovery of the Laws of Motion were, and however robust a template they provided for research methods in the natural or empirical sciences, they were not appropriate for investigating social phenomena.

The Baron de Montesquieu (1689–1755) further developed the idea of **human agency** by arguing that since society was produced through deliberate social action (rather than being a reflection of nature or a manifestation of Divine Will) it was necessary to understand how the various spheres of social action interact. Social reality is multidimensional in respect of the different spheres of action that give rise to it. As a result attempts at social order have to take account of the particular contexts of social action, contexts that continuously change as the various interacting factors are themselves altering. There can be no universal solution to the problem of social order because that which needs ordering continually shifts. A complicating factor, which we will not dwell on here, is that a crucial part of the context affecting social action is the current state of the society in which this action takes place. The current state of society is always a factor in the development of other forms of society. Methodologically, although the experimental method in the natural sciences makes it possible to isolate one particular object in order to analyse it, it is never possible to study social phenomena as if they are separable from the context in which they occur.

The Scottish Enlightenment

The key advance for social theory of this group of thinkers, David Hume (1711–76), Adam Smith (1723–90), Adam Ferguson (1723–1816) and John Millar (1735–1801), was that if society is produced through creative human social action, historical change must be determined in the same way. In suggesting this, they had identified another of the limitations of seeing human social life only in terms of God or nature, which is that things do not, or in fact should not, change very much (lest ye provoke the wrath of God). Making the assumption that there is such a thing as a natural or divine order to things, and that it is the duty of people and their leaders not to upset it, implies that any form of change will be disruptive to the natural order.

Time

One consequence of this naturalistic perspective is that historical time is seen as static or circular (or in the jargon of social theory **synchronic**), rather than dynamic or linear (or **diachronic**), in the sense that there is forward movement in historical time. Although society during the

18th century was still largely agricultural so that most people lived their lives according to the rhythms and cycles of the farming year (i.e. synchronically), the perception of the merchants and business classes in the towns and cities was increasingly that the tempo of life was, or ought to be, much more progressive or linear (diachronic). It became generally accepted that social action, and thus history itself, are controlled by people not by the turning of the seasons.

Having adopted the idea that society is a concrete manifestation of human action, and that this action has a dynamic property that pushes society forward into the future, this group of theorists focused its attention on the practical issue of how a scientific investigation could be made of the factors affecting social action. Taking on board current ideas about interaction and context just described, they suggested that it is necessary to distinguish between economic, philosophical and cultural factors, which certainly come together at the moment of interaction, but which also retain a degree of independence. The political and economic structures of society are closely related but it is still possible, for the purposes of investigation, to study them separately. These thinkers also emphasised that since a key practical problem for social actors is the tension between their own desires and what society will allow (a difficulty which gave rise to earlier notions of the social contract), this dimension should also be addressed in social theory. As we noted in Chapter One, along with the problem of social order, the action versus structure debate is still a main theme in social theory.

Collectively, but especially through the work of Adam Smith whose famous *Inquiry into the Nature and Causes of the Wealth of Nations* was published in 1776, this group also established a second main theme in modern social theory, which is that the quest for economic resources and the organisation of work and industry that goes with it are fundamental to the nature of society and to the quest for health, wealth and happiness. Expressing a view that became a basic principle of modern economics, Smith focused directly on the practical importance of the division of labour:

KEY QUOTE – Adam Smith, *The Wealth of Nations* (1776).
The greatest improvement in the productive powers of labour, and the greater part of the skill, dexterity, and judgement with which it is any where directed, or applied, seem to have been the effects of the division of labour. (Smith, 1970 [1776] p 42)

Stemming from this was an early humanitarian concern with the conditions of work and with the nature and causes of social inequality. Simply put, if society is determined by social action (albeit within the limits imposed by social and intellectual context), then inequality within society must also be attributable to that social action. There is a hint in the work of the early social theorists that social theory has a critical role to play in identifying both the nature and causes of social inequality. There is little doubt that the work of Karl Marx and Friedrich Engels in the 19th century, for example, was heavily influenced by their concern for the plight of the industrial working classes.

The following figure summarises the key developments in early social theory that we have discussed so far.

Figure 2.1: Key developments in early social theory

From	To
God as creator	Humankind as creator
Divine will	Human free will
Organic notions of human social life as part of nature	Realist notions of human social life independent of nature
Circular (synchronic) notions of time determined by the rhythms of nature	Linear (diachronic) notions of time determined by people themselves
Fate and chance	Reason
Metaphysics	Rational empiricism
Introspection	Positive knowledge
Speculation	Scientific investigation

The way forward

Through a combination of these new ideas, theorists reasoned that humankind controlled its own future, a future which could be changed through deliberate human action. This way of seeing things marks a radical departure form what went before, and is another important characteristic of the modern outlook. Instead of seeing the present as a repetition of the past, the strongly futuristic orientation, which accompanies the idea of progress, creates an entirely new conception of what the future could be like. There is no longer any need to assume that the future will simply repeat the past. The mood of progress was one of optimistic investigation, a hunger to see what *could be* discovered.

This vigorous spirit of enquiry provided social theorists with a new conceptual framework for understanding social development itself. Previous periods in history, previous manifestations of society, could be understood as the earlier stages, the stepping stones, of current society. Extending this perspective forwards, current society provides the foundation for the society of the future. Having taken human agency out of history it could now be put back in but this time as its driving force. Important questions remained, however, as to how social theory should go about conducting its investigations and what kind of knowledge it could produce. The first step was to establish the study of human social life and society as a distinct branch of knowledge in its own right.

Auguste Comte – 'positive science of society'

The first example of this new development was the work of the influential French social theorist and philosopher Auguste Comte (1798–1857). Comte is known as the father of sociology, a term he first used in 1839 to describe the new 'positive science of society' (*see also* **positivism**). Sociology was the first academic discipline to look specifically at human society. One of the major concerns of Comte (and a few years later of Émile Durkheim, another social theorist in the French positivist tradition, who we will be discussing in Chapter Three) was to develop a specific niche for social-theoretical knowledge as a distinct academic discipline rather than as a branch of philosophy or political theory. Sociology emerges as part of this process.

Born into a Catholic royalist family in Southern France, Comte developed a reputation as a scholar in Paris, before becoming secretary to Saint-Simon in 1817 (Saint-Simon's concept of 'industrial society' is discussed in Chapter Three). Comte occupies an important but somewhat ambiguous position in the development of sociological theory being strongly influenced both by the social philosophy of Saint-Simon, and the more empirical work of his contemporary British rivals Herbert Spencer (1820–1903) and John Stuart Mill (1807–73).

Comte argued that it was only possible to reach a firm understanding of society by looking at it in its entirety, as a complex unity of action and interaction, rather than just at its constituent parts. He contended that sociology (social-scientific knowledge) would be a 'positive science' in terms of:

- having a clearly defined subject matter and method;
- helping social progress;
- adding to the universal quest for knowledge.

Subject matter and method

Sociology would be positive as long as it could define a specific subject matter and appropriate methodology for developing knowledge of social phenomena. The issue of methodology is particularly important because in recommending that social scientists should use the empirical methods of the natural sciences, Comte is reinforcing the view that just as the natural sciences had been successful in uncovering some of the general laws of the natural world such as the laws of gravity or biological reproduction, social science would be able to reveal the 'laws of motion' of the social world. Indeed, according to this view of things, the success of the social sciences would actually depend on how well it was able to uncover such general laws of society. For Comte, social scientists should not only copy the methods of investigation of the natural sciences (observation, experimentation, deductive reasoning), but also accept a similar conception of what scientific knowledge is and what its purposes are.

We can distinguish between two basic modes of scientific reasoning. First, **deductive** modes of reasoning and investigation move from the general to the particular. This is the approach most often associated with the natural sciences, where, on the basis of things already known, the theorist begins with a hypothesis and conducts an experiment to 'prove' that she or he is correct. In this procedure, the theory tends to come first, and is followed by empirical investigation. Once the hypothesis has been proved or disproved (the null hypothesis) further theoretical work is done to generate further hypotheses and so the cycle continues. I might hypothesise, for example, that there are sufficient books in the library, and that people who claim that they cannot find the books they need are simply not trying hard enough. I might then design an experiment to test this hypothesis, perhaps by asking a sample of people from different disciplines to record how often they are or are not able to borrow a particular book. The results of this experiment would then give me some concrete data about whether there are enough books or whether there are not.

Second, and in contrast to deductive reasoning, **inductive** modes of reasoning and investigation tend to move from the particular to the general. If, for example, I observe that a particular student finds it difficult to grasp the fundamentals of social theory, I might conclude that *all* students find social theory difficult. I might then go on to argue that the reason for this lies in some property or characteristic of social theory, for example its tendency to be abstract, and conclude that *all* forms of **abstract** reasoning are difficult. In general terms, social theorists tend to use the inductive approach, and revert to the deductive approach in order to 'test' the validity of their arguments.

Making a 'positive' difference

The second way in which Comte claimed social-scientific knowledge was positive, was that once the results of its investigations had become truly scientific they could be used to make a *positive contribution* to social development. Having discovered the relationships between one phenomenon and another, and having uncovered the causal links between social actors and social contexts, social relationships could be made more productive. Comte writes: 'The positive Philosophy offers the only solid basis for that Social Reorganization which must succeed the critical condition in which the most civilized nations are now living' (Comte, quoted in Thompson and Tunstall, 1971, p 21). Writing during the mid-19th century when French society was coming to terms with the twin trauma of the French and Industrial Revolutions, Comte's claim that sociology could demonstrate the laws of harmonious social development would certainly have been very attractive.

The tree of knowledge

Comte's desire to provide an all-embracing framework for bringing together the different branches of scientific knowledge pushed him towards a conception of society as forming an all-embracing entity that was driven forward by an almost innate human predisposition to achieve ever higher levels of progress and civilisation. Social development was thus seen in terms of the development of knowledge, with social-scientific knowledge occupying the top position in what he called the 'hierarchy of the sciences'. As the first academic discipline to look specifically at human social life, sociology was itself a manifestation of human intellectual progress, and could not have emerged until the lower sciences of mathematics, astronomy, physics, chemistry and physiology (biology) had already developed. The emergence of sociology was proof that a higher state of knowledge was being reached.

Comte adopted a similar notion of hierarchical development (i.e. that the higher stages cannot be reached without passing through the ones below) in accounting for previous types of society. If knowledge itself evolved through theological (or fictitious), metaphysical (or abstract) and scientific (or positive) stages (what he referred to as 'The Law of Three Stages'), then society could be characterised as passing from a simple early stage largely dominated by military power, through an intermediate stage controlled by legal and Church power typical of medieval and Renaissance society, to modern society controlled by industrialists and 'moral science'. The civilising process, then, was largely driven forward by developments in knowledge.

This view of society as an integrated whole, and the associated idea that knowledge itself has an essential unity, is the third reason why sociology is a 'positive' science. It is the missing link, the necessary next stage of understanding the reality in which we live:

> In the final, the positive state, the mind has given over the vain
> search after Absolute notions, the origins and destination of the

universe, and the causes of phenomena, and applies itself to the study of their laws, that is, their invariable relations of succession and resemblance. Reasoning and observation, duly combined, are the means of this knowledge. (Comte, quoted in Thompson and Tunstall, 1971, p 19)

If the development of society itself depends on advances in scientific knowledge, then all the different branches of knowledge can, indeed, be integrated into a single system of knowledge as long as they are based on rational strategies of investigation. What the various sciences have in common is a shared conception of what knowledge *is* rather than just sharing similar techniques of investigation. Comte explains this by drawing attention to the basic correspondence between the positive sciences and their *common need* for understanding what lessons the past holds for the future:

The aim of every science is forethought. For the laws established by observation of phenomena are generally employed to foresee their succession. All men, however little advanced, make true predictions, which are always based on the same principle, the knowledge of the future from the past.... Manifestly, then, it is quite in accordance with the nature of the human mind that observation of the past should unveil the future in politics, as it does in astronomy, physics, chemistry, and physiology. (Comte, 'Plan for scientific work necessary for reorganising society', 1822, quoted in Kumar, 1983 [1978], pp 23–4)

If social scientists could discover the underlying processes of social development, this opened the possibility of using this knowledge to intervene in the next stage of progress. Social-scientific knowledge itself becomes a key ingredient *of* social development. Knowing about society is a prerequisite *for* social development.

John Stuart Mill's liberal positivism

The English philosopher John Stuart Mill (1807–73) broadly shared Comte's enthusiasm for the idea that the new science of society should be modelled on the scientific techniques of empirical observation and deduction that had been so successful in uncovering the laws of nature. Where Mill crucially differed from Comte was in his belief that the causes of social action could be traced back to underlying features of human psychology. The forces that drive social action are not the laws of nature but more specifically the laws of **human nature**. For Mill human nature is made up of the urges and passions, the desires and creative impulses, that are characteristic of the human being. These essential and irreducible inner drives are drawn out of social actors by the social contexts that surround them. Society provokes various behaviours, it elicits various responses, but the essence of action, and the predisposition to act, is a property that social actors already possess. Despite his willingness to accept the benefits of the positivist scientific method as providing objective and independent data about the social conditions of action, Mill's conception of social action is profoundly non-sociological since social context is rendered subordinate to a perpetual and never-changing human psychology. Social action varies from one place to another but the range of variation is ultimately bounded by the limits of human nature.

Mill's characterisation of society as a catalyst for the expression of inner drives inevitably underpins his other intellectual preoccupation (outlined in his most famous book *On Liberty*, 1859), which is with the nature of those social conditions. If the conditions of society are such that they cause social actors to act positively and productively then society can also be regarded positively. If, on the other hand, social actors are provoked into acting negatively then, despite their innate capacity to act otherwise, society is preventing social actors from achieving their full potential. Reflecting the utilitarian flavour of his own education (he was educated at home by his father James Mill and by Jeremy Bentham both of whom were central figures in the utilitarian movement), Mill argued that positive social conditions were those in which individuals could pursue wealth as long as this could be achieved without hindering the urge of other individuals to do the same. The good society in Mill's view is one where the pursuit of wealth is both morally justifiable and intellectually rational. The role of the **state** was to help create the right kinds of conditions where members of **civil society** could prosper. Like many other reformist and liberal social philosophers of the 19th century, however, and reprising issues discussed by social contract theorists like Rousseau, Locke and Hobbes, Mill also recognised the very great difficulty of creating the right conditions in society for balancing the rights of the individual with the common good. It is all very well to argue in an abstract philosophical way that ideally the state should play as small a role as possible in limiting the range and scope of actions in civil society, but practically this is a major challenge.

Herbert Spencer and the idea of social evolution

A third grand design for social theory and sociological theory we want to discuss here is that presented by Comte's other great British rival Herbert Spencer (1820–1903). One of the main ideas we have referred to a number of times in this chapter is that social progress can be understood as a kind of **evolution**. For us, living in the post-Darwinian world, this is a familiar idea. Organisms pass through various stages of development. Each stage has to be completed before the next can begin. Although successive stages are an advance on what went before, each stage still contains elements that were present in the previous stage. The rate and form of development is affected by the environment in which the organism lives. This environment is made up of a range of circumstances including the presence of animate and inanimate organisms. To understand evolution means understanding how these various circumstances interact with each other. Over time, and by looking at the causes and consequences of previous stages of development, it is possible to reach a fairly precise understanding of what is likely to happen next. The importance of the work of Charles Darwin (1809–82), in *Origin of the Species* (1859) and *The Descent of Man* (1871), was not so much the idea that life passed through a number of stages, but of *how* that process, the process of 'natural selection' as Darwin calls it, takes place.

Although all this is reasonable enough when dealing with the lower species of animals, it all gets a bit more difficult when you are dealing with *homo sapiens* (man the thinker), which has creative consciousness and **subjectivity** as an essential part of its being. Nevertheless, the idea of evolution, or more specifically of 'social evolution', was extremely attractive to the intellectuals of the 19th century. The main exponent of 'social evolution' was Herbert Spencer.

Background

Like J.S. Mill, Herbert Spencer was educated at home by his father who was an engineer. His childhood was also dominated by an extremely rigid nonconformist Puritan **utilitarianism**, which ultimately had a rather conservative effect on his political views. With this almost exclusively scientific background he trained as a mechanic and worked as an engineer for the London and Birmingham Railway Company between 1837 and 1846. He then worked as a sub-editor of the *Economist* magazine between 1848 and 1853 when an inheritance allowed him to devote himself to developing and publishing his ideas. Without taking a degree or holding any academic position, he became a 'gentleman scholar'. Spencer's main publications that deal with the concept of social evolution are: *Social Statics* (1851), *The Study of Sociology* (1873) and *The Principles of Sociology* (1876).

A common observation among Spencer's contemporaries was his rather peculiar habit of refusing to read anything that he did not agree with. He felt that the effort involved in this could be better used in thinking his own thoughts and developing his own ideas. This rather eccentric approach may have stemmed from a sense of exclusion from the formal academic world of which he had never really been a part, and from the initial reluctance of many of his contemporaries to take him seriously. More speculatively, it might have come from a desire to keep some distance between his own ideas and those of his contemporaries, most notably Charles Darwin, J.S. Mill and Auguste Comte, since there seemed to be some obvious overlap between their ideas. In combination, these factors contributed to the somewhat paradoxical position of Spencer in the history of social theory being seen by some as a Victorian dinosaur, and by others as one of its most progressive thinkers. Certainly the language and terminology used by Spencer are still part of the vocabulary of social theory.

Spencer's theory of social evolution

The basic principle of Spencer's theory is that primitive or simple society tends to be unstable, and is thus prone to failure (extinction), while forms of society that do survive are those which have become more complex and thus more stable. This stability is achieved as the different parts of the social organism ('society') become more clearly differentiated from one another, and, at the same time, become more fully integrated into the whole. Thus pre-modern society is characterised by **homogeneity** (similarity) and instability, while modern society is characterised by **heterogeneity** (differentiation) and stability. Society evolves from the simple to the complex, from homogeneity to heterogeneity, and from similarity to differentiation.

Using a unifying framework, which is noticeably similar to that used by Comte and by Mill, Spencer also believes that there is a fundamental unity or **holism** between all the different categories of organic and inorganic phenomena of which the world is made. Also like Comte, he includes in this unity the different types of knowledge that we have about these phenomena and arranges them in a hierarchy. At the base are the natural sciences (geology, physics and astronomy), which are concerned with identifying the origins and characteristics of inorganic matter. Next are the biological sciences (biology, botany and zoology), which are concerned with identifying the mechanisms of evolution of organic matter (plants and animals). Above these are the human or social sciences (sociology, anthropology and psychology), which are concerned with the mechanism of evolution of human social life.

In Spencer's scheme, of all the human sciences, sociology and anthropology are the most advanced since they are looking not just at the biological or physiological aspects of human behaviour (i.e. at human beings as a branch of the animal kingdom), but at the most advanced expression of human activity, which is its social aspect. As Spencer puts it: 'The study of Sociology [is] the study of Evolution in its most complex form' (Spencer, in Thomas and Tunstall, 1971, p 33):

> There can be no understanding of social actions without some knowledge of human nature; there can be no deep knowledge of human nature without some knowledge of the laws of Mind; there can be no adequate knowledge of the laws of Mind without knowledge of the laws of Life. And that knowledge of the Laws of Life, as exhibited in Man, may only properly be grasped, attention must be given to the laws of Life in general. (Spencer, in Thompson and Tunstall, 1971, p 36)

Where Spencer goes beyond Comte is in really pressing the idea that the process by which one stage is linked to the next is an *evolutionary process*. In the same way that Darwin explained why one species develops while another becomes extinct through a process of natural selection, Spencer hoped to show that a similar evolutionary mechanism determined which form of society prospered and which failed. Human progress and history *are also* part of an underlying evolutionary process. The unifying social theory Spencer is recommending includes not only the different categories of phenomena and our knowledge of them, but tries to account for the development of human societies *in the same terms* that biologists account for the development of all other organic phenomena:

> Using the analogy supplied by human life, we saw that just as bodily development and structure and function, furnish subject matter for biological science … so social growth and the rise of structures and functions accompanying it, furnish matter for a Science of Society….We saw, on comparing rudimentary societies with one another and with societies in different stages of progress, that they do present certain common traits of structure and of function, as well as certain common traits of development. (Spencer, in Thomas and Tunstall, 1971, p 34)

Just as biological evolution depends on how well or badly the organism or animal fits in with the natural environment, the evolution of society also depends on how well or badly members of that society are adapted to that stage in its development. Society is part of the environment in which people live: 'For every society, and for each stage in its evolution, there is an appropriate mode of feeling and thinking; and that no mode of feeling and thinking [which is] not adapted to its degree of evolution, and to its surroundings, can be permanently established'

(Spencer, in Thomas and Tunstall, 1971, p 36). From now on, then, we need to think about the role played by social and cultural factors in shaping the context in which social action takes place.

Assessing Spencer's contribution to social theory

Spencer's contribution to social theory is a little frustrating because, although he offers some very useful ideas about how to develop a theory of social development, other ideas produce some fairly misguided ideas about the constitution of society. Taking the plus points first, his evolutionary theory provides the basis for a new kind of comparative perspective in the social sciences. If all advanced societies are complex and characterised by increasing specialisation, then it is reasonable to conclude that 'complexity' and 'specialisation' are characteristics of, if not prerequisites for, social advancement. If a society is observed not to have these characteristics then, in comparison with those which have, this society has not yet reached the same level of advancement.

Building on this, and persevering with the idea of studying society as a social system, other necessary features of the system and how it works can be read off. For example, it stands to reason that the more complex a system is, the greater will be the need not just for individual functions to be integrated, but for integration to take on advanced forms. The level of **social integration** associated with an agrarian system of economic production, for example, in which a dispersed rural population make their living off the land, is likely to be less sophisticated than the system of economic organisation in an urbanised industrial society where mechanisms of employment and the organisation of work are certainly much more complicated. One kind of society can therefore be compared with another by examining the kinds of systems found in it. We can go further than this, and say that if there is little evidence of complex social integration, the society in question is not, and cannot become, much more advanced than it already is.

▸▸   We will have a lot more to say about the idea of social integration, and of **systems integration** when we discuss functionalist social theory in Chapter Six. Spencer's interest in how the various specialisms and functions of the social system hold together is his attempt to explain social order.

Third, Spencer recognises that the development of society also involves a process of what we can call cultural or intellectual adaptation to the conditions of society. Integration of the social organism is not just a matter of biological or physiological 'fit' with the various natural and social environments, it also depends on social actors having the right *attitude of mind*, 'an appropriate mode of feeling and thinking', to make the most of the developmental potential of those contexts. Although, compared with many other social theorists we are looking at in this book, Spencer provides a rudimentary account of the way that social and cultural environments are shaped by ideas, values and beliefs, he does at least help to bring these within the orbit of social theory. Concepts of 'civilisation' and 'social advancement' depend just as much on developments in intellectual capacity and curiosity as they do on technical developments like railways and microchips.

Looking now at some of the minus points of Spencer's social theory, in the same way that Mill tends to be anti–humanist in the sense that social action is limited by the parameters of human nature, social action in Spencer's theory is limited by the parameters of the evolutionary process. In neither case can the future be seen as entirely open, as something which is truly in the hands of social actors, since it is ringed–round by forces of nature that *homo sapiens* can never be free of. Spencer thus encounters a basic difficulty of all **systems theory** approaches to understanding society and social order, which is that social agency is plugged into a larger system that individual agents cannot control. Logically, any entity that is *part of* a natural system cannot at the same time be *in control* of that system. Ultimately, Spencer's theory allows only a limited opportunity for human agency to affect the overall direction of social progress.

The difficulty of modelling the social system on the kind of relatively closed and self-regulating system found in biological systems shows up particularly clearly when trying to explain the mechanisms by which **conflict** arises in a social system. Although pathological illness might result in crisis between parts of an organism, they cannot be seen as falling out with each other in the same way that different parts of society regularly do. It is difficult to accept Spencer's conception of systems equilibrium, when conflict and disequilibrium would seem to be the default setting of most social systems. The problem here is that the notion of 'balance' used to describe the steady state of biological systems is not the same as the concept of order necessary for describing conflict within social systems.

Spencer contributes a lot to social theory by emphasising that society provides the primary environment in which social action occurs, but his explanation of the emergence of society from nature obliges him to adopt an overly naturalistic notion of society. Society is always subjected to the environmental conditions of the planet but the whole point of cooperative social action is, where possible, to overcome the limits that these conditions impose on social action.

Comte, Mill and Spencer all suffer in varying degrees from the methodological difficulties of trying to adapt the positivist approach to social phenomena. The dilemma here is one of tending to assume that just because the various branches of scientific and social-scientific knowledge are all part of the great Tree of Knowledge, it does not follow that all explanations of particular social phenomena must also be traced back to a single unifying law of development or behaviour. For Comte everything is united by a single great quest for knowledge; for Mill everything derives from a unifying human nature; and for Spencer everything is united by a single great process of evolution. Positivism is a method that is designed to uncover laws of various kinds but it is a mistake to assume that just one law can explain all phenomena.

The most important gain for social theory in Spencer's work is actually awareness of the *im*possibility of treating social and cultural phenomena as if they are essentially the same as biological and natural phenomena. No matter how elegantly Comte and Spencer try to unite them, the natural world and the social world are two different orders of phenomena and because of this so are the traditions of knowledge, and the methods for developing knowledge, we have about them.

The modern idea of society and how to study it

So far we have been looking at the intellectual origins of social theory during the 19th century and the centuries before that. The purpose of this final part of the chapter is to consider how these grand ideas, and especially those about how the various branches of knowledge are related to each other, were reflected in the practical business of applying these ideas. Where, in other words, had social theory got to in terms of the kinds of strategies and specific lines of enquiry it wanted to follow?

Social theory and the comparative perspective

The most important strategy is, as we have just noted in respect of Spencer's work, that social theory would be *comparative*. Having realised that there is no single or universal reality that is out there for us to discover, and that we are not ultimately going to reach a perfect form of society, social theorists have to accept that social phenomena can only be studied in comparison with, or *relative to*, other social phenomena. For example, if we are interested in the different kinds of political systems used in different societies, there is little point in comparing them in terms of how they measure up to some perfect model of a political system that does not exist, but in terms of how the features of one (imperfect) system compare with those of another (imperfect) system. Such comparisons must take full account of the real circumstances, the actual conditions of existence, of the social phenomena under investigation.

An influential model of how to develop a theory of society based on making comparisons is provided by the German social theorist Ferdinand Tönnies (1855–1936). Like Spencer, Tönnies suggested that a useful starting point for social theory is to make comparisons between one instance of human social organisation, or one historical stage of society, and another. He concluded that there are important differences between the traditional 'communities' of the pre-modern period and the more complex 'societies' of the modern period. He distinguishes between *Gemeinschaft*, which translates as 'community' or 'communal relations', and *Gesellschaft*, which translates as 'association' or 'societal relations', or more directly as 'society':

KEY QUOTE – Ferdinand Tönnies, *Community and Society* (1887). The theory of the *Gesellschaft* [society] deals with the artificial construction of an aggregate of human beings which superficially resembles the *Gemeinschaft* [community] insofar as the individuals live and dwell together peacefully. However, in Gemeinschaft they remain essentially united in spite of all separating factors, whereas in Gesellschaft they are essentially separated in spite of all uniting factors. (Tönnies, 1957 [1887], quoted in Nisbet, 1967, pp 75–6; emphasis removed)

Tönnies is suggesting that one kind of society can be compared with another in terms of the kinds of social relationships that are found there. In communities (typical of rural, agrarian society) there is a sense of belonging, of being integrated into the lives of other people. Communities are literally places that are full of common experiences. In societies (typical of urban, industrial society) in contrast, 'there are no actions which, insofar as they are performed by the individual, take place on behalf of those united with him. In [society] everybody is by himself and isolated, and there exists a condition of tension against all others' (Tönnies, 1957 [1887], quoted in Nisbet, 1967, pp 75–6). The relations between people in society, and the various arrangements they come to in order to organise their affairs, are not natural or organic, as they are thought to be in communities, but are synthetic or fabricated. Developing at precisely the moment when these new synthetic and fabricated arrangements started to emerge, social theory becomes more and more focussed on these modern urban, industrial environments, and the forms of society that develop there.

Tönnies' opinion about the differences between one kind of human social group and another is very useful as it shows not only the early involvement of social theory with ideas about what constitutes a *modern* society (the above quotation is from 1887), but how social theorists began to establish the terms of reference for studying modern society; in his case, in terms of the kinds of social relations that are typical of it.

The centralising motif of 'the great transition'

Transition

A similarly popular comparative approach in social theory is the idea that, sometime during the hundred years from around 1760 to 1860, a fundamental and irreversible *transition* took place away from the traditional, typically rural community of the pre-modern period, and towards the non-traditional, increasingly urban society of the 19th and early 20th centuries. The key ingredients in this transition were the 'Industrial Revolution', which developed approximately between 1780–1840, first in England and then as it spread throughout Western Europe and the US, and the 'democratic revolutions' in France in 1789 (liberty, equality and fraternity), and to a lesser extent in the American 'Declaration of Independence' (life, liberty and the pursuit of happiness) of 1776, which emerged during the War of Independence against the British and French colonialists between 1775 and 1783. The transition approach is useful because it offers some useful *criteria* for distinguishing one type or stage of society from another. Modern societies are 'modern' because they are *not* traditional.

Figures 2.2 and 2.3 list some of the intellectual and material criteria that social theorists frequently use in comparing one type of society with another. Intellectual criteria can be regarded as making a significant contribution to the general intellectual perspective, belief system or world view of a society. Material criteria include the most important concrete or institutional features of a society, features which can also be used as a basis for making comparisons.

We can see, for example, that in terms of intellectual outlook or world view, societies can be compared in terms of how they see human nature (or indeed whether they have a concept of human nature), what kinds of organisations they regard as normal, and the ideas they have about civilisation, progress and change. If we compared the modern-day US with Ancient Egypt, we could use criteria like these to provide a framework for our analysis. Social relations in Ancient Egyptian society were based on the idea of absolute obedience to Pharoah who was regarded as a god. In the US, the presumption is that all citizens are equal and that the authority of the president is based on the will of the voters. In Ancient Egyptian society the economy drew heavily on the labour of slaves who had been taken through military conquest. Until the abolition of slavery in the US in 1865 economic production, especially in the southern states of North America, also relied heavily on the labour of slaves. The many fantastic monuments built by Ancient Egyptian society attest to the technical skills of that society. We also know, however, that these skills are quite different to those that characterise the modern American industrial division of labour. Societies fall into different categories *because of* the basic characteristics they exhibit.

Figure 2.2: Intellectual criteria used by social theorists for comparing societies

Intellectual characteristics
Types of knowledge i.e. rationality and materialism vs fate and religion
Philosophical ideas about the nature of humankind
Political-theoretical ideas about the organisation of society
Theories of social organisation
Theories about the nature of social relationships
Theories about the aims and purposes of society
Theories about social development and change

Figure 2.3: Material criteria used by social theorists for comparing societies

Material criteria
Organisation of economic production
Process of technological change
Actual relationship between the individual and society
Actual relationship between one person and another
Development of the state and state institutions
Nature and purposes of social institutions
Political system (emergence of universal suffrage and democracy)
Basic characteristics of social life including: • standards of living and styles of life • urbanisation • the family

Individualism

A common feature of many of the accounts we have looked at in this chapter is that the good society is a place where social actors can act as individuals. This is an enormously complex question and one that will recur in Chapter Three but it is useful to note at this point the sense in which modern society creates the notion of the individual. The emergence of the individual is one of the characteristics of modern society. This might seem somewhat paradoxical given that the theories of Comte, Mill, Spencer and to some extent Tönnies emphasise the centrality of society, which is often defined as a collective phenomenon. The problem of how social actors act as individuals rather than as part of a collectivity is an aspect of the general problem of social order, which provides social theory with one of its perpetual areas of investigation. Although none of the theorists we have been looking at in any way solves this apparent paradox they have sketched out for us the general parameters of a debate that ran throughout the 19th and 20th centuries in social theory.

The creation of the individual was a logical extension of the idea that if social actors are responsible for at least some of the conditions in which they live, then individual social actors must stand at the centre rather than on the periphery of society. This recognition of the role of individual social actors was, however, just the beginning and throughout the 19th century a thoroughly assertive theory of **individualism** was constructed. Individuals are not just particles of matter in the great social chemistry experiment they are the bearers of a complex range of political rights and moral entitlements that require adequate means of expression in society. The promotion of a robust and fully multidimensional concept of individuality, at the centre of which was a deliberate quest *for* individuality, tied in strongly with other important currents of 19th-century thought in political theory and philosophy, which were also highlighting the role of the individual in society. The introduction of the strong concept of society in social theory was accompanied by the introduction of an equally strong concept of the individual. It remains a moot point whether the emergence of one is a precondition for the emergence of the other.

Key points box – How to study society

- ☑ Social theory would be *comparative* because ideas and arguments about social phenomena only really make sense by comparing one instance or type of social phenomena with another.
- ☑ Social theorists would evaluate or assess social phenomena *relative to* other social phenomena rather than against some imaginary universal notions of perfection or destiny.
- ☑ In making such comparisons, it is often useful to develop broad categories or types of society to establish which sets or groups of characteristics are typical of one general type as distinct from another general type. Tönnies' distinction between community and society provides a very useful example of this approach.

☑ Also useful is the *transition approach*, which encourages us to look at social phenomena in terms of how one stage of development leads into a subsequent stage. We should reject the idea that the mechanism of transition is a kind of social evolution, but we can still usefully explore social phenomena in terms of the various sequences and similarities of their development.

☑ Social theorists can deploy various criteria as a convenient way of organising their analysis under various headings. As long as we remember that *in reality* beliefs about human nature, ideas about how to organise the economic and political systems, and about the impact of all of this on our social relationships, and so on are intertwined in complex ways, *in theory* it is alright to treat them as separate in order to conduct an investigation of them.

Practice box

⊃ Which of the early theorists thought society was 'organic'?

⊃ Who was the first person to come up with the idea of society as a 'social contract'?

⊃ Which group of theorists was the first to say that human beings could control their own destiny?

⊃ Give one of the reasons why Auguste Comte thought that sociology was a 'positive science'.

⊃ What did J.S. Mill believe was the underlying source of human social action?

⊃ Give one advantage and one disadvantage of the idea of social evolution discussed by Herbert Spencer.

⊃ Why is it useful to take a comparative approach when studying social phenomena?

⊃ Name two of the criteria social theorists use in comparing societies.

⊃ Would you rather live in a society or a community?

Further reading

Raymond Aron, *Main Currents in Sociological Thought*, 2 vols (Weidenfeld and Nicolson, 1965 and 1968).

Patrick Baert, *Social Theory in the Twentieth Century* (Polity Press, 1998).

Tim Benton and Ian Craib, *Philosophy of the Social Sciences: The Philosophical Foundations of Social Thought* (Macmillan, 2001).

Alex Callinicos, *Social Theory: A Historical Introduction*, 2nd edn (Polity Press, 2007).

Gerard Delanty and Piet Strydom, *Philosophies of Social Science: The Classic and Contemporary Readings* (Open University Press, 2003).

Anthony Giddens, *New Rules of Sociological Method*, 2nd edn (Polity Press, 1995).

Krishan Kumar, *From Post-Industrial to Post-Modern Society: New Theories of the Contemporary World* (Blackwell, 1995).

Alan Swingewood, *A Short History of Sociological Thought*, 3rd edn (Macmillan, 2000).

Websites

For general access to additional material try the Dead Sociologists' Society: http://media.pfeiffer.edu/lridener/dss/DEADSOC.HTML

A useful gateway into a comprehensive range of historical and bibliographical resources is the Virtual Library of Sociology: www.socserv.mcmaster.ca/w3virtsoclib/

Also useful for information about the European Enlightenment and its key thinkers is: www.wsu.edu/~dee/ENLIGHT/ENLIGHT.HTM

Biographical information about key thinkers such as Herbert Spencer and John Stuart Mill can be found in *The Internet Encyclopedia of Philosophy*: www.iep.utm.edu/

Also try the general social sciences resource Sociosite at: www.sociosite.net/

CHAPTER THREE

ÉMILE DURKHEIM AND THE COMING OF INDUSTRIAL SOCIETY

We ended Chapter Two by looking at some of the strategies and criteria social theorists use in comparing one society with another, and at some of the actual differences between the two types of society that matter most to social theorists, these being pre-modern and modern societies. In this and the next two chapters we turn our attention to a more detailed consideration of three of the most important contributions to social theory that came about as a direct consequence of the great transition from pre-modern to modern society. These are found in the work of the French theorist Émile Durkheim (1858–1917), and two German theorists, Karl Marx (1818–83) and Max Weber (1865–1920). We will compare them in terms of how they *explain* the emergence of modern society, and how they *describe* and *account for* the key characteristics of this form of society. In making these comparisons we will also reflect on the advantages and disadvantages of the *theoretical tools and strategies* they use and the choices they make about the subject matter of social theory.

It is difficult to overestimate the importance of Durkheim, Marx and Weber who are widely regarded as the 'founding fathers' of social theory in modern society. They occupy this privileged position for three clear reasons:

- First, they *consolidated* the position of social theory as an indispensable source of knowledge about the social world that really can make a difference to how we live.
- Second, taking the raw materials of social theory from the 18th and early 19th centuries, they developed much clearer *strategies* for developing social-theoretical knowledge. Many of the analytical tools social theorists use today are taken directly from Durkheim, Marx and Weber.
- Third, in their own analyses, they provide the first really robust *accounts* of the origins and nature of modern Western industrial society.

> ## This chapter is organised as follows. We will:
>
> Look at the intellectual context of Durkheim's social theory (Auguste Comte and Henri Saint-Simon)
>
> Find out about Durkheim's key concern, which is the relationship between individuals and society
>
> Look at Durkheim's general contribution to social theory

The intellectual context of Durkheim's social theory

Although Durkheim was aware of Marx's work, and was a contemporary of Max Weber (Durkheim died in 1917, Weber in 1920), his training and intellectual orientation were quite different. Marx built his social theory on the basis of the German **idealist** philosophy of Georg Wilhelm Friedrich Hegel, the British **political economy** of Adam Smith and David Ricardo, and the French socialist tradition. Weber's social theory developed out of the philosophical debates that dominated German intellectual circles in the 1880s (these intellectual contexts are discussed in the following two chapters). In contrast Durkheim stood as the successor to a quite different current of thought in the French **positivist** tradition.

Biography

Born into a modest Jewish family at Epinal in Northern France in 1858, Durkheim did well at school and persevered with his intention of following an academic career. His interest in the role of education brought him a teaching post in the Department of Education at the University of Bordeaux from 1887, and from 1902 at the Sorbonne in Paris. He was appointed as the first professor of Education and Sociology in 1913. He died in 1917 aged 59. In his own academic career, Durkheim combined a vigorous attempt to establish sociology as a distinct scientific discipline (summarised in *The Rules of Sociological Method*, 1964 [1895]), with the production of an extensive body of theoretical and empirical sociological investigation of his own, most notably *The Division of Labour in Society* (1933 [1893]), *Suicide* (1968b [1897]) and *Elementary Forms of Religious Life* (1968a [1912]).

Intellectual context

The context in which Durkheim developed his social theory was dominated by two key figures: Auguste Comte and Henri Saint-

Simon. From Comte he was inspired by the idea that it was possible and necessary to develop a knowledge of social phenomena that would be as rigorous, reliable and concrete as the positivistic knowledge provided by the biological and natural sciences. He also followed Comte in seeing human society in naturalistic terms as an organic unity. Although, in his later work, Durkheim used the organic analogy less often, he always believed that a central task of social theory was to understand the linkages and dependencies between one part or organ of the social body and another. A doctor might have a specialist interest in the digestive system, but this system can only be understood in the context of the other bodily systems with which it is connected. A similar challenge faces the social theorist in trying to understand how one social phenomenon interconnects with another.

Durkheim sets out his own view of these tasks in his influential book *The Rules of Sociological Method*, which was published in France in 1895. The key advance he makes on Comte's approach is to emphasise that it is possible to identify a category of social phenomena, or social facts as he calls them, which is objectively identifiable, and which can be studied quite independently of any grand system of analysis that might be applied to them:

KEY QUOTE – Durkheim, *The Rules of Sociological Method* (1895). Here, then, is a category of facts with very distinctive characteristics: it consists of ways of acting, thinking, and feeling, external to the individual, and endowed with a power of coercion, by reason of which they control him.... They constitute, thus, a new variety of phenomena; and it is to them exclusively that the term 'social' ought to be applied. And this term fits them quite well, for it is clear that, since their source is not in the individual, their substratum can be no other than society. (Durkheim, 1964 [1895], pp 3–4)

Unlike the grand theoretical universals used by Comte (unified theory of knowledge), Mill (human nature) and Spencer (social evolution), Durkheim insisted that social facts should be studied independently of such grand theoretical schemes. The investigation of social facts need not in fact have any necessary connection with any universal theory.

The second major figure for Durkheim was the French **utopian socialist** thinker Henri Saint-Simon (1760–1825) whom Comte had worked for as a secretary. Saint-Simon, who also influenced the early political views of Marx and Engels, was the first theorist to coin the term **industrial society** characterised by the division of labour. Like Mill, Saint-Simon also distinguished in his analysis between **civil society** as an autonomous, often privately owned, set of economic and cultural institutions, and the **state**, which he characterised as a centralised, bureaucratic and essentially parasitic institution. Setting a trend that Comte, Durkheim and others would follow, Saint-Simon suggested that progressive social organisation had to follow positivistic, rational and scientific principles.

Writing shortly after the period of turmoil that followed the French Revolution of 1789, Saint-Simon argued that the 'parasitic institutions' of the state (the Nobility, Church, Army and Government) had been shown to be conservative, reactionary and corrupt. He concluded that the most appropriate institutions for running society were to be found in civil society. Responding, as they had to, to the demands of the newly unfolding division of labour in industry, Saint-Simon believed that it was 'the producers', the entrepreneurs and business leaders, but also young intellectuals, scholars and artists, who had already acquired a rational, positive and progressive orientation, and so it was through their leadership that French society would move forward. The most advanced and progressive parts of civil society would provide the most advanced and progressive people to run society as a whole. Introducing a theme that would also be taken up by Comte, and especially by Durkheim, he also suggested that along with economic and political leadership went a responsibility for *moral leadership*.

For Durkheim, a strong and rational moral leadership or moral centre is one of the prerequisites for social order in modern industrial society. Social order depends upon three kinds of 'regulation' that prevent 'individual appetites' from exceeding what can be achieved: 'No living being can be happy or even exist unless his needs are sufficiently proportioned to his means' (Durkheim, 1968b [1897] p 246). These 'appetites' can be held in check by *material regulation*, which is simply the physical limit of what is possible, by *legal regulation* as set out in the laws of the land and backed up by various sanctions and punishments, and by *moral regulation*, which is set out within the belief system or world view of society.

There are two important points we should grasp about moral regulation. First, although it can provide the basis for physical and legal restraint, moral regulation embodies the idea that people in society voluntarily accept particular rules of social conduct. As a variety of social power, moral regulation is characterised as much by persuasion as by sheer force. Second, and showing a humanistic element in his theory, Saint-Simon follows the Enlightenment trend in seeing these rules of conduct as being essentially social and cultural in origin. Any notion that there are absolute principles of moral regulation originating from the Church or state, or that there are essential canons of action determined by human nature, is rejected.

Durkheim and the individual-versus-society debate

The key theme in Durkheim's sociological theory, the major theoretical issue he is concerned with throughout his work, is that of *the relationship of the individual to society*. For Durkheim, understanding the differences between pre-modern society and modern society cannot be separated from the question of what is happening to relations between individuals and society. For him, modern society is different from pre-modern society *because of* changes in the relations between individuals and society. The easiest place for us to begin is his most important work *The Division of Labour in Society* (sometimes translated as *the social division of labour*), which was published in France in 1893. In this book-length investigation, Durkheim analyses the individual-versus-society issue in terms of the different kinds of social solidarity that hold society and individuals together.

Durkheim begins his account by highlighting one of the recurrent dilemmas of social theory, which is to understand how the desire people have to act freely as individuals can be reconciled with the social pressure to conform. Durkheim recasts the general sociological preoccupation with social order into a more specific question about social relationships. If one of the things that makes modern society modern is the fact that demands for individual expression continuously increase, does this not suggest that the concept of society will eventually become redundant?

Social solidarity and social order

For Durkheim, the question of how individuals and society remain connected to each other is a question of **social solidarity**, by which he means the forces that hold individuals and society together and that give society its sense of coherence and orderliness:

KEY QUOTE – Émile Durkheim, *The Division of Labour in Society* (1893).
This work had its origins in the question of the relations of the individual to social solidarity. Why does the individual, while becoming more autonomous, depend more upon society? How can he be at once more individual and more solidary? Certainly, these two movements, contradictory as they appear, develop in parallel fashion. This is the problem we are raising. It appeared to us that what resolves this apparent antimony is a transformation of social solidarity due to the steadily growing development of the division of labour. That is how we have been led to make this the object of our study. (Durkheim, 1933 [1893], p 38)

The core of Durkheim's argument is quite simple. The type and quality of relations between individuals and society vary according to the kind of social solidarity that is characteristic of that kind of society. The sources of solidarity are to be found in the kinds of social organisation and cooperative practices that the individual is exposed to. These practices include practical things like family and community relations, institutions of government and administration, but also various cultural and religious beliefs and ideologies. The most important social practices found in society, however, those which are most indicative of social solidarity, are those derived from the division of labour; the forms of economic cooperation and working practices that ensure survival and prosperity.

In pre-modern society the division of labour is relatively undeveloped. Agrarian production close to home is the prevailing way of life, and working relationships and other kinds of social dependence associated with it are also largely immediate, local and uncomplicated. In this form of society the division of labour is not in fact able on its own to provide enough in the way of social solidarity. The remainder comes from what Durkheim calls the **conscience collective**, 'the totality of beliefs and sentiments common to average citizens of the same society' (Durkheim, 1933 [1893] p 79), which binds individuals together not so much in terms of their daily activity but of the religious and cultural beliefs, the social and political ideology, they share. In modern society, in contrast, the division of labour has developed to the extent that almost all the social contexts in which individuals operate are dominated by it. There is still a role for the collective or shared consciousness, for religion and ideology, but they play a far less important role than they once did (we will have more to say about this shortly).

The industrial division of labour has particular characteristics that give a particular *quality* to the social solidarity it provides; a quality that is reflected in the relations between individuals and society. Durkheim calls this more modern or advanced form of social solidarity 'organic solidarity' to capture the way in which the social relations it fosters are based on a mutual recognition of interdependence. The more specialised the individual becomes in her occupation or social role, the more *inadequate* she becomes at all the other tasks that need to be performed. Paradoxically, increasing specialisation of tasks causes greater **individuation**, or separating out occupational and social roles, but, at the same time, requires increasing *dependence* on the expertise of other people. The need to specialise, combined with awareness that specialisation makes the individual more dependent on other specialising individuals, gives social solidarity in modern industrial societies its organic quality. As he puts it:

> The most remarkable effect of the division of labour is not that it increases the output of functions divided, but that it renders them solidary. Its role in all these cases is not simply to embellish or ameliorate existing societies, but to render societies possible which, without it, would not exist. (Durkheim, 1933 [1893], pp 61)

This organic quality is not found in societies that have a rudimentary division of labour, because social solidarity in this form of society depends on the *conscience collective*, which imposes a much more directive and authoritarian form of social order. Durkheim calls this variety of social solidarity *mechanical solidarity* because, in these societies, individuals are held within society 'automatically', by the intimate, simple and relatively unchanging social contexts in which they live. There is less separating out (individuation) of roles and thus less opportunity for individual specialisation.

The limits of mechanical solidarity

The key reason why Durkheim was so interested in these two distinct types of social solidarity was that mechanical forms of solidarity, based on an all-powerful conscience collective, actually hinder social advancement. For intellectuals like Saint-Simon, Comte and Durkheim working in the post-Enlightenment period, these ossified belief systems do not even have the capacity for change. In historical terms, it was the unwillingness of the traditional mindset, together with the inflexibility of the mechanistic social solidarity it fostered, which meant that pre-modern society could not move on. Shared ideas, values and beliefs are still very important in modern societies, but their basic constitution is one that accepts the need for change. Modern ideas, one might say, are geared to the idea of change.

In the modern world view, for example, the increasing individuation, or separating out of occupational and social roles caused by the division of labour, is accompanied in the moral sphere by an increased acceptance of individual freedoms and appetites, forms of expression and motivation, which are largely inhibited under regimes of mechanical solidarity. As Durkheim puts it:

> Whereas [mechanical solidarity] implies that individuals resemble each other, [organic solidarity] presumes their difference. The first is possible only in so far as the individual personality is absorbed into the collective personality; the second is possible only if each one has a sphere of action which is peculiar to him; that is, a personality. It is necessary, then, that the collective

> conscience leave open a part of the individual conscience in order that special functions may be established there, functions which it cannot regulate. The more this region is extended, the stronger is the cohesion which results from [organic] solidarity. (Durkheim, 1933 [1893], pp 130–1)

Following an evolutionary model of social development that is reminiscent of both Spencer and Comte, Durkheim argues that the mechanical solidarity of pre-modern society tends to decay as the social division of labour becomes more complex. He is arguing that an advanced social division of labour is in fact incompatible with a strongly overarching *conscience collective*. At the point in history where strong claims to individuality appear, where the rights and responsibilities of individuality grow beyond the limits set by the collective conscience, mechanical solidarity breaks down. Since social solidarity is a prerequisite for social order of any kind, a new form of solidarity must emerge, and one which accommodates the strong notion of the individual and of individuality. For Durkheim, it is the social division of labour that performs this function:

> In sum, since mechanical solidarity progressively becomes enfeebled, life properly social must decrease or another solidarity must slowly come in to take the place of that which has gone. The choice must be made. In vain shall we contend that the collective conscience extends and grows stronger at the same time as that of individuals. We have just proved that the two terms vary in a sense inverse to each other. Social progress, however, does not consist in a continual dissolution. On the contrary, the more we advance, the more profoundly do societies reveal the sentiment of self and unity. There must, then, be some other social link which produces this result; this cannot be any other than that which comes from the division of labour. (Durkheim, 1933 [1893], pp 172–3)

One of the advantages of linking the individual-versus-society debate explicitly with the question of social solidarity is that it allows Durkheim to argue that developments in the demands of individuals and of modern notions of individuality, are actually complimented by changes in the nature of society rather than being in opposition to them. Durkheim sees the emergence of modern individuals, and of modern notions of individuality, as an inevitable corollary of the advanced division of labour in society.

New spaces for new individuals

Rather than driving a wedge between individuals and society the advanced division of labour gives rise to new kinds of individuals and endorses the strong notion of individuality. Modern society, just like modern industry, needs 'modern' individuals, just as individuals who want to behave in modern ways and to express modern attitudes and beliefs need an advanced division of labour where they can be expressed. The division of labour serves to reconcile the individual with society.

As Durkheim sees it, 'the problem of the individual' in modern society is that politicians and other intellectuals have been slow to recognise the emergence of this new kind of individualism. Like many other social critics, Durkheim believes that the earlier conception of 'acquisitive individualism' in which individuals are seen as selfish, egoistic and aggressively competitive, which had been popularised by utilitarian philosophers like Jeremy Bentham and John Stuart Mill, and liberal economists like Adam Smith and David Ricardo, had to be set aside. Utilitarian conceptions of competitive individualism were being superseded by a new and properly socialised conception. This is moral individualism (the influence of Saint-Simon is clear), in which individuals are seen as an embodiment of the core virtue of doing things for the common good.

The strength of modern individuality is not measured in terms of how much it promotes the selfish and **egoistic** interests of any particular individual, but in terms of the contribution the individual makes to the collective social body, that is, to society. Indeed, Durkheim goes so far as to suggest that the new cult of the individual becomes a central facet of the *conscience collective* of modern society. Just as it is the duty of the individual to work towards the social good, it is the function of society to provide individuals with fruitful opportunities to express themselves in as many ways as possible. The key point to grasp is that individuality and social opportunity cannot be separated one from the other.

Durkheim's contribution to social theory

Durkheim's analysis in *The Division of Labour* provided him with a starting point for further detailed studies of particular aspects of the individual-versus-society question. We can look briefly at a number of these and make some general points about the basic social-theoretical question of where the balance lies between the autonomy of the individual and the integrity of society. The presumption is that social order depends on there being a satisfactory resolution to this potential source of tension.

Durkheim's strong society thesis

Durkheim's social theory places great importance on society, not just in terms of the spaces and roles it provides social actors to express themselves, but also as a repository of collective phenomena. He tries very hard to establish a 'strong society thesis' in sociological theory. For him society is not just a useful way of summarising aggregates of individual social actors (in the way that herd and flock describe aggregates of animals), but a distinct entity in its own right. A form of reality having an existence that is independent of the individuals it contains.

In order to establish his arguments Durkheim constantly searches for examples of collective phenomena or social facts that exist quite separately from any particular individual. If such phenomena cannot be attributed to individuals and yet have a significant impact upon their lives, then they must come from somewhere else. Rejecting cosmic, divine and natural origins, and eschewing individual features of personality and psychology as having significant explanatory power, the answer must be that they come from society itself. A clear example of this, and one which we will be discussing in more detail in Chapter Nine, is language. The words I am writing and that you are now reading do not belong to me or to you but to the system of English language that we share. A little more abstractly, the *meaning* of the words and of the examples I am using was not created by me or by you but resides within the wider system of cultural signs that we also share. In this sense, the image I can create in your mind when I write 'the soft fluffy bunny frolicked in the summer sunshine' *proves* there is such a thing as society.

Religion and society

Durkheim's favourite example of such a social phenomenon, and one which he also uses to develop his explanation of how individuals and society are bound together, is systems of religious belief. His thoughts on the subject were published in France in 1912 as *The Elementary Forms of Religious Life: The Totemic System in Australia*, and in an earlier influential essay, *Primitive Classification* (1903), co-written with his nephew, the well-known anthropologist Marcel Mauss:

KEY QUOTE – Émile Durkheim, *The Elementary Forms of Religious Life* (1912).

The general conclusion of the book which the reader has before him is that religion is something eminently social. Religious representations are collective representations which express collective realities; the rites are a manner of acting which take rise in the midst of assembled groups and which are destined to excite, maintain, or recreate certain mental states in these groups.... There can be no society which does not feel the need of upholding and reaffirming at regular intervals the collective sentiments and the collective ideas which make its unity and its personality. (Durkheim, 1968a [1912], p 12)

What Durkheim is getting at here is that one of the functions that is performed by society, and one which cannot be provided by individuals on their own, is to offer a context in which the individual can express the ideas, values and beliefs that she holds in common with other individuals. By attending a collective event, such as a church service, community gathering, political rally or rock concert, the individual has the chance to recharge her sense of membership of a group that she is a part of, but which is also beyond her. In modern society, and recalling our earlier comments about the new moral individuality, collective events are not about the subordination of the individual to the group, but the individual reasserting her allegiance to the collectivity. Moreover, the motivation to do so is not simply because of a rationalist–utilitarian calculation that society membership benefits the individual in purely monetary terms, but because membership of society is rational–moral in the sense that the individual relies on society for her very sense of individuality. The payback to the individual of society membership is primarily moral and emotional and only secondarily material.

Representation

Durkheim uses the concept of *representation* to capture the more general sense in which society provides ideas, images and ritual practices that, a bit like a mirror, reflect back to the individual a sense of meaning and purpose, a set of guidelines that helps him or her to make sense of social reality. These representations are sometimes quite literal and sometimes more symbolic. Sometimes they are embodied in artefacts and sometimes in social practices and events. Literal artefact representations include such things as descriptions, maps or diagrams, even photographs and models, which provide us with a kind of record, a confirmation of how, in a practical sense, things are. Symbolic representations go further and provide us with an *interpretation* of how things are. The image or object is not just a copy, but also tries to show us the meaning it carries. For example, if we compared a painting of something with a photograph of the same object or event, the painting would convey a different quality of information than the photograph. In one sense, the eye of the artist sees the same thing as the lens of the camera, but the image on the canvas is embellished with a degree of creative transformation that a photograph cannot convey. What makes an artist 'great' is his or her capacity to get us to see the world, to represent it in our minds, in a way that we have not done before. Michelangelo and Pablo Picasso are great artists because they helped us see the world, to understand it, differently. Many cultural artefacts convey both kinds of representation at the same time. A statue of a famous person, for example, is a literal image of what that person looked like, but if it is placed on the top of a grand column or plinth, or stands in front of an important building, it becomes a symbolic representation, a celebration of the qualities of that person. Most famous statues signify military triumph, political success or religious or spiritual dignity.

The same combinations of literal representation and symbolic interpretation are also found in the various communal or collective events people take part in. Taking the communion service in Christian religious practice as an example, the congregation re-enact the events that are claimed to have taken place at the last supper. By literally eating a communion wafer and drinking wine at the alter, they make a copy of the original event but at the same time engage in the much more important symbolic aspect of the ritual, which is to imagine that the wine and bread are in fact the blood and body of Christ. In Durkheim's words, just quoted, both literally and symbolically, the communion service gives members of that particular society a means of 'reaffirming at regular intervals the collective sentiments and the collective ideas which make up its unity and its personality'.

The point Durkheim wants to make about all such representations, and especially those contained in structured, often ritualised, collective practices like religion, is that, both practically and symbolically, they cannot be anything other than *social* events. As examples of what most social theorists would now call **cultural practices**, such events and participations provide the individual with a vital source of collective knowledge and understanding. As Durkheim puts it: 'The important thing to know is not the way in which a certain thinker individually conceives a certain institution but the group's conception of it; this conception alone is socially significant' (Durkheim, 1964 [1895], pp xlvi, Preface to the 2nd edn). Cultural practices and artefacts literally and symbolically represent the extent of this general agreement.

▶▶ We can note in passing, that some social theorists in the 20th century, for example, the French structuralist Louis Althusser whose work we will be discussing in Chapter Nine, argue that societies produce an ideological image of the whole of society, not just symbolic representations of bits and pieces of it, which may in fact distort or otherwise deliberately misrepresent the real reality it claims to represent. Powerful groups use ideological misrepresentations to obscure the true picture in order to pursue their own particular interests.

Anomie

Aside from the artistic or esoteric purposes they might also serve, the primary function of religious and other collective representations is to consolidate the links between the individual and society. They are one of the varieties of social cement that bind the individual to society. In terms of the notion of moral regulation we introduced at the start of this chapter, they are, for Durkheim, a means of helping the individual keep his or her personal appetites and expectations within the limits of what can be achieved in society. The importance of regulation, and, more especially, the negative or pathological consequences it can have for the individual and for society if it does not work out properly, are addressed by Durkheim with his use of the concept of *anomie*. Anomie describes a state of limbo and uncertainty that critically undermines the individual's sense of security and well-being. It will be useful to look briefly at two parts of Durkheim's work that feature the concept of anomie.

Anomie and the limits of the division of labour

Despite his generally optimistic expectations about the beneficial effects of the division of labour, Durkheim acknowledges that the increasing individuation of social roles, and the new attitude of moral individualism associated with it, might cause some difficulties. He accepts that the division of labour has progressed too quickly for some, and yet too slowly for others. It is not enough, for example, simply to offer the individual an abstract choice about his or her occupational and other social roles, these choices have to be *real* choices. If the individual is not able to make choices for herself, then in effect she is being forced to do something against her individual will (and her will to participate in the new individualism). If the individual feels that the choices she is being offered are false she is also likely to regard the system that gives rise to them as illegitimate. At the other extreme, if the division of labour progresses too quickly, individuals might lose a sense of how these newly individuated and individualised roles correspond with the things they actually want to achieve. Under these circumstances the division of labour deprives individuals of a sense of connection with society.

ILLUSTRATION

We can illustrate this point by considering what happens when a new technology like personal computers or word processors are introduced at work. On the positive side, people can expect to receive training and so improve their skills. New ways of working might be introduced allowing more flexibility thus making work tasks more interesting and the working environment more convivial. Hierarchic divisions between one category of employee and another, which were developed in the era of bosses and typists, might be replaced by horizontal structures in which working relations are based more on co-working than on orders 'from above'.

On the negative side, however, retraining might not be very attractive to some people, for example, older workers who might prefer to carry on as before. They have acquired seniority based on experience and will resent being pushed out by younger, possibly less experienced, staff just because they have been trained on the new machines. Opportunities for moving jobs and for internal promotion might also be undermined once the new technology becomes the industry standard. Most worrying of all, employers introduce new technologies because they are more efficient. If it takes fewer people to do the same work, the likely result will be job losses. The positive experience of some employees therefore has to be balanced against the loss of security and well-being, the anomie, of others.

Anomie, regulation, solidarity and the suicide rate in society

Durkheim's interest in what might happen if the links between individuals and society break down led him to make an investigation of what is perhaps the most dramatic consequence of such a loss of social contact, namely, suicide. Again he uses the concept of anomie, but this time to describe situations where the individual feels they have lost their connection with society. In this important study (published as *Le Suicide* in 1897) of the social causes of the suicide rate in modern society, which is regarded by many as the first empirical study in sociology, Durkheim brings together several of the themes from other areas of his work. First, the study applies the methodological principles that he had set out in his *Rules of Sociological Method*. Most importantly, it treats the suicide rate, that is, the distribution of suicides among a given population as recorded in statistical data, as a social fact. Second, he defines the social causes of suicide (he regards the possible environmental and psychological causes as not being useful to sociologists because they have no discernible social pattern) very much in terms of how individual well-being is regulated by the quality of social relationships. Third, his analysis of the suicide rate and the conclusions he draws, depend for much of their qualitative substance on his earlier analysis of social solidarity. This study is not explicitly an empirical sociological testing of the more social-theoretical conclusions about social solidarity in modern society as described in *The Division of Labour in Society*, but one certainly helps us make sense of the other.

The study was based on comparing suicide rates in one part of the population with rates in another part. Durkheim found that rates were consistently higher among Protestants than among Jews or Catholics. Having compared various aspects of these different religious practices, Durkheim concluded that the major difference was that Protestantism places much greater emphasis on the *individual responsibility* of its followers for *their own* salvation, and that its practices are less solidary or communal than those of other religions. It is not, however, differences in the particular beliefs of different religions that are the most important factor where suicide is concerned, but the degree of integration and support that they offer to their followers: 'The essential thing is that they be capable of supporting a sufficiently intense collective life. And because the Protestant church has less consistency than the others it has less moderating effect upon suicide' (Durkheim, 1968b [1897], p 170).

Generalising from the characteristics of Protestant religious practice to the characteristics of social groups as a whole, Durkheim reaches the conclusion that the suicide rate is likely to be higher among social groups (or whole societies) where the individual feels that he or she is detached from the social group. If sources of social support and reassurance are weak, individuals are forced to rely much more heavily upon themselves and might resort to desperate measures at moments of crisis. Turning his attention to the likely causes of suicide in groups where individuals were highly integrated into society, Durkheim concluded that excessive integration could also be problematic if it did not allow people sufficient space to express individuality: 'Whereas [egoistic suicide] is due to excessive individuation, [altruistic suicide] is caused by too rudimentary individuation. One occurs because society allows the individual to escape it, being insufficiently aggregated in some parts or even in the whole; the other, because society holds him in too strict tutelage' (Durkheim, 1968b [1897], p 221).

Between these two types of causes of suicide Durkheim identifies a third, which arises not so much because of problems with social integration, but because of a failure to regulate people's behaviour and expectations. As we have already described it in this chapter, for

Durkheim, one of the most important functions of society is to help the individual realise that there are limits to what can be achieved: 'unlimited desires are insatiable by definition and insatiability is rightly considered a sign of morbidity. Being unlimited, they constantly and infinitely surpass the means at their command.... To pursue a goal which is by definition unattainable is to condemn oneself to a state of perpetual unhappiness' (Durkheim, 1968b [1897], pp 246–8). If these limits are not recognised then the result will be anomie expressed as disappointment, resentment and loss of a sense of emotional and personal security:

KEY QUOTE – Émile Durkheim, *Suicide* (1897).
Anomie, therefore, is a regular and specific factor in suicide in our modern societies; one of the springs from which the annual contingent feeds. So we have here a new type to distinguish from the others [egoistic and altruistic]. It differs from them in its dependence, not on the way in which individuals are attached to society, but on how it regulates them. Egoistic suicide results from man's no longer finding a basis for existence in life; altruistic suicide, because this basis for existence appears to man situated beyond life itself. The third sort of suicide ... results from man's activity's lacking regulation and his consequent sufferings. By virtue of its origin we shall assign this last category the name of anomic suicide. (Durkheim, 1968b [1897], p 258)

Individual versus society revisited

We conclude this chapter by returning to the core issue with which we began it; the relationship of the individual to society. One of the most important implications of Durkheim's analysis of the social causes of the suicide rate is that it forces him to confront again the central issues of the extent to which social life dominates the individual life. We know that society must be more than the sum of the individuals who live in it, because there are many social phenomena that cannot be expressed by individuals alone: 'It is not true that society is made up only of individuals; it also includes material things, which play an essential role in the common life' (Durkheim, 1968b [1897], p 313). At the same time, however, he goes to great lengths to stress that he is *not saying* that individuals do not exist as such, or that they are unimportant:

> We clearly did not imply by this that society can exist without individuals.... But we did mean: 1. that the group formed by associated individuals has a reality of a different sort from each individual considered singly; 2. that collective states exist in the

group from whose nature they spring, before they affect the individual as such and establish in him in a new form a purely inner existence. (Durkheim, 1968b [1897], p 320)

Whichever way you slice it, Durkheim is left in the rather uncomfortable position of trying to reconcile the opposing forces of individuality and communality, the push of the individual against the pull of society:

> Two antagonistic forces confront each other. One, the collective force, tries to take possession of the individual; the other, the individual force, repulses it. To be sure, the former is much stronger than the latter, since it is made of a combination of all the individual forces; but as it also encounters as many resistances as there are separate persons, it is partially exhausted in these multifarious contests and reaches us disfigured and enfeebled. (Durkheim, 1968b [1897], p 319)

The solution he offers is that the individual has a double existence. He or she exists in the real world as a concrete entity or object, but also, and at the same time, has a different kind of **subjective** existence, which exists in his or her head. Similarly, society has a double existence. It too exists as a concrete entity that is 'out there' but it cannot be purely separate from the individual because many of the social phenomena of which it is made (such as language) only 'exist' in the consciousness of the individual. At one level at least, society exists as a reflection of all the fragmentary consciousnesses that individuals have of it. Individuals are required, as it were, to bear witness to the existence of society; society is literally a figment of the collective imagination. Part of the challenge, then, faced by social theorists is to recognise that societies have distinctive characteristics that *are above and beyond* the individuals contained within or by them, but, at the same time, that individuals have to invest something of themselves in making the kind of society in which *they want* to live.

Key points box – Durkheim's contribution to the individual-versus-society debate

☑ All societies require some form of *social solidarity*, which holds individuals and society together.

☑ Modern society developed because of the emergence of a new basis for social solidarity, the division of labour in industry and in society more generally.

☑ In modern society occupational and social roles become more individuated and specialised.

☑ Increasing specialisation generates a new kind of cooperative integration between individuals and society.

☑ This new form of *organic* solidarity also develops at the level of the *collective conscience* around the idea of moral individuality.

☑ Society provides the context and many of the means of expressing moral individuality in which the social good and individual well-being are seen as being closely connected.

☑ Society also provides the individual *culture* as a place where shared ideas, values and beliefs can be developed and expressed.

☑ The solidarity individuals experience through the division of labour and cultural practice helps them regulate their behaviour and avoid anomie.

Practice box

⮕ Which of the key problems of social theory was Durkheim most interested in?

⮕ How does the division of labour provide a new kind of *social solidarity*?

⮕ The old individualism was based on the idea of competitive self-interest. What is the new *moral individualism* all about?

⮕ Why are cultural items and practices so important to the individual?

⮕ Give an example of a cultural social practice that has *symbolic meaning* for its participants.

⮕ What is *anomie* and how does society help the individual to avoid it?

Further reading

Émile Durkheim, *The Division of Labour in Society* (Free Press, 1933 [1893]).

Émile Durkheim, *The Rules of Sociological Method* (Free Press, 1964 [1895]).

Émile Durkheim, *Suicide* (Routledge, 1968b [1897]).

Anthony Giddens, *Émile Durkheim: Selected Writings* (Cambridge University Press, 1972).

Steven Lukes, *Émile Durkheim: His Life and Work* (Allen Lane, 1973).

Gianfranco Poggi, *Durkheim* (Oxford University Press, 2000).

Websites

For useful resources on Durkheim's life and work try:
wwwemiledurkheim.com

Also useful for summary information is the Émile Durkheim Archive at:
durkheim.itgo.com/main.html

CHAPTER FOUR

KARL MARX, CAPITALISM AND REVOLUTION

Durkheim played a decisive role in establishing the academic credibility of sociology at the turn of the 20th century. He also outlined its general field of enquiry and provided a repertoire of concepts that other social theorists continue to use in their own work. Outside the world of theory, however, Durkheim's name is little known, and apart from those who have studied *Suicide* as part of their professional training, his direct influence is minimal. The same cannot be said of the second of the big names we are looking at in these chapters, the radical German philosopher, social theorist and revolutionary thinker Karl Marx. One might even argue that, although it has been very large indeed, Marx's influence on social theory is nothing compared with his influence on actual world events. The historical importance and scope of his work is truly remarkable. Intellectually, and bearing in mind he was born a generation before Durkheim and Max Weber (who we will be discussing in Chapter Five), he draws on intellectual currents that began during the 18th century, he writes about events taking place during his own lifetime in the 19th century, and his legacy has had a profound impact on the history of the 20th century. Now, in the 21st century, we are still reading and writing about him and his ideas.

In an introductory book like this one, and given his almost unique status as a true giant of social theory, we need to be especially selective in looking at his contribution. One of the premises of Marx's own thinking is that real understanding only comes from looking at things in their historical context. He is much less interested in grand ideas and vague hypotheses than in the material reality in which events occur. We will adopt a similarly pragmatic approach here and explore just a few of Marx's key ideas very much in terms of the historical and intellectual contexts from which they arose.

In this chapter we will look at:

Marx's personal background

Key concepts of Marx's social theory (materialism versus idealism, alienation, theory of historical materialism, labour theory of value)

The impact of Marx's ideas on social theory

Marx's personal background

Karl Marx was born in 1818 in Trier in Germany into a prosperous middle-class family. His parents were Jewish but his father converted to Protestantism so that he could retain his job as a senior lawyer in the Court of Appeal. Aged 17 Marx left this comfortable home to study law first in Bonn and then in Berlin in 1836. His interests soon shifted, however, as he became involved with various radical socialist intellectual and political groups at university. He completed his PhD in 1841 but having fallen foul of the Prussian authorities, he had to abandon any hope of gaining an academic or even professional post, and he and his fiancée, Jenny, married and moved to Paris in 1843.

The move to Paris was crucial for Marx for two reasons. First, and still aged only 26, he wrote his most important philosophical work known as the 1844 *Paris Manuscripts*. Although these were not published until 1930 (and were not widely read until the 1950s), it is here that he introduced the concept of **alienation**, and laid the philosophical foundations for much of his later work. The second important event was meeting his lifelong friend Friedrich Engels (1820–95). Despite being heir to a flourishing textiles business with factories in Germany and a mill in Manchester, Engels had developed a reputation as a forthright critic of capitalist industry in his book, published in 1845, *The Condition of the Working Class in England*. Sharing many ideas with Marx, and certainly also favouring a socialist political outlook, Marx and Engels began a 40-year collaboration that lasted until Marx's death in 1883.

In 1845 Marx and his family were forced to leave Paris by the authorities there and they spent the next three years in Brussels. After a last unsuccessful attempt to return to Germany in 1848 (which was also the year in which Marx and Engels published *The Communist Manifesto*), the family moved to London in 1849 where they remained for the next 30 years. The picture we have of Marx spending long hours in the reading room of the British Library, while his near-poverty-stricken family had to get by on very irregular earnings from his journalism and financial support from Engels, is complete. The result for social theory was Marx's great work in economic theory *Das Kapital* (or simply *Capital*). The first volume was published in 1867 and volumes two and three, edited by Engels after Marx's death, in 1885 and 1894. Also important from the period around 1858 is his *Contribution to a Critique of Political Economy* and a collection of 'fragments' or 'notes', which were eventually published in 1953 as *Grundrisse*. A brief summary of Marx's and Engels' political activity is given in Figure 4.1.

Figure 4.1: Chronology of Karl Marx's and Frederick Engels' political activity

	Chronology of Marx and Engels and the Communist Party
1847	Marx and Engels join the newly formed Communist League
1847	Engels produces first drafts of the *Manifesto*
1848	Marx rewrites and edits final version of the *Manifesto*
1848	*The Communist Manifesto* published in German in London
1850	Addresses Central Committee of the Communist League
1850	First English version of the *Manifesto* published
1864-76	Founding of the First International by Marx
1883	Death of Karl Marx
1889	Second International formed by Engels
1893	Independent Labour Party founded in Britain
1919	First Congress of the Third International or 'Comintern' under Lenin

Key concepts in Marx's social theory

As is the case with all philosophers and social theorists, Marx's social theory was a critical response to the leading theories and intellectual traditions of the day. His approach was to become fully engaged with a particular set of issues, reach conclusions about them and then fashion his own variations. In many ways, Marx's impact on social theory comes from the fact that his theory does not simply amount to a moderate reworking of what went before, a slight modification here and a bit of tinkering there, but is instead a complete transformation of it. It is this radical intellectual technique that makes Marx *a revolutionary thinker* rather just than somebody who writes *about* revolution in capitalist society. Figure 4.2 charts the main stages in the development of Marx's social theory against four distinct periods of his life.

Figure 4.2: Karl Marx's intellectual development

Period	Place	Main focus of study & activity
1830s	University student in Berlin	The philosophy of GWF Hegel, **idealism** versus **materialism**
Early 1840s	Member of intellectual community in Paris	Theories of human nature and the concept of **alienation**
Later 1840s	Political exile in Brussels and London	Theory of **historical materialism**, *The Communist Manifesto* (1848)
1850s on	Years of study at the British Library	Critique of capitalist exploitation, 'labour theory of value'

The strategy we will follow in this chapter is to pick a central theme or concept from each of these four main periods and see how they add to the overall sum of Marx's social theory. The four we have chosen are:

■ the materialist view of knowledge and of society;
■ the concept of alienation;
■ the theory of historical materialism; and
■ the theory of capitalist exploitation as explained in Marx's 'labour theory of value'.

A common thread that runs throughout is Marx's preoccupation with conflict in society. One could say that, whether as a philosophy, an approach to social theory or as a political strategy, Marxist social theory specialises in the analysis of social conflict. This contrasts with the emphasis on social order in the work of Durkheim.

The materialist view of knowledge and historical development

When Marx entered university in the 1830s the German intellectual world was dominated by the work of the German **idealist** philosopher G.W.F. Hegel (1770–1831). In his key works, *The Phenomenology of Mind* (1807) and *The Philosophy of Right* (1821), Hegel developed a very ambitious philosophical system based on the premise that the ultimate purpose of human existence was to express the highest form of what he called the human **Geist** or 'Spirit'. This Spirit was not a physical or material entity but an abstract expression of the moral and ethical qualities and capacities, the highest cultural ideals, which, he argued, were the ultimate expression of what it is to be a human being. For Hegel, material life was the practical means through which this quest for the ultimate realisation of human consciousness, the search for a really truthful awareness of reality, could be expressed. Material life, and this included such things as the economy, the political institutions of

the **state** and other social organisations in **civil society**, are a means
to this higher end and not an end in themselves.

In saying all this Hegel was building on the philosophical system of
his great German predecessor Immanuel Kant (1724–1804). Kant was
a **rationalist** philosopher believing that the human mind is uniquely
equipped with the capacity to understand the exterior physical world
before we encounter it. This understanding is generally well organised
and sensible, and thus 'rational'. It is well-established, for example, that
all humans are born with the capacity to learn language. We learn the
words and grammar of a language through experience but *the capacity*
to do so in an orderly fashion comes before the learning process, or
is *a priori*, which would in fact not be possible without it. We do not
learn the capacity to learn, this is something that we already have. For
rationalists, and especially rationalist **idealists**, human knowledge and
understanding are more about what goes on inside our minds than
outside of them. Real reality, or the most significant version of reality,
is not the physical stuff that surrounds us, but the reflection of it we
hold or create in our minds. For Hegel, then, reason and thought are
not simply part of reality *they are reality*. It follows from this that the
laws and principles that govern human thought must also be the laws
and principles that govern the whole of reality.

▶▶   Kant tried to reconcile his **rationalist** view with the strict
      objectivism and **empiricism** of John Locke (1632–1704) and
      David Hume (1711–96) who argue that all our ideas and concepts,
      including both physical sensations and intellectual reflections, are
      derived from practical experience of the world around us and not
      from pre-existing capacities of the human mind. From an empiricist
      viewpoint, there cannot be any knowledge or consciousness until
      after we have had physical contact with the material world around
      us. This dispute over the two basic kinds of knowledge – knowledge
      derived *a priori* from within the conscious mind and knowledge
      derived retrospectively from sense perception – provides an
      important backdrop to debates about the nature of social-scientific
      knowledge.

Combining a strongly rationalist position with his own idealist
system based on the idea of Spirit as the search for a really truthful
understanding of human consciousness and its real relation with
material or objective reality, Hegel goes beyond Kant by suggesting
that, because the minds of all human beings are essentially the
same (physiologically and in terms of their wired-in capacities for
interpreting the exterior world), we are all part of *the same* overarching
consciousness. My consciousness of the highest human ideals and my

desire to find the most truthful ways of expressing them are essentially the same as yours because my consciousness works in the same way as yours does. If Hegel is correct in arguing that thought and reality are one and the same thing, and that the laws that govern human thought are therefore also the laws that govern reality, then in a sense all of humanity will eventually have the same thoughts. Differences between social actors in terms of their thoughts are to do with differences in their stages of development, how far they have progressed in the capacity for reason, not with differences in how they think.

Dialectic

The process by which this quest for the ultimate truth is carried on involves a *dialectical* process in which one state of awareness about the nature of reality (**thesis**) is shown to be false by a further and higher state of awareness (**antithesis**) and is finally resolved in a final and true state of awareness (**synthesis**). The idea of the dialectic comes from Ancient Greek philosophy and describes a situation in which truth is arrived at through a process of debate or conversation. A particular point of view is stated, this is challenged by an alternative view and eventually a third view emerges, which is superior to them both. Hegel refines the term to refer to the pattern or logic that human thought must follow. The dialectic is his explanation of the intellectual and philosophical process, inherent within and throughout human consciousness, by which social actors finally come to realise the truth of the idea that thought is reality. Hegel uses the same triadic approach in suggesting that the contradictions or imperfections of the family and of civil society (corresponding with thesis and antithesis) are finally resolved by the institutions of the state, which correspond with the new ethical synthesis. The state thus provides the practical means of expressing the universal Spirit.

Sublation

A further important analytical device used by Hegel is the idea of *sublation*. He uses this term to describe the need social actors have to feel at ease with their understanding of reality and how they fit into it. Lack of sublation shows itself as a feeling of estrangement, of not fitting in, of being at odds with the world and being confused about the nature of reality. Moving away from home for the first time, starting an unfamiliar job or being let down by a friend are all situations where, in Hegel's terms, the social actors experience a sense of estrangement and insecurity, a lack of sublation. Hegel felt that at its root, estrangement arose because uncertainty about the nature of reality 'out there' caused us to be uncertain about reality 'in here'. The extent to which we do not fully understand the objective world around us is also the extent to which we are ignorant about our own subjective inner nature. However much we live inside our heads and build up versions of reality there (and it is very difficult to see where else consciousness could come from), we are ourselves also physical objects that are a part of the exterior world we are trying to understand. We are both subjects (things that do things) and objects (things that have things done to them) at one and the same time.

Hegel believed that his system of idealist rationality offered a solution to this fundamental dilemma and that his ideas presented the highest synthesis of philosophical thought so far achieved. The fact that he had discovered the underlying principle of the dialectic process as it applies to the development of true human awareness of the nature of reality made Hegel even more convinced of the value of his contribution. The Spirit had become self-aware in terms of understanding the mechanism of its own creation.

Standing Hegel on his head

Although Hegel's work was extremely popular in Germany in the 1830s, not least because it led people to believe that the German state of the time represented the most advanced and civilised kind of society yet achieved, it was eventually challenged by a new generation of intellectuals who proposed a counter-thesis of their own. The Young Hegelians as they were known applied the triadic apparatus of thesis, antithesis and synthesis to Hegel's own philosophical system. The most influential of this group was Ludwig Feuerbach (1804–72), who argued that by subordinating the material world to the realm of consciousness and ideas, Hegel's obsession with the coming of the great universal Spirit was not in the least bit rational or objective in the scientific sense and was in fact nothing more than a form of religious mysticism. Rather than describing how social actors might overcome their sense of estrangement from material reality, Hegel simply made matters worse by suggesting that it was not objective reality that was the problem but simply the inadequacy of social actors' understanding of it. As Marx puts it: 'Feuerbach's great achievement is to have shown that philosophy is nothing more than religion brought into thought and developed in thought, and that it is equally to be condemned as another form … of the estrangement of man's nature' (Marx, 1975, p 381).

At university Marx soon became interested in the ideas of the counter-thesis group and of Feuerbach in particular and eventually rejected much of the Hegelian thesis. Crucial to his own development, however, Marx retained key elements and adapted them for his own use. While giving Hegel, 'that mighty thinker', credit for developing a number of very important insights, Marx argued that he had applied them incorrectly, and had thus reached incomplete conclusions about the true nature of real reality. Marx's social theory can be thought of as the new synthesis that emerged out of the collision of Hegel's thesis and the Young Hegelians' antithesis. The key to Marx's critique of Hegel is very simple; he takes a number of his most useful conceptual tools and uses them *the other way around*:

KEY QUOTE – Karl Marx, *Capital*, volume 1 (1867).
My dialectic method is not only different from the Hegelian, but is its direct opposite. To Hegel, the life-process of the human brain, i.e. the process of thinking ... is the creator of the real world, and the real world is only the external, phenomenal form of 'the Idea'. With me, on the contrary, the ideal is nothing else than the material world reflected by the human mind, and translated into forms of thought.... The mystification which dialectic suffers in Hegel's hands, by no means prevents him from being the first to present its general form of working in a comprehensive and conscious manner. With him the dialectic is standing on its head. It must be turned right side up again, if you would discover the rational kernel within the mystical shell. (Marx, 1954 [1867], p 29)

What Marx is getting at here, is that whereas Hegel, in common with all idealist thinkers, argues that the most truthful version of the world is the one that we hold in our consciousness, Marx proposed the opposite or **materialist** view, which is that the most real version must be the one we can actually touch and feel. For materialist thinkers, the really real world is not the one we create in our minds but the untidy, crowded, noisy physical matter that surrounds us. If we want to know about *real* reality, and provide a truthful account of it, social theory must begin with an analysis of real things and not become preoccupied with their 'ideal' representation in our thoughts. Even the most perfectly polished mirror needs something to reflect or it has no purpose at all. Worse still, it might be used to project a completely false image or **ideology**. So Marx reverses Hegel's approach by arguing that the quest for knowledge should not begin with abstract conceptions in the realm of ideas, but with a positive analysis of actually existing material things in the real physical world.

History

Marx's reversal of Hegel's idealist approach in favour of a materialist one has a number of important consequences for his own social theory. One of these is that it gives a real boost to the role of social action on historical development. Marx agreed with the rationalist perspective of Hegel (and thus with Kant and many other Enlightenment thinkers), that in coming to know the world, social actors make a practical difference to it. The mind does not simply reflect images of the world in consciousness without affecting them, but is actively part of that world and so affects the way things turn out. What Marx is less happy about, however, is the tendency of the idealist approach always to give priority to human intervention at the level of abstract conceptions and ideas, and correspondingly to underplay the significance of the impact of social action on material circumstances.

For Marx, it is quite inadequate to regard human history, the development of society itself, as merely a by-product of the quest for ultimate knowledge in the abstract realm of human consciousness. As far as he is concerned, all Hegel has discovered is 'the abstract, logical, speculative expression of the movement of history ... history is not yet the real history of man as a given subject' (Marx, 1975 [1844], p 382). Marx argues vigorously for the materialist view of things, which is that the most important ways in which social actors affect the world around them is not through 'abstract mental labour' but in their concrete and practical actions as 'real, corporeal beings with their feet planted firmly on the solid earth and breathing all the powers of nature' (Marx, 1975 [1844], p 389).

Shared experiences

Another important consequence of reversing Hegel, is that it affects Marx's understanding of what is the real substance of relations between the individual and society and between one individual and another. For him, the struggle that social actors have in trying to comprehend the material reality that surrounds them is not an intellectual or philosophical difficulty but a practical one. It is the material conditions in which social actors struggle to survive that should be the focus of our attention and not the struggle they might or might not have to reach a particular state of philosophical enlightenment. Indeed, any prospect of achieving the latter must depend, first of all, on achieving physical survival. What social actors have most in common, and which can most easily be observed, are the material conditions of society surrounding them. Marx's **realist** and materialist position points decisively towards the need for a detailed and non-mystifying account of material reality 'out there' and away from the 'abstract mental labour' of the idealist philosopher. Allowing the pendulum to swing fully in the direction of material phenomena, Marx famously makes the following declaration:

KEY QUOTE – Karl Marx, *Early Writings* (1975 [1844]).
The mode of production of material life conditions the general process of social, political and intellectual life. It is not the consciousness of men that determines their existence, but their social existence that determines their consciousness. (Marx, 1975 [1844], p 425; from the Preface to 'A Contribution to a Critique of Political Economy')

Conflict

We noted earlier that a key difference between the social theory of Marx, and of Weber, and Durkheim is that the former do not accept that human history simply unfolds in a gradual and benign fashion but that it is marked by periods of conflict and moments of crisis. The reason why Marx thought this can be traced straight back to the criticisms of Hegel and the idealist approach we have just been looking at. If the thing that really motivates social actors is the need to meet their basic survival needs, it follows that the most likely source of conflict between social actors in society will be to do with the struggle for material resources. Conflict might also arise over ideas, beliefs and values, but beneath all such disagreements will be some kind of rivalry over necessary resources. Marx completes his inversion of Hegel's ideas by taking the triadic model of conflict in the realm of ideas (thesis, antithesis and synthesis), or between the naive and mature states of consciousness of reality, and applies this to the *practical issues* that social actors have to deal with. History is driven forward by practical social action carried out in pursuit of necessary resources. A period of relative agreement over how the necessities of life can be provided becomes disrupted by a rival way of producing things and eventually a third alternative will emerge and social order will (temporarily) be restored. This historical cycle of balance, disequilibrium and resolution is likely to be endlessly repeated as the struggle for resources can never be finally settled.

From very early on in his intellectual development a preoccupation with the sources and nature of conflict in society became one of the core features of Marx's social theory. At the different stages in his career Marx discusses social conflict as occurring at the individual level, the economic level and at the level of society. Conflict at the individual level lies at the heart of the second main theme or concept developed by Marx that we want to discuss here, the concept of **alienation**.

Marx's concept of alienation

Having rejected the abstract Hegelian view of human nature as something that is expressed through the desire to find the universal Spirit, Marx turned his attention to finding an alternative. These deliberations were subsequently published in 1932, many years after his death, as the 1844 *Paris Manuscripts*. We noted in the previous section how Hegel uses the concepts of sublation and estrangement to describe the sense of insecurity or unease that people might experience at moments when they recognise the shortcomings of their mental understanding of reality. For Hegel, estrangement was a cognitive or psychological state of being whose resolution depends on acquiring a more thorough understanding of what reality is and how individual consciousness comes to terms with its place within it. As Marx puts it: 'All estrangement of human nature is therefore nothing but estrangement of self-consciousness' (Marx, 1975, p 387; from the section 'Critique of Hegel's Dialectic and General Philosophy'). Pressing on with his materialist alternative, Marx argues that estrangement, or *alienation* as he calls it (the two concepts are not quite identical), is less to do with how social actors meet their philosophical needs and more with meeting their physical needs. Human contentment requires a settled material life at least as much as a settled consciousness.

Consistent with his rationalist and materialist view, he argues that human beings are 'natural, corporeal, sensuous, objective beings' and that human–beingness is a profoundly practical and experiential thing. Unlike other animal species who similarly confront the material conditions of their existence, however, *homo sapiens* is unique because of its capacity *to imagine* what it wants to do before it does it. Social actors sometimes act instinctively and spontaneously but most often they act in order to achieve an outcome that they have already created in their mind:

KEY QUOTE – Karl Marx, *Capital*, volume 1 (1867).
We pre-suppose labour in a form that stamps it as exclusively human. A spider conducts operations that resemble those of a weaver, and a bee puts to shame many an architect in the construction of her cells. But what distinguishes the worst of architects from the best of bees is this, that the architect raises his structures in imagination before he erects it in reality. At the end of every labour-process we get a result that already existed in the imagination of the labourer at its commencement. He not only effects a change of form in the material on which he works, but he also realises a purpose of his own that gives the law to his *modus operandi*, and to which he must subordinate his will. (Marx, 1954 [1867], p 174)

According to this **humanist** view the experiences social actors have, the substance and quality of their lives and of who they are, are determined in a very direct way by the substance and quality of their actions: 'As individuals express their life, so they are. What they are, therefore, coincides with their production, both with *what* they produce and with *how* they produce. The nature of individuals thus depends on the material conditions determining their production' (Marx and Engels, 1991, p 42; from the section 'History: Fundamental Conditions'). If social actors are unable to realise their full potential (a potential incidentally that might not be known in advance of the action that expresses it) then, according to these humanist criteria, they would remain unfulfilled and resentful. Since in principle every social actor has roughly the same potential for creative self-expression through action, any lack of fulfilment must be something to do with the material circumstances in which social action takes place. Alienation is a consequence of negative social conditions not of philosophical confusion.

However advanced the processes by which social actors provide themselves with the basic necessities of life become, and however elaborate or sophisticated are the expectations that develop beyond bare necessity, the keenest sense of well-being always comes from satisfying the simplest survival needs:

> The first premise of all human existence, and therefore of all history [is] that men must be in a position to live in order to be able to 'make history'. But life involves before everything else eating, drinking, a habitation, clothing and many other things. The first historical act is thus the production of the means to satisfy these needs, the production of material life itself. (Marx and Engels, 1991, p 48; from the section 'History: Fundamental Conditions')

The four degrees of alienation

Marx used these new concepts in his critical analysis of the social contexts of action in modern industrial society in the mid-19th century. He identified one outstanding feature of that society that he argued was responsible for a dramatic increase in the extent and depth of alienation currently being experienced. That feature was **capitalism**. As noted in Chapter One, although modern society is defined in terms of the process of **industrialisation** it is also often defined as capitalist society because of the particular economic system within which industrialisation has taken place in Western society (the exception being the Soviet communist regime of Eastern Europe from 1914 to approximately 1985). Capitalism is an economic system in which commodities are mass produced for sale to consumers at a price that is greater than the costs of making them. The grossly uneven distribution of financial resources in society, a factor that Marx discusses in his critical analysis of economic classes and forms of property relations, means that a small capitalist class owns the **means of production** (see later) and can thus force the majority working class to earn their living through paid employment. Even despite the emergence of the welfare state in Western society from the middle of the 20th century the vast majority of workers have no choice but to work if they wish to achieve any reasonable standard of living. Compulsion allows employers to control the amount they pay in wages, and by controlling wages commodities can be sold for more then they cost to produce. This profit is retained by the capitalist who thus increases his already considerable financial resources and his power to coerce the working class. Competition between one capitalist and another stimulates a continual expansion of the productive system.

Marx felt that the conditions of employment used by capitalist employers, indeed the whole of its division of labour and ideology, caused alienation by placing unacceptable limitations on the capacity for social actors to express their creative potential in true cooperation with others. Marx went on to develop a detailed critique of capitalism as an economic system in his later writings, but even at this earlier and more philosophical stage in his development, he identifies *four* basic aspects of alienation as they might be experienced by a typical factory worker.

Products

First, paid work or labour in capitalism is alienating because the products that are produced do not truly reflect the creative energies of the worker but are merely objects that have been produced at the command of an employer. Workers cannot embrace the things they produce but end up resenting them. In capitalism, as Marx puts it, the products of labour confront the worker 'as something alien, as a power independent of the producer. [Work] appears as a loss of reality for the worker as estrangement, as alienation [*Entausserung*]' (Marx, 1975, p 324; from the section on 'Estranged Labour'). Worse still, the more people produce, the more they are surrounded by commodities that they are often unable to buy themselves, which only serves to remind them of how unsatisfying their working lives really are: 'the more objects the worker produces the fewer can he possess and the more he falls under the domination of his product, of capital' (Marx, 1975, p 324; from the section on 'Estranged Labour').

Act of production

Second, because the products of labour are alienating, so also is the act of production: 'The worker feels himself only when he is not working; when he is working he does not feel himself ... his labour is therefore not voluntary but forced, it is *forced labour*. Labour in which man alienates himself, is a labour of self-sacrifice, of mortification' (Marx, 1975, p 324; from the section on 'Estranged Labour', emphasis in original). We will have more to say about the compulsion to work and the exploitation of the worker later in this chapter, but the basic point is that in capitalist economies people have no choice but to work for wages in order to meet their basic needs.

Common purpose

The third aspect of alienation arises when another of the essential properties of human productive activity, its inherently social and cooperative dimension, is also taken away from them. As workers, social actors become alienated from other workers. That portion of life which is spent working for wages is also the portion where relationships with other social actors become debased.

Loss of humanity

Bearing in mind that in the Victorian society in which Marx was writing it was not uncommon for people to work more than 12 or even 14 hours a day in the mines, workshops and factories, prolonged exposure to these three aspects of alienation produce a fourth, which is a general and profound feeling of being estranged from the very essence of human-beingness. Alienated labour in capitalist society manipulates a worker's basic powers of creative and cooperative energy so that he can no longer achieve any true expression of his species-beingness and humanity. He becomes alienated from his own inner self:

KEY QUOTE – Karl Marx, *Early Writings* (1975 [1844]), on alienation. An immediate consequence of man's estrangement from the product of his labour, his life activity, his species-being, is the estrangement of man from man. When man confronts himself, he also confronts other men. What is true of man's relationship to his labour, to the product of his labour and to himself, is also true of his relationship to other men, and to the labour and the object of the labour of other men. In general, the proposition that man is estranged from his species-being means that each man is estranged from the others and that all are estranged from man's essence. (Marx, 1975 [1844], pp 329–30; from the section on 'Estranged Labour')

Marx's theory of *historical materialism*

The third key concept used by Marx that we want to discuss here is his theory of how to explain the emergence of modern industrial society out of the pre-modern agrarian society that came before it. In providing a rich account of this period of historical change Marx is at the same time establishing his *method* of analysis. The theory of historical materialism, as it is generally called, is more than a set of proposals about how to go about analysing social change through time but becomes an explanation of the factors that account for the emergence of industrial capitalism itself. The method, in other words, is embedded within the story he tells.

Marx produced more than one version of his account of the emergence of industrial capitalism. The earliest, subsequently published as *The German Ideology*, was written for a largely intellectual readership while Marx and Engels were living in Brussels in 1845–46. They were unable to find a publisher and, as Marx later recalled, they 'abandoned the manuscript to the gnawing criticism of the mice' (Marx, 1975, p 427). The book was eventually published long after their deaths in 1932. A second version, this time written very much for a popular audience, was published as *The Communist Manifesto* in 1848.

The basic structure of the account Marx and Engels provide draws directly on the Hegelian model in which one stage is challenged by another and replaced by a third. The 'materialist' bit in the theory of historical materialism reflects Marx's belief that the material conditions in which people live determine not only the nature and quality of their lives, but also the kinds of occupational and social relationships they have with each other: 'the mode of production of material life conditions the general process of social, political and intellectual life' (Marx, 1975, p 425). Although Marx is aware that at various times 'political and intellectual life' come to the fore, from this point in his career his analysis is almost exclusively about what goes on in the *economic sphere*: 'the multitude of productive forces accessible to men determines the nature of society, hence, the "history of humanity" must always be studied and treated in relation to the history of industry and exchange' (Marx and Engels, 1991, p 50). This is the most important realm of activity because it is here that social actors produce the things they need in order to have any kind of life at all. All of experience, of society, of human life itself, is built up from the economic base.

For Marx and Engels, industrial capitalism emerges at the point in history when agriculture ceases to be the main source of livelihood and is replaced by manufacturing, firstly in rural workshops, but eventually in large factories in the towns. As working life becomes less dominated by agriculture and more by manufacture and commodity production, there is a corresponding and inevitable shift in working relationships. The division of labour in farming, for example, is very different from the division of labour in industry because of the different types of work involved: 'the existing stage in the division of labour determines also the relations of individuals to one another with reference to the material, instrument, and product of labour' (Marx and Engels, 1991, p 43).

Change does not stop there, however, because a shift in the nature of economic relationships also has implications for social relations in society as a whole. Pre-modern agricultural societies are not different to modern industrial ones just because of changes in tools and techniques of production (the means of production as Marx calls them) and in the relations of production associated with them, but because the whole way of life of society has shifted from one **mode of production** to another mode of production; in the case we are interested in here, from a feudal mode of production to a capitalist one:

KEY QUOTE – Karl Marx, 'The Mode of Production'.
Social relations are closely bound up with productive forces. In acquiring new productive forces men change their mode of production; and in changing their mode of production, in changing the way of earning their living, they change all their social relations. The hand-mill gives you society with the feudal lord; the steam-mill, society with the industrial capitalist. (Marx, 'The Poverty of Philosophy', in McLellan, 1977, p 202)

For Marx and Engels, then, historical change shows itself as a progression from one mode of production to another. Just as the feudal mode replaced the ancient mode at the beginning of the Middle Ages, so the capitalist mode superseded feudalism during the 17th and 18th centuries. The key question of course is how does one mode of production displace the previous one? The theory of historical materialism specifies two underlying mechanisms that explain this process of change. One mechanism relates to technical and practical developments in the means and relations of production. The other must be traced back to the kinds of social relations or property relations that are characteristic of a particular stage of economic development.

Means and relations of production

The first mechanism of change builds on the relatively simple idea, which Marx adapts from the work of the influential political economist Adam Smith who we mentioned in Chapter Two, that over time people become better and better at organising their ways of working. This both raises the efficiency of work and creates opportunities for developing entirely new ways of working and different kinds of productive process.

For Adam Smith, and subsequently for Marx, Engels, Durkheim and many others, societies evidently progress because the industrial division of labour becomes more advanced. Changes in working relationships and the day-to-day organisation of work are intimately tied in with developments in the tools and techniques of production. Paraphrasing Smith, Marx concludes 'How far the productive forces of a nation are developed is shown most manifestly by the degree to which the division of labour has been carried. Each new productive force ... causes a further development of the division of labour' (Marx and Engels, 1991, p 43).

We can safely say that shifts from one mode of production to another are brought on by advances in techniques and the division of labour. But what causes these shifts to develop in the first place?

Imagination

Part of the answer is the sheer inventiveness of human beings and their natural capacity for creative imagination. The capacity for mechanical inventiveness in particular was given an additional boost during the 19th century because of advances in the realm of laboratory science. Great industrial innovators like Arkwright, Wedgewood, Stevenson and Brunel were as interested in the science of what they were doing as in its industrial application.

Clusters of innovation

A second element is that innovations in one aspect of work tend to hang together with innovations in another. The Industrial Revolution of the 19th century came about because of a *combination* of factors such as a rapid expansion in the production of coal and iron, a switch to mechanised factory production and the development of a transport and communications infrastructure for shifting raw material in and finished goods out. Technology transforms the whole of the productive system not just single elements within it.

Time for change

A third element is that as production becomes more efficient, people simply have more time and energy left over for inventing new things. Although there were innovations in agriculture during the Middle Ages these were very few and far between because agriculture was a very physical energy-sapping business and for most it was all they could do to keep body and soul together. There was also very little scientific knowledge to go on because modern research facilities like universities had not yet emerged. In fact the European Middle Ages lasted as long as they did (from around 1250 to 1650) precisely because changes in the means and relations of production were so slow to emerge. A similar observation could be made of many economies today, for example, in Africa, India, Pakistan and large parts of Asia, where agricultural practices have barely altered for thousands of years. Adopting the historical materialist approach one would say that it is because they have changed so little that they remain, in their rural locations at least, pre-modern, traditional societies.

Social or property relations

The second cause or mechanism of change identified by historical materialists relates to shifts in the wider economic and social relations between social actors. Recalling an important distinction we highlighted in the previous chapter, it is at this point that Marx and Engels turn their attention away from *industrialism* as a newly emerged set of techniques for producing things and towards *capitalism* as a specific set of economic and social relations that accompanied the arrival of European industrial society from around 1750. In principle at least, industrialism could have emerged in a society that was not a capitalist society. For Marx and Engels, the fact that industrial working is experienced by many as alienating is not to do with any inherently negative characteristics of industrialism as such, but with the fact that the economic and social relations in which it takes place are *capitalist relations*.

By focusing specifically on the origins and nature of capitalist relations we are also required to consider a further factor, and one which was singled out for particular attention by Max Weber whose work we discuss in Chapter Five, which is what *motivates* economic activity. At one level it is clear enough that developments in the means and relations of production will have a more general impact on the way people live. For example, changes in the infrastructure of the emerging industrial societies include a very substantial shifting of the working population into the towns and cities. Industrialisation is always associated with urbanisation. More significant for Marx and Engels, however, are the ways in which one group or **class** of people in society is formed in relation to other groups or classes, and how all of this is tied in with changes in the mode of production.

The simple answer is that throughout history the most powerful classes are those who quite literally own the means of production in the sense that they have legal entitlement to them and the things that they produce. With production comes wealth and wealth provides the means of purchasing all the other kinds of power in the political, military and even the religious spheres of society. Marx and Engels construct their analysis at the level of classes rather than of individuals because one of the central tenets of historical materialism is that people are most clearly identifiable in terms of the contexts, circumstances and experiences they have in common with those around them. And the most important determinant of social context, what social actors decisively have in common, is their location in respect of the means of production.

This is simply a question of acknowledging that if the main preoccupation of life is to satisfy basic needs, then the life experiences of one social actor will be most similar to, will have most in common with, those of other social actors who are trying to meet their needs from the same position in society. The key difference between a social actor who owns the means of production, let us say a feudal lord in medieval society or a factory owner in Victorian Britain, and the peasant or worker who works for them, is not the needs they have, their capacity for enjoyment or even their religious values, but how directly or otherwise they are able to make a living.

Ownership or property classes

Following this line of argument, Marx and Engels are able to link changes from one mode of production to another (say from feudalism to capitalism) to shifting patterns of ownership and thus to property or class relations. The earliest form of ownership found in the most rudimentary human settlements, they suggest, is 'tribal ownership', with chieftains at the top and slaves at the bottom. This gave way in Ancient Society to forms of 'communal and state ownership', in which private ownership of property, meaning the exclusive entitlement to land, property or business backed up by the law, became more common. People who owned slaves or land, for example, now had a shared interest, a common class interest, with other owners. Similar interests could be identified between the class of slaves who owned almost nothing, and the peasantry who, even though they depended on landowners for their jobs, were at least 'free'.

The third form of property ownership described by Marx and Engels is 'feudal or estate property'. In the countryside, the feudal system with its hierarchical structure of land ownership 'gave the nobility power over the serfs'. In the towns, a new kind of 'corporative property' emerged, which was based not so much on possession of tangible assets like houses and businesses, although these remained very important, but on the capacity to work. If a person owns none of the means of production his only remaining asset (unless he turns to crime or charity) is the capacity to work *for somebody else*. Some individuals are, however, better placed than others when it comes to selling their labour if, for example, they can offer particular skills or crafts or their skills are in short supply. It was in recognition of this new kind of common position based not on actual ownership of the means of production, but on possession of different assets *as an employee*, that the craft guilds emerged to defend the class interests of small artisans (the petty or 'small' bourgeoisie) both against the emerging class of proprietors and manufacturers (the grand or 'large' bourgeoisie), and the land-owning nobility in the countryside.

▸▸ Seeing economic assets in terms of marketable skills and qualifications, rather than just in terms of money, is something that Max Weber develops in his analysis of people's 'market position'. This idea was carried further forward during the late 20th century by Pierre Bourdieu who develops the notion of **cultural capital** to include a broader range of assets people use to distinguish themselves from others. We will discuss these ideas in Chapters Five and Twelve.

Capitalist property relations

The fourth type of property ownership Marx and Engels describe is that of capitalism itself. As the word 'capitalism' suggests, the most important characteristic of this form of property ownership is capital, that is, the availability of actual cash, which can be invested in businesses that will produce large profits and thus even more capital to fund further expansion of the enterprise. The capitalist class in Marx's day is thus that group in society who not only own between them the actual means of production (mines, foundries, machine-shops, factories, railways and so on), but who also share the desire, capacity and opportunity to make business investments. The capitalist class is itself made up of a number of competing capitalists or 'capitals' and competition between them also stimulates the expansion of capitalism.

As the scale of modern industry increases, the gap between this class and the other classes grows ever larger because only the very wealthy have enough capital to become capitalists. As the chances of a non-owner becoming an owner diminish there is a corresponding increase in membership of the class of people whose only asset is their capacity for work, that is, the working class. Although 'the great divide' between the major competing classes in each historical period has always been between the owners and the non-owners of the means of production, in capitalist society this divide becomes an unbridgeable chasm. On one side stand the capitalist class who have complete control over the means of production, and, on the other, the working class who have no control at all.

The capitalist revolution

The largely descriptive account we have been giving so far of the passage from feudal society to capitalist society might seem rather static. In order to understand the true dynamism of Marx and Engel's theory we need to look at how developments in the means and relations of production on the one hand, and changes in property or class relations on the other, sometimes come into conflict with sufficient force to generate a shift from one mode of production to another. We need in other words, to try to imagine these forces *in motion* rather than as separate and rather passive elements.

The basic argument developed in *The German Ideology*, and repeated in simplified language in *The Communist Manifesto*, is that since ownership of the means of production brings wealth, status and power, the class that at any particular historical juncture has this power is going to be very unwilling to let it go. As long as there is no significant change in the principal means of production in a particular society the *status quo* will be maintained. The agricultural mode of production in feudal society, for example, confers great power on the land-owning class. However, when an alternative means of production, an alternative way of making a living, begins to emerge this generates a great deal of conflict between the old agricultural way of life and the land-owning class, and the emerging industrial means and the capitalists who control them. An established property or ownership class thus comes into conflict with an emerging one: 'The history of all hitherto existing society is the history of class struggles' (Marx and Engels, 1952 [1848], p 40, 'Bourgeois and Proletarians').

Our epic story thus returns to the question of where the new means of production come from. Since it is not in the interests of the currently dominant class to encourage the development of any new means of production that might challenge the ones they currently benefit from, change is much more likely to arise outside that class. It is also highly probable that any really significant development in the means of production will depend on a combination of factors and historical circumstances rather than on any single factor. To these practical and technical issues we have to add what we might call the human factor. Social actors are especially motivated to develop new means of production if they feel it is in their own interests to do so. Once this motivation spreads to a whole group or strata of social actors in society, for example all of the entrepreneurs and business people, the search for new developments in the means of production becomes an expression of *class interests*. Developments in the means of production become inseparable from the class that stands to gain the most from their introduction.

The European Industrial Revolution of 1760–1850 arose out of just such an historically unique combination of technological and organisational development driven forward by the class self-interests of capitalists. During the 17th and 18th centuries new opportunities for profit making emerged in overseas trade and commerce, opportunities that were embraced by a new merchant and commercial class whose thirst for adventure and hunger for prosperity made them eager to discover valuable new commodities and to open up markets in which to trade them. These adventures made available large amounts of capital, which were then used to fund technical developments in domestic industry. Mechanised commodity production was the new kid in town.

Faced with new and highly profitable means of industrial production in workshops and factories, and with the associated growth of an urban business class who had control of them, the wealth, status and prestige of the land-owning classes began to diminish, first in favour of the new mercantile class and then the emerging capitalist and business class. Agriculture was still important as a means of providing food but in terms of the profits it could yield, and increasingly as a source of employment, it was becoming far less prominent. The feudal mode of production was in terminal decline as the capitalist mode gathered momentum.

This transition from one mode of production to another released further capital for investment and thus further advances were made in the means of production. During the 19th and 20th centuries, and notwithstanding the continuing influence of the merchant and commercial elements of capital, innovators, industrialists and entrepreneurs came to the fore who were keen to exploit the potential of the new scientific knowledge and developments in engineering, and thus develop even more variety in the means of production. The new powerhouse of profit making was manufacturing industry. What Marx and Engels refer to in the 19th century as modern industry provided the technological and organisational foundation for the even more hi-tech industries of the 20th century. They also revolutionised expectations of what could or should be produced by industry. The production of an ever-greater variety of commodities, many of which have only a very tenuous link with actual necessity, became the dominant feature of capitalist production. The class of direct producers was being transformed into the class of mass consumers.

The socialist revolution

The problem Marx and Engels identified with the apparently natural emergence of industrial capitalism is that the profits gained from increased efficiency, new ways of working and greater variety of commodities are not fairly distributed across the population. Most particularly, the class of people who do most of the work, that is, the class of direct producers or working class, actually receive very little from a production process that could not continue at all without the very considerable amount of effort they put into it. So obvious is this disjuncture between the productive capacity of the industrial means of production and the unequal distribution of the wealth it creates, and so essential were the skills and energy of the working class in making such a technically complex system possible, that Marx and Engels believed that a new cycle was about to begin in the fortunes of the property classes in modern society:

> Modern bourgeois society … is like the sorcerer, who is no longer able to control the powers of the nether world whom he has called up by his spells. For many a decade past the history of industry and commerce is but the history of the revolt of modern productive forces against modern conditions of production, against the property relations that are the conditions for the existence of the bourgeoisie and of its rule. (Marx and Engels, 1952 [1848], p 49, 'Bourgeois and Proletarians')

The capitalist class, which had been essential in the development of industrial capitalism, and which, as a result of this success, had taken economic and political power entirely away from the land-owning class that came before it, had, by the middle of the 19th century, itself become a reactionary force in society. As a class, it no longer looked for further improvements in the means of production but wanted to keep things as they were. As has been the case with all previous dominant classes in history, the self-interest of the class no longer depends on making changes but on keeping things just as they are. The class who *do* have a real and powerful interest in further transforming the industrial labour process is the industrial working class. Because so few people in the capitalist mode of production own the means of production it is inevitable that the class of non-owners is bound to increase. Even within the capitalist class, ownership of capital becomes concentrated into the hands of fewer and fewer capitalists as the size of the investments needed to stay in the game tends to increase. As far as Marx and Engels are concerned, the industrial working class, which was destined to become by far the largest class in society, was destined to become the dominant class of the future:

KEY QUOTE – Marx and Engels, *The Communist Manifesto* (1848). The modern bourgeois society that has sprouted from the ruins of feudal society has not done away with class antagonisms. It has but established new classes, new conditions of oppression, new forms of struggle in place of old ones.... Our epoch, the epoch of the bourgeoisie, possesses, however, this distinctive feature: it has simplified the class antagonisms. Society as a whole is more and more splitting up into two great hostile camps, into two great classes directly facing each other: Bourgeoisie and Proletariat. (Marx and Engels, 1952 [1848], p 41, 'Bourgeois and Proletarians')

The importance of the industrial working class can hardly be overestimated. First, as the real doers in industry, it was among them, rather than among the capitalist employers, that the practical skills and technical knowledge would be found to keep modern industry going and to push it on to the next stage. Second, the industrial working class were the first class in history whose power did not come from ownership of tangible property assets like land and factories but from *their capacity to work*; a capacity that included their technical knowledge, experience and skill. All social actors have a shared interest in making sure that the means of production are as advanced as they can because they share the same need to survive and the same desire to live as comfortably as possible. Third, because the capacity for productive activity is a universal characteristic of human-beingness, the working class is the universal class in the sense that through its collective productive energies its members most clearly express the basic premises of human existence. As a universal class there can be no other classes that are outside it. Morally and practically, the benefit is not for the private self-interests of any particular individual but for the whole of humankind. The emergence of the industrial working class thus signifies the end of class antagonism altogether:

> A stage has been reached where the exploited and oppressed class
> – the proletariat – cannot attain its emancipation from the sway
> of the exploiting and ruling class – the bourgeoisie – without,
> at the same time, and once and for all, emancipating society at
> large from all exploitation, oppression, class distinctions and class
> struggles. (Engels, 1888, Preface to the English edition of *The
> Communist Manifesto*, Marx and Engels, 1952 [1848] pp 20-21)

It is by means of this historical materialist narrative that Marx and Engels are able to make a direct connection between changes in the means of production and changes in class relations. The final historical connection, then, is between these two forces and a change in the *mode* of production itself:

KEY QUOTE – Marx and Engels, *The Communist Manifesto* (1848). The bourgeoisie cannot exist without constantly revolutionising the instruments of production, and thereby the relations of production, and with them the whole relations of society.... Constant revolutionising of production, uninterrupted disturbance of all social conditions, everlasting uncertainty and agitation distinguish the bourgeois epoch from all earlier ones. All fixed, fast-frozen relations, with their train of ancient and venerable prejudices and opinions, are swept away, all new-formed ones become antiquated before they can ossify. All that is solid melts into air, all that is holy is profaned, and man is at last compelled to face with sober senses, his real conditions of life, and his relations with his kind. (Marx and Engels, 1952 [1848], p 45, 'Bourgeois and Proletarians')

Having produced a painstaking account of how societies move on under pressure from developments in the means of production combined with changes in the nature of property relations, the simple message that Marx and Engels want to get across in *The Communist Manifesto* is that, as surely as night follows day, the capitalist mode of production is about to be replaced by a socialist or communist mode of production.

The only remaining question was exactly *when* this might happen and whether some kind of intervention might be required to make sure that it did. Marx and Engels certainly felt that by forming the Communist Party, and by spelling out the principles of historical change according to their own theory in the *Manifesto*, they could, as it were, give history a bit of a push in the right direction. The working class, it seemed, could not be relied upon to make history happen as it should, but would need the help of 'fresh elements of enlightenment and progress' (Marx and Engels, 1952 [1848], p 56) supplied even by the bourgeoisie to show them the way. There are also strong hints, at least in sections of the *Manifesto* drafted by Engels, that the overthrow of capitalism was unlikely to be a peaceful affair: the Communists 'openly declare that their ends can be attained only by the forcible overthrow of all existing social conditions. Let the ruling classes tremble at a Communist revolution. The proletarians have nothing to lose but their chains. They have a world to win' (Marx and Engels, 1952 [1848], p 96). Equally certain, however, is the fact that the validity of Marx and Engel's theory would have been considerably strengthened if a revolution *had* occurred in modern society during the latter part of the 19th century. The fact that this has not yet happened rather suggests either that the theory was not complete or that they had a poor sense of timing. As we shall see in later chapters, these issues are still hotly debated in social theory.

Capitalist exploitation and Marx's 'labour theory of value'

We have now arrived at the fourth main concept in Marx's social theory we are discussing in this chapter. Combining his materialist view of historical development with his philosophical concept of alienation, Marx spent the remaining and longest part of his career developing a very detailed analysis of how the capitalist labour process is able to exploit workers in the way it does. The major publications here are *A Contribution to the Critique of Political Economy* (1971 [1859]) and *Capital* (volume 1, 1954 [1867]). A key theme in this analysis was that capitalism was alienating and conflict-ridden because of the way it exploited the working class through work. Within the cool, hard, calculating mentality of the capitalist (his **instrumental rationality**, as Weber puts it), labour is no longer treated subjectively as the expression of creativity, but objectively as just another cost of production. The many qualitative dimensions of work are disregarded and replaced with a single quantitative dimension, which is how much product they can produce in a given time and what the minimum amount of wages is that they have to be paid for doing it:

> It goes without saying that political economy regards the *proletarian*, i.e. he who lives from labour alone as nothing more than a *worker*. It can therefore advance the thesis that, like a horse, he must receive enough to enable him to work.... Political economy knows the worker only as a beast of burden, as an animal reduced to the minimum bodily needs. (Marx, 1975, pp 288, 290; from the 'Economic and Philosophical Manuscripts')

Use values and exchange values

To understand Marx's version of the **labour theory of value** (a term first introduced by the influential British political economist David Ricardo [1772–1823]), we first need to clarify three different aspects of the notion of value as they appear in Marx's critique of capitalist commodity production (more recently Jean Baudrillard has suggested a fourth aspect, the symbolic or **sign-value** of commodities, which we will be discussing in Chapter Thirteen). The first aspect of value is **use value**. The use value of a commodity is a measure of how useful it is in meeting a particular need. The use value of a hammer or a saw, for example, is that they can be used to make things from wood. The second way of expressing the value of these items is their **exchange value**. This time we are not measuring their relative values in terms of how useful they are (it is actually quite difficult to say objectively whether a hammer is more or less useful than a saw), but in terms of their *comparative value* as commodities. If a hammer is for sale for £5, and a saw for £10, then the number of hammers I can buy for one saw (in this case two) is an objective expression of the relative exchange values of hammers and saws.

The importance of exchange values in capitalism is that, in combination with money as a universal medium for expressing them, it becomes possible to compare all commodities *in terms of* their relative exchange values. Hammers can be compared as easily with nails or footballs or train tickets as they can with saws. Expressions of actual usefulness are displaced by abstract expressions of comparable quantities: hitting a nail is concrete, wondering how many nails the hammer is worth is abstract. As long as commodities are still assessed at least partly in terms of their relative usefulness, it is possible to preserve something of the subjective and qualitative sense of how valuable something is. Within capitalism, however, the relentless rise of exchange values dramatically undermines the capacity for assessing commodities other than in terms of exchange. The point at which exchange values become universally accepted as the only reliable basis for comparing the value of commodities is also the point at which use values have to be entirely eliminated from the calculation.

Labour as a commodity

This merciless imposition of exchange values within capitalism is also applied to perhaps the most inherently valuable of all commodities and that is labour-power itself. The labour-power required in making bookshelves or writing books, for example, is no longer comparable in terms of the qualitative and subjective differences between these two kinds of activity (one might suppose that writing books is more difficult than making shelves to put them on) but only in terms of the *quantities* of labour-power each requires. The comparative value of book writing and shelf making is simply an expression of how much of one can be done in the time it takes to do the other:

> To measure the exchange value of commodities by the labour
> time they contain, different kinds of labour have to be reduced
> to uniform, homogeneous, simple labour; in short to labour of
> uniform quality, whose only difference, therefore, is quantity.
> This reduction appears to be an abstraction, but an abstraction
> which is made every day in the social process of production. The
> conversion of all commodities into labour time is no greater an
> abstraction, and is no less real, than the resolution of all organic
> bodies into air. (Marx and Engels, 1971 [1859], p xx)

Surplus value

The third aspect of value, and one which lies at the very heart of commodity production in capitalism, is **surplus value**. This aspect refers more particularly to a property of commodities, including labour-power as a commodity, which is released when they are exchanged in the marketplace. The principle of surplus value appears to be quite simple. If it is possible to sell a commodity for more than the cost of producing it then the difference between the sale price and the cost price is its surplus value. The whole point of capitalism is to produce commodities as cheaply as possible, sell them for the highest price, and thus make the greatest margin or profit.

Deploying his more complex version of the labour theory of value, however, Marx argued that this apparently natural explanation of where surplus value and profit come from was fundamentally flawed. He argued that what was missing was a distinction between the *labourer* (factory worker, fighter pilot, yoga teacher and so on), *labour*, which is the actual activity of doing something, and *labour power*, which is the capacity of the labourer to add value to commodities by virtue of expressing his labour-power as labour. What the capitalist buys with the wages she pays is not the labourer (capitalists do not own workers) but *the capacity* the labourer has to add value to the materials on which he works as a result of expressing his labour-power. Labour-power is elastic (or variable) in the sense that the addition of value through the exercise of labour-power can be greater or more limited depending on how hard the labourer labours. Only human labour has the capacity to add value in this way.

Necessary labour and surplus labour

It is also necessary to distinguish between necessary labour and surplus labour. Necessary labour is that quantity of expended labour-power that is required in order that the labourer can produce sufficient value (wages) to keep themselves alive. This value can be obtained by calculating the costs to the labourer of food, clothing, accommodation and so on. Besides necessary labour, however, labour power also produces surplus labour, which is the quantity of expended labour-power that exceeds the amount required by the labourer to keep themselves alive. By lunchtime, for example, sufficient necessary labour has typically been performed in order for the labourer to pay his bills and stop working. Workers are not employed only until lunchtime in capitalism, however; they are required to keep on working for the whole day. Since the wages the capitalist pays are only sufficient to pay for necessary labour (employers have little interest in employees other than to make sure they are able to turn up to work the next day), the extra or surplus value that is added to commodities, and for which workers are not properly paid, goes to the capitalist. By only paying wages that are sufficient for keeping the worker alive (the level of basic subsistence) the capitalist gets surplus labour for free.

Contrary to the opinions of the classical economists such as Adam Smith and David Ricardo, and as Marx was at pains to point out, although other factors such as changes in the price of raw materials or equipment, or variations in the supply and demand for any particular commodity, will affect the selling price of the commodity (and the price of commodities such as food and clothing will affect the living costs of the worker), this does little to alter the fact that the fundamental source of surplus value was the labour-power of the worker, a value that cannot be quantified until *after* the commodity has been sold and thus its surplus value realised. For Marx, therefore, profit is the most accurate way of measuring the value that the worker has added to the product, but for which she or he *has not been paid*. If the theory of alienation provides a qualitative assessment of the extent to which labour in capitalism is unsatisfying and dehumanising, the theory of surplus value provides an equally compelling quantitative measure of the extent of exploitation.

The explanation as to *why* the worker goes on working beyond the point at which he might otherwise choose to stop, is simply that having no direct access to his own means of production, he has no choice but to sell his labour-power to an employer and on the terms that are dictated. And, as we discussed in the previous section of this chapter, in modern capitalist society the terms of employment relationships are set by the social and wider property relations that hold between the capitalist class and the working class.

The impact of Marx's ideas on social theory

We conclude this chapter by making a number of observations about the impact of Marx's ideas on social theory and on the social theorists who came after him. The long-lasting significance of Marx's theory of historical materialism is that he goes far beyond the point of just adopting a materialist orientation in philosophical terms, but puts this approach to work in developing a detailed theory about the emergence of modern capitalist society. To the extent that Marx's theory accounts successfully for the emergence of capitalist society during the 19th century, this reinforces the general reliability, not only of his own theory of historical change, but of the materialist and **realist** approaches in social theory as a whole. For example, the strongly humanist theory of alienation proposed by Marx has been used consistently not only to explain feelings of dissatisfaction at work, but many other instances where cooperative productive activity is disrupted or withheld. Similarly useful is the linkage Marx identifies between the struggle for economic resources and class interests. Other kinds of resources and other types of social-group interests and conflicts, such as between ethnic or racial groups, between women and men and between political adversaries, can be analysed using exactly the same social-theoretical concepts. Marx provides a useful tool kit for understanding the conflictual nature of many kinds of social relationships.

Materialism versus idealism

One potential weakness of the materialist approach is its tendency to underplay the role of ideas, values and beliefs as a motivator of social action. Marx certainly felt he had 'settled accounts with our erstwhile philosophical conscience' by adopting a humanist view of human nature early on in his career. In his view, ideas are already part of social action in the sense that action is a manifestation in practical form of human cooperation and creativity. What he especially objects to is the idealists' claim that the realm of ideas or consciousness can be analysed *separately from* the actions they give rise to. As he famously puts it: 'the philosophers have interpreted the world, the point however is to change it'. One of the most difficult tasks of social theory is to identify where the balance lies, and what the direction of influence is, between ideas, values and beliefs on the one hand, and practical necessity on the other.

Individual and collective

Another kind of balance the historical materialist approach draws our attention to, is the balance between social actors as individuals, and social actors as part of a collective such as an economic class. Like Durkheim, Marx's social theory tends to come down on the side of the collectivising forces that affect social action and bind it together. Not surprisingly, and again like Durkheim, many of the tools and concepts in Marx's social theory are designed to look at this kind of social phenomenon. He is especially interested in the various ways in which social actors are bound together in groups or classes as a result of the kinds of social relations that surround them. Although the social position and life experiences of capitalists and workers are worlds apart, they are nonetheless closely bound together, because of the dynamics of the social and historical processes that they form an essential part of. Opposing classes are caught, as it were, in a perpetual embrace. These design features of the collectivist approach used by Marx and

Durkheim, mean that less attention is given to looking at the social collectivity as seen from the point of view of the individual social actor.

Base and superstructure

Whereas Durkheim's social theory has a very strong concept of society at its centre, such an explicitly sociological concept of society is less clearly developed in Marx. This brings us to Marx's influential description of 'society' as consisting of a massively foundational economic base above which, and on the basis of which, are constructed the various non–economic institutions of society:

> In every historical epoch, the prevailing mode of economic production and exchange, and the social organisation necessarily following from it, form the basis upon which is built up, and from which alone can be explained, the political and intellectual history of that epoch; that consequently the whole history of mankind ... has been a history of class struggles. (Engels, 1888, Preface to the English edition of *The Communist Manifesto*, Marx and Engels, 1952 [1848], p 20)

We can thus envisage 'society' topographically as a pyramid with a wide base on top of which are constructed other institutions that become increasingly distanced from the economy. However far the apex appears to be from the base, however, it is still fundamentally attached to, and thus determined by, the base. The economic base consists of all of the institutions of civil society that are involved in private capitalistic activity plus those aspects of the state that are involved in its regulation. The relationship between the economic base and the superstructure, particularly in terms of the various institutions that tend to operate at both levels such as the education and welfare systems, is obviously highly complex. The point to grasp, however, is that for Marx and for Marxists it is impossible to understand the superstructural features of the social collective 'or society' without first understanding the nature of the economic base, which always gives rise to them. Perhaps the guiding principle of Marxist social theory is that, in the final analysis, and whatever else might appear to be the case, the economic base is determinant.

Contexts and motivation

Marx's emphasis on the economic foundations of social action and social collectivity inevitably slants his social-theoretical investigation in particular directions. Consistent with his materialist and realist position, social action cannot be understood separately from the context where it takes place. Marx is encouraging us to look for the patterns of causation between contexts and action, and between one action and another; patterns that emerge *because of* the circumstances in which social actors act. Having identified these patterns at the surface the real work of social theory is to try to uncover their underlying causes. One such underlying causative force relates to the question of what motivates social action. Although it might sound rather simplistic to many people living in the richly materialistic and consumer-oriented society of today, the foundation of social action is largely unchanged: actors act in order, first of all, to satisfy their basic needs. The urge to survive plus the need to obtain resources in order to achieve this sometimes suggests that other possible sources of motivation are, if not absolutely less important, far less urgent.

The awareness that Marx and Durkheim share of the great significance of the collective aspects of social action is also evident in their concepts of alienation and **anomie**. These highly influential concepts have in common the idea that lack of properly fulfilling cooperative action has serious and negative consequences for social actors. At one level these negative consequences are personal in the sense that they disrupt the life-course of the individual. They also, and perhaps more importantly, depending on how strong a concept of society one wishes to deploy, have serious consequences for social order. Sociologically, for Marx, widespread alienation within the economic base might accumulate sufficiently to cause full-blown revolution. For Durkheim, anomie exists when society provides insufficient collective social adhesion among individual social actors. In both cases continuing social order depends upon the realisation through practice of a productive, cooperative and properly socialised context for social action.

Finally, and again much like Durkheim, Marx infuses his social theory with a certain moral expectation that a better society lies ahead as long as we are smart enough and energetic enough to reach it. This belief, which in Marx's case was self-evidently expressed through his personal political commitment to the Workers Movement, presents us with something of a paradox. As a good historical materialist Marx was reluctant to specify in advance what the good society, the communist utopia of the future, would be like (Engels tried to be a little more specific after Marx's death but still the picture is rather vague). Nonetheless Marx does envisage a future society that will produce greater happiness for the greater number. While this gives his social theory an optimistic tone, Marx seems pretty clear that this can only be achieved *on condition* that collective interests are placed ahead of individual ones. At this point, the objective examination of social phenomena with a clear mind and cool heart seems to have given way to a certain feeling of judgement as to how things *ought to be*. It is also a little ironic, given how critical Marx was of Hegel's idealism, that in openly suggesting that there is a perfect society up ahead somewhere, Marx himself becomes, along with Engels and Lenin, one of the great ideologues of the 20th century.

Key points box – The four main concepts we have looked at in this chapter are:

- ☑ That real reality is found in material things and not in the ideas social actors have about them.
- ☑ That because it is inherent in human nature that social actors essentially are what they do, anything that hinders the full creative potential of action will have negative consequences for the actor's sense of well-being (alienation).
- ☑ That one historical form of social collectivity or society is determined in crucial respects by the kind of society that came before it.
- ☑ In capitalist society, the value of things is assessed not in terms of how useful they are, or the kind of social purpose they serve, but abstractly and arbitrarily in terms of their exchange value.

Practice box

- ⮑ What was the main reason Marx disagreed with the theory of G.W.F. Hegel?
- ⮑ What did Marx mean when he said he had 'turned Hegel on his head'?
- ⮑ Did Marx think there was such a thing as human nature?
- ⮑ Why would writing a boring essay cause alienation?
- ⮑ Give a short definition of the two words 'historical' and 'materialism' as they are used in Marx's theory of 'historical materialism'.
- ⮑ Why does Marx prefer to talk about classes than about individual social actors?
- ⮑ Think of two activities and compare them in terms of their relative use value.

- ➲ Think of two commodities and compare them in terms of their use value *and* their exchange value.
- ➲ How did Marx argue that surplus value is a measure of exploitation?
- ➲ Why was Marx a 'revolutionary thinker'?

Further reading

Karl Marx, *Early Writings* (Penguin, 1975).

Karl Marx and Friedrich Engels, *The Communist Manifesto* (Penguin, 1967 [1848]), with an introduction by AJP Taylor.

David McLellan, *Karl Marx: Selected Writings* (Oxford University Press, 1977).

David McLellan, *Karl Marx: His Life and Thought* (Macmillan, 1973).

Leszek Kolakowski, *Main Currents in Marxism*, 3 volumes (Oxford University Press, 1981).

Websites

A vast range of material on Marx and Marxism can be found at: www.marxists.org/archive/

For detailed historical material on the political impact of Karl Marx and Friedrich Engels and the formation of the International Communist Movement in the 20th century see: www.marxists.org/history/international/comintern

CHAPTER FIVE

MAX WEBER, RATIONAL CAPITALISM AND SOCIAL ACTION

Introduction

It is difficult not to compare the work of the German social theorist Max Weber (1864–1920) with that of Karl Marx. It could even be suggested that a full appreciation of key aspects of Weber's work only emerges by making this comparison. These comparisons are inevitable since the writings of Marx, and the political claims of the Marxists who followed him, provided much of the academic and political context of Weber's own social theory. It is important to remember, however, that Weber's understanding of Marx was very limited since many of Marx's most important works (the *Paris Manuscripts*, *The German Ideology*, the *Grundrisse*) were not available during Weber's lifetime. The Marx that Weber did know was mostly based on his economic writings and *The Communist Manifesto*, and even these as they were being interpreted, rather simplistically, by the German Social Democratic Party in the 1890s. For Weber, Marx was the author of an original, but rigid and one-sidedly materialist, theory of historical development, a point that he tries to prove by offering an alternative explanation of the emergence of modern capitalism in his famous essay published in 1904/05, *The Protestant Ethic and the Spirit of Capitalism*.

Having boldly stated the need for comparing Weber with Marx we need to qualify this by saying that not all of Weber's work should be treated in this way. The comparison actually relates to the fairly specific topic of what social theory has to say about the origins and nature of modern industrial capitalism. To the extent that Weber's political concerns, his worries about the feasibility of **socialism** and the dominance of economic interests, can all be seen in terms of the rise of capitalism then the comparison is fair enough. Weber did have other interests, however, such as his analysis of German society and politics, his comparative history of the world religions, and the contribution he made to the methodology of social theory, which often have very little to do with Marx and Marxism.

In terms of our own approach to Weber's work, and aside from the fact that his style is rather awkward and much of his writing was either left unfinished or was published in a disorganised way by others after his death, we will follow the same procedure as the previous chapter and pick out some of Weber's key concepts that have made a special contribution to social theory.

In this chapter we will look at:

The biographical and political context of Weber's work

The intellectual context and Weber's contribution to method in social theory

Weber's account of the rise of modern, rational, capitalist society – 'rationality', *The Protestant Ethic* and bureaucracy

Weber's theory of social action: the role of values and beliefs

Concepts of political power – status groups and legitimate domination

Weber's contribution to social theory as a whole

The biographical and political context of Weber's work

The accusation that Weber produced bourgeois social theory as opposed to the proletarian social theory of Marx is partly based on the fact that Weber came from a wealthy establishment family, and thus had the benefits of a privileged education and good social and career prospects. Following his father (who was a member of the German Parliament), he trained as a lawyer in Berlin and then took a doctorate in economics in 1889. He gained his first academic post in 1893, and only three years later became professor of economics at Freiburg University in 1896 at the remarkably young age of 32 (he later held posts at Heidelberg and Munich). He then suffered the first of a series of serious bouts of psychological illness that forced him to give up his job and abandon academic work for the next six years. The period between 1905 and around 1915 was his most productive, beginning with the publication of two extended essays as *The Protestant Ethic and the Spirit of Capitalism* in 1904/05. He then worked intermittently on a number of detailed studies in economics, religion, the development of the legal system and other social institutions. These subsequently appeared in print as *Economy and Society* (1921), *The Religion of India* and *The Religion of China* (both published in 1916). *The General Economic History* (1927) was compiled from a series of lectures he gave in Freiburg during 1919–20, and *On the Methodology of the Social Sciences* was published posthumously in 1922 from a variety of articles and lectures given between 1903 and 1917. In most cases, complete English translations only became available during the 1950s and 1960s. Weber died from pneumonia in 1920 at the age of 56.

In terms of the kind of society in which Weber worked, the dominant political issue was the decline of the liberal, Protestant and highly individualist attitude of the established middle classes, and the emergence of an **authoritarian**, militarised, bureaucratic regime that accompanied the rise of the 'new Germany' following Bismark's unification of the German states in 1870. The success of the new regime rested on an alliance between the landowner class of Junkers (who were forced to rely on political power as their economic power declined), the military and the emerging classes of industrialists, financiers, bankers and career bureaucrats. In the last decades of the 19th century, Germany went through a period of rapid industrialisation, a process that was accompanied by the emergence of the German industrial working class although not, significantly, of an independent bourgeois middle class of the kind found in Britain, France and elsewhere. For Weber and many of his contemporaries, the demise of traditional liberal values of personal responsibility and autonomy, and their replacement with a much more paternalistic notion of national service, was a matter of great concern. Both Weber and his father made various attempts to express this opposition in the political sphere. The rather pessimistic tone of Weber's work, his sense that German society and its liberal values were in decline, certainly reflects his rather dismal political outlook.

The intellectual context and Weber's contribution to method in social theory

Intellectual background

Whereas Marx began his academic career by engaging with the abstract philosophical debates engendered by Hegelian **idealism**, Weber started out with the altogether more practical intention of training as a lawyer and economist. The emergence of a specifically social-theoretical emphasis in his interests really only arose after he had already begun to analyse specific topics as part of his professional work. Weber tended to deal with the more conceptual challenges of social theory on a need-to-know basis. In this sense, Weber was more interested in getting on with studying actual things than in devoting time either to establishing an entire account of historical development, as Marx had done, or to developing a set of principles for turning the study of social phenomena into a proper science, in the manner of Auguste Comte and Émile Durkheim. This approach accounts for why there is no unifying theme in Weber's work, no overall framework into which each of his concepts and ideas can be fitted. Whether he liked it or not, however, Weber could not help but become involved in the heated discussions about the role of social-scientific study, and the differences between this and the natural sciences, that were taking place in intellectual and academic circles in Germany around 1900.

Philosophical debates

These debates began with a revival during the 1890s, in Germany and elsewhere, of one of the old chestnuts of philosophy and social theory, which is the distinction between **empirical** knowledge, that is, knowledge that comes through physical sensation, and **rational** knowledge, that is, knowledge in the form of the ideas and other intellectual constructs through which it is made intelligible in the mind. Kant had argued that while knowledge of the real world was something that comes through our physical senses, it can only be made sense of once this information has been structured and organised by the mind. The human mind thus imposes a rational structure on the raw data of experience and feeling. All knowledge is thus a product of rational intellectual processing and as such reality cannot be regarded as a thing that is entirely distinguishable from knowledge of it. Reality 'in itself' cannot be known. (Recalling our discussion of Kant and Hegel in the second section of Chapter Four, Kant's position is **dualistic** because he accepts the necessary combination of sense perception *and* cognitive reason. Hegel is monistic as he emphasises the absolute primacy of intellectual reason alone.)

The younger followers of Kant or 'neo-Kantians' were faced with the problem of defending the rationalist approach, used in the historical, cultural and social sciences, against the **empiricist** approach of the natural sciences. The considerable success of the natural sciences during the 19th century (a success that was reinforced with every new advance in technology or feat of industrial engineering), allowed the empiricists to suggest that the kind of knowledge that was generated by the speculative, **metaphysical** and **inductive** approach of the social sciences, really did not constitute proper knowledge at all. Indeed, there was no reason to suppose that the search for the general 'laws of motion' of social phenomena should not be carried out using the tried-and-tested empirical methodology and methods of the natural sciences.

The neo-Kantians, and other interested parties including Max Weber, thus turned their attention to three issues:

- They wanted to challenge the idea that the kind of knowledge generated by the natural sciences was *the only* kind of knowledge available.
- They wanted to show that the two kinds of science had to be different because they were looking at two fundamentally *different kinds* of phenomena.
- If these points are valid, then it was obvious that two distinct *methodologies* were required to investigate them.

Different kinds of knowledge

Wilhelm Windelband (1848–1915), one of the leading neo-Kantians, argued that the kinds of knowledge generated by the natural and the social sciences were different because they were looking at two different levels of reality. Whereas the natural scientists were concerned with material objects and with describing the general laws that governed their origins and interactions, social and cultural scientists were concerned with the ethical realm of human action and culture. Although knowledge of natural phenomena could be achieved directly through observation and experimentation, knowledge of human motivation, of norms and patterns of conduct, and of social and cultural values, necessarily had to be based on a more abstract process of theoretical reasoning. You can only *infer* that somebody is in love; you cannot actually *see* 'love'.

The association of social phenomena with **values** was also considered by the German philosopher Heinrich Rickert (1863–1936) who strongly influenced Weber's views on the matter. Rickert (who was himself adopting a famous distinction between fact and value that had been made by the Scottish Enlightenment philosopher David Hume [1711–76]), argued that the natural sciences are 'sciences of fact' and so questions of value were necessarily excluded from the analysis. The social sciences, in contrast, are 'sciences of value' because they are specifically concerned with understanding why social actors choose to act in the ways that they do. While it is appropriate to disregard questions of value when studying the physical or chemical properties of things, it is certainly not appropriate to do so when studying human social action and its consequences. It is relatively easy to show what the properties of carbon are, where it comes from and what will happen if you combine it with some other material. What you never need to do is explain how carbon atoms *feel* about any of these things.

Interpretive understanding or 'Verstehen'

Distinguishing between two kinds of phenomena and two kinds of knowledge in this way had important implications for **methodology** (methodology is the *general approach* to studying something, **methods** are the *specific techniques* that are used). It is fair enough to study natural phenomena with a view to identifying the general laws that apply to them, and by using established empirical methods of observation and experimentation, because this was the appropriate way to study phenomena that had no capacity for acting on their own initiative. Equally, however, it is not sufficient to search for general laws of motion of social and cultural phenomena, or to use deductive empirical techniques alone, because social and cultural phenomena do have some capacity for independent action. They are just not the same as natural phenomena and their interactions are not regulated in the same way.

To stand any chance of understanding these social and cultural phenomena, it is necessary to adopt an **inductive** approach where the observation of an individual occurrence of something could be used to build up a picture of the whole. While some aspects of these phenomena can be observed, measured and described in the manner of a scientific experiment, only the inductive method can explain and account for the inherently subjective and 'unobservable' factors and judgements that underlie social action. Social scientists are therefore concerned with 'understanding' and 'interpreting' the actions of social actors and of trying to grasp what those actions mean to them. This method of interpretation, or **verstehen** as Weber calls it, is a defining characteristic of the social–scientific technique and one that is flexible enough to make room for the differences between social actors, rather than always seeing their actions as governed by universal principles.

●●●●●● ILLUSTRATION – DESCRIBING SOCIAL ACTION

How might we go about studying a person riding a bicycle? Adopting the techniques of a natural scientist we can measure how fast he is going, in what direction, how often he changed gear. We can say how tall or heavy he is, what the conditions are like and what kinds of materials the bike is made from. What we cannot determine just by looking at the cyclist, however, is *why* he is cycling. For this we need to adopt the approach of the social scientist, going beyond bare description in order to develop theories of action and motivation. Is the cyclist peddling quickly because he is late for a lecture in social theory or because he is trying to improve his fitness? Are he getting pleasure from cycling voluntarily, or is he having to do so because somebody has stolen his car? The full picture of cycling requires more than observation; it also requires interpretation.

Value-neutrality

A further major difference between the two sciences/types of knowledge/methods and methodologies also touches on the question of values, but this time as they affect the motives *of the scientist*. Weber brings these concerns together under the heading of 'value-neutrality'. He argues that since social science deals with phenomena that are value-laden, the researcher, both in choosing what to study and in reporting her findings, has to be aware of her own values and of the value-content of the phenomenon she is researching.

Beginning with the problem of choice, for Weber, and again following Rickert, all observations, whether as part of a deductive or of an inductive procedure, are necessarily preceded by a judgement on the part of the observer about what is worth observing. Scientific knowledge, therefore, does not come about in an orderly fashion and following some carefully planned strategy that all the scientists in the world agree upon, but is a much more haphazard affair that reflects subjective judgements made by members of the scientific community. What we know is essentially a product of what we want to find out. Weber takes this line of reasoning a little further and argues that since it is impossible to grasp every tiny detail about a particular phenomenon, social scientists also have to be very selective when making more immediate decisions about which aspects of a phenomenon to study and in how much detail. Social-scientific knowledge can in fact only ever be partial and selective.

Second, and this time looking at value-neutrality in terms of how the observer handles the value-content of the research, Weber notes that values are not objective material entities and cannot be assessed, measured or compared in an entirely logical and dispassionate way. Adopting a rationalist approach to things, since knowledge is actually only a representation of some phenomenon or other in the mind, this representation is always arbitrary. The thing itself is not identical with the idea one has about it. Although conceptual arbitrariness is not so much of a problem when conducting experiments among things that have known and invariable properties, it makes quite a big difference when ideas, values and beliefs are the objects of the analysis. The social researcher cannot disregard her own values, nor can she avoid studying values as they present themselves as social phenomena and as the motivators of social action. Being aware of the value-content of social-scientific methodology and of the subject matter itself, what the social researcher must strive to do is remain neutral in respect of the values that are in play. Social-scientific research fails and social-scientific knowledge is critically undermined if social researchers fail to keep their opinions to themselves. Social-theoretical knowledge, then, is the product of subjective judgement, is partial and selective, and, in at least some respects, arbitrary. Natural scientists would be utterly perplexed if the knowledge they sought to produce was described in this way.

Ideal types and methodological individualism

Weber made two further contributions to the methodology of theory-building in social theory. The first of these was a by-product of the conceptual arbitrariness problem we have just mentioned. Although social theorists are always faced with the dilemma that there is a reality gap between the ideas and concepts they use and the really real world 'out there', which they hope to explain by using them, Weber suggested that this could sometimes be turned into an advantage. Given that we are free to make up whatever concepts we like, it might be useful for social theorists to develop concepts that represent the purest form, or 'ideal type', of a particular phenomenon. Although there is no expectation that any particular instance of that phenomenon can match the ideal type, it nonetheless provides a useful intellectual tool for thinking about what the most essential or typical characteristics of a particular event or action might be. For example, in making sociological comparisons between different types of family in a particular society it can be useful to refer to different general types of family rather than attempting the impossible task of describing each and every family individually. Sociologists have developed the ideal-typical descriptions of 'nuclear family' and 'extended family' as part of their methodology. Ideal types provide a way of conceptualising differences even if the ideal type is never observed in its pure form. Weber uses the technique of ideal type in his own analysis of bureaucracy (see later).

Individual analysis

Weber's second additional contribution concerns a similar set of issues but this time in terms of acknowledging that individual variations might also be important. Despite the usefulness of general concepts, social theory should also remain sensitive to variations at the **micro level** of analysis. Furthermore, while it was perfectly reasonable to choose to investigate social phenomena at the level of collective actions and events (as Durkheim and Marx generally do), it was also reasonable to investigate things from the point of view of the individual social actor. Social actors might often be compelled to act in one way rather than another but even on these occasions there remains an element of **voluntarism** in what they do. The interpretive or 'verstehen' technique described earlier is designed to improve the prospects of really understanding what actions mean to the social actors carrying them out. Weber can thus be described as a 'methodological individualist' in the sense that he wants to try to include in his analysis an account of social phenomena as they appear to social actors themselves. **Methodological individualism** also dips into the rationalist definition of knowledge discussed earlier since it is not unreasonable to argue that if all knowledge is a product of cognitive reasoning, then the only perception of the exterior world that is available is an individual one. Even the most intimate social act remains personal since the feelings, impressions and thoughts of the participants are always separate.

Weber's account of the rise of modern, rational, capitalist society: 'rationality', *The Protestant Ethic* and bureaucracy

As we noted in the introduction, it has become standard procedure in learning about social theory to compare Weber's explanation of the emergence of modern industrial capitalist society with Marx's account. We have to be interested in this comparison because the question of the causes and consequences of historical development remains a central part of the subject matter of social theory. Notwithstanding the fact, as already noted, that Weber was only familiar with a portion of Marx's work and was undoubtedly influenced by the simplified German Social Democratic Party reading of Marx, there were very few modern accounts to choose between and certainly Marx's historical–materialist analysis was a leading contender. Weber was, however, unhappy about the historical–materialist account for a number of reasons. A number of necessarily simplistic comparisons can be made.

First, Weber thought that it was highly unlikely that history develops according to any kind of grand plan, let alone the one that Marx describes. For Weber, human action is much more contingent than this in the sense that nobody can predict what all the circumstances and contexts of action will be. If you cannot specify the context, then there is little chance of foreseeing the action that will take place within it. The basic inability to specify what will happen next also applies to the consequences of action, many of which are quite unintended. Just because social actors hope that things will turn out in one way rather than another does not guarantee that they will. Regarding Marx's idea, for example, that capitalism must follow feudalism, Weber pointed out that capitalism is not in fact unique to modern society. Much of his historical analysis is concerned with showing that different forms of capitalistic or profit-making behaviour have characterised earlier forms of society. Modern industrial capitalism in other words, is just one type, one variety, of the different kinds of capitalism that, under different historical circumstances, could have developed. Weber is therefore inclined to be cautious about the contribution to social theory of the historical-materialist method.

A second weakness of the historical-materialist approach, as Weber saw it, was that it gave too much attention to the economic realm and thus underestimated what goes on in other aspects of social life. In trying to understand the origins of modern capitalism it is necessary to look at developments in the political, legal and religious spheres as well as in the economic sphere. Rather than accepting Marx's topographical representation of society as a pyramid with the broad economic base providing a foundation for all other superstructural phenomena, Weber is more inclined to see society as a series of overlapping realms, none of which has the power to control or dominate all of the others. He accepts the very great significance and influence of the economic sphere but does not see this as causative of all other phenomena in the way that Marx does.

A related weakness, according to Weber at least, is that while materialist theories inevitably give priority to material phenomena, ideational phenomena, including ideas, values and beliefs, but also the way social actors construct intellectual representations of reality in their minds, also need to be taken into account. One could press this point and suggest that at the point ideas become realised through practice, they also take on a material existence.

Having made these criticisms of the historical-materialist approach, Weber felt compelled to offer an alternative. After all, history had to develop in one way or another, and just because historical materialism fell short in its explanation this did not mean that other social theorists should not give it a try. We will look at Weber's alternative under three headings:

- his comments about the development of a new kind of **rationality**, which became integral to the Western world view from the 16th century onwards;
- his detailed description in *The Protestant Ethic and the Spirit of Capitalism* of how a new variant of the business or commercial spirit of capitalism coincided with the emergence of a particular kind of Protestant religious ethic in Northern Europe at around the same time;
- his comments about the inevitable spread of **bureaucracy**.

Rationality

Weber agreed with Marx that modern capitalism had become the dominant characteristic of modern industrial society. It was (and in fact still is) not possible to think of modern society without also thinking about the capitalist business enterprise that lies at the heart of it. Where he disagreed with Marx was over the explanation of how this state of affairs had come about. For Weber the originating cause, the fundamental root of this development, was not 'men making history' or 'the class struggle', but the emergence of a new approach to life based around a new kind of **rational** outlook. This new rationality had its roots in the various intellectual currents that emerged during the European Enlightenment.

The main intention of the new rationality was to replace vagueness and speculation with precision and calculation. This was a profoundly practical kind of rationality in which social actors no longer behaved spontaneously or emotionally but only after making a careful consideration of the various alternatives available to them. The new rationality took the Enlightenment idea that people could control their own destiny and turned it into a strategy for action. It was all about controlling the outcomes of action, of eliminating fate and chance, through the application of **reason**. Weber called the new outlook **instrumental rationality** because it took the degree to which it enabled social actors to achieve the ends they had identified as its main criteria for judging whether an action was or was not rational. A characteristic of modern society is that actions are defined as rational as long as they are effective in achieving particular ends. The new instrumental rationality was also a 'universal rationality' in the sense that it affected the way in which decisions to act were made, not just in economic affairs, but across the full spectrum of activity. Weber argued that instrumental rationality had become a foundation for a new and highly rationalistic way of life or world view.

Rationalisation

In the same way that the term industrialisation describes what happens when economies take on industrial techniques, Weber uses the term rationalisation to describe what happens when the different institutions and practices that surround social action take on the techniques of instrumental rationality. Modern society is modern because it has undergone this process of rationalisation. Although, as we have already noted, Weber agreed with Marx about the great significance for historical development of developments in the economic sphere, he argued that the massive expansion of the economic sphere as it entered its industrial stage was itself a consequence and not a cause of the spread of the new instrumental rationality. Weber noted, for example, that instrumental rationality was not confined to the economic sphere but also affected the development of democratic systems for electing governments, the rationalisation of government into different departments and the increasing use of bureaucracy as the most instrumentally rational way of organising complex organisations. The legal and medical professions, universities and research institutions and so on, are all similarly drawn under the influence of instrumental rationality. The uptake of instrumental rationality through rationalisation can be seen to be a driving force behind all forms of modernisation in modern society.

While factors identified by Marx, such as property relations, class conflict and developments in the means of production, clearly play an important part in how, at a lower and more descriptive level of analysis, the specific consequences are worked out, each of these is, according to Weber, an outlet for the underlying urge to become increasingly rational. Recalling Durkheim's analysis of social solidarity and the new **individualism**, discussed in Chapter Three, one might say that the instrumental rationality identified by Weber provides an important source of collective consciousness in modern society. Rationalisation and its consequences regulate the behaviour of social actors and thus contribute to social order.

Formal and substantive rationality

Before moving on to look at two detailed examples Weber provides of the actual impact of rationalisation on real situations (the capitalist business enterprise and the rise of bureaucracy), we should pause to make one further point about the new instrumental rationality. As ever, this requires some preliminary philosophical reflection on the qualitative dimensions of instrumental rationality. This concerns the distinction between **formal rationality** and **substantive rationality**. There is a tendency to assume that in describing the new instrumental rationality Weber somehow approves of it and of its effects on social life. This is partly unavoidable precisely because Weber goes to great lengths not to offer his own opinion (he would regard this as a serious transgression of the principle of value-neutrality discussed earlier). Quite unlike Marx, he does not supplement his account of the origins and nature of capitalism with a *critique* of capitalism. Nor does he wish to offer any suggestions about how things could be organised differently (although he is generally critical of the socialist alternative as he thinks the mode of bureaucratised social organisation it envisages would restrict individual freedom).

He does, however, make an important distinction between the rationality of something in terms of how useful it is in a purely practical sense (its formal rationality), and how rational it is in terms of the ends it serves (its substantive rationality). For example, it is clear that the industrial division of labour is a more technically efficient, a more rational, way of producing things than feudal agriculture. What is less clear is whether the decision to apply this type of organisation is an entirely rational one given that there is no guarantee that the general quality of life is also bound to improve. Just because social actors make sensible choices between the various techniques for doing something this does not necessarily help us decide if the ends they want to achieve are, in a more substantive sense, also rational. The atomic bomb is the most effective means of mass destruction but mass destruction is hardly a rational objective.

This dilemma runs parallel to the issue of value-neutrality discussed in the previous section of this chapter. For Weber, one of the most difficult challenges of social theory is to account for the judgements social actors make, not so much over the best means for achieving something, but over which ends they feel are worth pursuing. The potential conflict between formal and substantive rationality is itself a consequence of the modernist perspective that emerged from the European Enlightenment. In pre-modernity crucial decisions about ultimate ends simply did not arise because the originating force in the universe was taken to be either nature or God. Having displaced nature with society and having marginalised the notion of the divine presence with the introduction of a strong concept of human self-determination, social actors in modern society have to make choices without reference to supra-human forces; choices that have been created by the powerful new technical means at their disposal.

▶▶   We will return to this topic of means and ends when we discuss the global environmental impact of modern industry and the 'risk society' in Chapter Fourteen.

It was the apparently indissoluble nature of these tensions between the formal and substantive rationalities of modern society, and between the rationalities of the different spheres of social action, that caused Weber to be extremely pessimistic about what the future might hold. If bureaucratic procedures cause a loss of liberty, or if, as Marx showed, the division of labour in industry causes alienation, would it be better not to use these techniques? Most fundamentally, and reflecting the instrumentality of the new outlook, Weber felt that as social actors become more and more obsessed with expressing formal rationality by improving the techniques they have for doing things, they become less and less interested in why they are doing them. The connection between means and ends becomes increasingly weakened even to the extent that ends come to be defined in terms of the unquestioned desirability of developing yet more means.

The ways in which these underlying tensions in the concept of instrumental rationality played themselves out in society provided Weber with a powerful way of theorising the sources of social conflict. Whereas Marx had correctly defined social conflict in terms of the struggle for economic resources, Weber added that important struggles also took place between one value system and another. The resources, in other words, over which social actors come into conflict, are not just economic ones but ideational and conceptual ones as well. Capitalism dominates modern society not just because it is red hot at developing new techniques for producing things (it expresses very high levels of formal rationality, or in Marx's terms is very dynamic in developing the means of production), but because it engages sufficiently at the level of ideas for social actors to believe that this is a rational way to proceed.

The 'rationality' of modern capitalism

Dropping down a level from Weber's more abstract development of the concept of rationality to describe the general causes of the process by which modern society develops, we can look at two examples of how Weber thought these principles worked themselves out in practice. The first is his influential description in *The Protestant Ethic and the Spirit of Capitalism* (otherwise known as 'the Protestant ethic thesis') of how a particular set of business interests coincided with a specific religious orientation to produce the modern rational variant of capitalism (the second is his critical analysis of bureaucracy, which we will be looking at shortly). Along with his influential contribution to methodological issues in the social sciences, and of his analysis of rationality and social action, Weber's reputation as a major social theorist rests heavily on the two extended essays he published under this title in 1904 and 1905. In them, and drawing on the ideas and arguments we have just been looking at, he offers his description of the origins of modern capitalism:

KEY QUOTE – Max Weber, *The Protestant Ethic and the Spirit of Capitalism* (1976 [1904/05])
In the last analysis the factor which produces capitalism is the rational permanent enterprise with its rational accounting, rational technology and rational law, [complemented by] the rational spirit, the rationalisation of the conduct of life in general and a rationalistic economic ethic. (Weber, quoted in Andreski, 1983, p 128)

This brief quotation usefully summarises Weber's analysis of what is peculiar about *modern* capitalism. In contrast to earlier forms of profit making, the modern form is profoundly *rational* in the sense that its advocates try to keep risks to a minimum, behave in a highly calculating way when making business and investment decisions, and, perhaps most essentially, continue to make profits even when they have already passed the point of satisfying their own immediate needs. Reflecting the problematic nature of instrumental rationality as discussed in the previous section, profit making within modern capitalism becomes *an end in itself* rather than a means to an end. Recalling Marx's description, this amounts to a shift from the production of commodities that are valuable because of their practical use [or **use value**], to the production of commodities whose value lies in their abstract capacity for exchangeability [**exchange value**]. The production of use values is limited by the needs they satisfy, whereas the production of exchange values is unlimited.

The spirit of capitalism

We can list the basic features of the modern rational business enterprise as follows:

- Most important is the use of rational calculation as the basis for doing business. This is a 'means–ends relation', meaning that decisions about how to act are based on a mathematical calculation of costs and benefits. It is an instrumental orientation.
- The medium for achieving this level of economic instrumentalism and regulation is *money*: 'From a purely technical point of view, money is the most "perfect" means of economic calculation. That is, it is formally the most rational means of orienting economic activity. Calculation in terms of money is thus the specific means of rational economic provision' (Weber, 1978 [1921], p 86).
- In order to be able to calculate accurately, the capitalist also needs ownership, or at least complete control over the business, access to reliable technical and scientific knowledge, including knowledge of a comprehensive accounting system (double-entry bookkeeping), and a rational legal and administrative context within which to work.
- The capitalist must also have access to a source of workers who can be relied upon to sell their labour power: 'People must be available who are not only legally in a position to do so but are also economically compelled to sell their labour on the market without restrictions. [Only then] can the costs of production be unambiguously determined in advance' (Weber, 1983, p 110).

The Protestant ethic

These practical requirements of the modern rational business enterprise only tell half the story. The other half is made up by the attitudes and expectations, the ideas, values and beliefs, of the fortunate folk who own or control them (in Marx's terms 'the owners of the means of production' or bourgeoisie). As Weber tells it, these values and beliefs arose within a particularly vigorous and **ascetic** variety of the Protestant faith, which developed in Northern Europe, and later in North America, during the 16th and 17th centuries. 'Asceticism' is an attitude of self-restraint, even self-denial, which imposes strict limits on the kind of enjoyment a person may take in the products of his or her work. For Weber, it was the historically fortunate coming together of this religious code of conduct or 'ethic', and the 'spirit' of the newly emerging and instrumentally oriented variety of capitalism, that launched rational capitalism into the modern world.

Individual responsibility

The originality of this new ascetic Protestantism lay not so much in ideas about living a good earthly life and having faith in the possibility of spiritual salvation, principles that had been around for quite a while already, but in the self-administered and thus psychological nature of the fear of not achieving spiritual salvation. Central to the Protestant faith is the idea that it is the individual and not the Church who carries responsibility for spiritual destiny. The concept of individual conscience and individual responsibility was built around the idea of 'the calling' developed by the initiator of the Protestant faith, the German theologian Martin Luther (1483–1546). As Weber interprets it: 'The only way of living acceptably to God was through the fulfilment of the obligations imposed upon the individual by his position in the world. That was his calling' (Weber, 1976, p 80).

  This key principle was supplemented soon after by the idea of 'predestination', put forward in the teaching of another Protestant theologian John Calvin (1509–64). According to this principle, the soul of some individuals had been marked for salvation 'by his gratuitous mercy, totally irrespective of human merit [and by] a just and irreprehensible, but incomprehensible judgement' (John Calvin, *Institutes of the Christian Religion*, 1838 translation, pp 128–9, bk 3, Ch 21, para 7; quoted in Tawney, 1960 [1926], p 108). Those who had not been chosen were destined never to achieve spiritual salvation. At first sight this position seems paradoxical. If spiritual salvation has been settled in advance then what is to be gained from pursuing earthly toil in a Godly manner, why not simply lead a life of pleasure and idleness?

Calvin emphasised, however, that precisely since there can be no certainty of salvation, individuals must prove their spiritual salvation by leading an exemplary life on earth. Moreover, this proof could not simply be demonstrated abstractly by believing in the possibility of salvation hereafter, but through concrete action in the present. Intense worldly activity thus became indispensable 'as a sign of election': '[It is] the technical means, not of purchasing salvation, but of getting rid of the fear of damnation' (Weber, 1976, p 115). Through frenetic devotion to one's calling, the individual is provided with a means of demonstrating how certain they are about being saved. Conveniently, 'the earning of money within the modern economic order is, so long as it is done legally, the result and the expression of virtue and proficiency in a calling' (Weber, 1976, p 54). Ascetic Protestantism thus unequivocally ties spiritual destiny to a profoundly practical and energetic ethic of hard work:

KEY QUOTE – Max Weber, *The Protestant Ethic and the Spirit of Capitalism* (1976 [1904/05]), on the Protestant ethic and 'the calling'
In truth this peculiar idea, so familiar to us to-day, but in reality so little a matter of course, of one's duty in a calling is what is most characteristic of the social ethic of capitalistic culture and is in a sense the fundamental basis of it. It is an obligation which the individual is supposed to feel and does feel towards the content of his professional activity, no matter in what it consists, in particular no matter whether it appears on the surface as a utilisation of his personal powers or only of his material possessions (as capital). (Weber, 1976, p 54)

Increasing capital

Irrespective of whether salvation is actually achieved through hard work, the practical outcome of the idea that it might gave rise to a work-obsessed class of entrepreneurs and business people whose earthly desire for commercial success ran parallel with their religious desire for spiritual redemption. Since the enjoyment of wealth is considered sinful, the only legitimate use for the increasing revenue is to reinvest it in the business itself. The pragmatic saving of capital is justified by the higher substantive aim of the saving of souls. For Weber, it is this coincidence within the Protestant ethic between obsessive hard work and an ascetic attitude towards the wealth it generates that lies at the heart of the 'elective affinity' or sympathetic association between Protestantism and capitalism:

When the limitation of consumption is combined with the release of acquisitive activity, the inevitable practical result is obvious: accumulation of capital through ascetic compulsion to save. The restraints imposed upon the consumption of wealth naturally served to increase it by making possible the productive investment of capital. (Weber, 1976, p 172)

The hard-working, hard-saving, soul-searching mentality embedded within the Protestant work ethic filtered down the social hierarchy eventually establishing itself as the most practical and legitimate way of achieving prosperity in modern society. Making good use of time, being busy not idle, avoiding frivolity, self-indulgence and wastefulness, are common principles of behaviour that have undoubtedly shaped the mentality of modern Western society.

In summary, then, the argument Weber puts forward in his Protestant ethic thesis tries to provide a multidimensional explanation of how modern capitalism really got going. The basic point he wants to get across is that although the very large amounts of capital that capital*ism* needed to get started did, from a technical point of view, come by way of developments in the versatility of the division of labour and the efficiency of the means of production, these developments *were themselves* a result of a qualitative change in the general approach to life and work; a general approach based on new ideas, values and beliefs. Weber's explanation can be much more precise about the timing of the whole modern capitalist adventure (Northern Europe in the period 1650–1750), because the release of spare capital is tied to a specific coming together of commercial attitudes and the religious teaching of Luther and Calvin. Unlike the historical-materialist account, which relies on the theoretical construct of developments in the means and relations of production to predict the emergence of capitalism from feudalism, Weber's thesis gives the whole event a real sense of historical actuality. Modern rational capitalism emerged because of the collision at a particular time and place of a particular set of real *but unpredictable* circumstances. Some of these circumstances were material ones (technical innovation, new commercial opportunities), but others came from the realm of ideas.

Getting back to Weber's underlying argument that the whole ethos of modern society changed with the emergence of the new rationality, he felt that what the twin beliefs in saving one's capital and saving one's soul had in common was the fact that they both defined rationality in highly instrumental terms. If by working hard it is possible to achieve earthly comfort, *and* enhance one's sense of having a spiritual future thereafter, then hard work becomes the pivotal activity of one's life. Hard work is legitimately regarded as having very high levels of formal rationality because it is the practical means of achieving the substantively rational goals of prosperity and salvation. Nobody in the

West is ever criticised for working too hard because hard work is the best means of achieving these highest ends.

Bureaucracy

The second detailed example Weber provides of the actual impact of rationalisation on real situations is the rise of bureaucracy. Having begun to define modern society in terms of the spread of instrumental rationality, Weber goes on to argue that as society becomes more and more complex (both in terms of its economic arrangements, and in terms of its increasing institutional sophistication), the quest for an appropriately rational means of organisation also becomes increasingly urgent. Since the most rational means of organisation is bureaucratic organisation, he felt it was inevitable that bureaucracy would become an ever more dominant feature of modern society. The importance of this development for Weber's social theory is that bureaucracy provides a fine example of a technique of formal rationality that is found in all spheres of social life. In fact, whether in the economy or in the legislative and administrative functions of the state, progress comes to depend on the availability of bureaucratic means of organisation and administration.

The main characteristics of the ideal-type bureaucracy as envisaged by Weber can be summarised as follows:

- Bureaucracy is an expert system of administration based on detailed documentation and record-keeping.
- The operation of bureaucracy is governed by a legalistic framework of formal rules and regulations.
- Decisions are made through the application of specific procedures designed to eliminate subjective judgements.
- The legitimacy of bureaucracy and of bureaucrats is based on a strict separation of individual personality from the task being done.
- Authority is a characteristic of the post not of the post holder.
- Bureaucracies have a rigidly hierarchical organisational structure with clear lines of communication and responsibility.
- It is not possible to become a bureaucrat without the correct formal qualifications and credentials.

In strictly practical terms there is nothing unexpected about these developments since the application of bureaucracy is entirely rational in the sense that it offers the best technical solution to the problem of organising large quantities of information. Bureaucracy is widely perceived as a legitimate way of making decisions and of running things because the personal interests of bureaucrats are kept separate from the decisions they make.

Even at the level of formal rationality, however, Weber felt problems were likely to arise because few bureaucracies ever match up to the ideal type. The substance of many decisions is likely to be based on subjective judgement, even if the process is intended to prevent this. Sometimes rule-governed procedures can become rule-bound in the sense that too much red tape prevents decisions being made quickly. Even more seriously, to the extent that the personal career interests of bureaucrats depend on the status of the bureaucracy itself, they have a vested interest in putting the particular aim of increasing the power and authority of the bureaucracy ahead of the universal ends that were supposed to be served by the bureaucracy. Civil servants might become more concerned with protecting the status of the civil service, even of one government department against another, than with delivering a decent service to the public.

In terms of its political and cultural impact, Weber was also very concerned that bureaucracy has irrational tendencies in the sense that it might override individual freedom and integrity. Based on his own analysis of what was happening in German society during the 1890s, he feared that as more and more aspects of the decision-making process became gathered into fewer and fewer hands, bureaucracies, and the bureaucrats who ran them, would smother personal freedoms resulting in the emergence of what he famously called 'a new iron cage of serfdom' (Weber, 1978 [1921] p 472). In the political sphere, the turn towards democracy also meant the spread of detailed procedures for conducting democratic elections, which in turn entailed greater reliance on the electoral process and electoral officials. This tension between the wider purposes (substantive rationality) of the political process, and the narrow functional priorities (formal rationality) of bureaucracy, is a good example of the kind of value conflict we discussed earlier in this chapter.

Weber was greatly concerned that aided by the increasing centralisation of authority, a new class of professional bureaucrats might be tempted to subvert bureaucratic authority for their own ends. His major reservations about the prospects of a socialist Germany were less to do with the values of the socialist belief system, than with the practical problems it would create through the yet further **bureaucratisation** of society. As it turned out, the concerns expressed by Weber were amply substantiated in respect of the version of socialist/communist society that emerged as the Soviet Union during the 20th century. This society was profoundly criticised because of the way the bureaucracies of party, state and military contrived, so it seemed, to deprive citizens of representation, rights and liberty.

Weber's theory of social action: the role of values and beliefs

As we noted in the first section of this chapter, Weber wanted to develop social theory in a way that tried to examine social action from the point of view of the social actor. Although Weber shares with Marx a desire to develop what we can call a theory of social action, that is, a coherent account of how and why social actors act as they do, aspects of Weber's explanation differ from that offered by Marx. Whereas Marx describes motivation as the expression of human-beingness through productive activity and the desire to survive and prosper, Weber argues that social action also provides social actors with opportunities to live out their values and beliefs. There is no question that social actors act in order to survive, but for many the quality of life also depends on some of the more esoteric and abstract aspects of human consciousness, qualities that are often expressed as values and beliefs. For example, if a group of social actors share a particular set of religious or spiritual beliefs, notwithstanding the fact that they still need to survive, such beliefs are likely to shape the way in which they manage their survival. Even the concept of 'survival' might be modified to include ideas about spiritual well-being. A social theory that seeks to explain social action in that context has to include some account of needs and desires, which exist alongside basic economic ones.

Following this line of argument, and placing this in the context of his analysis of the relentless spread of instrumental rationality in the modern world, Weber's theory of social action centres around an analysis of the rationality or otherwise of different types of action. If individuals are indeed immersed in a rationalised and rationalising social world, then presumably this has an important impact on the way they act. The basic point of departure for Weber's theory of social action is that actions can be distinguished one from the other depending on which kind of rationality the actor is trying to express. Unsurprisingly he concludes that in modern society the variety of rationality that most often guides social action is instrumental rationality. Being modern or acting in a modern way means acting according to the modern principles of instrumental rationality.

Four types of social action

Weber refers to four basic types or 'determinations' of social action. Brubaker summarises these for us:

> Traditional action is determined by longstanding habits; affectual action, by strong feelings; *wertrational* action, by conscious belief

in the intrinsic value of acting in a certain way, regardless of the consequences of so acting; and *zweckrational* action, by a consciously calculating attempt to achieve desired ends with appropriate means. (Brubaker, 1984, p 50)

While the distinction between 'traditional' and 'affectual' action is clear enough (we can all think of times when we have acted out of habit or emotion), the distinction between *wertrational* (or value-rational) action and *zweckrational* (or purpose-rational) action is more complex. The distinction Weber is trying to identify is between actions that are inherently satisfying as an end in themselves, that is, actions that are worth doing primarily for the experience of doing them, and actions that produce a desired result even if in themselves they are not particularly satisfying. Again following Brubaker:

> *Value-rational* action is oriented to an act's intrinsic properties, *purpose-rational* action to its anticipated and intended consequences. Value-rational action presupposes a conscious belief about the intrinsic value or inherent rightness of a certain way of acting, purpose-rational action [presupposes] conscious reasoning in terms of means and ends. (Brubaker, 1984, p 51)

Although there is no reason why an action cannot be both an end in itself and a means of achieving a desired end (a concert pianist presumably enjoys playing the piano as well as playing in order to earn a living), Weber is suggesting that these two types of rational action correspond with two sometimes quite different kinds of values that the actor is trying to express. Some actions are in themselves an expression of value in the sense that the enjoyment they bring is actually experienced at the moment the action is performed. Other actions express a belief in the desirability of results that have yet to be achieved. They express an acknowledgement of deferred rather than immediate gratification. Thinking about our concert pianist again, the joy of playing is felt during the performance itself. As a means of earning a living the reward of being paid for playing comes some time after.

Picking up on the discussion of rationality/rationalisation earlier in this chapter, we can follow the logic of Weber's idea that since one of the features of modern society is a dramatic increase in the practical facilities needed for achieving certain goals (the division of labour, rational accounting procedures, a formalised legal system, institutional bureaucracy and so on), social actors become increasingly inclined to pursue the kinds of action that allow them to express their belief in the value of purpose-rational action. Priority is given to actions that have instrumental intent rather than immediate fulfilment. In the world of work, for example, many people are prepared to tolerate dull, tedious and boring jobs so long as they pay well. Higher pay at the end of the week is accepted as compensation for having to do unsatisfying work. The apparent irrationality of grinding out a miserable working life is overridden by the instrumental rationality of earning money that can be spent at some later time. Work has become a means to an end rather than an end in itself.

The limits of rational understanding

As should be clear even from the few simple examples we have given the task of sorting out which variety of values come into play for any particular action is potentially very complex. One might ask, for example, whether there are limits to the extent to which social actors are prepared to forgo immediate satisfaction in order to achieve some longer-term aim. Marx clearly felt that the working class had already reached the end of its tether and was about to reject capitalism altogether. It also seems likely that many actions express more than one kind of rationality at the same time. Just because a social actor acts in order to express some form of traditional belief that she feels strongly about (tradition plus affectual rationality) does not mean that the action cannot also provide her with a degree of immediate satisfaction (value-rationality) and express her belief in the value of achieving some longer-term goal (purpose-rationality). Other actions, such as an adult reprimanding a child, seem to contradict other values, such as wanting to protect children from stressful situations.

Conceptual ideal types

The level of complexity here can certainly be quite intimidating but the thing to remember is that, in building his theory of social action, Weber uses the different kinds of rationality and the values they are thought to express as conceptual ideal types. When looking at social action in the real world, however, things are much more untidy and so one would expect there to be a lack of 'fit' between what seems to be going on, and the theorist's ideal-typical explanation of it. It is because Weber is so conscious of this lack of fit that he tries to make room for it in his method. Although it is possible to make an objective assessment of whether one course of action is preferable to another in a practical sense, it is not possible to make objective assessments of whether an actor made the right kinds of subjective choices. Was the cyclist in our earlier illustration right in thinking that cycling would make him fit or save the planet from further harm? Does cycling make his actions morally superior? By definition, actions that bring satisfaction in themselves (value-rational actions) can really only be assessed by the actor themselves. Unless the scientific observer is reflecting on her own actions she has no access to such subjective impressions at all. As Weber puts it:

> Even such simple questions as the extent to which an end should sanction unavoidable means, or the extent to which undesired repercussions should be taken into consideration … are entirely matters of choice and compromise. There is no (rational or empirical) scientific procedure of any kind whatsoever which can provide us with a decision here. (Weber, *The Methodology of the Social Sciences*, quoted in Brubaker, 1984, p 59)

Concepts of political power: status groups and legitimate domination

As we noted in Chapter One, one of the central concepts social theory tries to use is the concept of **power**. We suggested that power can be defined as the struggle for control over resources, and that different kinds of power thus relate to the resources that are being fought over. The concept of power encompasses the use of direct physical force and its more subtle expression as persuasion. This definition of power is **pluralistic** in the sense that it accepts that there is more than one kind of power and more than one way of expressing it in society. Looking at the situation of women in modern Western society, for example, feminist social theorists argue that men attempt to control the lives of women by exercising different kinds of power over them. They try to prevent women having access to economic power by keeping the best-paid and most prestigious jobs for themselves. Until the 20th century at least, men exercised political power by withholding the right of women to vote in elections. They even attempt to exercise power over women's bodies by developing a male-based science of biological reproduction. In the last resort, men, it is suggested, exercise physical power over women by using the threat of violence. For some feminist social theorists, these four aspects of power are combined to develop a theory of **patriarchy**, which is the idea that, above all else, men seek the subordination of women. (We will be looking at the concept of patriarchy in Chapter Eleven.) We can learn quite a lot about how Weber thinks about the concept of political power by looking briefly at two parts of his work. First is his analysis of 'status groups', and, second, his ideas about 'legitimate domination' and political leadership.

Marx and Weber on power

One of the advantages of the pluralist conception of power of the kind that Weber uses is that it allows for the fact that power in society is exercised in varying degrees by different groups, and also depending on particular circumstances. One might have thought, for example, that the likelihood of one political party being elected rather than another mainly depends on the credibility of the candidates, their track record in office and even the policies they hold. There is strong evidence, however, that each of these factors can be manipulated by the mass media, which political parties have to rely upon to get their message across. Although it would not be sensible to argue that the mass media are more powerful than political parties, or that the kind of power exercised by the mass media is greater than the power exercised by the political sphere, there are key moments when the mass media do hold the upper hand. There are different types or centres of power, and the relations between them vary according to the relative importance, at any given time, of the different kinds of resources they represent. Alliances can also be made between the different sources of power. For example, a right-wing government might introduce legislation that benefits employers because many politicians are from the same social background as employers, and therefore have shared economic interests with them.

One of the main differences between the concepts of power used by Marx and by Weber is that Weber is more inclined to accept variation in the types and sources of power as they apply to different situations, whereas Marx defines power primarily as control over economic resources. This is the decisive source of power in society and he conceives all the other struggles that take place as being supplementary effects of this. Struggles in the cultural and political spheres are conceived as part of the more fundamental struggle between groups for control over the economy. A historical-materialist interpretation of the struggle between women and men described earlier, would be that it is in the interests of the capitalist class to make women economically dependent on men, in order to increase the pressure on men to turn up for work to support their families. Similarly, women accept the need to provide their partners with domestic support so that they will be able to keep on working. One of the best ways of seeing the differences between Marx's rather uniform concept of power and Weber's more variegated approach is to compare their analyses of 'classes', 'status groups' and 'parties'.

Marx on class

You will recall that, for Marx, class relationships are determined in a very direct way by the objective fact of whether a person does or does not own (or control) the means of production. The owning minority (the capitalist class or bourgeoisie) are able to compel the non-owning majority (the working class or proletariat) to work because this is the only way that the latter can make a living. Not working means privation and starvation. The relationship between these two great classes of modern society is inherently exploitative, because the capitalist pays the worker less for what he or she has produced than the the profit the capitalist gets from selling what has been produced. Capitalists accumulate surplus value and profit, which enables them to increase their domination over the economic realm. For Marx, and irrespective of the other social or political conflicts that may arise as a result of this underlying economic relationship, all members of the working class have a mutual interest in regaining control over the means of production. Thus his famous opening theorem in *The Communist Manifesto* that 'The history of all hitherto existing society is the history of class struggles'. It is because members of a particular class share the same interests that they become members of that class.

Weber's criticisms of Marx

Weber rejected this conception of how different groups come into conflict in society on a number of grounds. First, he argues that groups might come into conflict for many reasons and certainly not just because of the struggle over economic resources. Struggles over political and cultural resources might be just as important. From his own analysis of the manoeuvrings of the various economic and political groups in German society at the turn of the 20th century, Weber felt not only that these other kinds of resources sometimes override interests of a purely economic kind, but might even go directly against them.

Second, and this time focusing on how Marx uses the concept of class, Weber felt that Marx made the mistake of confusing the analytical category 'class' with the actual groups of real social actors that the theory presupposes were members of that group. Marx is thus accused of confusing a term for analysis ('class') with an actual historical entity having effects to an extent independently of its individual members. Just because historical materialism assumes there are such things as economic classes, and even feels able to predict how they are formed, it does not mean they really do exist. They might, but they might not. In the jargon of social theory, Marx takes a **realist** position, because he thinks the conceptual entities he describes, such as 'class', are things that actually exist. Weber takes an alternative **nominalist** position, in the sense of merely applying a 'nomos' or name to a particular phenomenon for the purposes of analysing it, but without claiming that it has a form of existence independent of the term used to describe it. Using a nominalist approach Weber uses notions of 'class' and 'status group' in the manner of an ideal type and for the purposes of analysis and comparison, not as an attempt to record and categorise actual things in the way that botanists or geographers do.

Third, and related to this basic conceptual principle, Weber makes a distinction between the objective sociological factors that social actors and theorists use in identifying which groups social actors fall into (type of job, level of qualifications, standard of living), and the much more subjective criteria that determine the qualitative aspects of group identity (shared ideas and beliefs, judgements of 'social honour' and lifestyle). It is perfectly possible, for example, for the theorist to place a person into a particular category without that person even realising that such a category exists. Statisticians spend much of their time doing precisely this. It is also important not to confuse objective location in a particular group with assumptions about subjective affiliation or loyalty either to the group as a whole or to other individual members of it. Even Marx, who is certainly tempted for political reasons to make this assumption, recognises that much political persuasion is needed to turn an objective class 'in itself' into a subjective class 'for itself'.

Weber feels that because historical materialists take such a literal view of class, and make such a direct link between historical change and the class struggle, they must also commit themselves to a somewhat restricted account of how power affects the distribution of social actors in society and its effects on social relationships. Weber wants to move beyond economic sources of power and the two-class distribution of social actors it produces, and to think about the relational and distributive effects of non-economic sources of power. In order to do this he develops a stratification model of social distribution in which each social strata is identified with, and defined in terms of, other sources of social power. Analytically, there are as many strata as there are identifiable sources of power in society.

Life chances

Weber begins by developing the concept of 'life chances' to add more detail to what we already know about the struggle for economic power and resources: 'A class is a number of people having in common a specific causal component of life chances. This component is represented by economic interests in the possession of goods and opportunities for income under conditions of the market' (Weber, 1978 [1921], p 927). Weber is trying to capture the sense in which social actors in a similar economic situation are likely to have similar opportunities. This is an objective view of their situation that does not assume that individuals sharing the same life chances are particularly aware of this fact or are committed in a more subjective sense to others in the same life-chance situation.

The important point to note from this quotation is that for Weber, the distribution of economic life chances (and correspondingly the distribution of social actors according to their objective life-chance situation) is determined not just by the ownership of property ('the possession of goods') as Marx had correctly identified, but also by other 'opportunities for income' in the market. These opportunities come in the form of talents, skills and experience, which give some social actors economic advantages over others. A senior manager or skilled technician, for example, may not own their means of production in the Marxist sense, but they do gain a distinct economic advantage from the possession of highly marketable skills and technical knowledge. They are 'positively privileged' compared with junior managers and unskilled workers who are thus 'negatively privileged'. In modern society, with its advanced division of labour and bureaucratic forms of organisation, possession of formal qualifications becomes an increasingly important determinant of life chances.

Status groups

The second thing Weber does is look beyond economic power and economic classes and towards groups that are formed on the basis of other, often more subjective, criteria of the kind we have just been discussing. These include such things as taste, lifestyle, social and cultural values, or what Weber refers to as 'estimations of social honour': 'Every typical component of the life-fate of men that is determined by a specific, positive or negative, social estimation of honor' (Weber, 1978 [1921], p 932). A common feature of these estimations or judgements is that they tend to be made about actions and behaviours that take place in the realm of consumption rather than in the realm of production. They are social determinants caused by the way social actors spend their money rather than of how they earn it.

'Parties'

Weber also wanted to include in his analysis of the effects of power social groups that form with the explicit purpose of actively pursuing their interests as a group. He refers to these as 'parties' and their main mode of operation in modern society is the political campaign. Sometimes parties coincide with economic classes and/or status groups (for example a socialist political party aligned with the economic interests of the working class and immersed in working-class culture). The decisive factor is that although party membership is an objective fact, social actors make a judgement to get involved with them rather than being objectively oriented in a way that presupposes that their membership is automatic. Examples of parties include professional bodies, trade associations or trade unions taking up 'the political struggle' in the economic sphere, or political parties who conduct the political struggle in the traditional sphere of public elections. Parties might also be more loosely organised pressure or campaign groups, which form specifically to achieve a particular aim. In the case of single-issue pressure groups, once the issue has been settled, their aims have been fulfilled and so they disband. Although parties or pressure groups might try to use physical force to press their case through a strike at work, a protest march or civil disobedience, and make use of legal entitlements such as the right to free speech, their main strategy is to try to attract popular support by getting other social actors to see something from their point of view. In this sense at least parties make use of power as persuasion rather than power as physical force.

Legitimate domination and legitimate leadership

The final example of Weber's theory of power we want to look at here relates to control over the decision-making processes in society. For Weber, and much like the notion of civil consensus developed by Saint-Simon and later by Durkheim, the capacity of an individual or group to become dominant in modern society, depends less on their ability to overcome physical resistance from rival groups, and more on persuading the dominated to accept this fact. Domination is accepted as legitimate as long as it is seen as such by those affected by it.

▸▸ A similar theory of leadership or domination, based on the willing compliance of the population to be dominated, was put forward by the Marxist theorist Antonio Gramsci (1891–1937). He used the concept of **hegemony** to describe how, in modern societies, social change comes about as much by attracting people to a particular point of view as by threatening them with physical force. This theory is discussed in Chapter Eight.

Traditional and charismatic leadership

Weber identifies three kinds of legitimate domination, which in some respects reflect three of the basic types of action (traditional, affectual and purpose-rational) discussed in the previous section. First is 'traditional domination' of the kind associated with monarchy. The population accepts the authority of the ruler to rule largely on the grounds of historical precedent, inheritance, custom and so on. Second is 'charismatic leadership', under which the exceptional personal attributes of the leader (military, spiritual, magical) are accepted as being sufficient to warrant submission and obedience. Many of the great leaders in history are categorised as 'great' precisely because, as individuals, they had exceptional qualities of leadership. In both these cases the manner in which authority is exercised might very well include a certain amount of physical coercion and threat of punishment.

Rational-legal domination

The third kind of leadership Weber describes, and the one which is most characteristic of modern society, is 'rational-legal domination'. This is the kind of authority that emerges in parallel with bureaucratic organisation. Since, in modern society, it is the bureaucracy of government and government officials that control the decision-making process for society as a whole, political power becomes the most important form of power, and 'leadership' amounts to 'political leadership'. (This is not to say that economic power, or the ideological and cultural power of the Church or mass media, cease to exist, just that in modern society, of all the different kinds of power, political power comes to the top of the heap.)

People are prepared to accept the authority of the political leadership, not primarily because of the personal qualities of its individual members or the physical forces they can apply, but because they have been elected by means of the correct procedures sanctioned by legal arrangements. Those who exercise this kind of legitimate authority (presidents, prime ministers, government ministers), do so by virtue of having the right kinds of formal credentials and technical knowledge to get themselves elected. Although there is no reason why an elected president or prime minister cannot also have a certain charismatic authority (a property that might have helped them get elected in the first place), their authority is not personal to them but is an attribute of the office they hold. As long as the procedure for making the appointment is sound, and as long as post holders do not abuse the power associated with it, then they will be accepted as legitimately exercising the power which that position confers.

The essence of rational–legal domination, therefore, is the separation of authority from personality and its embedding in the structure of the organisation or system. The processes of electing a leadership are designed to reduce the impact of subjective judgement and to increase reliance on objective criteria such as formal qualifications. The fact that society has these procedures in place for electing a leadership also shows that the need for physical coercion has been greatly reduced. Indeed any attempts to take control by force would immediately discredit the perceived legitimacy of that group at least in terms of rational-legal authority (they might still find support on account of their charisma). The efficient functioning of the social apparatus is protected by a framework of rules enforced by the police and other security agencies of the sate and sanctioned by courts of law. As Weber puts it, it is the state and the state alone that has 'a monopoly on the legitimate use of violence' (Weber, 1978 [1921] p 637).

Weber's contribution to social theory as a whole

As should be clear from this introduction to Weber's work his influence on social theory has been considerable. First, in terms of methodology, Weber extends the conceptual tool kit of social theory by drawing attention to the uniqueness of social phenomena and especially to their qualitative and subjective dimensions. While recognising the difficulty of doing so, he recommends that social phenomena need to be seen from the point of view of social actors themselves, and not just from the abstract vantage point of the social theorist. His discussions of *verstehen*, of value-freedom and of ideal types are intended to assist in this process.

Second, Weber extends the analysis of social development offered by Marx in order to include not only material economic factors, but intellectual ones as well. It is the struggle over ideas that fuels social development not just technological innovation. Raising an issue that has been taken up by social theorists such as Anthony Giddens during the 20th century, Weber also draws attention to the fact that social events are much more contingent than we might like to think they are. He still tells us an interesting and persuasive story about the historical origins of modern capitalism, but all the while insists that things could have turned out quite differently. Social theory needs to work at the level of actual events rather than trying to interpret events in order to substantiate a general theory of how things ought to or must have developed.

Third, Weber adds to his account of how society develops a similarly detailed account of individual social action. His theory of social action builds on the materialist conception that people are motivated by their basic struggle over access to necessary resources but he adds an idealist counterbalance by arguing that some of those resources, and the motivation to have access to them, comes in the form of ideas, values and beliefs. Corresponding with his methodological recommendation of trying to understand social action from the point of view of the individual social actor Weber strongly supports the need for social theory to include non-material phenomena. He thus prepares the way for a much more forthright analysis of the importance of the **hermeneutic** or meaning-laden aspects of social phenomena that was to follow later in the 20th century.

Fourth, Weber's methodological individualism also sets him apart from Durkheim and Marx, both of whom adopt a strongly collectivist interpretation of social action. Although Weber accepts that social actors often act together, and with shared ideas and common aims in mind, he resists the idea that individuals are drawn towards particular ways of acting by the pull of collective forces. Weber's social theory is more **voluntaristic** in the sense that social actors choose how to act rather than being compelled to do so by social forces beyond their control. For much the same reason, Weber concentrates on a theory of social action and not on a theory of society.

Finally, and in terms of his own sociological analyses of modern society, Weber identifies the crucial significance in social development of the general concept of rationality, which was central to Enlightenment thought and the idea of **reason** (see Chapter Two). He then refines this into a robust and thoroughly modern concept of instrumental rationality. Although opinion differs over the exact formula of instrumental rationality it is widely accepted that this is the kind of rationality that is most characteristic of modern society. One of the major preoccupations of **critical social theory** and the **Frankfurt School** (see Chapter Eight), and of Jürgen Habermas (see Chapter Twelve), is to continue to explore the negative impact on modern society of the idea of instrumental rationality described by Max Weber.

Key points box – the key ideas we have looked at in this chapter are that:

☑ While it is important to think about how the actions of individuals fit in with 'the bigger picture' of social life, it is also crucial to try to explore social phenomena as they appear to individuals themselves (*verstehen* and methodological individualism).

☑ Social life and historical development are as much to do with thoughts and ideas as they are with changes in the techniques and organisation of work.

☑ One of the strongest motivators of social action is a desire to express values and beliefs. Values and beliefs constitute an essential qualitative dimension to the purposes of social action.

☑ Developing theoretical explanations of ideas, values and beliefs is problematic, first, because many of these are experienced subjectively and, second, because it is very difficult to assess one instance of substantive rationality against another.

☑ Weber believed that instrumental rationality had become the basic organising principle of social life in modern society.

☑ Weber was pessimistic about the impact of rational-legal domination as he felt that it would lead to the 'disenchantment' of the world.

Practice box

➲ Would it be fair to say that Max Weber provided a middle-class version of the working-class social theory of Karl Marx?

➲ What differences does Weber see between the methods of the natural sciences and the methods of the social sciences?

➲ What is the most important feature of Weber's concept of *verstehen*?

➲ What is 'instrumental rationality'?

➲ Summarise the main reasons why Weber thought modern capitalism was 'rational'.

➲ Why was Weber suspicious about the spread of bureaucracy?

➲ Can you think of an example of what Weber calls 'rational-legal domination'?

Further reading

Stanislav Andreski, *Max Weber on Capitalism, Bureaucracy and Religion: A Selection of Texts* (Allen & Unwin, 1983).

Reinhard Bendix, *Max Weber: An Intellectual Portrait* (Heinemann, 1979).

Karl Löwith, *Max Weber and Karl Marx* (Allen & Unwin, 1982).

Gordon Marshall, *In Search of the Spirit of Capitalism* (Hutchinson, 1982).

Frank Parkin, *Max Weber* (Routledge, 1982).

Mark J. Smith, *Social Science in Question* (Sage, 1998).

Richard Henry Tawney, *Religion and the Rise of Capitalism: An Historical Study* (John Murray, 1960 [1926]).

Max Weber, *The Protestant Ethic and the Spirit of Capitalism* (Allen & Unwin, 1976 [1904/05]).

Max Weber, *Economy and Society*, 2 volumes (University of California Press, 1978 [1921]).

Sam Whimster, *The Essential Max Weber* (Routledge, 2003).

Websites

In addition to the general sites listed at the end of Chapter Two try the Max Weber *Verstehen* website at: www.faculty.rsu.edu/felwell/theorists/weber

A useful set of resources on Max Weber (and many other social theorists mentioned in this book) can be found at the academic resource Sociosite: www.sociosite.net/sociologists/

CHAPTER SIX

TALCOTT PARSONS, FUNCTIONALISM AND THE SOCIAL SYSTEM

The classical tradition in social theory we have been looking at in Chapters Three to Five clarified many of the pivotal issues of social development and offered some of the first explanations of what constitutes a modern society. In terms of the questions they asked, the concepts they deployed and the strategy they used for analysing social phenomena, these writers set the agenda for social theory as it entered its modern period. As we move further into the 20th century, and especially if we look at developments in social theory in North America, new concepts and ideas were developed to look at some of the different kinds of social phenomena that surrounded social actors living in mature, rather than newly-emerged, modern society.

Although these new approaches can often be traced back to the classical tradition of European social theory, and especially to the work of Marx, Weber and Durkheim, a number broke away from it and established important new perspectives on the challenges of modern society and modern living. During the 1940s and 1950s the centre of gravity of social theory had moved away from Europe and towards North America. Two distinct schools of thought developed there at this time. One was oriented around the **functionalist** or 'general systems theory' perspective of Talcott Parsons (1902–79) and Robert Merton (1910–2003), and the other around the **social interactionist** perspective of George Herbert Mead (1863–1931), Charles Cooley (1864–1929) and Herbert Blumer (1900–87).

> **In this chapter we will:**
>
> Introduce the basic differences between conceptions of knowledge in functionalism and social interactionism
>
> Look at the concepts of function, structure and system
>
> Look at Parsons' general systems theory
>
> Consider the limits of functionalist social theory
>
> Briefly assess Parsons' contribution to social theory

Basic differences between functionalism and social interactionism

Functionalism and abstract general theory

There are a number of significant differences between functionalism and social interactionism but perhaps the most important is that they take very different positions about what social theoretical knowledge is (the problem of **epistemology**) and about how to develop social theoretical knowledge (research strategy). For those like Parsons and Merton adopting a **rationalist** perspective (which as we saw in our discussion of the Age of Reason in Chapter Two includes the idea that knowledge is a product of the rational processing of information in the mind of the observer rather than a simple record of things that are 'out there'), knowledge depends very heavily on the theoretical framework within which such knowledge is produced. As a variety of rational knowledge, social-theoretical knowledge must begin with the theoretical framework that gives knowledge an intelligible form. Conceptual terms such as function, **structure** and **system** owe their existence to the theoretical frameworks from which they emerge.

Although social phenomena clearly exist independently of the thoughts we have about them, it is the process of thinking about them that makes them available to our senses in an orderly rather than disconnected and chaotic way. Thinking introduces discipline and organisation into a process that would otherwise be utterly anarchic and, beyond the rudimentary impact of phenomena on the physical senses, unknowable. Rational knowledge is not the only way of knowing the world, since many social practices are based on faith and emotion rather than reason, but it is the only way of knowing the world rationally. As we also saw in Chapter Two in our discussion of August Comte, rational knowledge is also positive knowledge in the sense that it is concerned with uncovering the universal laws of social action and social development. It offers propositions about social life in the belief that they can be shown to be scientifically valid.

The rationalist approach that functionalist social theorists adopt has a number of important consequences for the kind of social-theoretical knowledge that functionalists are able to offer. Typically, functionalist theory takes the form of generalised and often quite sweeping propositions about the nature of social phenomena and the general laws that govern them. It is called **general theory** because it attempts to develop a theory covering the whole range of social phenomena. Functionalist theory is thus a theory not just of this or that social phenomenon taken in isolation, but of the social world as a whole. This is a top-down approach where the theory is developed well in advance of any detailed examination of real data. As the name suggests, functionalism posits 'functionality' as a fundamental and indispensable characteristic of social action and social systems (see later). Functionalists begin their work by developing an all-embracing general theory of functionality and only later try to substantiate it with data.

It is also a characteristic of this approach that the language used to outline general theory tends to be quite obscure. There are three reasons for this. First, because the theory is constructed at a very general level it has to make use of concepts that are also quite abstract. Abstract concepts tend to require abstract language to describe them. Second, high levels of precision are required in describing the relations between one abstract concept and another because, even more than is the case when describing physical objects, the theory only has real substance in the words and concepts used to describe it. The existence of the physical phenomenon of gravity can be seen when objects fall to the ground (are being pulled onto the earth's surface), whereas, *the theory of* gravity is an abstract phenomenon.

Third, the relations between different parts of the theory, and indeed the way in which the theory develops, involves a process of *logical abstraction* in the sense that the likely properties of actually existing social phenomena are deduced from the theory. The observation that stable social systems are more successful than unstable ones bears out the theoretical proposition that 'stability' and 'success' are positively linked. The theory might also point towards some useful places to look in order to find out why this tends to be *a general rule* in human social organisation but this need not be its main purpose.

▸▸ The most abstract version of rationalist and **positivist** reasoning is known as **logical positivism**, which emerged in Vienna in the early part of the 20th century. For members of the Vienna Circle knowledge is very closely bound up with the underlying logic of the statements scientists make about the phenomena they are studying. The rules of logic that determine whether a statement makes sense and is therefore true are seen as providing the logical framework of knowledge itself.

The interactionist alternative

In direct contrast to this rationalist top–down approach, interactionist social theorists argue that knowledge is not really about theory but about making clear descriptions of concrete situations. It is about real-life encounters between actually existing social actors having real physical presence. The version of social-theoretical knowledge favoured by social interactionists develops from the bottom up. They begin their work by looking first at particular examples of a social phenomenon, and only later do they attempt to build up a more general theory of what might be going on. Theory is induced from the evidence rather than evidence being deduced from the theory. If done properly (i.e. without too much bias on the part of the researcher, or too many faults in the research design), this method will produce a genuinely accurate representation of the real world 'out there'. The whole point of the strictly empiricist inductive method, the virtue of the empirical knowledge it produces, is to entirely eliminate the distortions produced by the creative imagination of the observer. The mind of the observer is required to 'observe', not to 'imagine'.

Again in contrast to the realist conception of knowledge in which, as we have seen, concepts and technical language are themselves a constitutive part of theoretical knowledge, the language and concepts used in the empiricist conception have far less influence over the data, but are simply used as a convenient means of describing actually observed reality. There is less need to create a parallel universe of technical language and complex ideas for describing the real world. All that is required is that the terminology used is recognised and agreed. It is also a characteristic of the bottom–up approach that 'theory' is about much smaller pieces of the social world than is the case with general theory, which tries to include everything in a single grand design.

Uneasy compromises

If we stand back a little from these alternative definitions of knowledge and strategy it is clear that neither is entirely satisfactory. Against the rationalist conception it can be argued that, unless one is prepared to accept the possibility that rational general theory might be a complete fantasy, some actual data are bound to be included in the analysis somewhere even if these are based just on the personal experiences of the theorist. If the kind of social theory one is most interested in is one based on abstract reasoning rather than on examination of actual data, then that is fine as long as one does not claim later on to have said anything particularly concrete about real society. For this kind of theorist, the primary object of social theory is not so much society or actual social phenomena like families or bureaucracies, but the various ideas and propositions that are made about the constitution of society. Against the empiricist conception, one has to acknowledge that planning and carrying out a piece of research, let alone describing and analysing the data that it produces, must involve some degree of theoretical and thus rational reasoning on the part of the researcher/ theorist. The idea of theory-free or 'pure' data is just as silly as the idea of data-free or 'pure' theory.

It can also be argued that despite attempts to eliminate the subjective input of the researcher, the best that can be hoped for is to keep this to a minimum. As we saw in our discussion of **value-neutrality** and the 'interpretive method' (**verstehen**) of social enquiry proposed by Max Weber in Chapter Five, a model that is often used by social interactionists, the study of social interaction almost inevitably requires a degree of interpretation about the meaning of what is going on. Social researchers have to guard against allowing their own ideas and values from distorting the observations they make. Furthermore, even if social interactionists are able to collect their data objectively, the analysis of the data is a creative and thus inherently subjective process. Things are doubly difficult if the object of the research is to investigate the subjective meaning for social actors of the interaction they are participating in.

ILLUSTRATION – THE THEORY JIGSAW PUZZLE

We can look a little more deeply into these matters by using the analogy of completing a jigsaw puzzle. Imagine that one only had a few pieces of what was known (logically, because of simple common sense, or because of the content of the parts that were known) to be a giant jigsaw puzzle. However interesting each of the pieces are, in order to make sense of them it is necessary to imagine, to hold in the mind's eye, some kind of image of what the whole might look like.

When doing real jigsaw puzzles we immediately calculate the probable size of the finished picture by looking at the size and detail of the pieces we have. A few large bold pieces suggest a simple puzzle. We see the individual pieces (sense perception), but use this information in the mind's eye (rational deduction) to develop a sense of scale. General theory is all about putting forward suggestions as to what 'the bigger picture' looks like. An outline or structure into which the few found and very many yet-to-be-discovered pieces might fit. Since no single piece of the puzzle can, on its own, tell us what the whole looks like, individual pieces of the puzzle must be regarded as partial, as mere fragments, when compared with the full knowledge that 'the bigger picture' is presumed to yield. Talcott Parsons' general theory of social action and the social system, characterised by the idea of functionality, is one such attempt at doing this. Parsons is trying to design for us a picture of what the total theoretical explanation looks like, an explanation that makes the individual pieces meaningful.

If we now imagine that we are working on a picture of the social world in its empirical dimension, that is, as it actually is (or appears to be) rather than as a construct of rational knowledge, a different mode of construction is required. The empiricist begins with the individual pieces that are already known and, assuming that sufficient time and reliable investigative techniques are available, proceeds to try to discover the other pieces. There is no need to spend too much time imagining what the full picture of actual reality might eventually look like since its discovery is simply a matter of time. The process of observation is not conditional on already having 'the full picture'. Individual pieces make sufficient sense in themselves and when seen in relation to the other pieces they immediately connect with.

In learning about social theory, then, we need to bear in mind that there are two distinct approaches to investigating social phenomena, two techniques for puzzle-solving, which exist side-by-side. One uses rational–theoretical deduction and reasoning and the other empirical observation and induction. There might be moments of happy coincidence when the knowledge claims of rationalists coincide exactly with the knowledge claims of empiricists, but the two are not necessarily or logically connected. Pieces of one puzzle cannot 'prove' or 'complete' the other because they have different conceptions of what the bigger picture is and indeed of whether it is necessary to have such a thing.

Having looked into some of the basic differences between functionalist and social interactionist approaches in terms of their alternative conceptions of knowledge we turn our attention in the next section to the central concepts of functionalist social theory.

The concepts of 'system', 'structure' and 'function'

System

The basic idea of a **system** is quite easy to grasp. If we take the example of the central-heating equipment in a house, we can observe that it consists of a self-contained and readily identifiable structure of pipes, radiators and a boiler, together with an electrical control system, fuel system and water supply. This structure becomes a system when we envisage it in operation. The boiler is lit, the cold water is heated, the pump pumps and hot water circulates around the radiators. The thermostat and boiler control system switch things on and off in accordance with the settings made by the homeowner, settings that reflect ideas about what is a 'normal' temperature for houses in that location.

The heating system comprises part of the overall system, or set of systems, of the house, and is itself dependent on the satisfactory functioning of other subsystems such as the electrical system and the supply of water and fuel. For the house to function as a satisfactory dwelling for the people who live there (and again reflecting expectations of what is 'normal' in that time and place), the heating system and its various subsystems must all function in the way that they are expected to function. In turn, their functioning depends on there being reliable systems for supplying this and the other houses in the neighbourhood with basic amenities and utilities. The domestic electricity supply, for example, depends on a complex system of cables, transformers, substations, pylons and ultimately a national and even an international grid of power stations that are generating electricity for people to use in their homes.

Although we have chosen an example of a mechanical system to illustrate the general properties of systems, the basic concept, as it is applied to social systems, draws very heavily on what we know about biological systems. Showing its close association with biological models of how various elements fit together, and with shades of Victorian evolutionist models of development popularised by Charles Darwin and Herbert Spencer (discussed in Chapter Two), the concept of system used by functionalist social theorists at the start of the 20th century presumes that systems have a rather naturalistic and organic character.

Organic systems also tend to be 'closed systems' in the sense that although integrated at a higher level, one system is, at least in terms of how one might describe its inner workings, separate from all the other systems. Regarded as a system, a living plant is made up of several subsystems for taking up water, processing nutrients, photosynthesising from sunlight and so on. It also has systems for growing and reproducing itself. Internally, each subsystem depends on all the others so that organic body-systems (plants and animals) constitute systems of mutual co-dependence. Externally, plants form part of the natural environment, which in turn forms part of the global organic system (or Gaia as it has been called).

Structure

We will have a lot more to say about how social theorists have used the concept of structure when we look in detail at theories of **structuralism** in Chapter Nine, and at Anthony Giddens' theory of **structuration** in Chapter Twelve. For now we can simply note that **structure** is qualitatively different to 'system' because systems are literally 'in motion' or 'on the move' while structure implies components that are connected together statically but not yet 'set in motion'. The various components of the central-heating equipment form an identifiable structure, but only become a system when the boiler is switched on.

An example from the organic realm would be the difference between the physical structural anatomy of a dead body being examined in the morgue by a pathologist, and the living body of a patient being examined by a doctor in the consulting room. Both are interested in the systems that go into making the body-system but there is a qualitative difference between a living body and a dead one. Seeing the various structure-systems of the body in motion is more than seeing them on the dissection table. Some of the body subsystems are in fact only observable when the body is alive. Frankenstein would not be much of a horror story if The Creature could not get up and walk away.

We should add that although structure typically implies a tangible entity made up of rigid components like the bars of a cage, it is also often used in social theory to convey the idea of regularities and patterns of action that are much more fluid and dynamic. The rules in a game of ice hockey, for example, are fixed in as much as they are written down in a book of rules, but the impact they have on the game itself is neither static nor predictable. Other theorists have developed a notion of structure that is not conceived as something that social actors can see and touch at all, but which comes into being only at the moment that social actors make use of these structures of rules and resources in their actions. The common example used to illustrate this more virtual idea of structure is language, which is clearly structured in terms of the grammatical rules that tell us how to construct sentences, but which only take on a concrete form when they are being used. Latin is often regarded as a dead language not because its rules and structures are no longer known (because they obviously are) but because the language is no longer in common use.

Function

At its most general level, the concept of function is intended to capture the idea that objects and actions can be understood in terms of the function they perform. For social theorists adopting a functionalist perspective, 'functionality', or the capacity to fulfil a particular function, lies at the heart of the substance of things. The utility or purpose of things coincides with their function, which is why it is rare to find objects and actions that have no function. When new functions emerge, or when new ways of performing established functions are developed, the old ways become redundant and fall out of existence. Recalling our discussion of Max Weber in Chapter Five social action that has no purpose would be irrational.

Strategy

The idea of function also provides a strategy for analysing and comparing different objects and actions in terms of the different kinds and levels of function they perform. Functions, and thus the objects and actions that enable them to be performed, can be understood quantitatively (and hierarchically) in terms of the simpler functions on which they are based and of the higher functions that they contribute to. They can also be understood in more qualitative ways to compare the different ways in which similar functions can be performed and indeed of the different ways in which notions of 'function' and 'purpose' acquire their meaning. (Anthropologists who adopt a functionalist perspective are especially interested in how certain essential social functions are met in different ways in different cultures. We will say more about this in the section on the 'social system' later.)

Connectedness

If the first principle of function is that the fundamental purpose of things is the function they perform, the second principle is that there is an essential connectedness between one function and another. Functionality implies very high levels of integration and co-dependence between one function and another (hence the strong association in functionalist theory with the concept of 'structure'). Looking again at our central-heating example, the fuse in the plug that connects the boiler thermostat to the electrical system of the house has a relatively simple function, but one that profoundly affects the rest of the system. If the fuse is blown, the thermostat will not work and so the boiler cannot be switched on and the water will remain cold. Function is thus a very inclusive concept because the purpose of each individual function contributes towards the functioning of the entire system. In this sense, the overall function of the central-heating system, that is, to keep people warm, is implied in the functioning of each and every component of the system. Even the function of the humble clip that holds the fuse in place in the plug on the boiler thermostat can be defined in terms of the need to keep people warm.

System-maintaining functions

This view of function as integration, and the associated idea that there must be such things as between-system functions, draws attention to a third important principle of the idea of function, which is that the satisfactory functioning of the overall system depends upon the correct functioning of its individual parts. Here we enter the realm of objects and actions whose primary function is to maintain the system itself. Even in the case of very simple systems, 'systems maintenance' is a prerequisite for the system to be able to perform any of the other purposes that it was brought into being to serve (mechanical and social systems) or that led to its evolution in the first place (biological systems).

Systems maintenance is an integral feature of functionality at two levels. First, and as we have just noted, some systems have the specific function of maintaining the system. In the body-systems of animals, for example, the immune system has the function of protecting the body from illness or disease. At a second level, all systems and subsystems have a more indirect part to play in maintaining the overall system either by making small contributions to it or at least by not interrupting the satisfactory functioning of systems that are directly concerned with servicing or maintaining the overall system. In the human body-system, the circulation system is obviously integral to the functioning of the whole body, but the way in which the heart pumps blood can have an impact on systems maintenance. What we are referring to here is the efficiency or integrity with which each system operates, the assumption being that if all systems are running at optimum levels, the risk to systems maintenance is bound to be low. The reason why acquired immune deficiency syndrome (AIDS) is so devastating is precisely because it interrupts the capacity of the human body-system to resist infection, thus causing widespread systems failure.

System needs and shared or collective purpose

At this point we need to sound a cautionary note. Although it is obviously sensible to accept that small amounts of systems maintenance are implied in the performance of any function, the functionalist analysis of social systems sometimes goes further than this and implies that the social system has what we could loosely call 'needs of its own' or 'system needs'. While such a notion is useful in describing features of systems in terms of their mechanical workings it is not such a large step from this to the implication that the 'needs' of the system take priority over the needs of the social actors who brought these systems into being in the first place. We saw an example of this in Chapter Five where Weber warns that bureaucracy may become an end in itself rather than properly serving the purposes it was designed for.

The idea that functionality can be regarded as a kind of collective undertaking that all the systems and subsystems make towards the correct functioning of the overall social system is essentially a positive one. It is also positive to see function in terms of how the various components of the social system help people fulfil their various needs. What is less positive, however, is the idea that 'functionality' *is itself* an expression of shared purpose, or, even more mistakenly, that the social system can have a shared purpose in the same sense that human social actors do. Social systems do not have any kind of intentionality of their own, let alone one that expresses collective purpose. We will talk more about the limits of functionalist analysis in a later section of this chapter. As we turn our attention towards Talcott Parsons' version of functionalist analysis it will be useful to bear in mind that what goes for organic systems, and even mechanical ones, might not always go for social systems.

Talcott Parsons' functionalist 'general systems theory'

Background

Born in 1902, Parsons grew up in the rather strict atmosphere of a traditional Protestant household in small-town rural America. He began his academic career aged 18 at Amherst College in Massachusetts in 1920 where he took biology as his major subject. He spent a year at the London School of Economics in 1923/24 (where he would have met the influential Polish-born functionalist social anthropologist Bronislaw Malinowski) before taking up a fellowship to study for his PhD at Heidelberg University in Germany in 1925. In 1927 aged 25 he moved to Harvard University where he remained for the rest of his career. The first Department of Sociology in Harvard was established in 1931 and Parsons became Professor of Sociology there in 1938 and Chairman of the Department in 1942. He retired in 1973 and died of heart failure in 1979 aged 77. Parsons published a very large number of books and articles during his long career (over 160 published items). The most important are: *The Structure of Social Action* (1937), *The Social System* (1951) and, with E. Shils, *Toward a General Theory of Action* (1962).

General systems theory

Talcott Parsons was through-and-through an advocate of the rationalist deductive approach to social theory. Drawing initially on the work particularly of Max Weber and Émile Durkheim (he also read Karl Marx, Werner Sombart and Thorstein Veblen but regarded their approach as insufficiently 'scientific'), Parsons spent his whole career trying to develop a general theory of social action and of the social system by means of which, and within the limits of which, social action takes place. Parsons' approach can be described as 'synthesising' in the sense that he draws together into a single grand design what he regarded as the key insights of the leading European social theorists. Developing what became known as **general systems theory** his objective was to devise a theoretical framework for making sense of all aspects of human social action within a single explanatory framework. The grand design would, he hoped, provide a blueprint for a universal sociological understanding of social action. It is useful to think of Parsons' work not so much as a theory that tries to explain social action as such, but as a *theoretical schema* into which theoretical explanations can be fitted. It is a grand design *for* theory rather than just *of* theory.

The possibility of developing such a grand design obviously also meant having a conception of 'society' or 'the social system' as a single unified system. The different systems, structures and functions could be looked at separately, but essentially they never are separate because they all fit together into one overall system. In this conception the combined entity of the total social system must also be regarded as greater than the sum of its parts in the sense that social systems have 'emergent properties' (for example, the sentiments expressed at public celebrations) that cannot be attributed to any individual component when looked at individually. Very much following Durkheim's strong conception of society as an entity that has a real existence which exceeds that of its individual components, the meaning and purpose of the individual parts is lost unless they are seen in the context of the larger system. The human liver, for example, is fascinating as a piece of anatomical matter, but to really understand its significance it has to be seen in the context of the body it is part of.

For Parsons, then, the unit of analysis of social theory is the total social system. Although the system, the subsystems that it is made up of and the various functions they perform are massively complex, Parsons thought it was possible for social theorists to identify features that are found in all the systems of a particular society, and possibly of all forms of human society, and to describe some of the always-repeated characteristics of how functions are performed. For Parsons, the main effort of social theory should be directed towards perfecting our understanding of these systems, structures and functions. General systems theory provided theorists who were more interested in developing specific hypotheses about the nature of social action (sometimes referred to as 'middle-range' theory) with a higher-order theoretical map of the social system, thus giving empirical researchers a framework within which to make sense of their empirical data. Although we must be very careful not to confuse social phenomena with natural ones, a reverse example (i.e. one that goes from empirical observation to grand theory) is the general theory of evolution through natural selection developed by Charles Darwin. Following his painstaking observation over many years of fossils and living organisms, Darwin put forward what is now regarded as the basic template for understanding the process of development in all natural organisms. Parsons is attempting the same kind of result for sociology.

The unit act

Looking at Parsons' own theoretical scheme of social action and the social system, his first step, described in *The Structure of Social Action* (1937), is to specify that the basic building block of all social action is 'the unit act'. This was 'the smallest unit of an action system which still makes sense as part of a concrete system of action' (Parsons, 1937, p 731). He identifies four basic elements, all of which have to be included for a particular piece of behaviour to be counted as action for the purposes of his theory of action. There might be other elements, and some other theory might not include all of the ones he does, but as far as Parsons was concerned, a true general theory of action must start out from the following combination of the basic elements of the unit act:

- An **agent** or actor.
- A goal or **ends** (which must be different to the situation that currently exists).
- Responses made to situational **conditions** (these can be thought of as the means to achieving particular ends). Some conditions cannot be controlled by the actor (biological make-up, some environmental conditions) and some can (the resources and techniques we have at our disposal).
- The business of acting to achieve a purpose by responding to environmental conditions has to be done in a way that conforms to the prevailing **norms** of that society. There has to be what he calls 'a normative orientation to action' in the sense that when making choices over how to act, and assuming that alternatives are available, the making of choices is guided by social norms.

In addition, all of the elements have to take place in a knowledgeable or informed way so that the action-choices social actors make can be regarded, not as passive and random responses, but as consciously made rational choices. Part of what makes a choice of action rational is whether or not it conforms to the social norms of that society. If a social actor is unable to make rational and informed choices they are likely to be categorised by others as irrational or possibly as mad.

The action frame of reference

Parsons refers to his approach as an 'action frame of reference' as he is keen to specify that he is developing a theoretical framework not only for making objective assessments of social action in the manner of a positivist (observing the mechanical actions of a cyclist), but also to include the subjective or **voluntaristic** dimension of action as well (why cyclists cycle). He regards social actors as conscious, knowledgeable and intentional. This is why he makes a sharp distinction between sociology and psychology, and especially **behaviourist psychology**, which had become very popular in America at this time. As soon as social actors are recognised as acting in accordance with value-laden social norms (item 4 in the above list), human action cannot be adequately explained in terms of psychological or biological causes alone. As Parsons describes it, 'normative orientation is the *motor* of social action' (Parsons, 1937, p 142).

In terms of the concepts used by classical social theorists discussed in the previous chapters, the first three constituents of the unit act (agents, ends and conditions) correspond with a fairly straight forward positivistic and **utilitarian** conception of action in which social action is explained in terms of the ends actors seek and the means they employ to achieve them. It is by introducing the fourth element, the key idea that all of this takes place in the context of, or is oriented in terms of, identifiable systems of norms and values, that Parsons really moves social theory forwards. Metaphorically speaking, if classical social theory (Marx, Weber, Durkheim) provides the basic spokes of a theory for describing social action in terms of a series of means–ends relationships, Parsons adds the rim of the wheel by asking what the relationship is between these various 'ends'. As far as Parsons is concerned, patterns of norms and values are the means by which the different spokes of social action are combined into something that really can rock and roll.

Parsons is combining the Weberian notion of the voluntary or subjective aspect of social action with the Durkheimian notion of the objective contexts of action in society. From the Weberian side, social actors do act in a rationalistic means–ends kind of way and make knowledgeable choices in order to fulfil various goals and objectives. Often these goals and choices are to do with the ideas, values and beliefs they hold. From the Durkheimian side Parsons takes the idea that social actors cannot act in an entirely free way, because the resources at their disposal, and the rules and conventions that they have to follow if their actions are to be effective, are, to a greater or lesser extent, regulated by society.

If we take the example of language again, there is nothing to prevent a social actor from making whatever vocal sounds they like. If, however, they want others to understand these sounds, they need to accept the rules and conventions of the language system around them. Making linguistic sense to others means accepting the limits of their language code. The language code does not belong to any particular social actor, but to society (for Durkheim the rules of language are a social fact). Human action can be regarded as free in the modified sense that once social actors *have accepted* the limitations imposed by the rules and norms of society, they can express themselves in any way they like up to those limitations.

The social system

Having described the basic building blocks of his theoretical grand design by developing the descriptive analytical concept of the unit act, Parsons proceeds in his later key works (*The Social System* [1951] and *Towards a General Theory of Action* [1962]), to discuss a theoretical framework of the overall social system where action takes place. His intention is to move his scheme forward from being one that simply organises various descriptions of action, towards one that also gives a sense of coherence to theories that offer *explanations* of action as well. As we have already noted, the key concepts he uses to energise his theory in this way are the concepts of **system** and function.

Functional prerequisites of a social system

Beginning with his most abstract general conception of the system itself, Parsons suggests that in order for it to function as a society (rather than as a random collection of institutions and events), society must fulfil four basic functions. Since society cannot function without them they can be described as the four *functional prerequisites* of all social systems. Taking the initial letter of each, this is known as the AGIL system:

- **A**daptation (broadly the economic function)
- **G**oal attainment (broadly the political function that controls the allocation of resources to meet agreed goals)
- **I**ntegration (the norms and rules that regulate the system and the between-systems functions that hold the whole thing together)
- **L**atent pattern maintenance (the transposition or conversion of individual values into social values and vice versa, usually by symbolic means)

Parsons also lists the four major subsystems that are devised for meeting these functional prerequisites. Each of these subsystems has particular functional responsibilities of its own, which are in turn based on further subsystems.

First, **A**daptation to the environment and conditions in which social actors find themselves is brought about through the *behavioural system*. This is most easily understood as the economic system through which actors obtain the resources they need in order to live.

Second, **G**oal attainment, which refers to actors being able to live in a way that they want to live and to express themselves beyond the simple needs of survival, is served by the *personality system*. This is the function that allocates resources between individual social actors and motivates them to meet their goals. The way in which actors respond to external (i.e. social) and internal (i.e. psychological) controls over their actions is also included in the personality system. (The personality system contains shades of what Durkheim describes in his social theory as 'the regulation of appetites'.)

The third functional prerequisite of social **I**ntegration is carried out by the *social system*, which concentrates on maintaining the linkages between one system and another, and on bringing social actors into line with those systems and the social roles they might occupy, often by establishing the norms and values of the system. The process of socialisation by which especially children are introduced to the norms of society operates through this system, as does the legal system, which imposes a more rigorous form of integration on individual social actors. In some ways the social system is the key subsystem (which is why Parsons writes a whole book about it), as its function is to hold all the other functions together. Referring back to our analogy with the spokes of a wheel, this is the system that provides the rim holding all the other components together.

Fourth is the *cultural system*, which provides a realm of symbolic meanings and representations by means of which social actors can express agreement over the purpose and significance of their actions. Although quite unfamiliar, the term **L**atency is intended to capture the more subtle, even subconscious, cultural processes that hold individuals together in society and give actions a sense of legitimacy.

One way of imagining how these four major subsystems are arranged is to think of them as a series of schematic diagrams representing areas of social action at a fairly low level of magnification. Below the general level, are further levels showing the various systems and subsystems at ever-increasing levels of magnification. The smallest component (i.e. the highest level of magnification) that makes any sense in a theory of social action is the unit act. The largest component (i.e. the least magnified level) is that of the whole social system where only the broad outlines are shown. If we take the economic system as an illustration, this system supports Adaptation (one level up) and is itself supported by various subsystems (one or more levels below), which provide systems, among other things, for getting and transporting raw materials, systems for manufacture and production, systems for employment and so on. 'Below' the employment subsystem are further subsystems such as the trade unions and employers' organisations, which help organise groups of employees and employers. Systems of training and education are also required to provide a suitably skilled workforce, and even below this are instructors, counsellors and tutors who support individual workers.

Social actors in the social system

One might well ask at this point, where are the social actors in Parsons' theory of social action? In one sense the short answer is that there are none. It is a framework for organising *theories of* action, not a theory of how real social actors actually behave. Parsons never claims that there will be an exact match between what his theoretical scheme suggests about how actors behave, and their actual behaviour. (The closest it comes to being a theory that can be empirically tested against actual data is in terms of the Weberian notion of the **ideal type**.) In another sense, however, social actors are always there in Parsons' scheme, since the basic point of his work is to help us understand how there can be such a thing as social order given that the social system seeks to organise the actions of millions of separate actors who are often preoccupied with exhibiting their individuality, not their collectivity. The concepts that come closest to bridging the gap between his theoretical framework of action and the actions of real actors are those of 'system' and 'pattern'.

For Parsons, as we have seen, it is possible to identify a certain logic operating between the systems and functions of the social system. Systems and subsystems are logically and functionally interdependent (or 'systematised') in the way we have been discussing (the basic principles of bureaucratic administration tend to be repeated whichever organisation is using them). This logic also provides a means of identifying certain patterns in the way the system and its parts work together (all bureaucrats follow formal rules). Adding the actors back into the analysis, Parsons is suggesting that the patterns of logical association that can be identified in respect of the parts and functions of the social system are bound to influence the way actors behave (bureaucrats behave 'bureaucratistically'). Regarded as knowledgeable and rational, the choices actors make are strongly influenced by the patterns and structures of the social system where their action takes place (actors in modern society often describe their actions and society as 'rational'). In their turn, these how-to-act choices become embedded in the various institutions in society, which further reinforces the system of patterns and linkages that hold society together (rationality is endorsed as a feature both of how institutions operate and of how actors act). According to the logic of the functionalist conception of the total social system this must be the case since there can in fact be no such thing as action that takes place *outside* the system. (There is a problem of **tautology** here, which we will come back to shortly.)

Pattern variables

Of central importance, and again showing the significance of the voluntaristic dimension of the action frame of reference that Parsons took from Max Weber, conformity with these patterns draws heavily on agreement about the *norms and values* associated with different systems and their functions, including those that come to be identified as the value-system or world view of the whole of that society. To repeat an earlier point, the difference between actors operating like robotic components in a mechanical system, and actors acting in a social system, is that the latter make choices that always involve some kind of engagement with values. For Parsons, the value-choices that guide social action become embedded in the institutions of society.

The general value-orientations that hold the various systems and subsystems of society together can be imagined as taking the form of a series of choices between two extremes on a series of continuums. It is possible to identify certain patterns within these choices or *pattern variables* as Parsons calls them, and he considers that four of these are essential to the satisfactory functioning of the social system:

■   *Affectivity verus affective neutrality* (i.e. the level of emotion or rational detachment 'that is appropriate in a given situation').
■   *Diffuseness versus specificity* (whether 'the range or scope of obligations in an interaction situation' is broad or narrow).

■ *Universalism versus particularism* (whether 'evaluative standards' are based on universal criteria or the beliefs only of a particular society).

■ *Achievement versus ascription* (whether social status is assessed in terms of 'performance criteria', i.e. how successful actors are in their achievements, or of 'forms of endowment', i.e. labels and categories based on something other than merit).

The implication of pattern variables for Parsons and his followers was that it appeared that American society of the 1950s had reached the highest level of social and institutional sophistication yet achieved. Society operated on the principles of rational detachment, which characterised the modern approach to life in general. Social action was also relatively specified (rather than diffuse) in the sense that it was focused on and regulated by the functional requirements of specific social roles. The general value-system exhibited high levels of universalism (rather than particularism) as it tried to enact the basic civic principles of 'life, liberty and the pursuit of happiness'. The irrational claims of selfish individuals and particular groups were prevented from eclipsing the collective interest of American society as a whole. Finally, society had become fully meritocratic in the sense that actors could be rewarded for their own achievements in society rather than being pigeonholed into ascribed categories such as class, race and ethnicity; categories over which they had no control. Using the technical jargon of Parsons' theory, America in the 1950s could be described as having reached the advanced and sophisticated pattern of 'universalistic-achievement'.

Bringing 'the internalisation of institutionalised values' into the foreground, Parsons links these four key pattern variables into his broader analysis of the four major subsystems that support the functional prerequisites of the AGIL system (**A**daptation, **G**oal attainment, **I**ntegration and **L**atency). So, for example, within the personality system, which supports the largely economic function of **A**dapting to the environment, the process of **socialisation** introduces children at a young age to what they can expect in terms of the economic roles that might be available to them, the kinds of values that are necessary to be successful at work (i.e. Protestant work ethic), and the kind of attitude they should adopt towards other social actors (an individuated meritocratic orientation). Other linkages and patterns are also established between 'the modes of orientation in the *personality* system', and the 'normative requirements in the *social* system', and the 'value-patterns of the *cultural* system' (Parsons, 1937, pp 48–50, emphases added). Economic roles are obviously linked to social roles, and in order to be successful, both of these have to be consistent with the general patterns of values in society as a whole.

Social development

For Parsons, these pattern variables, and especially the universalism–particularism and achievement–ascription pairings, can be used as a basis for making bold comparisons between one society and another, and about how society changes over time. Echoing a kind of description we have already come across in the work of Herbert Spencer, Auguste Comte and Émile Durkheim, Parsons suggests that as society becomes more advanced it also becomes more specialised in its individual functions. As individual functions become more specialised, so also do levels of systems integration (which is another way of saying that the integrity of the social system becomes increasingly dependent on the integrative function). There is a clear parallel here with Durkheim's observations about how the increasing **individuation**, or separating out of tasks and roles in modern society (functional specialisation), goes hand in hand with the emergence of a new variety of **individualism**, which acknowledges collective and social, rather than selfish, interests. Developments also take place in the value-orientation that characterises the system in the sense that more complex social systems have a capacity for supporting the expression of higher or more advanced kinds of collective values. These value-orientations, along with the capacity for running sophisticated organisations, result in high levels of systems integration across the institutions of modern society.

The problem of social order

Correspondence both between the action-choices of one social actor and another, and between the action-choices of actors in general and the continuing satisfactory functioning of the overall system, also helps Parsons account for the apparent stability and continuity of the social system. A basic condition of the existence of society is that there is sufficient coincidence between individual actors and the collective value-orientation that characterises that society. One might say that this aspect of Parsons' theory is actually a highly detailed account of how value judgements are arrived at, and how consistency in making such judgements (a consistency that he identifies through the concept of patterning) renders social systems, and the place of actors within them, stable. As Parsons puts it:

KEY QUOTE – Talcott Parsons, *The Social System* (1951).
The problem of order, and thus of the nature of stable systems of social interaction, that is, of social structure, thus focuses on the integration of the motivation of actors with the normative cultural standards which integrate the system, in our context, interpersonally.... The basic condition on which an interaction system can be stabilized is for the interests of actors to be bound to conformity with a shared system of value-orientation standards. (Parsons, 1951, pp 36–7)

The limits of functionalist social theory

Given the very grandness of Parsons' theoretical scheme, it is not surprising that both it and the functionalist approach it represents have generated much controversy among modern social theorists. In this section we will look at three main areas of dispute (which will also give us some clues as to how the interactionist alternative, which we will be discussing in Chapter Seven, began to develop):

- First, we can identify a number of problems with the abstractness of Parsons' grand design.
- Second, is the problem of how to explain the unintended consequences of action.
- Third, functionalism adopts an inherently conservative attitude towards social action and thus seems poorly equipped to explain social conflict.

Problems with the abstractness of the grand design

Abstraction and distraction

First, despite wanting to develop a grand theoretical scheme that others with a more empirical orientation could use to develop testable hypotheses (middle-range theory), Parsons leaves too much of a gap between the two. The theoretical scheme is just too far removed from any empirical investigation for there to be any easy movement between one and the other. Bridging this gap means making up all sorts of intermediate concepts and strategies that inevitably fall short of the exacting standards of the original design. If, for example, we were interested in the linkages between systems for personal development and systems for formal education, it is not clear how one might develop testable hypotheses that distinguish between what are claimed to be separable functions. A common-sense view might be that education and personal development cannot really be treated as separate and that the notion of function is insufficiently subtle to capture the real processes that are involved. In order for the principles of functionality to make sense social reality has to be described at a very high level of generality. The closer to the action one moves the less adequate the notion of functionality is for describing it.

There is what we might call an excess of theory in the sense that having developed key concepts like function, system and structure all explanation has to be provided in terms of these concepts. A preoccupation with the logic of systems, functional prerequisites, pattern variables and so on leaves very little space for alternative scenarios of explanation. Even though Parsons tries to make room for the voluntaristic dimension in his description of value-orientation and pattern variables, the more subtle and subjective qualities of decision making are still theorised using technical terms and concepts that are not very well equipped to deal with them.

Making moral judgements about technical systems

A second underlying difficulty, and one that is associated with the tendency not to acknowledge the difference between biological systems, mechanical systems and social systems, is the temptation to slip out of the realm of describing systems and how they work, and into the realm of evaluating social systems and the various functions they contain in terms of how 'good' or bad' they might be. This tendency to roll a judgement about social phenomena up behind a description of them is something that also hindered the kind of earlier functionalist analysis proposed by Durkheim. In his description of the 'health' or 'sickness' of society, for example, Durkheim is obviously borrowing terms that are more usually used for referring to the condition of biological organisms. Although he substitutes the terms 'normal' or 'pathological' to describe how well or badly the overall system is functioning, and takes care to define 'normality' in terms of statistical likelihood rather than some more elusive subjective criteria like 'nice' or 'happy', the door is always left open for assessments of functionality that use evaluative criteria. In place of objective measures of 'efficiency' or 'effectiveness', which make sense for describing the quality of mechanical or even biological systems, the successful functioning of society is described in terms of how 'good' or 'civilised' it is thought to be.

As we saw in our discussion of pattern variables at the end of the previous section, also typical of Parsons and Durkheim (who in turn got it from Comte and Saint-Simon), is the tendency to compare the well-being of one society with another very much in terms of 'moral integrity'. Modern functionalists like Parsons avoid saying directly that some social systems are better than or higher than others but there is still an underlying hint that functionality has a strongly moral dimension to it. Stretching this point a little, it is rather like saying that central-heating systems are not only technically superior to other methods of keeping warm but that keeping warm is, in a moral sense, the right thing to do.

Ultimate purposes

Further confusion over differences between organic and social systems arises over judgements about what the overall or ultimate purpose of the social system is. In biological systems the question does not arise in quite the same form because purpose is bound up with the general reproduction of the organism. The purpose of biological systems is inherent in those systems in the sense that they occur in nature because they can. The function of the various subsystems of the plant- and body-systems is simply to keep the organism alive and give it a chance of reproducing itself. As Darwin pointed out, the organisms that survive are the ones best fitted to the environments in which they occur. Over time they develop particular features that increase their ability to fit in. The difference between *homo sapiens* and other biological species is that humans are conscious of the incentive to survive and are able to do something constructive about it. Very often that something includes making some pretty significant changes to society and to the natural environment itself.

The key confusion here is between organic systems, which are self-regulating in the sense that they naturally adjust their internal functioning in order to maintain the degree of fit between the organism and its surrounding environment (these are sometimes called **homeostatic systems**), and non-biological systems, which require intervention by agents who are not part of the system (for example the heating engineer who fixes the boiler). Although it is possible to refine the idea of homeostatic biological systems to distinguish between the most basic forms of stimulus–response and slightly more advanced forms where part of the system makes a kind of intentional adjustment (the production of antibodies to fight an infection), this is not in the same league as the much more sophisticated kind of deliberate and reflexive self-awareness that human social agents express in modifying the social system wherein they act. Such interventions cannot really be described as natural or automatic and so the question persists as to where human society gets its sense of purpose from. (We will have more to say about **reflexivity** when we discuss the work of the British social theorist Anthony Giddens in Chapter Twelve.)

System needs

A crucial distinction, then, between organic systems and social systems is that social systems have no survival instinct equivalent to that found in biological systems. A more patient consideration shows that even if the objectives of a particular part of the social system (for example the economic system) seem to coincide with the needs of social actors, social systems are merely the means developed by social actors to meet their survival needs. This is not to say that, viewed as a social system, society does not have what Parsons describes as 'emergent properties', that is, features that only emerge at the level of society as a whole. In many interesting respects, society must be greater than the sum of its individual parts, and certainly than the individual social actors who live there. It is more a question of avoiding the assumption that these emergent properties provide evidence of the needs of society, needs that only become apparent at the level of the overall system (or when the overall system becomes the unit of analysis). Social systems always serve the needs of social actors and not the other way round.

Universal value-orientation

If we take these four difficulties together (too much theory, value judgements, the question of ultimate purposes, problems with the 'needs' of the system) we can see how Parsons arrived at a point in his later writings where he implies that all social systems might converge towards the dominant model of American society at the midpoint of the 20th century. What we are talking about here is a **teleological** dimension within functionalist social theory, which implies that, using a mechanism of continual adaptation to its environment, society is on its way to a definite end-point rather than just moving around in time and space in an essentially directionless way.

This issue of the trajectory human society might follow becomes particularly problematic when thinking about the proposed existence of a 'universal value-orientation' (an all-society-wide set of values and beliefs) of the kind referred to by Parsons. Modern social theorists are generally highly sceptical about the presumption that there ever could be a universal value-orientation that acts as a kind of guiding star for human social development. As we know already from looking at Max Weber's analysis of the different kinds of rationality that social actors draw on in making decisions about how to act, there are no universal standards for making choices between one value-system (different manifestations of substantive rationality) and another. Taking religious belief systems as an example, would a universal value-orientation have a Christian, Muslim, Hindu or Buddhist flavour to it, or would it be an atheistic value-system?

As we have described it in previous chapters, having come to regard human society as separate from nature (i.e. as not being part of an even more spectacularly grand programme of evolution), and having taken the notion of Divine Will out of the equation, modern social theorists have pretty much given up the idea that society has any particular destination. Despite itself being a variety of social theory that relies quite heavily on notions of wholeness and adaptation, the limitations of functionalist social theory have tended to reinforce a general scepticism about seeing society in these terms.

The unintended consequences of action

Our second group of reasons for doubting Parsons' functionalist grand theory questions the way in which the theory can cope with the unintended consequences of social action. The problem for Parsons here is that in wanting to emphasise the voluntaristic aspect of action (which is crucial to his action frame of reference), he must also accept that social systems do not in fact behave as predictably as mechanical or even biological systems. The radiator or kidney might quite reasonably be expected to 'act' in accordance with the clear functions they serve. Unless they are broken or ill, in which case they need to be fixed or cured, they cannot deviate much from the path set out for them. Social systems, however, are always at risk from the perverse and unexpected choices that, even within the limits imposed on them by the various systems of society, actors express through action. Social actors might believe that their actions have produced some anticipated and desirable outcome when the very opposite might actually be the case. Conversely, there are likely to be instances where actors contribute positively to the performance of a particular function but without themselves being fully aware that this is what they are doing. The fact that social action is unpredictable is rather challenging to functionalist accounts because they tend to presume that the primary purpose of action has already been determined by the demands of the system. If, however, there is more than one way of performing a particular function, or if there is more than one function that can be performed to achieve a particular end, or if more than one end is achievable, choices have to be made. Furthermore, the making of these choices involves reference to the kinds of norms and values, the beliefs and expectations, of the actors making them, and as such have an inherently qualitative and subjective aspect to them.

Manifest and latent functions

The difficult question of social actions that have unpredictable consequences, some of which have to be viewed as operating against the social system or one of its components, has been explored by one of Parsons' first, and perhaps most influential, PhD students, Robert K. Merton. Merton (1949) introduced a distinction between what he calls **manifest functions** and **latent functions**. Manifest functions are ones where the observable practical outcome of an action is consciously intended and recognised by the actor. Latent functions are functions where the outcome is not intended or recognised by them. Merton then introduced the terms 'dysfunction' and 'non-function' to accommodate situations where the consequences of an action (manifest or latent) either had no beneficial effect for the system, had effects that were actively harmful to it, or were simply irrelevant to it.

The colour of a private motor car, for example, has no impact on its mechanical functioning; repainting it would be non-functional in this respect. Painting over the windows, however, would obviously be dysfunctional in terms of driving the car safely. Painting emergency vehicles in bright colours *is* functional because it makes them more conspicuous. If an actor painted his car in order to make it look like an emergency vehicle (i.e. deliberately in order to deceive people), then the outcome would be manifestly functional for him (although perhaps rather perverse), but obviously dysfunctional for the rest of us. Turning the flashing lights on so that the ambulance can get through the traffic more quickly is manifestly functional for the driver and patient, but if the flashing had the unexpected effect of causing a passer-by to have an epileptic seizure, then this could be described as an unintended or latent consequence of turning on the flashing lights.

Advantages of Merton's approach

A first clear advantage of Merton's contribution was that it relaxed what many functionalist models, and especially those developed in structural-functionalist anthropology by Bronislaw Malinowski (1884–1942) and Alfred Radcliff-Brown (1881–1955), tended to assume was always a fairly direct link between the action-choices of individuals and the satisfactory functioning of society as a whole. The assumption, that is, that there is a more-or-less perfect match between what is functional for social actors and what is functional for society. Developing the idea of non-function and dysfunction, Merton was able to suggest that, actually, there might be a number of outcomes of action that were functional for social actors while being quite dysfunctional for society. Similarly, not all individuals or groups can be expected to benefit to the same extent from each of the many functions of the overall social system. The notion of latent function also suggests a way of thinking about the many instances where actors do things that have outcomes (harmful or beneficial, dysfunctional or functional) that they were not aware of. For example, we go to school to learn to read and write, to play games and to meet our peers, but at the same time we are socialised into the prevailing social norms of discipline and conduct, and are assimilated intellectually into the prevailing value-system.

Second, although Merton's ideas could be interpreted as weakening the functionalist model, they tend in fact to strengthen it by making the idea of functionality more subtle. In the political system, for example, although it might appear that opposition parties threaten the stability of society (and indeed many of the most radical opposition groups put social transformation at the centre of their plans), part of the function of the political system is to give vent to these pressures. The overall function of the political system is to arrive at some kind of workable consensus, not to try to produce passive universal submission to the prevailing view.

A third advantage of Merton's approach, and again one that relaxes some of the rigidities of basic versions of the functionalist model, is that it accepts that although there probably are functional prerequisites of the kind described by Parsons (functions that have to be performed if social systems are to operate properly), different ways of performing these functions might be found in different forms of society. There need not, in other words, be a presumption that all forms of society develop identical systems for fulfilling the same functions, and thus no need to assume that all social development is mapped onto the same trajectory.

There might very well be coincidence between social actors at the level of the objective or manifest functionality of their actions (for example earning money to pay the rent), without there necessarily being complete coincidence in terms of the more subjective or latent differences between one job and another. The universal benefits of working are income, sense of well-being, creativity and social contact, but there is much variation both between jobs and the different measures of each of these benefits they provide, and between one person and another in terms of the benefits they require.

Issues of power and conflict

The third and final area of criticism we need to look at here, is the argument that functionalist approaches in general, and Parsons' approach in particular, place too much emphasis on balance, equilibrium and consensus and pay insufficient attention to issues of power and conflict. Although Parsons responded to this question by pointing to his notion of pattern variables as the mechanism through which various kinds of social conflict are resolved (universalist rather than particularist value-orientations, achievement versus ascription and so on), it remains the case that his grand plan appears to be generally conservative in political terms, and always implies that social systems invariably revert to a state of normative harmony. The conservative and conflict-free tendencies in Parsons' theory can be traced back to the basic tension he tries to reconcile in his action frame of reference between objective conditions that restrain action on the one hand, and the desire social actors have to make free choices on the other. The main contribution to this critique has been made by the British theorist David Lockwood (born 1929) who proposes (1964) that the problem of power and conflict can be tackled if one makes a distinction between **systems integration**, understood in functionalist terms as stability within and between the various components of the social structure, and **social integration**, defined as consensus in society between individuals and the groups or classes they form.

Developing his critique from a Marxist or **conflict theory** perspective, Lockwood suggests that systems integration is to do with the satisfactory state or otherwise of material conditions and with how well the various institutions of society achieve their ends. If and when these aspects of the social structure begin to fail or relations between them deteriorate (in Merton's terms, when they become dysfunctional), the possibility emerges that various levels of conflict will emerge at the normative level between social groups. For example, if unemployment rises because of restructuring in the economic sphere, this is likely to cause tensions in the political sphere as employers, employees and government try to figure out how to resolve the problem. A failure to do so might result in a general strike, the fall of the government and even social revolution. This sequence of cause and effect might work in the opposite direction if a breakdown in normative integration between groups results in a breakdown of social institutions. The Green Movement of the 1980s, for example, raised sufficient public concern over economic practices, use of natural resources, pollution and so on that economic institutions were forced to change some of their practices. In this instance a change in the value-consensus of society brought about by conflict over ideas, values and beliefs was reflected in a change in the way that the institutions of the social structure 'function'.

Parsons' contribution to social theory

In many ways, and at least until the mid–1980s, the importance of Talcott Parsons in the development of social theory is that in eventually rejecting his theoretical schema social theorists also turned decisively against both the functionalist perspective, and even more significantly against the whole idea of general social theory, that is, a theory of all the social action in society. This reorientation can be associated with the publication, in 1959, of C.W. Mills' (1916–62) influential book, *The Sociological Imagination*, which was highly critical of the Parsonian approach, recommending that it should be replaced by a much more bottom-up style of social research. Mills' book certainly hastened the dramatic fall in the popularity of Parsons' work during the 1970s and prefigured a new trend in American and British sociology at this time, which was pretty much to avoid looking for 'the bigger picture' altogether. Whatever 'the whole' is, the general presumption has been that its discovery no longer provides the point of departure for the research process. The ground workers of social research no longer felt they needed to justify their activities in terms of some grandiose theoretical project. This separation between theory work and grounded research has largely remained in place.

Taking to heart Weber's observation that social research is inherently selective and partial, and that there are whole areas of personal and subjective experience about which it is extremely difficult to give a coherent account, social theorists adopted the view that having a few pieces of the puzzle, especially if they can be related to a few others, is enough to be going on with. There is plenty of room for theorising at a relatively moderate level of abstraction ('middle-range' theory) without necessarily having to fit this into a grand scheme at all. Moreover, the 'grandness' of Parsonian general systems theory is challenged by other rationalist theorists who reject the suggestion that there is only one theory-type picture of society that can be drawn. In addition to there being at least two types of picture (the rational and the empirical), it is possible to picture the social world theoretically in non-Parsonian ways. Accepting a more relaxed definition of rational knowledge, that it is not always logically necessary to take a view on what the whole looks like as a precondition for understanding the individual parts, the knowledge claims made by social theorists no longer depend on their scale and inclusivity, but reflect other qualities such as groundedness, relevance and policy application. 'The bigger picture' is no longer regarded as being as 'big' as it once was.

Despite these criticisms there is no doubt that Parsons' work constituted a major contribution to the general body of material that social theory is made of. His ideas are now part of the intellectual stuff that social theorists who came after him have inevitably had to address. Even more deliberately than this, a number of social theorists have taken on the task of trying to identify the weaknesses within Parsonian functionalism in order to move functionalist theory into its next stage, for example, Jeffrey Alexander has made a very significant contribution to the development of **neo-functionalist** social theory during the 1990s.

A final point relates to Parsons' method of developing his social theory. Much like Jürgen Habermas and Anthony Giddens, whose work we discuss in Chapter Twelve, Parsons excavates the work of previous theorists in order to find new combinations and compromises. Although Marx gets less of a look-in, the work of Weber and Durkheim in particular provide important conceptual compass-points that Parsons uses to navigate his way and ultimately develop his own theory. There is a sense in which Parsons has provided social theory with a very social-theoretical way of building theory. The break between theory and research just referred to could be seen as a necessary stage in this process. Having problematised the relationship between theory and research, and having made social theory more autonomous, social theorists no longer need to abide by the criteria of empirical testing used in the natural sciences at all. Post-Parsons, social theory is allowed to be much more self-referential.

Key points box – The key ideas we have looked at in this chapter are:

- ☑ Functionalism and social interactionism use different conceptions of knowledge and strategy in looking at social phenomena.
- ☑ Functionalism thinks about society as an integrated social system made up of various subsystems.
- ☑ The integrity of the social system depends on necessary functions being carried out and on the integration of these different functions.
- ☑ Talcott Parsons developed the most sophisticated account of society as a social system.
- ☑ The smallest component of the system is the unit act, which is made up of a social actor who aims to satisfy particular ends by particular means and in specific social contexts.
- ☑ The social context includes expectations about what constitutes 'normal' action.

☑ The largest components of the system are the behavioural system, the personality system, the social system and the cultural system.

☑ These four systems are tied to the four functional prerequisites of Adaptation, Goal attainment, Integration and Latency, or *AGIL* for short.

☑ Parsons suggests that social systems can be compared by looking at the kinds of value-choices made by social actors (*pattern variables*).

☑ Functionalist social theory has difficulty in explaining *dysfunctions* in the system arising from *unintended consequences* and possibly resulting in *social conflict*.

Practice box

➲ Why are some types of social theory described as 'top-down' and some as 'bottom-up'?

➲ What is the main difference between the concepts of 'structure' and 'system'?

➲ Does the social system have needs of its own?

➲ What are the four components of the unit act?

➲ Give a brief definition of one of the four *functional prerequisites* identified by Talcott Parsons.

➲ Which of the four functional prerequisites is matched with *the behavioural system*?

➲ Which of the four major systems is concerned with norms and values?

➲ What is the importance of the four *pattern variables* described by Parsons?

➲ Give an example of something that might be *non-functional*, and something that might be *dysfunctional*, for the social system.

➲ Why does functionalist social theory have difficulty dealing with the idea of *conflict*?

Further reading
Peter Hamilton, *Talcott Parsons* (Tavistock, 1983).
Robert K. Merton, *Social Theory and Social Structure* (Free Press, 1949).
Charles Wright Mills, *The Sociological Imagination* (Harmondsworth, 1970).
Talcott Parsons, *The Structure of Social Action* (Free Press, 1937).
Talcott Parsons, *The Social System* (Routledge and Kegan Paul, 1951).
Neil J. Smesler and A. Javier Travino (eds) *Talcott Parsons Today: His Theory and Legacy in Contemporary Sociology* (Rowman and Littlefield, 2001).

Websites
There is no single archive of the work of Talcott Parsons available on the internet and so the most profitable internet search strategy is to use the search engines to look for references to 'Talcott Parsons'. Also use the sites listed at the end of Chapter Two.

CHAPTER SEVEN

SOCIAL INTERACTIONISM AND THE REAL LIVES OF SOCIAL ACTORS

We noted at the start of the previous chapter that in the early part of the 20th century the main developments in social theory were taking place in North America. At the same time that Talcott Parsons was building the **functionalist** tradition at Harvard, other key researchers were developing a very different approach at the University of Chicago. Collectively referred to as 'The Chicago School', the emphasis here was far less on grand theory of the kind Parsons advocated, than on a much more empirically grounded, down-to-earth approach to studying the social world.

In this chapter we will look at:

Basic elements of the social interactionist perspective

The social interactionism of George Herbert Mead and the symbolic interactionism of Herbert Blumer

The phenomenology of Alfred Schutz and the ethnomethodology of Harold Garfinkel

Erving Goffman and the dramaturgical approach

The contribution of social interactionism to social theory

Basic elements of the social interactionist perspective

Social action in context

Although not all Chicago School social theorists had identical interests and methodologies, and although theorists working in this perspective during the mid- and later parts of the 20th century pushed key ideas in new directions, we can use the term **social interactionism** to refer collectively to their approach. Interactionism starts out from the premise that the real stuff of social investigation is not abstract theoretical speculation but the much more mundane day-to-day encounters that constitute the real lives of actual social actors. As the name suggests, interactionism highlights the fact that all of social action takes place between social actors in particular contexts. It follows that the ideas actors have, their sense of meaning and purpose, and the decisions they take as to how and when to act are a product of contextualised social encounters. Decontextualised and non-interactive phenomena are not part of social action.

Rather than trying to explain human social action in terms of psychological responses to external stimuli (behaviourism), or of passive compliance with the social roles and functions of the social system (**functionalism**), social interactionists insist that social action has to be understood in terms of actors' consciously expressed desires, values and expectations. Human social interaction is thus regarded as a creative, dynamic and sometimes rather spontaneous process that has a strongly real-time and live-action feel to it.

The micro level of analysis

The strong focus on studying real social events in their own context highlights a first important issue for social interactionists, which is the scale at which different social theorists conduct their analysis. General systems approaches, like those used by functionalists and **structuralists**, are pitched at a relatively high level of generality because the kind of social theory they try to develop is based on finding broad patterns and similarities between various instances of social interaction. If such similarities can be identified, the task of the theorist becomes one of identifying and explaining the general principles that are in play at the **macro** level of analysis. As we saw in Chapter Six, functionalist social theorists argue that the most general organising principles of social action are those of **system** and function. With these principles very much in mind functionalists go in search of instances of social interaction that can be explained in terms of system and function.

One difficulty with this approach is that there are many aspects even of a relatively simple piece of social interaction that cannot be explained adequately in terms of two or three simple principles. Social interactionists claim they have the advantage here because they go into the research process with a much more open mind about what they might find. For them, the many aspects of social action that seem to fall outside the functionalist template support their view that the functionalist template is too narrow. Investigating the more intimate and detailed aspects of social interaction has to be carried out at the **micro** level of analysis.

ILLUSTRATION – MICRO OR MACRO?

Imagine we are observing a group of people enjoying themselves at a restaurant. Social interactionists would argue that the essence of what is going on is largely embedded within the social interaction itself. The meaning that this activity has for the people taking part (pleasure, enjoyment and relaxation) can be inferred through direct observation of their interaction.

An alternative functionalist explanation might be that 'restaurant-going', in common with other kinds of social downtime in public places, has the function of providing social actors with a chance to rest and recuperate. The difference between one instance of restaurant-going and another, or between going to the bar, golf club or soccer game, is less important than the fact that they share the common purpose or function of relaxation. Such social events are similar because they serve the same function.

A social interactionist reply to this explanation might be that although it is possible to explain going to the restaurant in terms of the function it serves within the social system, a more immediate explanation is that, for most social actors most of the time, going out for a meal with friends is simply about having fun. The difference between one otherwise very similar socialising event and another, and indeed between one particular instance of it and the next, is that each one constitutes a social-interactive event that is meaningful in and of itself. Meaning is part of the event and not something that has to be explained in terms of elaborate external forces like functionality.

Gathering the raw materials

From an interactionist perspective, then, the task of the social investigator is to study in great detail, and with as much precision as can reasonably be achieved, exactly how these social encounters take place, what is involved in them and how they are affected by context. The basic methodology of social interactionism is therefore **empirical**. The primary source of information about social phenomena is hard data usually gathered by close observation of human subjects in action. The theory that might subsequently be inferred from these observations is regarded as valid because of the empirical clarity of the data and not because of the logical integrity of its arguments. The task of the social researcher is not to look for data in order to support a theoretical explanation, which has been developed speculatively in advance of 'doing the research', but to observe and record social phenomena at face value and in their unique context.

A combination of micro-level analysis together with a sensitivity about uniqueness of context does, however, raise a significant problem for interactionists, which is whether they will ever be able to offer much in the way of theoretical explanation given that there are an infinite number of social encounters that could be described. If all social encounters are unique where does one begin looking for common features? We encountered this difficulty when reading about Max Weber's views on the **verstehen** or interpretive method in Chapter Five. Weber suggests that since it is impossible to record each and every instance of a particular social phenomenon, social theorists inevitably have to be selective in what they choose to investigate. The theory that might eventually emerge from an interactionist/**interpretivist** perspective is bound to be partial because it is based on inferences from only a limited selection of examples. In the end, both macro and micro approaches can be criticised for making generalisations; it is more a question of understanding whether they make their generalisations at the macro or the micro level of analysis.

The insider–outsider problem

This brings us to a third key element in social interactionist thinking, which is the idea that although social actors carry ideas and values with them as they enter social situations, social interactionists define 'meaning' as a particular characteristic of the social-interactive situation. Meaningfulness is one of the most important qualitative products of social interaction. There are no social interactions that are not imbued with meaning and similarly this sense of meaning does not exist outside the interactive situation. This raises the important issue of what the special properties of socially-constructed meaning or meaning-in-context are, as distinct from the more personal sense of meaning that individual social actors have of the social situations they are engaging in. If Max Weber is correct in suggesting that one of the things that makes action meaningful is the opportunity it provides to express ideas and values (see Chapter Five), then it is not unreasonable to presume that actors have a sense of meaning that develops separately from social interaction. It seems likely that more than one variety or level of meaning is involved when social interaction takes place.

The suggestion that there are different species of meaning raises an important methodological question, which is whether it is possible for the theorist or researcher to really understand the meaning of what is going on during social interaction unless they themselves are part of that interaction. **General systems theory**, like functionalism and

structuralism, tends to assume that the social researcher is in a rather privileged position compared with the social actors whose interactions are being researched. Social theorists are trained professionals who are expertly placed to help the amateur general public understand what is really going on. Social interactionism attempts to combat this air of superiority by always trying to stay as close as possible to the action. This raises some challenging issues about what Weber described as the **value-neutrality** of the researcher, since even a very experienced investigator might struggle to prevent his own ideas and values from affecting how he sees things. As we shall see in the following sections of this chapter, leading social interactionists have spent a lot of time devising better ways of investigating the social world. How successful they have been remains an open question. Ultimately, no matter how hard the social researcher tries to become an 'insider', he always remains an 'outsider' in the situation he is studying.

Having looked briefly at these key elements in social interactionist thinking (focus on events at the micro level, the meaning of the situation and the insider–outsider problem) we now turn our attention to leading examples of the kind of social theory it has produced.

The social interactionism of George Herbert Mead (1863–1931) and the symbolic interactionism of Herbert Blumer (1900–87)

Some background

The first phase of work by members of the Chicago School was led by W.I.Thomas (1863–1947) and R. Park (1864–1944), who had a strong sense that social organisation was the best way of achieving 'the good society'. During the first decades of the 20th century Chicago became one of the first truly modern American industrial cities and underwent rapid and very substantial economic and social transformation in terms of its physical environment and population. Concentrating on the expanding urban centre, Park, Thomas and their colleagues made numerous field studies of the city during the 1920s and 1930s and of the people who came to live there. It was hoped that this new urban **ethnography** would provide important information for city planners and others about how best to organise the new urban social environments where the vast majority of Americans were now living.

The second main strand of the first phase of social interactionist thought at Chicago, also at the turn of the 20th century, emerged from the social-psychological perspective of George Herbert Mead. Although he was born roughly a generation before Talcott Parsons

(Mead was born in South Hadley, Massachusetts, in 1863, Parsons in Colorado Springs in 1902), both were sons of congregational ministers. Mead graduated from Oberlin College aged 20 in 1883 and spent three years working with surveyors on the Minnesota to Saskatchewan railway before returning to study at Harvard University in 1887. He studied and travelled in Germany before taking up a teaching post at the University of Michigan in 1891 (where he met and worked with influential social psychologist Charles Cooley [1864–1929], and the philosopher John Dewey [1859–1952]). For much of this period abroad he was primarily interested in physiological psychology and studies of animal behaviour. (J.B. Watson, who also studied under Dewey at Chicago in 1900, published his highly influential book, *Behaviourism*, in 1925, and B.F. Skinner's [1878–1958] equally important text, *The Behavior of Organisms*, was published in 1938.) In 1892, aged 31, Mead moved to Chicago University where he remained until his death from cancer in 1931.

Mead never published a book-length piece of work. The main texts we have of his ideas were all published after his death from various notes and accounts mostly from his university lectures on what he called 'social behaviourism'. The most important collections are: *The Philosophy of the Present* (1932), *Mind, Self and Society* (1934) and *The Philosophy of the Act* (1938). One of the main popularisers of Mead's work was Herbert Blumer (1900–87) who developed a slightly modified approach that he called (in 1937) 'symbolic interactionism' (Blumer, 1969). The importance of Blumer is that he sought to bring together both the urban ethnographic orientation of Park and Thomas, and the more social-psychological approach developed by Mead. The name **symbolic interactionism** (rather than just *social* interactionism) captures the idea that human social interaction is not only performed in order to convey practical purposes and intentions (an idea that lay at the heart of Cooley and Dewey's system of **philosophical pragmatism**), but is also central to the whole business of creating and exchanging *meanings*. Even if people do sometimes act in a stimulus–response kind of way, they also take time to interpret their actions. Meaning, so to speak, is one of the practical consequences of social action. Rejecting behaviourist and functionalist characterisations of social action as mechanistic responses lacking dynamism and spontaneity, Blumer insists that without the creative-evaluative element of human decision making, action would have no real meaning but only functionality.

G.H. Mead on self and society

We can identify two main innovations in Mead's contribution to the interactionist perspective; his development of the idea of the profoundly social nature of the self, and his recognition of the importance of symbolic communication, particularly language.

The self

Rejecting some rationalist representations of selfhood as a profoundly isolated thing embedded within individual consciousness ('I think therefore I am'), Mead wanted to stress instead that our sense of who we are, our sense-of-self, is profoundly social. In essence, we cannot have any sense of ourselves outside of the social contexts where we interact with other people; society is a precondition for sense-of-self. It is by interacting with others that we get feedback from them about who we are, and we use this information to develop our sense of who we are. Like Robinson Crusoe, a person who had nobody else around to reflect back to them a sense of who they were would soon experience a very impoverished sense-of-self. Think how disturbing and inconvenient it would be if you looked in the mirror and there was no reflection looking back at you:

KEY QUOTE – G.H. Mead, *Mind, Self and Society* (1934).
The self is something which has a development; it is not initially there, at birth, but arises in the process of social experience and activity, that is, develops in the given individual as a result of his relations to that process as a whole and to other individuals within that process.... The individual experiences himself [as an individual], not directly, but only indirectly, from the particular standpoints of other individual members of the same social group, or from the generalized standpoint of the social group as a whole to which he belongs. For he enters his own experience as a self or individual, not directly or immediately, not by becoming a subject to himself, but only in so far as he first becomes as object to himself just as other individuals are objects to him.... The process out of which the self arises is a social process which implies interaction of individuals in the group, implies the pre-existence of the group. (G.H. Mead, 1934, pp 135, 164)

Mead calls the sense-of-self we get from digesting other people's impressions of us the 'me'. The 'me' is, so to speak, the social side of the self. There is, however, a second crucial part of the self, which Mead calls the 'I', which can be thought of as the essential nugget of a person that he comes to know through his own immediate subjective consciousness of self. The self is thus made up of an external aspect, the social 'me', which a person comes to know by receiving feedback from others, and an internal aspect, the personal 'I', which he comes to know through his subjective sense of being. It is not possible to experience the 'I' (inner self) unless one is already experiencing the 'me' (the socially-reflected aspect of self). We come to know the intimate, subjective and personal side of the self by means of the public, objective and impersonal side.

Mead develops the idea of the 'generalised other' to describe the audience who give us back our sense of who we are. The notion of the generalised other is distinct from the Freudian notion of the 'significant other', which refers usually to only one or two very specific 'others' (often mother or father) whose opinion we take very seriously when we think about who we are. From a Meadian point of view, one might say that what makes the Freudian 'other' significant (apart from keeping the infant warm and fed) is the fact that it provides them with their sense of 'me'.

Introducing an idea that played a major role in Blumer's adaptation of Mead's ideas, Mead goes on to describe how these two aspects or phases of the self (the 'I' and the 'me') establish a kind of internal dialogue that gives us our capacity for self-reflection. By testing the 'I' against the various versions of the 'me' that we get back from our social interaction with other people (from partners, family, friends, workmates and strangers) we develop the capacity for self-monitoring and self-control. By rehearsing our sense-of-self in this way, we can reach decisions about how to act, and thus who to be, in the social encounters that follow. There is always an elusive quality to this internal dialogue and the sense-of-self that arises from it, however, because the self never reaches a point when it is finally settled. The 'I' is always on the move between one experiment with the 'me' and the next. The 'I' always lags behind the 'me'. As Mead puts it: 'I cannot turn around quick enough to catch myself' (1934, p 174).

Symbolic communication

Mead's second main innovation was to emphasise the importance of language (or vocal gestures as he sometimes calls them), understood as a medium for symbolic communication between people. The development of symbolic communication, and the social contexts in which it occurs, are central to Mead's ideas about how the self is formed. Symbolic communication is the medium through which we receive feedback from others about our sense-of-self, and is also the medium through which we conduct our internal dialogue between 'me' and 'I'. When we say 'I was just thinking ...', that thinking takes the form of language (which poses the interesting question of whether it is possible to think before one can speak). Although it is a difficult idea to grasp, the provisional or elusive nature of the self partly results from the symbolic or abstract quality of the mode of communication (usually language) that we use to think about who we are. As we shall

detail in Chapter Nine, to the extent that language and
ct systems of communication are socially constructed,
e the objects one is speaking about (including the self).
¹ nature of the medium through which we come to
the self must always be provisional; we never reach
of selfhood.
olic communication, and especially language, plays an
e process by which individual selves are integrated
e two aspects to this. First, the language we use in
rom others about our selves, and for conducting
rsations between 'I' and 'me' (our thoughts), are
drawn from the community we are part of and so the way we express
ideas through language are already a product of that communal
undertaking. There must always be something communal about sense-
of-self because the production of the self relies on the communal
resource of language. For Mead, socialisation is enabled and social
order maintained by the fact that through symbolic communication
between our selves and the generalised other, and in our own heads
between the 'I' and the 'me', we are all 'talking the same language'.

Second, and this time focusing on the content of those ideas,
language is itself a social construction that reflects the general culture
of society. To the extent that sense-of-self is a direct reflection of what
other people think, and that 'thinking' takes place in the context of
prevailing cultural norms and values, sense-of-self is already integrated
into the wider culture. As Mead puts it 'the attitude of the generalized
other is the attitude of the whole community' and it is in this form that
'the community exercises control over the conduct of its individual
members' (Mead, 1934, p 155). If a sense-of-self develops that is at odds
with the wider community, then that individual will find it extremely
difficult to 'fit in'. Using a Darwinian analogy, their sense-of-self is
not 'best fitted' to the culturally imbued environment of selfhood that
surrounds them.

Mead and social theory

Although Mead's ideas about social behaviourism were mainly
intended for consumption in the field of social psychology rather than
social theory, his comments about the reflexive capacity of human
consciousness, the importance of symbolic communication and
language, and how individual selves become integrated into the wider
society through language and culture are certainly familiar territory
within social theory. A little ironically, given the general expectation
that social interactionists avoid the mistakes made by functionalists, one
of the main weaknesses of his ideas, from a social-theoretical point of

view, is that he has very little to say about situations where social actors deviate from the norm, or how or why they behave in unpredictable ways. A bit like Parsons, Mead assumes that social actors express such high levels of social conformity that deviant selves hardly ever emerge.

The same criticism can be made about his characterisation of society as a place that seems to exist in a permanent state of equilibrium and integration. Although, a bit like Durkheim, it makes a lot of sense to emphasise the importance of the 'generalised other' or 'community' as a way of understanding how actions are positively regulated and conformity achieved, unlike Durkheim, Mead has relatively little to say about what happens when these regulatory forces become negative and repressive. The usual solution in social theory is to envisage social actors existing in a constant state of dynamic tension, suspended between their urge for perfect individuality and autonomy, and the pressure to conform.

Again bearing in mind his background in social psychology, Mead's intellectual approach to the autonomy–conformity problem (the problem of **social order**) is to see the development of the self very much in terms of the biological and psychological well-being of the individual, and to frame all of this within a rather naturalistic account of social development. Herbert Blumer followed a very similar path here, arguing that, beyond the facility for symbolic communication, what binds social actors together is a tendency for them to interpret things in the same way. This capacity for shared meanings, expressed through symbolic communication, is very much the essence of Blumer's theory of symbolic interactionism.

Up to a point, the organic metaphor used by Durkheim, Parsons and others in the functionalist/positivist tradition, also lurks within Mead's approach to social interaction. There is a good deal of similarity, for example, between the ideas we have just been discussing and Parsons' description of the 'latency function', where he makes great play of the fact that social order crucially depends on the assimilation of prevailing social norms and values by individuals as they grow up. It is not unreasonable to suggest that social and symbolic interactionism provide a study of how, as a key mechanism of the latency function, the socialisation process takes place. The Chicago tradition is thus working on just *one part of* the overall system of knowledge about society that Parsons' general systems theory is trying to outline. They have chosen different levels of generality in looking at what is essentially the same key issue.

Finally, and anticipating an issue we will be looking at in more detail in Chapter Nine, if Mead and Blumer are correct in identifying the importance of language and of shared meaning as key structures that bind society together, one might have expected them to enquire about the other kinds of structure (for example the economic structure) that perform an equivalent kind of function in different spheres. This is something that they largely fail to do.

The phenomenology of Alfred Schutz and the ethnomethodology of Harold Garfinkel

Whether or not they made an entirely successful contribution to social theory, Mead and Blumer certainly consolidated the position of interactionism, and especially its interest in the importance of shared meanings. This theme was carried forward by another key figure in the interactionist camp, Harold Garfinkel. Like the functionalist theorist R.K. Merton, who we looked at in Chapter Six, Garfinkel (born in 1917) also studied at Harvard under Talcott Parsons, before establishing a centre for ethnomethodology at the University of California Los Angeles in the 1960s. Garfinkel's most widely read work, *Studies in Ethnomethodology*, was published in 1967 (Garfinkel, 1967).

The procedures of meaning

The special focus of Garfinkel's work, and again he was much more interested in empirical investigation than theory-building, was not so much on the content of the meanings that social actors develop through social interaction, although he certainly thought these were very important, but on the procedures by which they are arrived at. The basic insight here is that the consensus social actors reach about meaning is partly to do with the kinds of shared ideas and beliefs they have (ideas and beliefs that, as Mead and Blumer pointed out, are embedded in a common culture), but is also very much to do with the fact that they arrive at these shared views by using very similar ways of thinking. Members of the same culture tend to follow the same mental routines as they make decisions. An important part of the socialisation process involves training children to use these particular patterns of thinking. Similarity of mental procedure helps produce similarity of meaning and interpretation. If it were not for this similarity, social actors would find it very difficult to act together at all. Ways of thinking are part of what meaning is.

Similarity of procedure derives partly from the fact that one human brain works very much like another. Culturally, we also share particular habits of thinking such as a tendency to think about things in terms of binary opposites, or by using particular world views, such as the kind of instrumental rationality we discussed in Chapter Five when we looked at the social theory of Max Weber. At another level, however, Garfinkel wants to emphasise that social actors reach consensus about meaning because in their thinking they make full use of a special kind of thinking called **common sense**.

Common sense

Common sense is a special mode of thinking because it is very much directed towards solving practical day-to-day issues in a direct almost automatic way. A leading influence on interactionist views about common sense, and especially for Garfinkel, is the phenomenological philosophy of Alfred Schutz (1899–1959). Schutz suggests that in their day-to-day activities, social actors ordinarily reach decisions and make judgements, not by applying complex procedures of scientific rationality, but by applying a much more direct kind of practical rationality. They arrive at their decisions by adopting a common-sense approach to things, and by drawing on the knowledge they already have. This knowledge is 'practical' in the sense that it tends to be based on experience rather than on abstract reasoning. It is also 'common' knowledge because it arises out of previous shared experiences.

One of the key features of practical rationality (as distinct from scientific rationality) is the presumption that things actually are as they appear to be. Common sense means taking things at face value rather than worrying whether there are multiple versions of reality. Following the phenomenological philosophy of Edmund Husserl (1859–1938), Schutz also believed that the sociological investigation of the meaning of social action had to focus on how reality appears from the point of view of social actors acting together. The process of meaning-construction is a mutual undertaking that proceeds on the basis of a common 'stock of knowledge' built up from previous experiences. Social life is thus anchored within a process of meaning-construction as social actors strive to make sense of their actions and in the context of the actions of others. Social reality has to be regarded as a profoundly active and creative process of meaning-construction rather than as a battle between individual subjects and an exterior world of objective structures.

There is an obvious consistency between this phenomenological perspective offered by Schutz, the pragmatist philosophy of Charles Cooley and John Dewey, who see meaning as determined by practical purposes and intentions, and the interactionist perspective developed in the social psychology of Mead and Blumer. They all seem agreed that social order derives from shared meanings and shared procedures for arriving at this common understanding. 'Common sense' quite literally means an understanding that is held in common by social actors who share the same culture, and which is arrived at by applying common patterns of thinking and communicating.

Garfinkel moved the interactionist perspective forward by showing that an important part of the decision-making procedure (another of the special properties of common sense) is the capacity to see things from the point of view of the others involved in the interaction. Although we are quite familiar with the psychological notion of empathy, which is the ability to identify emotionally with others, Garfinkel wants to emphasise that, at a day-to-day level and operating in common-sense mode, 'meaning' can be regarded as a form of consensus. The world is made to be as it appears because the day-to-day social encounters of social actors require it to be so. Social life would be impossible without agreement between social actors about the nature of reality, and if reality did not conform to this view, social life would be in a permanent state of uncertainty and crisis. Furthermore, embedded as they are in everyday life, 'meaningfulness' and 'orderliness' cannot be regarded as separate, objective phenomena having any existence that is independent of context (a property Garfinkel calls 'indexicality'). Social order emerges out of a perpetual process whereby **reflexive** social actors continuously make and remake a sense of reality by drawing on embedded or sedimented common sense.

Erving Goffman and the dramaturgical approach

Interactionist ideas about common sense, the grounded nature of social reality and the way in which sense-of-self is largely a product of social encounters played a major part in the theory of the last big name we are looking at from the Chicago School, Erving Goffman (1922–82). Goffman completed his PhD at Chicago in 1953 having spent several years doing detailed field research including a year-long spell living on the Shetland Isles off the UK mainland. Like other members of the Chicago School, Goffman's main intention was to provide detailed studies of specific examples of social interaction rather than spend a lot of time trying to develop elaborate theoretical explanations. In his first major field study, *The Presentation of Self in Everyday Life* (1959), he commented, for example, that 'scaffolds are to build other things with and should be erected with an eye to taking them down' (Goffman, 1959, p 42). To this extent, his contribution to social theory is something that other social theorists have attributed to him and not something he was directly preoccupied with himself. His other best-known studies are *Asylums* (1961) and *Stigma: Notes on the Management of Spoiled Identity* (1964).

The 'theory' that Goffman does produce is found in the terminology he uses for classifying the very large number of detailed descriptions he gathered about the techniques and rules social actors use to 'perform' various social roles; social roles that provide opportunities to express a sense-of-self. Discussing 'communication out of character', for example, Goffman has four categories that he labels 'treatment of the absent; staging talk; team collusion; and realigning actions' (Goffman, 1959, p 181). His theory is thus a kind of classificatory scheme for the different procedures and techniques social actors use to illicit impressions of themselves from other actors. The internal structure of the system of classification, and the relations between one part of it and another, is where we can look for elements of a more abstract kind of theoretical formulation. We are interested in Goffman's work in terms of what it adds to the interactionist perspective in general.

The dramaturgical approach

The main organising device Goffman uses in sorting out his observations is to describe social behaviour as a 'theatrical performance'. 'I shall', he says, 'consider the way in which the individual in ordinary work situations presents himself and his activity to others, the ways in which he guides and controls the impression they form of him, and the kinds of things he may or may not do while sustaining his performance before them' (1959, p ix). Like Garfinkel who emphasises process over content, Goffman emphasises that it is the procedures and techniques of self-presentation that interest him, rather than 'the specific content of any activity' or with the part that a specific activity plays in the 'interdependent activities of an on-going social system' (1959, p 13). The drama he is interested in, in other words, is not about one role or character rather than another, or particularly about how an actor's role as 'worker' or 'mother' fits in either with the other social roles she may have or with any notion of wider social function. Goffman is only concerned 'with some of the common techniques that persons employ to sustain the impressions other people have of them and with some of the common contingencies associated with the employment of these techniques' (1959, p 13).

There are three main participants in this drama: the actor who is performing, other co-performers who Goffman often refers to as 'members of the team', and the audience who witness the performance. Although the individual performer relies on other members of the team (or cast) to bring off her performance successfully, the audience is perhaps the key participant for Goffman because it is from them that the individual actor hopes to gain some kind of positive approval of her performance. Goffman suggests that social roles are built up on the basis of the repeated performance of clearly identifiable 'parts' or 'routines'.

Using an analogy with circus performance, the utterly familiar slapstick routine played out by the clowns establishes the social role of 'circus clown'. The success of the actor playing this role will depend on how closely the performance matches up with what the audience are expecting to see. A margin for innovation is allowable but in its essential parts the routine must fit the audience's expectations of the stereotypical template of clowning. The social roles of student, lecturer, police officer and bureaucrat can be described in similar fashion as routinised performances of familiar parts. In both the circus and the 'real world', the routines are in place in the minds of the expectant audience *before* they are performed by any particular individual actor or social-role occupant.

The performance

Looking at the performance itself, Goffman suggests a key distinction between 'front stage' or 'front region', and 'backstage' or 'back region'. (There is also a non-stage area that he calls 'the outside', which is rather vaguely defined as everything else that is neither front nor back region.) He defines front stage as 'the expressive equipment of a standard kind intentionally or unwittingly employed by the individual during his performance' (1959, p 19). Front stage includes both the setting where the action takes place and the 'personal front' of the performer. This includes visual props or attributes such as a uniform or specific equipment required in that role, personal attributes such as age and gender, and 'appearance', which is a term Goffman uses to refer to the social status of the performer. Personal front also includes other often non-verbal requisites such as manner, expression, posture, decorum and so on.

These props and attributes cue the audience in to what the performance will be. Once the setting, personal front, props, attributes and manner become sufficiently routinised, the front 'becomes a "collective representation" and a fact in its own right' (1959, p 24). We do not particularly have to study the performance of the secretary and the refuse collector, and certainly not of each and every one of them, in order to make a pretty good guess about what the routines they perform will involve and how they will differ. Performances are thus '"socialized", moulded, and modified to fit into the understanding and expectations of the society in which it is represented'. They will tend to 'incorporate and exemplify the officially credited values of the society' (1959, pp 30–1).

The backstage or back region is where the performer prepares his or her performance. In one sense it is a props room where the various bits of physical equipment, clothing and so on are kept. In another it is a place where performances can be rehearsed out of sight of the audience. It is here, as Goffman put it, that 'the performer can relax; he can drop his front, forego speaking his lines, and step out of character' (1959, p 98). A key characteristic of the back region is that it is a place 'where the performer can reliably expect that no member of the audience will intrude', 'it is typically out of bounds to members of the audience' (1959, pp 98, 111).

Goffman as an interactionist

Looking at Goffman's analysis in the context of interactionist ideas in general, there would seem to be three clear points of correspondence with Mead's ideas.

A tale of two selves

First, the self is not something that emerges from within the social actor, it is not an outward projection of an inner unique property of personhood, but can more accurately be described as something that is projected onto the person by the community. In Mead's terms, the 'I' only takes on a concrete form because the 'me' is there to provide a vehicle for it to do so. It is impossible for social actors to express the 'I' at all without feedback from the collective other. There might be an essential subjective consciousness in there somewhere, but one that has yet to take on a concrete form. As previously noted, the 'I' hovers perpetually between one bodily incarnation and another but without ever acquiring a permanent, settled concrete form.

For Goffman, although in a simple sense all social actors are 'playing the part' as they go about their daily routines, it is the collective other, this time called 'the audience', that makes the playing of the part worthwhile and meaningful. Acting would be an exceptionally dull occupation if there were no audience. Logically, and although Goffman does discuss exceptional circumstances in which the audience is absent, it is the audience that creates the need for the performance, and likewise the meaning and purpose of the performance are also down to them. Goffman's distinction between 'performer' and 'character', and his specification of 'character' as that which is elicited from the audience by the actor playing the part, is quite close to Mead's distinction between the 'I' and the 'me'. Rather than seeing 'self-as-character as something housed within the body of its possessor' Goffman argues that 'the performed self', which the individual plays to the audience while in character, 'is imputed to him' (Goffman, 1952, p 91).

KEY QUOTE – Erving Goffman, *The Presentation of the Self in Everyday Life* (1959).

This self itself does not derive from its possessor, but from the whole scene of his action, being generated by that attribute of local events which renders them interpretable by witnesses. A correctly staged and performed scene leads the audience to impute a self to a performed character, but this imputation – this self – is a *product* of a scene that comes off, and is not a cause of it. The self, then, as a performed character, is not an organic thing that has a specific location, whose fundamental fate is to be born, to mature, and to die; it is a dramatic effect arising diffusely from a scene that is presented, and the characteristic issue, the actual crucial concern, is whether it will be credited or discredited. (Goffman, 1959, p 223, original emphasis)

Common understanding

A second conspicuous similarity between Goffman's analysis and interactionism in general is that social interaction depends on very high levels of common understanding between participants about the purpose, meaning and significance of what is going on. As he puts it: 'The key factor [in the structure of social encounters] is the maintenance of a single definition of the situation, this definition having to be expressed, and this expression sustained in the face of a multitude of potential disruptions' (1959, p 225).

To the extent that, like Mead, Blumer, Schutz and Garfinkel, Goffman is happy to define social order subjectivistically in terms of the systems of shared meaning and understanding that give rise to symbolic order in society (as distinct, that is, from objectivistic forms of social order defined as external structures of socio-economic or socio-political power), identifiable patterns and regularities in the way social actors elicit views of themselves from others make a clear contribution to social order. Even in the expression of personality, for example, he seems clear that performers have to comply with socially-accepted versions of themselves: 'The expressive coherence that is required in performances points out a crucial discrepancy between our all-too-human selves and our socialized selves ... a certain bureaucratization of the spirit is expected so that we can be relied upon to give a perfectly homogeneous performance at every appointed time' (1959, p 49).

Reality in action

A third area of overlap emerges from Goffman's treatment of how social reality is also something that is created by and through social interaction. We have encountered one version of this idea already in the pragmatist philosophical views of Dewy and Cooley, and the **phenomenology** of Schutz and Garfinkel. These authors emphasise that any uncertainty social actors might have about which version of social reality they are dealing with tends to be resolved at the point when actors get involved in purposeful social interaction. They are free to speculate about social reality abstractly, but in order to act constructively, social actors have to plump for one particular version of it. In the same way that social interaction depends on everyone (or nearly everyone) having a shared attitude towards what is going on, what the purposes of the interaction are and so on, so also must social actors converge in their ideas about social reality. An important theme in two of Goffman's later studies (*Asylums* [1961] and *Stigma* [1964]), is what happens when individual social actors' ideas about reality no longer converge sufficiently for them to be able to interact in ways that are defined by the wider group (the audience) as 'normal'. Goffman's early analysis of 'the performative self' implies that it is at 'the moment of performance' that social actors resolve doubts about which version of their sense-of-self they really want to be, so also actors resolve worries about different versions of social reality at the moment when they finally act. Final or actual reality is, as it were, held back until the moment of performance.

At the heart of Goffman's dramaturgical approach is the assumption that actors are motivated to perform various social roles by their desire to receive back from the audience a positive and supportive confirmation of who they are. Social actors go to a great deal of trouble to fine-tune their performance-of-self in order to maximise this sense of being socially accepted and worthwhile. Although Goffman is reluctant to go much further than describing the techniques and characteristics of how actors bring off a successful performance, one can certainly say that successful performance is a means to a further end, which is the development of a socially validated sense-of-self. Quite unlike Cooley, Mead, Blumer, Garfinkel and other members of the Chicago School, Goffman has no theory of the psychology of the self as such, but it is clear that the quest for sense-of-self, a quest that often requires expertise in the techniques of performance described by Goffman, lies beneath many of the performances he describes and analyses.

Some critical comments

It is relatively easy to find fault with Goffman's work. His method of gathering data and of analysing it was largely unique to him and, as he himself was quick to acknowledge, fell far short of the standards of rigour and objectivity generally associated even with broad-brush ethnographic fieldwork. His style of presentation and written expression is also peculiar to him and is thus very different to conventional academic prose. We have also already noted that Goffman is very clear that he has little interest in developing, let alone in proving, general theoretical propositions, even to the extent of avoiding any clear theoretical discussion of the nature of the self or other basic elements in the interactionist perspective. Goffman is true to his aim, which is to describe a very specific dimension of social interaction. The fact that in his work this fragment seems quite large is because he describes it in so much detail. A bit like zooming in from a satellite image of the globe, to a continent, a country, a city and an individual apartment, Goffman really is working at the micro level of analysis.

From the point of view of our present concern with Goffman's contribution to interactionist social theory, we can group our criticisms under two headings; problems with the micro level of analysis, and the dramaturgical analogy.

Limitations of micro-level analysis

First, and accepting as we must that Goffman was quite clear in specifying the limited range of his analytical interests, there are nonetheless problems that arise from the micro-analytical level at which he works. In order to really understand the particular segment or fragment of social interaction one has chosen to analyse, it would be useful to express even in general terms some thoughts about what goes on either side of or 'beyond' the particular bit that is being analysed. As we have already hinted, this deficit shows up in Goffman's analysis particularly at the point where it would be extremely useful to know what kind of entity he thinks the self is.

If, as Goffman suggests in the key quote earlier, there is no inner subjective self (the 'I' in Mead's analysis), then what, one might ask, is the point of producing successful performances of that (apparently non-existent) self? Goffman could be interpreted as presenting a radicalised version of social interactionism in which real social reality and a real sense-of-self only acquire concrete existence for fleeting moments. On this reading, social interaction does not build up into anything, but only exists 'in the moment'. This is a very transitory and existential representation of social reality where social interaction is not 'for' anything or anyone, but is only temporarily there when the action is taking place or when the self is actually being performed. This seems to suggest that, like the theatre, once the audience has gone home 'society' is little more than an empty venue that is of very little interest in itself. Clearly, however, like the circus tent and the theatre, performances cannot take place without suitable venues.

At some points in his analysis Goffman goes so far as to suggest that the self disappears altogether since performers 'merely provide a peg on which something of collaborative manufacture [i.e. the various social roles people perform] will be hung from time to time' (1959, p 223). Since pegs lack any dynamic abilities of their own, the self not only depends on the 'interpretative activity of the audience', but can only exist at the moment when the interpretation is being made. Goffman seems to be likening social actors to string puppets, having no personality or **biography** of their own and only activated as a device for performing various roles and characters at the behest of the audience. Mead offers a concept of the self that has both an outer shell ('me') and an inner core ('I'), Goffman's concept only has the outer shell.

Looking at what happens after a particular isolated episode of face-to-face interactive performance has taken place, Goffman's micro-level perspective commits him to silence over any cumulative effects, long-term consequences or broader significances of these face-to-face interactions. We already know that Goffman is not developing a theory of the psychology of the self, or a theory of society, but he also seems unwilling to reflect on the implications for social life in general of particular performances. In what ways, for example, are the stage scenery and settings of social performance determined by circumstances that are beyond the actors' control?

Limitations of the dramaturgical analogy

A second group of criticisms arise from within his own use of the dramaturgical analogy. It is clear enough that the rules and techniques of performance, the stagecraft that professional actors use in the theatre to illicit positive appreciation of the characters they are playing from the audience, are largely the same as the techniques social actors ordinarily use when playing-out the social roles they occupy in real life. From Goffman's dramaturgical point of view, and in terms of analysing what is going on during these performances, it makes little difference whether one is observing real life or theatre. It also makes sense to envisage a backstage area where the paying audience cannot go so that the illusion of the illusory element of the performance can be maintained (that it is in fact a play and not real life).

However, if what Goffman says about the interdependence of the performer/performance and the expectations of the audience is correct, then the audience already knows what goes on backstage. The backstage is symbolically or ceremonially disregarded in the theatre but in real life the audience has full knowledge of it. This must be the case since members of the audience are just as often performers themselves. As Goffman himself remarks, there is necessarily a kind of conspiracy of agreement in performance not only between members of the team or cast, but between them and the audience.

The dramaturgical perspective thus relies very heavily on a kind of universal suspension of disbelief. Goffman makes no comment about the interchangeability of social actors as performers, as members of the team and as members of the audience, and yet it is clearly the case that while making a performance to the audience 'out front', the performer is also seeking confirmation of his or her integrity as a stage performer and as a person from other members of the cast 'back here'. It is not clear in what sense the backstage area is actually free of performance. In the end the dramaturgical metaphor is limited because although professional actors in the theatre use the same techniques and devices as ordinary social actors, the relation between professional actors and the paying audience is not the same as the relation between ordinary social actors acting, and ordinary people watching them. They are performers, members of teams and members of audiences simultaneously, not sequentially. To the extent that differences in these kinds of relationship do make a significant difference to the performance, Goffman's analysis is incomplete.

Categories of action

If, as we noted at the start of this section, the theory in Goffman's work relies heavily on the categories he uses, then its wider usefulness would certainly be compromised if its categories were incomplete. One example of incompleteness is that although he gives detailed descriptions of the front stage and backstage areas, he says very little about the non-stage area, or about how social actors experience their sense-of-self in intimate situations or if there is no audience at all. In intimate situations where selves rely heavily on feedback from a significant other, one might expect the dynamics to be quite different than when performing other social roles in front of anonymous others. If there is no audience present, does this mean that persons cease to experience any significant sense-of-self at all?

Continuity and change

There is also a major issue with innovation in Goffman's account because if, as he repeatedly suggests, social actors habitually rely on preconceptions of how they should or ought to perform particular social roles, one might pose the question what is the process by which new social roles emerge and how can these become absorbed into common understanding and common interpretation? This is not to say that Goffman's scene lacks dynamism; it is after all about face-to-face encounters in real time. The point is that it would be useful to have some suggestions about whereabouts in the 'habitual routines of daily life' novelty can develop. The characters and selves in the drama Goffman describes sometimes appear to resemble the passive role-obedient individuals that Parsons was much criticised for presenting in his **general theory**. A related point could be made about the unintended impressions that performers give off, which Goffman acknowledges can have an important bearing on how the performance is judged. If the success of the performance depends on social roles being largely predetermined then un-choreographed happenings, or unintended impressions created in the mind of the audience, would seem to pose a considerable challenge to the notions of continuity and regularity Goffman uses.

Goffman's contribution to interactionist theory, and thus to social theory in general, remains an open question. What we can say is that his work is very thought-provoking and does encourage us to continue thinking about whether detailed micro-level analysis can provide insights into the nature of the more general problems in social theory. Despite the very large amount of detail, there is, one might say, a lot of surface in Goffman's work and relatively little depth. Is the surface he describes thick enough to make a strong contribution to general theoretical issues?

Anticipating a line of analysis we will be exploring in detail in Chapter Nine, the integrity of social interaction, the fact that it is orderly and meaningful to social actors, seems to depend quite heavily on there being identifiable structures and rules that they can apply when trying to sort out reality. Sometimes these rules are linguistic, sometimes they are to do with shared or common cultural interpretations, and sometimes, as Goffman has identified, they are rules of social and symbolic performance.

The contribution of social interactionism to social theory

We have been looking at some of the strengths and weaknesses of the various contributions to interactionist social theory as we have gone along and so we need not repeat them here. We can, however, attempt a more general evaluation of the contribution of the interactionist perspective.

First, the interactionist movement, which developed at Chicago, shifted the balance of interest in social research away from general social theory of the kind being developed by Talcott Parsons and others at Harvard and towards a much more empirically grounded approach. This consolidated an intellectual division of labour between micro-level empirical investigations on the one hand, and macro-level abstract theorising on the other. The empirical and ethnographic approach sponsored by developments in social interactionism became progressively more and more oriented towards an applied, policy-oriented perspective. The advantage for social theory was that it gave theorists free rein to develop ideas and concepts independently of the need to devise specific hypotheses for empirical testing.

Second, the interactionist perspective highlighted the importance of seeing social action as dynamically embedded in the contexts where it takes place. In particular, it argued that the sense social actors have that events and experiences are significant for them is very much an effect of action in context. 'Meaning' should not therefore be seen as an independent property, which is added to the event like salt and pepper to a Sunday lunch, but as something that is actively created as social action unfolds. In this respect, the meaning of the action, and, to the extent that action is driven along by the quest for meaning, the motivation for acting, are not only socially constructed but very much at the moment when they occur. Adopting the pragmatic philosophical perspective of Charles Cooley and John Dewey, social interactionism supported the idea that meaning and purpose are closely tied to the practical outcomes that social actors aim to achieve.

This perspective becomes increasingly important in social theory during the 20th century because it provides support for the idea that social action is not driven along, as some elements in Enlightenment thinking suggested, by the quest for universal truths. Meaning is conceived in an essentially practical, rather than abstract, way. The anti-Enlightenment trend is keenly developed, particularly in post-structuralist and later in postmodernist social theory, which establish a conception of meaning and purpose as having no universal centre at all. It would be stretching the point to say that social interactionism provided a foundation for postmodernism, but they do tend to share an anti-Enlightenment conception of knowledge as relative rather than universal; as subjectively determined rather than objectively given.

Third, and clearly showing its grounding in the field of social psychology, social interactionist theory provides a multidimensional perspective on the nature of the human self. This is important for two reasons. First, it concentrates attention on the individual thus balancing out the obsession in general systems theory with structures and functions; it puts social actors at the centre of the analysis rather than the social systems that surround them. Second, it introduces the idea of the self as a dynamic entity that emerges out of a combination of psychological and experiential elements. This concept of the self as a 'reflexive project', a dynamic and creative undertaking, plays an important part in the thinking of **contemporary modernist** social theorists such as Anthony Giddens, whose work is discussed in Chapter Twelve.

Key points box – In this chapter we have looked at how:

☑ Social interactionists concentrate on gathering empirical data (rather than on 'theory') from actual events in context at the micro level of analysis (ethnography).

☑ Mead developed a notion of the self as comprising an inner core, or personal 'I', within an outer shell, or social 'me'.

☑ The self is profoundly social because the sense of 'I' only develops as a result of feedback social actors get from others about the 'me'.

☑ The meaning of social action is seen as being embedded in the interaction situation itself; meaning is not an external property that is added to the interaction from outside.

☑ The phenomenologist theorists Schutz and Garfinkel argue that 'meaning' must therefore be profoundly practical (common sense) rather than abstract.

☑ Social integration occurs because the sense of meaning actors have about sense-of-self, and the means of communicating it to others, are embedded in the social context.

☑ Even taking features of individual biography into account, the social context determines the kind of sense-of-self social actors can develop.

☑ Goffman develops a dramaturgical approach suggesting that actors 'perform' their sense-of-self to an audience.

☑ The self is thus shaped by the expectations both actor/ performer and audience have about what particular performances involve.

Practice box

⊃ Why do social interactionists concentrate on 'research' rather than on 'theory'?

⊃ George Herbert Mead sees the self as having two elements; what are they?

⊃ Why does Mead think that the self is a profoundly 'social' thing?

⊃ Give an example of how social actors develop a sense of who they are from other social actors

⊃ What role do Mead and Herbert Blumer think that 'symbolic communication' plays in social integration?

⊃ Which interactionist theorists introduced the idea of phenomenology?

⊃ How would you define phenomenology?

⊃ What is 'common' about common sense?

⊃ In what ways does Erving Goffman see the self as a performance?

⊃ What is the difference between the 'front stage' and the 'backstage' in Goffman's description of the self?

⊃ Outline briefly two main criticisms of Goffman's theory.

Further reading

Peter Berger and Thomas Luckmann, *The Social Construction of Reality* (Penguin, 1966).

Martin Bulmer, *The Chicago School* (University of Chicago Press, 1984).

Tom Burns, *Erving Goffman* (Routledge, 1992).

John Heritage, *Garfinkel and Ethnomethodology* (Polity Press, 1984).

Ken Plummer (ed) *Symbolic Interactionism*, 2 volumes (Edward Elgar, 1991).

Robert Prus, *Symbolic Interactionism and Ethnographic Approach* (State University of New York Press, 1996).

Roy Turner, *Ethnomethodology: Selected Readings* (Penguin, 1974).

Websites

There is no dedicated web-based resource for the Chicago School of sociology so the most positive internet search strategy is to use the search engines to look for references to 'The Chicago School'. Also use the sites listed at the end of Chapter Two including: www.Sociosite.net/topics/sociologists

An exhaustive list of scholars and philosophers in the tradition of phenomenology, including major figures discussed in this chapter such as Alfred Schutz and Harold Garfinkel, can be found at: www. phenomenologyonline.com/scholars

CHAPTER EIGHT

WESTERN MARXISM, ANTONIO GRAMSCI AND THE FRANKFURT SCHOOL

Chapters Seven and Eight on **functionalism** and **social interactionism** have described key developments in social theory that took place in North America in the first decades of the 20th century. Back in Europe meanwhile, which is where the foundations of modern social theory had been laid by August Comte, Émile Durkheim, Max Weber, Karl Marx and others, social theory had been taking a different path.

> ### In this chapter we will be looking at:
>
> Basic contrasts between Eastern and Western Marxism
>
> Lenin and Georg Lukács – ideology and false consciousness
>
> Antonio Gramsci and the concept of *hegemony*
>
> The Frankfurt School and critical theory
>
> Influence of critical theory on social theory

Basic contrasts between Eastern and Western Marxism

The development of modern society in Europe at the turn of the 20th century was taking place against a background of continuing rivalry between powerful nation-states vying for control over vital economic resources and colonial possessions. The intense political and subsequently military conflict that ensued, seemed to many observers on the political left to illustrate just the kind of crisis of modern capitalism that had been predicted by Karl Marx and Friedrich Engels a few years before. There was also strong evidence of increasing tension between the industrial working class and the capitalist class in all of the leading manufacturing economies of Europe including in Britain, Germany, France and Italy. Although still a vast and predominantly agricultural economy, which had yet to achieve levels of manufacturing typical of modern industry in Western Europe, tension was also evident in the emerging industrial centres of Russia. The various **socialist** parties and movements that emerged across Europe all drew inspiration from the work of Marx and Engels but there were some significant differences between them.

The most basic difference was between the Eastern or Soviet interpretation of Marx and the Western interpretation. Drawing on what it regarded as Marx's scientific theory of social change as set out in his great economic work *Das Kapital*, Soviet Marxism premised its analysis of modern society on the historical inevitability of revolutionary change. Leaders of revolutionary socialist and communist groups throughout Europe took literally Engels' exhortation that Marx had discovered the theory of the laws of motion of human history, a discovery that was just as significant as Darwin's theory of evolution by natural selection.

The key political development beyond Marx came from the great Bolshevik leader and hero of the Russian Revolution of 1917 Vladimir Illich Lenin (1870–1924). Lenin proposed that, especially in a country like Imperial Russia, the working class and the peasantry could not achieve full consciousness of the need for radical social change spontaneously, but needed to be brought to this scientific truth by a revolutionary political leadership. Following Lenin's death in 1924, and Joseph Stalin's takeover of the newly-emerged soviet leadership, the Communist Party became both in theory and in reality the prevailing force in Soviet Communism. The totalitarian regime in Soviet Eastern Europe, dominated by the Communist Party and supported by massively robust military forces, remained in power until the early 1980s.

In contrast to soviet or scientific Marxism, Marxists outside the Soviet Union took their inspiration from a different period of Marx's work. Broadly speaking, and without underestimating the variations and differences that persist within Western Marxism, it is the early philosophical Marx, the period of the *Paris Manuscripts* (1844) (see Marx, 1975) and the *German Ideology* (1991 [1845]), that provides the point of departure for their critique of modern capitalist society. Central to their thinking is the **humanist** conception of human nature as species-being and the concept of **alienation**, which are discussed in detail in Chapter Four.

Notwithstanding the fact, as all Marxists see it, that the exploitative character of capitalist industrial production is the root cause of oppression and conflict in modern society, Western Marxism emphasises the need to confront the intellectual and **ideological** forces of oppression that also provide support for capitalist regimes. The struggle for freedom from capitalist oppression needs to be fought among the hearts and minds of oppressed social actors and not just by mounting the barricades of direct confrontation. Advocates of this position tend to be unconvinced by the idea that social change can only be achieved by immediate violent revolution alone and argue for a more gradual concept of change. Real and lasting social change, so it is argued, is something that requires a range of tactics, including political reform of key aspects of currently-existing society and ideological countermeasures to undermine the perceived legitimacy of capitalist regimes. The final moment of revolution will eventually arrive (a moment that may or may not be violent), but its success depends on the gradual and reforming preparatory work that creates the final conditions for revolutionary change.

Lenin and Georg Lukács: ideology and false consciousness

Writing at a time when the potential for revolution seemed to have reached its peak, Lenin and Georg Lukács (1885–1971) were deeply concerned with the ways in which adverse ideological influences upon class consciousness might interrupt the revolutionary process. Lenin believed that the full development of class consciousness could only be achieved if the industrial working class or proletariat developed a distinctive ideology and political consciousness of its own. He also recognised that in the West, bourgeois ideology represented a powerful force that acted directly against this possibility. The extent of this influence was in proportion to the fact that the middle classes or bourgeoisie not only had access to far greater resources with which to propagate their world view, but were also much better organised: 'Bourgeois ideology is far older in origin than socialist ideology, it is more fully developed and has at its disposal immeasurably more means of dissemination' (Lenin, 1947, p 42). He was therefore very doubtful that the proletariat would be able to develop an alternative ideology 'spontaneously' as Marx had suggested, and even if it was able to, thought that this ideology would be contaminated and thus weakened by aspects of bourgeois ideology, albeit in residual form: 'There is much talk of spontaneity. But the spontaneous development of the working-class movement leads to its subordination to bourgeois ideology ... for the spontaneous working-class movement is trade-unionism ... and trade-unionism means the ideological enslavement of the workers by the bourgeoisie' (Lenin, 1947, p 41).

Having identified the limitations of spontaneous consciousness Lenin goes on to develop the idea of a 'political and theoretical form of consciousness', which is 'developed by intellectuals outside the spontaneous movement of the class' (Larrain, 1983, p 65). This higher consciousness would be brought to them by an intellectual revolutionary vanguard who would enlighten the working class and so nurture a truly alternative proletarian ideology. The intellectual vanguard thus emerges as the agency through which the working class can pursue the ideological and political struggle.

Reflecting Lenin's concern that the new ideology might be contaminated as a result of the bourgeois milieu within which it develops, the Hungarian Marxist social theorist Georg Lukács suggested that one of the means by which bourgeois ideology is propagated within the consciousness of the proletariat is through the device of substituting a false and incomplete account of social reality for a real and complete understanding. He therefore advocates the development of a holistic or all-inclusive description and critique of social reality in order to neutralise and ultimately reverse the development of what he famously refers to a **false consciousness**. True class consciousness can only be developed by a united class; a class acting for itself as a class rather than as an assembly of associated groups or craft-based unions.

Having argued that a holistic conception is essential at the level of critical theory and consciousness, Lukács suggests that in terms of practical strategy it is not possible to dissolve bourgeois ideology, achieve true consciousness and engage in revolutionary practice in a single spontaneous outburst:'The self education of the proletariat is a lengthy and difficult process by which it becomes "ripe" for revolution, and the more highly developed capitalism and bourgeois culture are in the country, the more arduous this process becomes because the proletariat becomes infected by the life-forms of capitalism' (Lukács, 1968, p 264).

Achieving true consciousness must depend upon the prior development of an alternative conception of the world, a proletarian world view that can reveal the real and fundamental contradictions of working and living within capitalist society. As long as this new world view is based upon universal concerns, and as long as these concerns are expressed by a united class, the limitations and self-defeating tendencies of false trade union consciousness can also be overcome. Once the revolutionary process is under way, the practical experience of a socialist alternative to capitalism will lead to a greater understanding and appreciation of the new world view, the legitimacy of which will be correspondingly enhanced.

Taken together, Lenin's recognition of the significance of the struggle within the political sphere between alternative ideologies, and Lukács's concerns over false consciousness, establish a new paradigm in the Marxist analysis of social change centred around a set of closely related issues:

■ the significance of ideas and their combination in the form of ideologies;

■ the origins, development and propagation of ideas and the ways in which they become materialised through practice;

■ the role of intellectuals as the practitioners of a new universal and positive ideology and the means by which they can or cannot convey their perceptions of reality to other members of society; and

■ the probability that radical social change can only be achieved with the prior formation of an alternative world view.

Antonio Gramsci and the concept of *hegemony*

Much of the social theory of the Italian Marxist Antonio Gramsci (1891–1937) is an attempt to develop a revised strategy for revolutionary social change that takes these new considerations fully into account. He moves the new paradigm of intellectual and ideological persuasion forward by introducing the concept of **hegemony** (a term that he takes from Lenin [*gegemoniya*] who uses it to refer to the universal world view that is necessary for full class consciousness) to describe the unifying conception of the world that any social group must have if it is to gain power and hold on to it.

Gramsci begins by arguing that although the concept of ideology has been used by Marx and others in a generally pejorative and negative way to describe 'the arbitrary elucubrations of particular individuals', the concept of ideology can be viewed in a more positive light as an intellectual and cultural force that helps the development of a sense of solidarity around shared beliefs and adherence to a new collective world view. Gramsci defines these as 'historically organic ideologies ... which are necessary to a given structure' and therefore have 'a validity which is "psychological"; they "organise" human masses and create the terrain on which men move, acquire consciousness of their position, struggle, etc' (Gramsci, 1971, pp 376–7).

Organic development

We can note three basic characteristics of hegemony. First, hegemony is an organic phenomenon that continues to develop as circumstances change. Hegemony is not a metaphysical force or spirit lying beyond the control of social actors, but is actively created, maintained and reproduced by them. Hegemony describes a grounded process of conscious intellectual reflection and synthesis, which leads to a greater understanding of material reality and to the development of a new form of political strategy and action. In this sense hegemony is a form of praxis, a realisation through action of conscious, critical self-reflection.

Force and consent

Second, Gramsci sees hegemony as a kind of 'intellectual and moral unity' that provides the essential ideological glue required for holding emergent social groups together. Although necessary for group solidarity, ideological coherence is not, however, sufficient to bring about social change. For this to happen, the emerging group or new alliance or 'historical bloc', as Gramsci calls it, must also exercise more traditional forms of direct economic and political control:

KEY QUOTE – Gramsci, *Selections from the Prison Notebooks* (1971). The methodological criterion on which our own study must be based is the following: that the supremacy of a social group manifests itself in two ways, as 'domination' and as 'intellectual and moral leadership'. A social group dominates antagonistic groups, which it tends to 'liquidate' or to subjugate perhaps even by armed force; it leads kindred and allied groups. A social group can and indeed must already exercise 'leadership' before winning governmental power (this indeed is one of the principal conditions for the winning of such power); it subsequently becomes dominant when it exercises power, but even if it holds it firmly in its grasp it must continue to 'lead' as well. (Gramsci, 1971, pp 57–8)

There is therefore a dialectical strategy available to the dominant group in society. Either it can use direct physical force to overcome its opponents, or it can gain support, as it were, voluntarily by persuading oppositional groups to accept and assimilate the norms and values of its own prevailing world view. Hegemony can be defined in terms of these positive aspects of social control.

Third, leadership does not emerge spontaneously but has to be actively created. If a social group is to be successful in its aims, it must exercise leadership before the critical moment of social upheaval. The extent to which it can lead depends upon the extent to which it is genuinely representative of a cohesive and purposeful alliance, or 'historical bloc', of social groups and their aspirations. Furthermore, an emergent historical bloc will only be able to take power once it has developed a universal perspective that transcends the particular self-interests of its component parts. Although the interests of the various groups that make up the new alliance are principally concerned with structural or 'economic-corporate issues', as Gramsci calls them, these concerns will inevitably be reflected in the political and moral spheres. The new political and moral leadership must recognise, and be prepared to engage with, practical and ideational issues within both the economic structure and the political superstructure.

War of position and war of manoeuvre

Recalling the tumultuous political and economic circumstances in which Lenin, Lukács and Gramsci were working at the start of the 20th century, Gramsci is constantly preoccupied with how or whether the successful revolution in Russia might spread across Western Europe. Before Stalin adopted a policy of 'socialism in one country', many Marxists followed Leon Trotsky's (1879–1940) theory of permanent revolution, which simply asserted that the Russian revolution signalled the beginning of a domino effect in which capitalist leaderships throughout the world would collapse. World Communism would develop like an irresistible political-economic tsunami. Being an enthusiastic student of history, however, Gramsci soon realised that this was unlikely. The failure of the German and Hungarian Communists to mount a revolution of this kind in 1919 and 1921, despite the massive trauma of the First World War of 1914–1918 *and* the fact they had the Russian example to follow, confirmed the truth of this observation. Gramsci therefore became one of the main advocates of the need for a new strategy, and much of his later writing is devoted to this problem: 'In war it would sometimes happen that a fierce artillery attack seemed to have destroyed the enemy's entire defensive system, whereas in fact it had only destroyed the outer perimeter; and at the moment of their advance and attack the assailants would find themselves confronted by a line of defence which was still effective' (Gramsci, 1971, p 235).

Gramsci thus distinguishes between two distinct strategies or phases of revolutionary action. First, an all-out frontal attack, or 'war of manoeuvre', designed to take control of society in one move by overthrowing the coercive agencies of the state and its military forces in particular. Coercive force is needed to counter coercive force. Second, a more gradual and subversive 'war of position', whose object is the progressive undermining of the 'trench systems', 'earthworks' and 'permanent fortifications' of civil society. Since the control exercised by these civil institutions is primarily consensual, they must be tackled in and on their own terms through ideological and political 'attack'. The choice between these two tactics is determined by the institutional complexity of the society over which control is being sought. If, as in Tsarist Russia in 1917, the institutions of civil society are 'primordial and gelatinous', a war of manoeuvre is appropriate. In societies where civil institutions and the democratic structure in particular are well-established, a war of position is appropriate, at least in the first instance, since the defences of the state merely constitute an outer ditch.

Having made this distinction between two types of revolutionary practice, Gramsci warns that waging a war of position, a 'passive revolution', will be particularly arduous: 'The war of position demands enormous sacrifices by infinite masses of people, so an unprecedented concentration of hegemony is necessary' (Gramsci, 1971, p 238). War of manoeuvre and war of position are two phases of the revolutionary struggle that will vary according to the particular combination of economic, political and ideological forces that are in play.

In summarising Gramsci's contribution, we can identify three key aspects of the concepts of power and social order associated with his concept of hegemony. First, and in relation to the concept of historical bloc, Gramsci emphasises that the successful overthrow of one social group or class by another (in this context of the bourgeoisie by the proletariat), depends upon the prior formation of solidarity both within that social group itself, and between it and other sympathetic groups. Most importantly, the new historical bloc must transcend the particular interests of its component parts and establish a new and universal world view. In order to win the support of the population at large, that is to say, of other groups who are not initially part of the alliance, the emergent social group must give leadership and direction before, during and after the crucial moment of frontal attack. When these conditions are fulfilled the new social group can be said to be hegemonic. The extent to which the revolution is likely to succeed, and more importantly to last, is the extent to which hegemony has been achieved. Although Gramsci argues that social order in modern society tends towards the hegemonic form, the relationship between hegemony and historical bloc remains problematic since society inevitably produces a whole series of economic and political alliances based upon mutual interest, only very few of which will actually become dominant. It is the requirement for historical blocs to be genuinely hegemonic that separates the truly successful from the rest.

Second, he uses the concept of hegemony to describe the various modes of social control available to the dominant social group. He distinguishes between coercive control, which is manifest through direct force or the threat of force, and consensual control, which arises when individuals 'willingly' or 'voluntarily' assimilate the world view or hegemony of the dominant group; an assimilation that allows that group to be hegemonic. He then goes on to discuss the institutions and practices through which these two basic forms of control operate. In their purest form, coercion is exercised physically through the repressive institutions of the state, most notably the army, police and penal system, while consent is exercised intellectually through the institutions of civil society such as the Church, the education system and the family. Most importantly, however, Gramsci recognises that all institutions have both a material and ideational impact upon individuals, and therefore that, in reality, coercion and consent tend to combine. The association of coercion with the state and of consent with civil institutions, in other words, is ideal rather than absolute.

Third, and having emphasised that the bourgeoisie in modern democratic Western society maintains power primarily through consensual or hegemonic control, Gramsci argues that a challenge to their power must, at least in the first instance, take place on the political and intellectual terrain of both the structure and the superstructure. He therefore proposes that the emergent group should wage a war of position aimed both at freeing individuals' minds from the distortions of bourgeois ideology through a process of hegemonic critique, and at freeing their bodies from the contradictory practices of bourgeois society through the gradual subversion of these practices. Once these positions have been won, and once the new hegemony has been established, the earlier tactic of frontal attack can be used to achieve the final and, if necessary, violent overthrow of the bourgeoisie's military defences. For Gramsci, the formation of an emergent historical bloc based upon an effective and realistic counter-hegemony constitutes, in the context of the evident relapse in the proletarian struggle after 1917, the only feasible strategy for revolutionary practice.

The Frankfurt School and critical theory

The widespread feeling on the political left in Europe from the 1930s to the 1950s was that the emergence of fascism in Germany, Spain and Italy, of totalitarian communism under Stalin in the Soviet Union, together with global conflict from 1939 to 1945, signalled decisively that the moment of socialist revolution had passed. In reaction to this many turned away entirely from direct involvement with workers' movements and socialist political parties and put their efforts instead into ideology critique. The lines of political engagement had shifted away from debates about revolutionary strategy and mobilisation and towards an entirely intellectual strategy of exposing the negative ideology of capitalism; an ideology that Lenin, Lukács and Gramsci had all recognised blocked the way for a true rather than false understanding of its exploitative nature. Freedom from capitalist oppression required a thorough intellectual analysis of the ideological and cultural superstructures of modern society.

Taking a lead in this change in direction in Western Marxism was a group of academic theorists based in the Frankfurt Institute for Social Research, which first opened in 1923. Max Horkheimer (1895–1973) became Director in 1930 and other leading members were the musicologist and theorist Theodore Adorno (1903–78) and the cultural theorist Herbert Marcuse (1898–1978). The rise of Nazism forced members of the Institute to leave Germany and they carried on their work in exile at Columbia University, New York State, from 1931 to 1947. The Institute relocated to Frankfurt in 1947 although some of its members remained in America. In their general theoretical orientation the group was influenced especially by Marx's early philosophical writings, and by Lukács's development from Marx of the concepts of praxis (the realisation through action of creative human essence) and reification (the tendency for human subjects to become objects or 'things' within capitalist society). They also drew on the work of the Hungarian theorist Karl Mannheim (1893–1947) (who was himself influenced by Georg Simmel [1858–1918] and Max Weber [1864–1920]), and his ideas about the crucial role of intellectuals in historical change. Sigmund Freud's work in psychoanalytic theory also influenced the ideas of Frankfurt-School associates like Eric Fromm (1900–80). Marcuse's book, *Eros and Civilization* (1955), for example, attempted a fusion of Marx and Freud.

Although the initial activity of the Institute was to develop studies of the economic and cultural experiences of the German working class, under Horkheimer's direction the work of the Institute became increasingly philosophical and theoretical in nature and was concerned exclusively with the cultural and aesthetic dimensions of social experience. Using Marx's characterisation of society as base and superstructure (see Chapter Four), the focus of research moved 'up' from the socio-economic milieu of the economic base and to the 'higher' cultural milieu of the superstructure. Debates about revolutionary strategy were recast as debates over how to expose the negative ideology of capitalism and its dehumanising culture. Having turned away from practical politics and towards intellectual reflection, however, much of the work produced by members of the Frankfurt School offers a pessimistic and despairing reading of the prospects of emancipation.

Although the Frankfurt School laid the foundations for the later development of popular disciplines in social and cultural studies, and critical media studies, many of their own writings are complex and challenging to read. According to Adorno the arduous intellectual struggle that is necessary for getting to grips with the aesthetic experience of cultural forms is itself part of the process of re-enlightenment. His major philosophical work, *Negative Dialectics* (1973 [1966]), for example, makes major demands of the reader both in terms of prior knowledge and in terms of its literary style. Despite Adorno's strictures, in the following sections we look superficially at two leading themes in Frankfurt-School thinking, themes that have given Western Marxism its distinctive character. First is its critical orientation and, second, the idea of anti-enlightenment characteristic of mass society.

Critical theory

In a defining essay called 'Traditional and critical theory' (1972 [1937]), Horkheimer emphasises that the analytical work produced by the Institute would be thoroughly critical (hence 'critical theory') in the sense that it assumed from the outset that, within capitalist society, the outward appearance of phenomena inherently disguises their inner essence. It might appear that capitalism produces economic wealth but in essence, as Marx had pointed out (see Chapter Four), profit is a measure of exploitation at work. Profit signifies the immiseration of the worker both in material terms, since he is not properly paid for the labour he performs, but also, and perhaps more significantly, in personal terms, as he becomes alienated from his inner social and creative nature. In the intellectual domain also, Horkheimer argued, capitalist society was permeated by traditional theory, which merely served to legitimate the status quo. Standing in opposition to traditional theory, critical theory, in contrast, strives to imagine alternatives, to find new ways of getting beyond traditional theory in order to look back at social reality with fresh eyes. Critical theory thus presupposes the possibility of emancipation as a basic characteristic of ideology critique.

From the point of view of developments in social theory, the key question being addressed by critical theory here is which social actors are in a position to be able to tell the difference between the false view and the real view of society? Clearly there is no shortage of alternatives so how does one tell which is the right one? As we have seen, Lukács had argued that it was the industrial proletariat that occupied the highly privileged historical position of having true rather than false consciousness. This optimism is not shared by Horkheimer who argues that precisely because of the oppressed position they occupy in the social structure, the working class are least likely to be able to see beyond their own immediate situation. They are intellectually disabled by the overpowering reality of their day-to-day lives.

If not the proletariat, then who? One possibility is found in the work of Karl Mannheim who, in a collection of essays called *Ideology and Utopia* (1936 [1929]), suggested that the processes of modernisation and industrialisation produced a strata of 'free-floating intellectuals' who are sufficiently detached from particular class interests that they are able to produce a more independent, truthful and insightful account of social reality. Mannheim argues that the intellectual strata operate as informed observers of society and have the capacity to identify which ideas and values in circulation at any particular historical moment are helpful in the search for general or universal 'truth'. Unfortunately, however, and expressing the now familiar pessimism, Mannheim concluded that even though the emancipatory utopianism of intellectuals in the period of revolt against capitalism was potentially much more positive and enlightened than bourgeois ideology, it could never break free from the actual historical circumstances that gave rise to it. The emancipatory potential of an independent-minded intelligentsia is continually thwarted because proper knowledge of events can only become known after they have occurred. There is no possibility in Mannheim's scheme for intellectuals (or anyone else for that matter) to get sufficiently ahead of events in order to make a real difference to how things turn out.

Although Horkheimer rejected the historicist implication in Mannheim's analysis that particular ways of seeing the world, particular styles of thought, are fundamentally constrained by the historical period where they occur, he agreed with the general idea that intellectuals play a crucial role in, and are primary bearers of, critical awareness. Reasserting the linkage between experience and knowledge, critical theory offers a pragmatic view of knowledge as something that emerges from direct experience. This is quite different from the **positivistic** or scientistic view of knowledge, which views knowledge as something that exists independently of subjective experience and that social actors 'come to know' through observation and experimentation. Standing against the positivist view of knowledge and the instrumental rationality that it serves to legitimise, critical theory emphasises the socially constructed nature of knowledge. This view of critical knowledge also recognises the significance of the **hermeneutic** dimension of knowledge-construction, meaning that all knowledge involves a process of interpretation. Knowledge cannot be insulated from the mind of the knower, a mind that is already saturated with ideas and experiences.

Linking the idea of critical knowledge with the idea of enlightenment and emancipation, Horkheimer goes further and argues that the particular interpretation of knowledge as instrumental positive science put forward by the gainers in capitalist society is not at all motivated (as perhaps the quest for knowledge ought to be) by a desire genuinely to know social reality in the interests of the common good, but is a particular (and thus false) interpretation serving only the interests of the bourgeoisie. Maintaining this façade of respectable knowledge also means suppressing the emergence of alternative views of knowledge, including the critical version offered by critical theory. Becoming properly aware of this situation is a crucial first step in moving outside the false paradigm of bourgeois theory. Critical theory thus begins with the problematic nature of the role of intellectuals in the class struggle already identified by Lenin, Lukács and Gramsci, but goes a stage further and develops an analysis of the competing forms of knowledge that are at stake in the struggle for freedom in modern society. Ideology critique becomes a major preoccupation for critical theorists because in developing the new form of knowledge produced by critical theory they also have to offer a systematic critique of bourgeois ideology that has itself been deployed to disguise the partial and false character of instrumental rationality.

Mass society and anti-enlightenment

One of the most influential contributions of Frankfurt-School thinking to social theory is the suggestion that modern society is inherently anti-enlightening because of the way it suppresses alternative definitions of knowledge and views of social reality. The domination of the imagination in modern society by positivist definitions of knowledge and of instrumentalist definitions of rationality seriously inhibit the development of alternative views. In their influential treatise *The Dialectic of Enlightenment* (1972 [1947]), Horkheimer and Adorno apply the principles of critical theory in trying to understand how it is that capitalism is able to insulate itself intellectually and culturally from what seems to be the perpetual threat of its own collapse. The answer, they suggest, is that modern society has become suffused with a form of compliance culture in which the *status quo* is accepted as entirely legitimate and inevitable. The majority of social actors in modern society are, so it is argued, rapidly losing their capacity for independent critical discourse. In Gramsci's terminology, it seemed as though the capitalist regimes of the world had become so thoroughly hegemonic, had achieved such high levels of willing compliance with the norms and values of capitalism, that the possibility of opposition was being entirely lost.

Central to this argument is the idea of anti-enlightenment, which suggests that the free space required for intellectual and cultural reflection in and about modern society has been progressively closed off. Referring again to the important role of an independent intelligentsia, Horkheimer and Adorno suggest that whereas the ideas of the European Enlightenment had been driven forward during the 18th and 19th centuries by free-thinking, well-educated, often independent, professionals and intellectuals, the subsequent development of capitalism and of instrumental rationality into the 20th century had resulted in further and more thorough incorporation of these groups into the mainstream. The continuing **rationalisation** of modern institutions and administrative structures (see the discussion of Max Weber's ideas in Chapter Five), especially their professionalisation and bureaucratisation, also served to reduce the space for free and critical thought. These changes are structural in the sense that, following Weber's analysis, instrumentalism and rationality have become fundamental precepts of social action in modern society. Not only, then, was the process of enlightenment through critical social knowledge being hindered in modern capitalist society, but the whole process was shifting into reverse; social actors were becoming *less* critically aware, *less* able to pursue the quest for full and thorough knowledge of social reality.

Praxis

There is a clear continuity here between critical theory and the idea of **praxis** used by Gramsci and especially by Lukács. Originating with Marx, this is the idea that the essence of human-beingness becomes manifest at the moment when ideas are translated into action. Despite a superficial resemblance, whereas instrumental rationality is a linear process where means are devised for achieving particular ends, praxis describes a much more experiential and multidimensional instant in which thought and action become, even if only momentarily, united. The moment of praxis is the moment at which social actors experience the real vitality of their lives; when essence and appearance genuinely coincide. Marx's theory of alienation (see Chapter Four) is essentially an analysis of the negative consequences that arise when this fundamental creative process is interrupted. Although in his later writings Marx applies himself to showing how the capitalist labour process is inherently alienating, Horkheimer and Adorno follow Lukács in using the concept of praxis to describe how other domains of social experience (for example the development of class consciousness) are seriously inhibited in capitalist society.

Culture industry

Applying these ideas to cultural experience, for example, and drawing on parallel ideas developed by Walter Benjamin, Adorno and Horkheimer argue that the unimaginative routines of repetitive working, and the banal commodities that are produced, create a kind of aesthetic alienation where art and culture are stripped of their critical potential. Like bars of soap, the culture industry manufactures cultural artefacts for mass consumption. If there is no variety there can be no sense of contrast, and if there is no sense of contrast, then concepts of difference and opposition cannot develop. For Marx, much of the negativity (alienation, anti-enlightenment) that is so characteristic of capitalism relates to the way in which relations between social actors and what they produce, and between one social actor and another, are treated as if they were merely relations between things. This process of **reification** tends to accelerate in societies of mass production and mass consumption because everything appears to be available as one or another form of commodity. Other criteria that might be used for assessing the value of things, such as usefulness and creative potential, are disregarded in favour of the single abstract criteria of **exchange value**.

From their vantage point as foreign observers of the developing mass-consumer culture in American society during the 1930s and 1940s, Horkheimer and Adorno noted how, in what is perhaps the most blatant example of appearance masquerading as essence, the enjoyments of consumption served to distract attention from the inequalities of industrial work in capitalist society. Capitalists literally buy the consent of workers by tantalising them with an ever-increasing range of consumer goods. Mediating between production and consumption, a host of new occupations arose in the first decades of the 20th century in product design, marketing and advertising with the specific purpose of persuading workers to become consumers. Horkheimer and Adorno soon concluded that mass-produced popular culture consolidates the general condition of anti-enlightenment in modern society. It is yet another of the conditions of living that closes off critical space. Mass-produced ideas and mass-produced ideology ensured compliance not resistance.

Influence of critical theory on social theory

The Frankfurt School played an important part in the development of a Western alternative to the state-sanctioned interpretation of Marx that characterised the largely totalitarian regime of the Soviet Union from the 1920s to the 1980s. Despite the highly pessimistic tone of much of their work, and their abandonment of practical political action, these theorists suggested some new directions for theoretical critique. First, they strongly promoted the idea that social theory cannot do without its critical dimension. Understanding social reality means getting beneath the surface of things in order to reveal discrepancies between appearance and actuality and to discern elements of social reality that can lead to the transformation of that reality. Although Adorno's negative dialectics express his own conviction that such a process has virtually come to an end in modern mass-produced consumer capitalism, the very fact that he is able to make the point offers hope that alternative views can still be developed.

Second, up to a point, the Frankfurt School instigated a technique of conceptual leverage within Western Marxism in the sense that they legitimated the use of some basic Marxian concepts like alienation, reification and praxis for the purposes of ideology critique, rather than using them in the traditional way as tools of revolutionary strategy. This process of adopting established concepts in Marxian social theory and refining them for new purposes is also a feature of post-structuralist and postmodernist styles of theory-building (for example Jean Baudrillard and Jean-Francois Lyotard, see Chapter Thirteen), which use their revolutionary potential not in order to mobilise the revolution, but to revolutionise perceptions of social reality itself.

Third, and although the Frankfurt School tends to work in a relatively abstract rather than grounded dimension, it nonetheless produced an early version of the mass-society thesis, which identifies some novel features of modern society as it enters is consumption-oriented phase. In this sense, Adorno and Horkheimer, and certainly Herbert Marcuse in his influential book *One Dimensional Man* (1964), base their analysis on some careful, almost empirical, observations of the changing nature of social reality. They express themselves philosophically, but the subject matter is not exclusively abstract. One important aspect of this, and one that has had an important influence on the development of the academic study of popular culture, is an acknowledgement of the role of the mass media in crafting public opinion. Ideology critique now includes the instruments of transmission as well as the content of the message. The shifting of ideology critique into the universities has resulted in very little in the way of revolutionary planning, but it has outlined a new paradigm, an alternative and critical perspective from which to explore social action in modern society.

Key points box – In this chapter we have looked at:

☑ How Soviet and Western Marxism developed in different directions during the 20th century.
☑ Lenin's theory of the revolutionary role of the intellectual vanguard.
☑ Lukács's distinction between true and false class consciousness.
☑ Gramsci's concept of hegemony as a form of political and ideological alliance requiring both force and consent.
☑ Gramsci's ideas about the difference between a war of manoeuvre and a war of position in political strategy.
☑ The development of the Frankfurt School and its ideas of critical theory, anti-enlightenment and the mass-society thesis.

Practice box

➲ What were the key historical events that resulted in the development of Soviet Marxism?
➲ Why did Western Marxism turn away from revolutionary action and towards ideology critique?
➲ What is the difference between 'true' and 'false' class consciousness?
➲ What were the key elements in Gramsci's political strategy?
➲ What is 'critical' about critical theory?
➲ What are the main features of the 'mass-society thesis'?

Further reading

Stephen Bronner and Douglas Kellner (eds), *Politics, Culture and Society: A Critical Theory Reader* (Routledge, 1989).

Antonio Gramsci, *Selections from the Prison Notebooks* (Lawrence and Wishart, 1971).

David Held, *Introduction to Critical Theory* (Polity Press, 1990).

Martin Jay, *The Dialectical Imagination: A History of the Frankfurt School and the Institute of Social Research, 1923–1950* (Heinemann, 1973); and *Adorno* (Harvard University Press, 1984).

Douglas Kellner, *Critical Theory, Marxism and Modernity* (Macmillan, 1989).

Leszek Kolakowski, *Main Currents in Marxism*, 3 volumes (Oxford University Press, 1981).

Jorge Larrain, *The Concept of Ideology* (Hutchinson, 1979); and *Marxism and Ideology* (Macmillan, 1983).

Vladmir Ilych Lenin, *What is to be Done?* (Progress Publishers, 1947 [1901/02]).

Paul Ransome, *Antonio Gramsci: A New Introduction* (Harvester Wheatsheaf, 1992).

Websites

A comprehensive range of material on Georg Lukács, Antonio Gramsci and the Frankfurt School and its members can be found within the vast Marxism resource: www.marxists.org/subject/frankfurt-school/index.htm

For detailed historical material on the formation by Lenin of the Third International or Comintern in Moscow in 1919 see: www.marxists.org/history/international/comintern

CHAPTER NINE

LANGUAGE, STRUCTURE, MEANING

Whether we choose to define reality as a series of small-scale or **micro** events, or as a large-scale or **macro** entity into which everything can eventually be fitted, and whether we emphasise the objective or subjective dimensions of knowledge and experience, we are still faced with the major problem of how, as social theorists, we are able to produce reliable and intelligible accounts of that reality. In many ways running parallel to the kinds of issues raised by interpretivist and **constructivist** social theorists in Chicago during the first decades of the 20th century (see Chapter Seven), theorists working in Europe were developing new ideas about how our descriptions of reality are crucially dependent on the language we use to compose and communicate those accounts. Also at this time, and reflecting some of the ideas associated with Parsons, Merton and the functionalist tradition at Harvard University (see Chapter Six), there was renewed interest in studying society in terms of structure. Although these two areas of interest (language and structure) are not identical, the overlap between them attracted much attention among social theorists. The essential reason for this was that language itself is highly structured; it provides a powerful illustration of, and possible justification for, the argument that the parts do in fact mean very little unless one also has a conception of the whole.

There are a number of strands to this important change of direction or 'linguistic turn' in social theory. This chapter describes these strands and looks at a number of individual contributions to the debates that surrounded them. It also looks briefly at **post-structuralist** ideas and their accompanying concern with culture and **meaning** ('the 'hermeneutic turn').

In this chapter we will be looking at:

The 'linguistic turn' in social theory during the early 20th century

Language and meaning (Ferdinand de Saussure, Ludwig Wittgenstein and Peter Winch)

The concept of **structure** in social theory

Structure and the emergence of **structuralism**

Claude Lévi-Strauss and the structuring of culture

Sigmund Freud, Jacques Lacan and the structuring of the conscious mind

Louis Althusser and the decentring of the subject

Some limitations of first-wave structuralism

The linguistic turn in social theory during the early 20th century

The linguistic turn in social theory came about as a result of increasing awareness of the role of language in how social actors see the world. It is very difficult to think of how actors can build up mental representations of reality, to describe and make sense of it, if they do not have the words to do so. This would be a bit like trying to paint a picture without paints or to play a tune without notes. A number of important consequences can be identified here.

Self-awareness

Language is essential to the processes through which social actors develop a sense-of-self. Much of the internal conversation actors have with themselves (between the 'I' and the 'me' in Mead's theory) relies on the human capacity for language. A sense of biography, for example, the personal story of how an actor came to be as they are, includes sensations and mental images, but it also relies heavily on being able to give a narrative account of the life experience. Without language there can be no narrative. Without narrative there can be no biography.

Communication

At the heart of language is the intention of conveying a sense of meaning to others. There is almost universal recognition, for example, of common gestures like waving, beckoning and pointing. There is also a widely shared set of facial expressions like staring, smiling and frowning that, in their basic forms at least, are easily interpreted. Language represents a major advance on these more basic forms by providing a distinct set of signs and symbols, or 'vocal gestures' as Mead calls them, which, once the rules and conventions belonging to the set have been learned, can be used to communicate. In an important sense knowledge and communication at anything other than a very rudimentary level are impossible *without* language.

Social integration

In each of the above respects language has the effect of integrating people into society. The language social actors use during their internal conversations is socially constructed and as such it uses ideas and concepts that have been communally produced within society. The integrative capacity of language is also emphasised by Herbert Blumer in his theory of **symbolic interactionism**, and his strong suggestion not only that people use the same kinds of symbolic tokens when they communicate through language (language is a form of common currency), but also that they tend to *interpret* them in the same way (see Chapter Seven).

Decision making

Language is also key to Schutz's and Garfinkel's conception that people tend to resolve day-to-day decisions through the rather phlegmatic application of common-sense reasoning. Most of the time, most conversations are fairly simple constructions using plain language and avoiding unnecessary jargon and detail. This is likely to be quite distinct from the more specialist language used, for example, by social theorists who are not using language to arrive at practical solutions in quite the same way. This is why social actors often feel excluded or locked out of the conversation if those around them, for example lawyers or medical professionals, are using obscure words that they do not understand. Language thus integrates social actors when they search for their own sense-of-self, as a shared medium for communicating and as a key purveyor of shared norms and values in society.

Language and structure

In addition to what we might call the practical uses of language for communicating meaning and integration (i.e. what language *does*), 'language' is also of interest to social theorists as a social phenomenon *in itself* because it is an ideal example of a socially-constructed phenomenon that is highly structured. There are two key features here. First, language is not generally random and superfluous, but is a deliberate, organised and systematic undertaking. Language is integral to many, if not all, necessary cooperative tasks. Second, successful communication depends on members of the language community being aware of and prepared to use the various rules and conventions associated with language. Language provides a highly versatile means of communicating, but is itself highly structured and rule-governed.

Language and meaning

Ferdinand de Saussure and the science of signs

Discovering the sign

One of the first European intellectuals to develop a distinctly modern approach to the study of language was the Swiss-French philosopher of language, or theoretical linguist, Ferdinand de Saussure (1857–1913). He was among the first to characterise language as being much more than a useful historical inheritance that enabled social actors to speak to each other. His most important book, *Course in General Linguistics*, based on his university lectures, was published two years after his death in 1915. Saussure's main claim to fame was to establish **semiotics**, 'the science of signs', as a distinct aspect of the study of language or linguistics. For Saussure, language is most usefully regarded not as a kind of linguistic mirror for representing the world, but as a system of **signs**. We use signs as a way of referring to objects in the real world (or **referents** as philosophers usually call them). Looking more closely at the sign itself (typically a particular word although, as we shall see shortly when we look at the work of Roland Barthes, there are other kinds of signs as well), Saussure noted that each sign is made up of two closely linked elements. The first is the **signified**, which is the mental or cognitive image we have in our heads of the thing or object being referred to. The second is the **signifier**, which is a particular combination of vocal sounds or written characters that is used to represent the object. The two aspects of the sign, the signified/signifier, form one entity. Signifiers cannot exist without their signifieds; a non-expressed signifier would simply be a blank page or silence. Written words and sounds give the otherwise abstract mental or cognitive entity 'language' its own material form.

It is important to be quite clear that in Saussure's science of signs, the sign is *not the same as* the real object. Signifieds are different from referents (i.e. the things that they refer to). In the sign–system, signs simply *stand for* the objects to which they are conventionally attached in a particular language. When I write the word 'motorcycle', for example, the entity that has just come into your mind is obviously not actually a motorcycle, but your mental image of one. If you have no knowledge of the object called 'motorcycle' then equally obviously you are now wondering what on earth I am writing about!

The arbitrary properties of signs

Returning to our discussion of language as a way of describing the world 'out there', although we can reasonably presume that signifiers would not exist if there were not a concrete something that needed signifying (it is surprisingly difficult to invent a word for an object that does not exist), it is precisely the possibility of slippage between the real object 'out there' and the word–sign social actors use to capture a sense of it in their minds that drew Saussure towards his most innovative observation about the nature of language. This is the highly *symbolic* nature of human language. What this means is that the word–signs actors use, either in their written form or as vocal sounds, are *arbitrary* in the sense that they have no necessary, and certainly no physical, relationship with the real objects, concepts, feelings and so on to which they are attached. For example, speakers of the English language have got used to the idea that the word–sign or signified/signifier 'cat' refers to a species of furry mammals, some of which live wild and hunt in the jungle, and some of which we keep in our own homes as companion animals. However, the association we make between this animal and the letters that make up the word–sign 'cat', and the vocal sounds we make when we say 'cat', is merely a linguistic convention. There is no actual 'catishness' in the word 'cat'. Although, as we shall see shortly, differences in the words used to represent 'cats' in different languages might mean that the French view of these animals cannot be identical with the Welsh or Cantonese view precisely because they use different words, the fact that more than one word–sign is available to represent the entity 'cat' confirms that the connection between the animal and the word is indeed arbitrary.

Relations between signs

Looking a little more closely at the interior structure of language itself, and bearing in mind what we have just said about the arbitrary nature of the relationship between word–signs and the real objects that they represent, Saussure went on to argue that word–signs only become significant when considered in relation *to other* word–signs. Although, in other words, word–signs are arbitrary in respect of objects in the real world, they are *not* arbitrary in respect of other word–signs in the language system. Each number in a set of numbers, for example, has significance (or relative **sign–value** as Saussure puts it) only in relation to the other numbers in that set; 'nine' means nothing unless there is also an 'eight' and a 'ten'. If we try to insert the Welsh word 'saith', this means little unless we also know that saith is the number 'seven' in the Welsh language. As long as we *do know* the words for numbers in different language sets we can, however, reconstruct a useful set; one, deu, drie, quarto, pimp, six, saith, ocho, nine, dix.

Signs for concepts

Although up to this point we have used examples of word–signs that refer to objects like mushrooms and pencil sharpeners, it should be clear that language also supplies social actors with word–signs for other, more abstract or conceptual, properties as well. For example, if a child was asked 'what is a banana?', and they replied 'it's yellow', we know that the child has grasped the idea that yellowness is one of the properties of bananas. They have learnt to use the concept of colour as a way of differentiating between objects in terms of how they are affected by the reflected spectrum of light. Having learnt the appropriate set of word–signs used in a particular language to differentiate between one colour and another, the child would now be able to describe all bits of reality in terms of the property 'colour'.

A little more abstractly, and again with experience and practice, the child might also learn to associate the concept of colour with other kinds of concepts. The mental image of 'banana' tends to bring to mind a sensation of something that is sweet-tasting. The concept of colour might also be associated with particular moods or emotions, for example red is often associated with warmth and passion, in contrast to green, which connotes coolness and calmness. Although actors would still be able to see, taste and feel without language, language gives them the means of organising these experiences and, most importantly, of expressing them to others.

Difference

Continuing with the theme of how the sign–system helps social actors make sense of the world, Saussure emphasised that signs identify objects not so much by telling social actors what they are, as by telling them what they are not. What is significant about the word–sign 'cat', for example, is that it affirms a distinction between cats, 'dogs', 'broomsticks' or any other object, concept or feeling an actor might want to express. By saying 'cat' an actor is in effect saying '*not* dog', '*not* broomstick', '*not* love'. Although this is a difficult idea to grasp, Saussure is suggesting that the sense social actors have that there really are concrete things around them comes about because language gives them the ability to comprehend that a particular object or thing is what it is because it is not, and in fact cannot be (and very certainly not at the same time), something *else*. A crucial property of signs in the system is that they signify *difference* between objects, and it is this sense of difference that gives us a sense of meaning.

Sequences and paradigms

We need, finally, to be aware of a further important distinction made by Saussure. This is between the horizontal or **syntagmatic** dimension of language, and the vertical or **paradigmatic** ('associative') dimension. The former refers to the linear or sequential arrangement of words as they appear in a sentence or phrase. The meanings of the elements take their sense from the presence of the other elements in the sequence. The rules of grammar and syntax govern which arrangements make sense. Thus the phrase 'the cat sat on the mat' makes sense to members of the English-language community, but 'mat the sat cat the on' does not. The vertical or paradigmatic dimension is more difficult to grasp but refers to the way that each element also conjures up in the mind at least some of the absent alternatives that have not been used. For example, in the phrase 'the black cat sat on the mat', the sense this coveys of what black cats look like borrows a little from other colours that cats might be, such as grey, tabby or marmalade.

Saussure refers to these 'associations' as a 'constellation' to emphasise that these non-present alternatives do not have any particular order to them. In a sense, they form a reservoir of meaning, from which the item that has been selected by the writer or speaker, acquires some of its meaning. When, for example, a social actor makes a statement that others do not appear to understand, the speaker will very often repeat the statement but this time making a slightly different choice of words in the hope that the audience will then be able to hook onto what they are saying.

A slightly unexpected implication of the associative or paradigmatic dimension of language is that although the speaker gets to choose between the alternative words available for expressing something, the choice they have is actually restricted by the number of alternatives in that particular set or paradigm (a spectrum of colours or a sequence of numbers, for example). In addition, once a social actor has started speaking or writing, and quite in addition to the syntagmatic or sequential restraints placed on them by the rules of grammar and syntax, in order for what they say to remain meaningful they need to stay within the bounds of meaning established by what they have already said. I can vary the sentence 'the cat sat on the mat' by replacing 'sat' with 'stood', but to say that 'the cat stood on the helicopter' is at a minimum rather obscure and verges on the meaningless. In a manner of speaking, the further an actor goes along a particular linguistic path, the more closely his subsequent choices are imposed on him by the language set he is using.

Language structures meaning

And the implication of *this* Saussurean conception of how social actors grasp reality and find meaning in it, is that reality and meaning are both things that fundamentally depend upon, or emerge out of, the internal structures of language itself. If one of the properties of language is that it has a logical regularity to it (i.e. that it is built around a framework of identifiable rules without which it would have little practical use), then the rules that govern the relations between the sets of word-signs and other features of language such as syntax and grammar *might also be* the rules by which social actors come to know reality itself; language literally creates a sense of comprehension and meaning. Language is not a passive tool social actors use to communicate, but is an active part of their comprehension of the world around them. The rules of language are also, so to speak, the rules of how the world can be known at all. Not surprisingly, Saussure recommended that the systematic study of structural linguistics was the fast track to understanding reality.

Getting back to the impact of all of this on social theory, following Saussure, many theorists came to accept that it was no longer sufficient to regard language as having some literal connection with the objects social actors describe by using words (connections that could be discovered by tracing language back to its early origins). Nor, having given the whole matter something of a philosophical twist, was it reasonable to assume that language, or the objects, ideas and emotions it is used to describe, remain unchanged over time. Although theorists of language prior to Saussure had only studied language 'diachronically' or historically as a kind of social-cultural sediment that builds up over time, or studied the origins of particular words (etymology), it was also important to study it 'synchronically' as a here-and-now kind of phenomenon. In this sense, language, and the power it has to facilitate and regulate communication, to conceptualise reality and so on, is entirely simultaneous with the moment it is being used.

Ludwig Wittgenstein: language and 'language games'

The emergence of a more energetic appreciation among social theorists of the importance of language and the role it plays in allowing social actors to make sense of things was given a further push by the work of the Viennese-born philosopher Ludwig Wittgenstein (1880–1951). Wittgenstein spent much of his career studying and teaching at Trinity College, University of Cambridge. His most influential work, and the only one to be published in his own lifetime, was his *Tractatus Logico-Philosophicus* (1961 [1921]). His principal interest was how language, and the rules that make language what it is, actively control the concepts and meanings actors use to describe the world around them.

Wittgenstein's main argument was that social actors should be much more sceptical about assuming that the language they use does actually give them the capacity to make reliable interpretations of the outside world. Language itself needs to be treated as one of the external phenomena that, potentially at least, controls social actors. Language is not a neutral and unproblematic device, which is used like an inert tool for describing the world 'out there', but is heavily implicated in the whole process of meaning formation. (One way of thinking about this is to consider how different media used in fine art – clay, bronze, oil paint, watercolour, pencil – result in the production of often quite different representations of the same object. The original subject is radically transformed by the medium used to represent it. The medium becomes *part of* the representation.)

Wittgenstein illustrates this idea by referring to language in his later work as a 'language game'. He suggests that just like any game, for example a game of chess, the game cannot be played and positive outcomes cannot be achieved unless participants know and follow the rules of the game. To make sense when actors write or speak they have to abide by the rules of language; rules that are not negotiable. Although, in principle, language seems to offer an infinite number of possible permutations and combinations, only some of these will actually make sense. The business of 'making sense' is, in a manner reminiscent of Saussure's analysis of language, dependent on the number of meaningful utterances made permissible by the rules of the language game as played in a particular language community. Moreover, the criteria by which a particular utterance can be judged successful are also internal to that language. Using the game analogy, what constitutes a legitimate move in a game of poker, for example, is entirely created within the rules of poker. It would be ridiculous to try to play a game of poker using the rules of some other game, such as American football or golf. One cannot use the language rules of ancient Sanskrit to judge the meaning of modern Portuguese.

Raising an issue that was subsequently developed by Peter Winch (see later), Wittgenstein was also concerned to show that although philosophers and other specialists develop specialist terms and concepts, and thus have at their disposal an extended vocabulary, if they want their utterances to make sense, they are still bound by the general grammatical and syntactical rules that apply to everyone else who uses that language. Philosophers and social theorists might use specialist terminology, but it is questionable whether their understanding actually goes much beyond that which is commonly available to everyone in their language community. It is the rules that give the language game a sense of structure and continuity, and, arguably, it is the same rules that give a sense of structure and continuity to reality also.

Peter Winch: different accounts, different realities

Moving a step beyond the idea that words are crucial for describing reality, the English philosopher Peter Winch (1926–97) emphasised that, to the extent that what and how social actors think about phenomena depends on the words they use to describe them, language must also be a prerequisite for developing *any* overall conception of reality. In his book *The Idea of Social Science and its Relation to Philosophy* (1958), Winch considers whether the social sciences are more akin to philosophy than to science. One of his main arguments is that debates over the nature of 'science', 'proof', 'evidence' and so on are not so much about the validity or reliability of theoretical statements or propositions about things 'out there', but are actually conversations about different ways of defining and conceptualising things as 'external' to us. If philosophers, social theorists, academics and so on cannot even agree as to how to distinguish between things as being 'out there' rather than 'in here', then what chance is there of developing any kind of reliable and concrete knowledge of the world at all?

ILLUSTRATION – DIFFERENT WORDS, DIFFERENT REALITIES

Winch argues that human beings use language to solve the general problem of how to describe the world in order to make sense of it. However, each language community (English, Chinese, Polish and so on.) produces and reinforces a particular, and in some sense unique, conception of that world. For example, if an explorer from Egypt was having a conversation with an Inuit in the Arctic Circle about what kind of snow was likely to fall that day, the Egyptian might well say 'The usual kind, what other kind is there?' To an Inuit, however, whose immediate experience is very much dominated by snow, it would be essential to distinguish between one kind of snow and another. Similarly, the Egyptian would probably be able to describe several different kinds of sand because, living in a largely desert environment, his reality might very well vary depending on different sand conditions. Without the words to describe them, one could certainly argue that different kinds of snow do not actually exist for Egyptians, nor different kinds of sand for Inuits.

Important variations might also emerge *within* the same broad language group. Different youth cultural groups, for example, develop particular kinds of slang vocabulary and ways of talking (informal idioms) to distinguish themselves from other youth groups and perhaps the adult majority. To take another example, although Spanish is a global language inasmuch as it is commonly spoken in parts of Europe, the US and Central and South America, it is obvious that there are important differences between these locations despite the fact that people there speak the same basic language. This shows us how language intersects with **culture** to produce variation between different language groups; language may be used to assert differences in the way that social actors see the world. The fact that a person from Spain could easily communicate with a person from Mexico also demonstrates for us the fact that Spanish has certain 'universal' properties that do not belong to any of the language groups who use Spanish. In the terms that Durkheim uses, 'language' provides proof of the existence of a category of social phenomena that not only lies beyond the control of any particular individual, but also beyond the control of any particular actually existing society.

An important implication of Winch's arguments for us as social theorists is that it is naive (he thinks logically, but implies in practical terms as well) to claim that the various alternative accounts of reality given by social theorists are any more 'truthful' or 'reliable' than those given by other specialist groups such as physicists or philosophers. Because all such accounts rely on language for their expression, and because, just like other cultural groups, different specialisms each have their own language, science, philosophy and all the rest are best regarded not even as different constructions of the same reality, but different constructions of *different realities*. This leads us into the highly relativist dilemma that everything has to be understood as relative to everything else because there is no independent referee or ultimate judge (presumably using a 'mega-language' or a 'language-plus') with which to show us which account is more true than another.

Although then, for Winch, there might be value for us in some personal sense in analysing society in the way we do, and although the specialist concepts and tools we use to do so give our accounts some unique properties that are not found in other kinds of accounts, we are claiming too much if we believe that our account is more privileged than any other.

The concept of structure in social theory

Several times in this chapter we have referred to language in terms of structure. We also referred to structure a good deal in our discussion of the functionalist approach to social theory developed by Talcott Parsons in Chapter Seven. We have also referred a number of times to structures of meaning and to the various ways that meaning, in other words, our active comprehension of the world around us, is structured. We will have more to say about structure and meaning in the final two sections of this chapter and in Chapter Ten, but at this point it will be useful to elaborate a little on what we might call the family resemblance between these uses of the concept of structure, and to make some general points about their place in what it collectively referred to as **structuralist** social theory.

Essentially the concept of structure has been used by social theorists to convey the idea that the purpose, significance and indeed meaning of social phenomena are best understood in terms of the larger whole of which they are a part. As we have just seen in our discussion of the sign-system called language, each individual element in the **system**, such as a word or sentence, is insignificant and meaningless until it is seen in terms of the larger linguistic structure it is a part of. It is language 'as a whole' that gives purpose to the individual components of language.

If we do feel able to conceptualise social phenomena in terms of the larger whole of which they are a part, then it is a relatively short step from this to describing the purpose of things also in terms of how they fit into, and what role they play in, the broader totality. We have already come across this way of explaining things in the **functionalist** approach (see Chapter Six). Functionalists argue that purpose is pretty much the same as function in the sense that the main reason why social phenomena come into being in the first place, and why they take the particular form that they do, is directly related to the functions they perform. Much else in functionalist social theory is about deciding what level of the system and its functioning the researcher wants to focus their attention at.

Whether or not one chooses to describe social phenomena and to interpret social actions exclusively in terms of their function the sense remains, first, that there is such a thing as a larger entity that exists 'over and above' the parts, and, second, that there is some kind of identifiable orderliness among those parts. Unlike concepts such as 'category', 'type' or 'class', which group things together on the grounds of common traits or properties, the concept of 'structure' assumes that the various bits of the structure are held together in clearly identifiable ways. Structure implies orderliness and predictability in the way that this process of holding-together is accomplished. For example, the various struts, brackets, bolts and wires of an electricity pylon constitute an observable structure having the properties of repetition, regularity and symmetry. The same rules of construction and functionality apply to all pylons, and so 'pylon' can be used to refer in a generic sense to this kind of mechanical structure. The stream that runs beneath the pylon in the countryside, however, cannot be described as a structure as it exhibits none of these properties of orderliness.

Structure and the emergence of structuralism

From structure to structuring

It is quite common for social theorists to use the term structure in a relatively casual way for representing social phenomena that can usefully be thought of in terms of how the various bits are held together, for example, 'the class structure' or 'the family structure'. As a more formal mode of academic analysis, however, and especially among structural*ists*, the term has a more precise meaning, which is to investigate *the nature of the connections* between the parts. In saying this we are thus moving away from using structure as an adjective for describing things (pylons have structure, streams do not) towards *structuring* used as a verb. Structure *is*, but structure also *does things* to the various parts that turn out to form a structure.

In this kind of investigation it is the process of structuring that becomes the object of enquiry. The parts, whether they be words and phrases in language, moves in a game of chess, parts of a ritual or elements in a literary text, become relatively unimportant *other than* because they reveal the nature of the structuring process that holds them in place. If we are prepared to accept suggestions from Saussure,

Wittgenstein and Winch that the significance and meaning of the parts really does depend upon, or emerge out of, the kind of structuring that goes on among those parts, then as a method of academic enquiry, **structuralism** is largely about working out the nature of the linkages between the parts. Structuralism asks how this particular kind of structure does its structuring. In what ways are the outcomes of the structure (such as the purposes it serves, the significance it has, the meanings it generates) a consequence of the way it structures its parts?

New structures of investigation

During the 20th century, first in linguistics, then in social anthropology and sociology, later in literature and cultural studies, structuralism emerged as a mode of investigation that could, potentially, be used to understand any natural or cultural phenomena that displayed some form of orderly connectedness. And what connected each of these fields of investigation together was a shared desire to identify what was special about how each kind of structure did its structuring. For Saussure, for example, and in addition to the rules of grammar and syntax that specify the correct sequence the words have to go in (the horizontal or syntagmatic dimension of language structuring), the special feature of the structuring properties of the linguistic structure is that it does its structuring by using the special properties of 'difference' and 'absence'. Word-signs mean what they do because they do not mean something else. The paradigmatic (vertical) meaning of each word-sign is generated by all the other signs in the set that are implied but not directly mentioned by name. We understand what it means to say a cat is black because we also know what it means to say it is tabby or grey or white or marmalade. Paradigmatically speaking, and assuming we are not talking about an invisible cat or one that has pigmentation never seen before, if it is not tabby, grey, white or marmalade, it *must be* black.

Beneath the surface

Greater awareness of how particular underlying properties of the structuring process directly affect the final arrangement of the parts as they appear on the surface also started social theorists thinking about the different levels at which these processes take place. Again beginning with Saussure's model of linguistic structuring, a distinction is often made between **deep structure**, which social actors might not be very conscious of, and **surface structure**, where structure becomes useful to us as a tool for communication and where, in a more philosophical or analytical sense, meaning is constructed or 'revealed'.

Saussure distinguishes between langue, meaning the underlying form and structure of the language or language-system (its deep structure), and parole, or more simply 'speech', which is the 'surface' or more immediate spoken form of language actors use when they speak.

A similar distinction has been proposed by the influential linguist Noam Chomsky (born 1928), who argues that it is fruitful to distinguish between 'language competence', which is the innate and inbuilt capacity human beings have for language, and 'language performance', which is language in the form of what social actors actually say and write. The fact that it is perfectly possible, and indeed quite commonplace, for social actors to learn and use more than one language, is taken as a basis for inferring the existence of an underlying competence to use language. Human brains are, as it were, wired for language. This provides a foundation for the further argument that if each language system is just an example of the generic human capacity to handle linguistic structure, then it is just as probable that the human brain can also handle other kinds of structure as well, for example in music or mathematics. Arguably, the human brain has a predisposition towards structured forms of comprehension and thus actively creates systemic phenomena like language, music and mathematics in order to express this capability. Randomness and chaos are not privileged in this way.

The basic supposition that we can come to 'see' or 'know' what lies hidden beneath by examining its effects at the surface has also been highly influential not just within the social sciences and humanities, but also in natural science and especially the field of developmental psychology. The general structuralist principle adopted here is that the nature of extremely important and yet very difficult to observe phenomena, such as intellectual and cognitive processes, emotions and even the human capacity for **reason**, can be inferred by looking at their effects at the surface. If deep structure determines what happens at the surface, then, applying the process in reverse, an analysis of surface events should reveal the nature of the underlying structuring process.

Claude Lévi-Strauss and structuring of culture

Running alongside these developments in the quest for underlying properties of structure, one of the most ambitious applications of the structuralist approach emerged in the work of the French cultural **anthropologist** Claude Lévi-Strauss (1908–2009). Much impressed by developments in structural linguistics and phonetics (the systematic study of vocal sounds and how they are structured to form speech), Lévi-Strauss applied this approach in his detailed fieldwork investigations, mostly carried out among indigenous peoples living in the Amazonian region of South America, in which he compared one culture with another in terms of their kinship systems and their forms and uses of art, taboo, myth and ritual. His leading publications are: *The Elementary Structures of Kinship* (1969 [1949]); *Tristes Tropiques* (1973 [1955]); *Structural Anthropology* (1963 [1958]); *The Raw and the Cooked* (1970 [1964]); and *The Savage Mind* (1966).

Using a version of the notion of deep structure, he wanted to see whether it was possible to uncover universal deep features of human culture through an analysis of how they appeared, albeit in different surface forms, in different cultures. The incest taboo, for example, which seems to appear in all human cultures, could be regarded as just such an instance of an underlying structural node of human culture. All human cultures have to deal with the problem of preventing sexual intercourse between close family members, and so, universally, they have developed an incest taboo. In his book *Structural Anthropology* (1963 [1958]), for example, he asks 'if the content of a myth is contingent [i.e. the product of local circumstances], how are we going to explain the fact that myths throughout the world are so similar?' (Lévi-Strauss, 1963 [1958], p 208).

Lévi-Straus also relied heavily on the parallels, as he saw them, between features of linguistic structures and cultural practices. He suggested, for example, that various common elements in human kinship systems, such as rules about who can marry and when, the various conventions and obligations of marriage or community attitudes towards marriage, not only acquired significance and meaning by being part of the more general cultural system of which they are a part, but demonstrated the presence of an underlying process of cultural structuring. As with linguistic structure, what appears at the surface reveals the influence of something more fundamental, even universal, below.

Although there is variety among the different subjects that Lévi-Strauss investigated, a general theme that runs through his work is a quest for what we might call 'pure structure'. Different types of cultural structuring were of interest to him not just because of the effects they had on particular social phenomena or types of social organisation, but because they implied the possibility of a deeply-rooted set of organising principles that underlie our capacity *for* structure. Language, ritual, kinship, taboo and all the rest point towards a preoccupation with, and urge to express, structure. The quest for knowledge thus becomes an investigation into the different forms of structuring that hold matter together in time and space, and into whether there are rules that govern the relations between these different types of structure. At its highest (deepest) level of abstraction, the question we would be asking is what the particular properties of the structuring process are that govern the arrangements of the different kinds of structuring we have been able to identify so far. (Are the structuring processes that produce language, music, mathematics and so on themselves underpinned by an even deeper structuring process?)

Sigmund Freud, Jacque Lacan and the structuring of the conscious mind

One of the most influential attempts at applying structuralist principles (although he is not generally classified as a structuralist theorist) is in the work of the Austrian psychiatrist Sigmund Freud (1856–1939). Freud developed a clinical analytical technique that operates on the principle that mental disorder or neurosis, which shows itself in the behaviour of adults, can be traced back to significant moments of personality development in early childhood. Freud sees personality as comprising three elements: the Ego, which is the ordinary conscious sense-of-self; the Superego, which is partly conscious and exercises a monitoring or supervisory influence over the Ego; and the Id, which is a largely unconscious phenomenon made up of the basic instincts and drives especially those associated with sexual expression. Using hypnosis and other techniques the psychoanalyst attempts to lead the adult back into his unconscious mind in order to uncover and thus alleviate features of his past that have become repressed.

Freud's ideas were carried forward in the work of the French social theorist Jacques Lacan (1901–81) who applied a deep-structuralist approach in his studies of psychoanalytic theory. Lacan finds a parallel between Freud's notion that the hidden unconscious mind exerts an important if often unacknowledged influence over conscious activity at the surface, and the structuralist perception that surface forms are produced by underlying structuring forces, in this instance of emotions, meanings and feelings. Lacan sees Freud's concept of the unconscious as a highly persuasive way of describing part of the deep or underlying structure of personality and the self. As a therapeutic technique, psychoanalysis seeks to bring back to the surface elements that are hidden within the unconscious mind, elements that might help the individual develop a new awareness of where his or her own development deviated from that which usually underpins so-called normal development. Lacan tries to develop this basic Freudian concept further by suggesting that the unconscious mind is not a jumbled depository of random thoughts and memories, but is itself a kind of structure. Using insights from the structuralist analytic method, it should be possible, he thinks, to develop an understanding of the ways in which the unconscious mind does its structuring.

As a basis for his ideas about how what we might call psychic structuring or the structuring of personality takes place, Lacan, like all good first-wave structuralists, borrows key insights from Saussure's description of linguistic structuring. Indeed, he goes so far as to suggest that 'the unconscious is structured like a language' (Lacan, 1998 [1773] p 48). The way Lacan adapts these ideas can be somewhat difficult to grasp, but the underlying principle he uses is to regard the words and actions social actors express in their conscious surface behaviour, including events and objects they refer to in their dreams or while under hypnosis during a therapy session, as signifiers that might or might not be satisfactorily lined up with particular signifieds, that is, with the true emotions, meanings and feelings the person meant to convey. A simplified version of this notion is commonly referred to as a 'Freudian slip' in which a mistake in what an actor says reveals what he or she was actually thinking.

This perspective reflects the basic presumption in Freudian psychoanalysis that past events and experiences have been interpreted by the individual in such a way that they have not developed a normal or properly adjusted adult personality. The key idea Lacan uses here is the idea of 'slippage' between signifier and signified. This can occur both in terms of differences between what a person meant to express deep down and what he actually said, and between the general manner in which a particular individual developed his own sense-of-self or personality but yet in a way that is at odds with the usual conventions for personality-formation that surround him.

On the presumption that in order to take part effectively in society, social actors have to be properly adjusted to those circumstances, the structuring of personality is also and inevitably embedded within the wider and more general social processes through which particular interpretations and meanings come to be regarded as normal in that society. In order for a social actor to be 'normally adjusted', there must obviously be some kind of society–wide agreement about what, in terms of personality, constitutes normality. This is a particularly complex issue because the emergence in society of agreements about what constitutes a normal personality is obviously affected by the social actors living in that society. Which comes first, the 'personality' of society, or individual personality? (We will be looking at the linkages between the kinds of underlying structurings that produce society-wide constructions of meaning, and underlying structurings that produce normally-adjusted individual personality in Chapter Ten.)

ILLUSTRATION – THE MEANING OF DREAMS

For example, a social actor might have a dream about losing his cat when what he is really anxious about is failing to turn up to give a lecture on time. If that person repeatedly had dreams about losing things, it might subsequently emerge through therapy that he had developed an unnecessarily acute sense of anxiety about being late. To the extent that 'being late' is a social construct that social actors learn during socialisation, this particular individual could be regarded as having developed a mild personality disorder as a result of misinterpreting the idea of 'lateness' at an earlier stage in their development. The signifier 'lost cat' is thus misdirected both from the real underlying meaning or signified (in this example, anxiety about being late), and from what is held in that society to be normal expectations about punctuality. The purpose of therapy is to help the participant retrace his footsteps, develop a different interpretation of past events, and thus arrive at a revised or 'new' personality that does fit in more comfortably with life around him.

In terms of how the structuring process of personality actually does its structuring, Lacan suggests that much of this takes place within the unconscious mind. This obviously presents the theorist with considerable difficulties because, by definition, the unconscious mind and much of what goes on there lies largely beyond our ordinary reach. Lacan's solution is to try to infer or read-off underlying content from surface forms. He thus presents a somewhat abstract conception of the self as a property that emerges from and expresses the interplay of emotions, feelings and meanings held within the unconscious. Personality, self and behaviour, as they appear at the surface, provide us with clues as to who we really are and what we really think and feel 'deep down'.

The self, signifiers and signifieds

Up to this point, we could say that Lacan's use of the surface–deep structure mode of analysis is fairly conventional. Where he becomes much more radical, however, is in terms of what he sees as the relative importance of the signifier compared with what is being signified. For Saussure and his followers, the usual presumption is that, within the sign-system, signifieds (i.e. those things that are being signified) are more important than the signifiers (i.e. the ways in which they are being represented). Lacan suggests a reversal of this presumption arguing that, actually, the signifier is more important because without signifiers there can be no representation of underlying meanings (signifieds) at all (without the word-sign 'cat' it would not be possible to conceptualise the furry mammal this sign refers to at all). For Lacan, therefore, meaning, signification and all the rest of what we regard as knowledge and reality is created within and between the relations of one signifier and another. For Lacan, it is not enough to give priority to the study of surface forms as a way of uncovering the underlying structurings that have given rise to them, but, *within the sign itself*, priority must also be given to the surface form of the sign (signifier) rather than to the signified that, although intimately connected with it, lies beneath (the word-sign 'cat' and the relations between it and other word-signs in the same system is more important than any actually existing entity conventionally referred to as 'cat').

Applying this more radical approach in terms of what it might tell us about the underlying structurings of self and personality, and bearing in mind that we are talking here about processes that lie beyond the reach of direct observation, Lacan sees these phenomena as existing within, or as emerging out of, the gaps between the emotional or psychic signifiers and signifieds that originate in the unconscious. It is precisely because we can only come to know about what lies in the unconscious part of the mind by inferring its properties from what appears at the surface of a person's behaviour, that *the means of its expression* become so very important. It is thus signifiers rather than signifieds that ought, for Lacan, to engage our attention the most. Even emotional states such as feeling guilty or anxious would seem to lie beyond conscious comprehension *until* word-signs have been invented to give them a reality. The very many unfamiliar emotions and sensations experienced by young children quite literally only become 'hunger', 'pain' and 'anger' once they have been socialised into using names for them.

Louis Althusser and the decentring of the subject

One of the main criticisms raised against the structuralist approach we have been discussing in this chapter is that analysis becomes progressively less focused on actual social actors and their conditions of living and more preoccupied with the intellectual and philosophical puzzles of the theory. In one sense this criticism is unfair because structuralism is about developing techniques *for* analysis rather than necessarily always providing analysis *of* particular social phenomena. Besides, Saussure, Lévi-Strauss, Chomsky, Lacan and many others adopting the structuralist approach have produced detailed accounts of how the underlying structural organisation of language, culture, the intellect, cognitive development, personality and so on affect social actors at the surface level of their daily lives. It is true to say, however, that the detailed accounts provided by structuralist researchers often retain a strongly abstract flavour in the sense that the conceptual machinery of the structuralist technique requires a good deal of abstract reasoning even before one actually gets down to carrying out investigations of 'real things'.

Along with Lacan, decisive moves towards what has been called the 'decentring of the subject' in social theory, a move that challenges the long-standing assumption that social actors can be regarded as free-thinking, autonomous subjects who have control over the events around them, occurred in the work of the French Marxist-structuralist social theorist Louis Althusser (1918–90). Preparing the way for **post-structuralism** (discussed in Chapter Ten), Lacan and Althusser introduced the radical suggestion that the biographical subjective self does not remain fundamental and essential, but is a much more temporary phenomenon created within the spaces formed by underlying structures.

Louis Althusser: structure and superstructure

Althusser sought to apply what we might call the deep-structuralist method in his reading of the key works of Karl Marx (*Reading Capital*, 1969 [1965]; *For Marx*, 1969). In terms of his general conception of society or 'social formation', Althusser argues that in the same way that it is possible to uncover the underlying rules and patterns of linguistic structuring (langue/language competence) by examining surface utterances (parole/language performance), the same approach can be applied in tracing back from the actual institutions and practices that surround social actors in search of the underlying structuring forces that have given rise to them. For Althusser, Marx's great achievement was to be the first theorist to show how a particular arrangement of social forces at the surface, for example **capitalist society**, arises directly from the presence of underlying economic forces that have the effect of structuring surface institutions in particular ways. Althusser also retains the strongly historical emphasis in Marx's work, which is that the present can be regarded as a kind of surface form that has been created by the past (hence Marx's use of the term **historical materialism** to describe his theory). In both Marx and in Althusser the historical past, which has become embedded within institutions and social practices, is seen as continuously imposing itself on the present (Marx's ideas are discussed in detail in Chapter Four).

From this point of view, Marx's detailed exploration of the practices of capitalism is a first attempt at working out the underlying or deep rules of social structuring that give rise to particular surface forms of society. To take a simplified example, Marx identifies that a particular combination of the forces of production with the relations of production will give rise to a particular mode of production. Modes of production give rise to historically identifiable types of society, such as ancient society, feudal society and capitalist society. We can infer the underlying rules of economic structuring by examining the nature of these different types of social formation as they occur at the surface. (For structuralist Marxists, the outline Marx provides of the principal features of the underlying processes of economic structuring are, in an analytical sense, equivalent to characteristics such as 'difference' and 'absence' in Saussure's description of linguistic structuring.)

The four instances of social formation

In terms of his own analysis of the capitalist surface formation at the midpoint of the 20th century, Althusser suggests that the social formation (society) is made up of a number of areas or instances of social practice. At the most general or aggregated level in the theory these are the economic, the political, the ideological and the theoretical instances. The economic and political instances (or 'fields' as some later social theorists call them) are reasonably familiar. The 'ideological instance' refers to the common-sense awareness people have of social reality (similar to the **conscience collective** in Durkheim's theory), which is produced by institutions such as schools, churches, trade unions, political parties and the mass media. The 'theoretical instance' refers to specialist, scientific or professional **discourses**, including most importantly specialist discourses in the academic and political fields of social theory, where 'non-ideological' knowledge develops (of which more later).

Looking at the relations between one 'instance' and another, Althusser suggests one instance and its associated institutions are relatively autonomous in respect of the other instances, which accounts for why the relations between, for example, churches and political parties vary from one society to another. The underlying structuring processes are also relatively autonomous in the sense that the ideological instance is not produced by exactly the same process of structuring as is the political instance or the theoretical instance. The operative term here is *relative* autonomy because, again following Marx, Althusser argues that the political, ideological and theoretical instances are **overdetermined** by the economic instance. He does not mean by this that always and everywhere the economy is dominant (a view often mistakenly applied to Marxism), but that the economic instance plays a crucial role in determining which of the various instances assumes a leading role in society at particular moments. A rise in levels of unemployment, for example caused by industrial restructuring, will have political ramifications not just for trade unions and employers' organisations, but for national governments. Any ensuing crisis might also affect relations between one nation-state and another. When Althusser famously declared that the economic instance is determinant 'in the last instance', he is expressing his main conclusion about the nature of social structuring, which is that the structuring processes that give rise to the different instances at the surface are themselves linked together at an even deeper level by an underlying process of economic structuring. In Althusser's conception there is a hierarchy of structuring processes below the surface, the deepest and thus most pervasive of which is economic structuring.

Ideology

Although the idea that society has economic and political instances is relatively familiar to us, Althusser's inclusion of a distinct and separate 'ideological instance' and a 'theoretical instance' is less so. Their inclusion in such a bold way shows us that Althusser believes that two of the principal characteristics of the underlying processes of social structuring (like characteristics of 'difference' and 'absence' in Saussure's theory) are ideology and theory. Although the concept of **ideology** is often used in a negative way, it is important to note that, for Althusser, and in fact for many social and political theorists, ideologies can be both negative and positive. Racism, for example, is a negative ideology, whereas environmentalism is generally regarded as a positive ideology (an important positive concept of ideology is contained in Antonio Gramsci's theory of **hegemony**, which is discussed in Chapter Eight). Althusser describes most of the conscious understanding social actors have of events around them as 'ideological' as his way of emphasising the generally-accepted point that there is always a gap between events and the way people become conscious of them. The distinction the specialist or theorist is able to make, then, is between an accurate or true understanding of reality and an inaccurate or false one.

The notion of non-ideological knowledge is very important in Althusser's analytical system because he believed that another of Marx's outstanding achievements was to show how the vested interests in capitalist society (the owners of the means of production, their agents and co-conspirators) create a false impression in the popular imagination of the true nature of those underlying economic forces and interests. The consciousness social actors generally have of what goes on around them in capitalist society is, in Marx's terms, not real but **false consciousness** (the concept of false consciousness is associated especially with Georg Lukács whose work is discussed in Chapter Eight). Whereas we might suppose that language is honest or neutral in respect of how deep structural forms affect surface utterances, the same cannot be said of how capitalism appears to be at the surface.

According to Marx's and Althusser's critical perspective (critical in the sense of challenging whether things have to be as they currently are), the impression social actors have of capitalism is largely false and ideological in the sense that its real underlying essence (i.e. that it is predatory, exploitative and prone to conflict and crisis) is kept from view.

The role of theory

Althusser's inclusion of a distinct theoretical instance follows quite naturally from his interest in ideology. If, as he supposed, the role of Marxist intellectuals is to explain the true reality of capitalist exploitation, something that Marx and Engels attempted to do a century or so earlier in writing *The Communist Manifesto*, then a theory of society must give a special place to the development of theoretical skills and activities. These tasks, and the intellectuals and theorists who carry them out, cannot be regarded as ancillary or supplementary to the wider processes of social structuring, but are an integral part of it.

In common with structuralist approaches in whatever field of analysis, a special place is thus reserved by Althusser for those who, suitably equipped with the tools of the structuralist trade, can carry on the necessary work of retrieving the mysteries of deep structure by examining its effects at the surface. Structure creates a space for theorists who can reveal the glorious thing that structure is.

Role of theory and of the intellectual

Seeing himself as fulfilling the role of specialist intellectual (i.e. as occupying a space in one of the grids at the surface that has been created by underlying social structuring) and believing that he is carrying forward crucial insights developed by Marx who was also so engaged, Althusser makes the crucial observation that despite their relative autonomy, and the assumptions they make about their subjective integrity, social actors are heavily constrained by the surface outcomes and effects of the underlying structuring process. In his famous analysis of the 'Ideology and ideological state apparatuses' (1984 [1971]), that is, of the surface institutions like the media, Church and schools, which supply taken-for-granted, or common-sense, understandings that enable social actors to make enough sense of what it going on around them in order to live their lives, Althusser introduces the idea of **interpellation**.

Interpellation

This slightly elusive concept describes the sense in which Althusser believed social actors are drawn into, or impelled towards, prevailing or dominant understandings of reality. Again his conclusion here is that the underlying processes of structuring that produce cultural values and meaning open up spaces into which actors allow themselves to be drawn. This is not a crude process of indoctrination or brainwashing, of social actors being swamped by a relentless tide of state propaganda, but a much more subtle process where the ideological instance and its institutions meet the need social actors have to be provided with some kind of plausible explanation of social life. Again, this is reminiscent of Gramsci's concept of hegemony (see Chapter Eight).

Some limitations of first-wave structuralism

As we have previously noted, structuralism relies on the idea that it is possible to infer the principles of different kinds of underlying structuring processes by looking at their surface forms. It is, therefore, an inherently abstract technique because the main object of its analysis, that is, structuring processes, can never be observed directly. This raises a number of difficulties.

The privileged position of the structuralist social theorist

Despite strong indications from Peter Winch and others that it is a mistake to assume that one specialist academic discourse is any more truthful or accurate than another (or even that they are describing the same reality), the structuralist approach continues to give the impression that the structuralist theorist really is in a more insightful position than everyone else. The popularity of the structuralist method during the midpoint of the 20th century, the fact that it seemed applicable to so many different spheres of investigation into language, culture, economics, politics, ideology and personality, strongly reinforced this sense of structuralism as producing the foundation for a new kind of universal truth. It is by no means a coincidence, for example, that Althusser includes the 'theoretical instance' as a distinct sphere of activity, and argues that specialist structuralist observers emerge to occupy spaces created for them by the structure.

If it is the case, however, that individual subjects are drawn into social spaces created by underlying structuring processes that make those role-occupants 'necessary', then the fact that a particular social actor becomes aware of this situation would seem to reflect a property of the individual and not of the social space they occupy. Can we really accept that the structure produced a unique space that had Marx's or Althusser's name on it? For Althusser's approach to work, there has to be a category of spaces duly filled by especially enlightened and privileged observers who are sufficiently 'beyond' or 'outside' the structure to be able to look back and observe it.

Lacan is open to a similar criticism in respect of the role of the therapist. Although ordinary social actors are presented by Lacan as being perpetually ignorant of their real selves because the gap between their conscious selves and the structuring of it that occurs at an unconscious level is so difficult to bridge, the therapist is in the privileged position of being able to do just that. Like the analytical Marxist-structuralist, the Lacanian psychotherapist seems to be outside the process of psychic structuring and is thus able to develop a level of self-awareness that is not generally available. Is it plausible to accept that the structuring process creates spaces in which a privileged few can develop special insight, an insight that seems to be denied to the majority?

The problem of historical time

Structuralism is a mode of analysis that is designed primarily to investigate the construction and expression of meaning. Since the experience of meaning is a present-time phenomenon the structuralist mode of analysis has to emphasise the synchronic, or present-time, dimension of experience, rather than the diachronic or historical dimension. It thus leaves relatively little room for the influence of past events or 'history'.

At the same time, however, some attempts in applying the structuralist mode of analysis promote the idea that the present is a kind of surface that has been produced by the deep structure of the past (which is very much how Marxists see things). The present does appear to be determined, to a large degree if not entirely, by the past. This would seem to justify concentrating on the diachronic (historical) mode at the expense of the synchronic (present-time), which is a very un-structuralist thing to do. Althusser tries to get around this problem by using the Freudian notion of **overdetermination** to suggest that it is only 'in the last instance' that the economic realm finally asserts itself (history finally determines the present). It is a little confusing to suggest that although ultimately the present is determined by the past, in the meantime we can proceed with a detailed analysis of how social actors cope with the pressing and immediate matters of the present. In many respects, structuralist analysis never fully deals with the problem of historical time.

What is an individual subject?

Ever since the European **Enlightenment** and the emergence of the idea that **reason** is more powerful than God or nature (see Chapter Two), theorists and philosophers had tended to regard individual social actors as relatively free-thinking, autonomous and dynamic beings who were pretty much aware of, and in control of, what was going on around them. This view of the proactive, subjectively conscious individual fitted in with prevailing ideas about the nature of society, about progress and about individuality. The idea of the new kind of moral individualism developed by Émile Durkheim towards the end of the 19th century, for example, certainly presupposed that although society imposed itself on social actors in various ways, there was a kind of balance of mutual interest between the needs of social actors and the 'needs' of the social system. Drawing also on organic and biological conceptions of the nature of things, this image of the individual was multidimensional in the sense that actors had an awareness of their own development over time. They had, in other words, a sense of their own *biography*.

Within first-phase structuralism this conception of social actors as active, biographically-aware subjects came under increasing pressure. In the structuralist conception, social actors are typically seen as living out their lives within spaces created by underlying structuring processes of which they are only vaguely aware. The concept of structuring being used here imposes on the theory an image of social actors as entities that lack spontaneity and initiative and are severely limited in their actions by the form and function of underlying structuring processes of various kinds. According to Lacan, for example, even at the level of the self and personality social actors are presented as having little autonomy and freedom because everything about their psychic make-up is determined by processes within the unconscious mind that social actors barely understand let alone have control over. Social actors are not simply ignorant of how important aspects of their lives are governed by underlying structurings because they have not thought about it enough, but because access to the unconscious mind is closed. The therapeutic situation offers the only means of access to the unconscious realm.

In the same way that structuralist theory tends to suppress the diachronic or historical dimension in order to study phenomena synchronically at a fixed moment in the present, it also tends to suppress the notion of biographical experience that builds up over time. When an insistence on the present-time analysis of structuring processes is pushed to its limits, the only kind of social actor that can be fitted into the analysis is one that lacks imagination and biography altogether. The notion of a biographical subject is replaced by a much more thinly drawn image of social actors as subjects acting in accordance with underlying forces over which they have little control.

As far as its impact on the development of social theory is concerned structuralism occupies an ambiguous position. Although it offered an exciting new approach to carrying out investigations of social phenomena it remained quite closely aligned with many of the traditional preoccupations of social theory. Approaching phenomena as holistic entities in which the parts are best understood in relation to the whole, for example, invokes the kind of model of society that Marx and certainly Durkheim would have easily recognised. Similarly, the idea that the particular form that social institutions and practices take on can be traced back to the underlying purposes or functions they serve was already well-established in functionalist approaches. The idea that social actors often find themselves being propelled along by events over which they have little direct control, or that they sometimes act in accordance with underlying systems of belief that they are not always conscious of, were familiar territory to Marx and Weber. Far more important was the fact that first-wave structuralism provided a stepping-off point for what turned out to be the much more radical ideas developed by second-wave or post-structuralist theorists. This is the topic of Chapter Ten.

Key points box – in this chapter we have looked at:

- ☑ How social theory was attracted by developments in the study of language and how language shapes the way social actors see and describe social phenomena.
- ☑ Saussure's key concept that language is a sign-system and that signs have an *arbitrary relationship* with the real things (referents) that they stand for.
- ☑ All signs have two components: the *signifier* (actual words and sounds) and the *signified* (the mental image of the referent).
- ☑ Signs are bound together in sign-systems (the relationship between signs in a system is *not* arbitrary).
- ☑ The rules of the sign system govern both its grammatical form (syntagmatic dimension) and the meanings that the sign-system allows us to communicate (paradigmatic dimension).
- ☑ The surface form of language (*parole* or speech) is structured by deep structures (*langue* or linguistic competence).

☑ Wittgenstein described the rules of language as a language game to emphasise that all members of a language community must see the world in essentially the same ways because they are bound by the same language rules.

☑ Althusser and Lacan use the structuralist model to explore whether, like language, the surface forms of society and personality can be analysed to infer the presence of underlying structuring processes.

☑ Disadvantages are that structuralism assumes that theorists who observe structure are in a privileged position, it struggles to cope with historical time and it implies an impoverished conception of the social actor.

Practice box

⮕ List two of the main features of the 'linguistic turn' in social theory.

⮕ Give an example of a sign and describe what it stands for.

⮕ What is the difference between a sign and what it stands for?

⮕ What is the difference between one sign and another sign?

⮕ Saussure showed that language was controlled in its horizontal or *syntagmatic* dimension by grammatical rules. What other dimension of 'rules' does he describe?

⮕ Which theorist introduced the idea of the language game and why did he do this?

⮕ Give an example of a structuralist social theorist who argues that the surface form of society can be analysed to reveal the underlying forces of economic structuring.

⮕ Why does Althusser suggest that there are ideological and theoretical 'instances' as well as economic and political ones?

⮕ Give an example of how Lacan's idea that personality is a surface form of the unconscious mind might be useful in understanding social action.

⮕ Give one advantage and one disadvantage of the structuralist perspective in social theory.

Further reading
Malcolm Bowie, *Lacan* (Fontana, 1991).
Ian Craib, *Psychoanalysis: A Critical Introduction* (Polity Press, 2001).
Jonathan Culler, *Saussure* (Fontana, 1976).
Peter Gay, *The Freud Reader* (Vintage, 1995).
Terrence Hawkes, *Structuralism and Semiotics* (Routledge, 1978).
John Patrick Kenny, *Wittgenstein*, revised 2nd edn (Blackwell, 2006).
Edmond Leach, *Lévi-Strauss* (Fontana, 1974).
Claude Lévi-Strauss, *Tristes Tropiques* (Jonathan Cape, 1973 [1955]).
John Sturrock, *Structuralism and Since: From Lévi-Strauss to Derrida* (Oxford
  University Press, 1979).

Websites
For access to general website information enter the terms 'structuralism'
and 'semiotics' into the search engines.

For a gateway into a very comprehensive resource on Sigmund Freud
and psychoanalysis, including the work of Jacques Lacan, go to: www.
freudfile.org

For links to sites of interest on Louis Althusser, and links to other theorists
discussed in this chapter, such as Claude Lévi-Strauss and Ferdinand
de Saussure, start with the vast Marxists resource: www.marxists.org/
reference/archive/althusser/index.htm

CHAPTER TEN

DISCOURSE AND POWER: POST-STRUCTURALIST SOCIAL THEORY

In Chapter Nine we discussed the important change of direction that took place in social theory during the first decades of the 20th century resulting from growing interest in how language shapes both our understanding of the world and our ability to communicate these meanings. Saussure's analysis of how language is actually a surface phenomenon, which is in effect controlled by underlying processes of linguistic structuring, and Levi Strauss's work on the underlying structuring of cultural practices, provided a terrific boost to the credibility of the structuralist method in many areas of academic research including social theory. We concluded that even if it might be going too far to suggest that the lives of social actors are entirely governed by social structures and the structuring processes that lie beneath the surface, it is not such an unreasonable idea that, within a relatively short period of time of their becoming established, social practices do take on 'a life of their own'. A life, moreover, that often has the appearance of **structure**.

Seen in this light, **structuralism** is not so much a paranoid investigation of how social actors are being controlled by structures, but an attempt to develop a systematic analysis of how structures set the limits within which people act. As a method it can help identify variation between one mode of structuring and another (structuring of economy is different from structuring of culture), and the degree and manner in which structuring processes limit or enable the capacity of social actors to act with freedom and autonomy. In this chapter, and following a review of where our discussion of first-wave structuralism left off at the end of Chapter Nine, we will look at second-wave or post-structuralist social theory.

Specifically we will be looking at:

The movement from first-wave to second-wave structuralism

Roland Barthes and the power of signs

Michel Foucault on discourse, discursive practice and power-knowledge

Jacques Derrida on logocentrism, différance, decentring the subject

Overview and chapter summary

The movement from first-wave to second-wave structuralism

In the sections that follow we will be continuing with our discussion of how social theory deals with the problem of meaning by looking at important developments in social theory during the 1970s and 1980s. Many of these followed the basic premises of first-wave structuralist social theory before carrying them off in new directions. Although the three theorists we will be talking about in the sections that follow (Roland Barthes, Jacques Derrida and Michel Foucault) do not generally like being labelled as **post-structuralist**, it is difficult to avoid using a term that is widely deployed in referring to ideas and theories that take structuralism as their common point of departure.

We will be using an alternative term 'second-wave structuralism' to emphasise how post-structuralism (literally structuralism that came *after* the first wave) could not have emerged unless there had been a first wave. Although post-structuralists certainly do not have a shared agenda, their work does have in common a tendency to develop some radical implications from original structuralist ideas. Developing structuralist ideas, which were already regarded in their own time as pretty revolutionary, into dramatic new ways of exploring social phenomena, is a defining characteristic of social theories that are generally labelled as 'post-structuralist'.

One of the main preoccupations of first-wave structuralism was that, in the treatment of social actors within social theory, and especially the extent to which they do maintain a significant degree of control over events around them, much still depends on how the theorist deals with the issue of **meaning**. Since neither structures in themselves, nor even structuring processes, are inherently meaningful it would seem sensible to accept that it is social actors who supply this missing ingredient.

If social actors are regarded as the necessary suppliers of meaning within social structures, it does not automatically follow, however, that the meanings they express are freely chosen by them. A dog's capacity to fetch and carry things gives the impression of autonomy, but if it is merely following the commands of its owner, the dog could not really be regarded as having control over its actions, and even less so over their meaning and purpose. Althusser's emphasis on **ideology** and on the specialist role of the theorist in revealing 'the truth' to ordinary people, pointed the way towards a new variety of critical exploration of **culture** as the primary site where such meanings are produced and contested. The analysis of culture became a major focus of attention for social theorists despite the fact that first-wave structuralism declined sharply in popularity after the 1970s.

Differences

One way of understanding the progression from first-wave to second-wave structuralism is to consider some of the differences between the two. The most obvious of these is that the second wave was more interested in *the content* of the sign-system, in actual examples and instances of meanings that have been made and communicated, than in the mechanisms underlying their creation and communication.

A second difference is the tendency within post-structuralist thinking to consider structuring processes, and especially **semiotic** ones that underpin the production of mental phenomena like thoughts and meanings, as a source of enormous *variety*. This contrasts with the general intention in first-wave structuralism to look for the unifying rather than diversifying tendencies of structuring processes. In the second wave, the quest for underlying processes of structural simplicity, regularity, unity and thus predictability gives way to a view of structures-of-meaning (semiotic structuring) as expressing enormous complexity, variety, difference and surprise.

This feature ultimately caused major problems for the post-structuralist approach, however, as it is difficult to hold that ideas, thoughts, language, meaning and so on are limited in important ways by the underlying structuring processes that give rise to them, and yet at the same time to claim that these self-same underlying processes generate variety. One is bound to ask how much variety can there be before the continuity of the underlying structuring process is lost altogether? As with many key problems in social theory much depends on *the scale* the theory is working at. One might claim to be able to find general patterns in the way that the Pacific Ocean behaves but it would be ridiculous to claim to predict the movement of each of its individual waves.

In common with the first wave, second-wave structuralism has an appetite for adding new terms to the social-theory phrasebook. While this is not always very helpful to people who are just beginning to get a grip on social theory, there is some justification on the grounds that one of the characteristics of post-structuralist theory is to overturn, to make more radical, some of the taken-for-granted terms and concepts that have been used by social theorists in the past. If new things need to be said it is reasonable to make up new terms with which to say them. In the following sections we will explore the most important new terms and constructs that provided a centre of gravity for much European social theory during the 1970s, 1980s and early 1990s by looking at the key authors involved in this movement. A movement that in its turn paved the way for the idea of **postmodernity** (discussed in detail in Chapter Thirteen).

Roland Barthes and semiotics or 'the science of meanings'

One of the most influential instances of the shift in social theory away from the mechanisms of linguistic structuring, and towards a study of the **meanings** that sign-systems produce, is the work of another French theorist Roland Barthes (1915–80). Concentrating specifically on the **semiotic** properties of sign-systems, that is, on the meanings that signs carry, what they stand for or *connote*, Barthes argued that since language is just one of the various rule-governed systems social actors have devised for communicating with each other, the principles of structural linguistics provide a universal platform for the study of signs in whatever form they take. The task of semiotics is to analyse and codify these sign-systems of meaning in the same way that linguistics tries to codify the structuring properties of language. Although we have to recognise that there is a difference between the cognitive version of reality that social actors have inside their heads, and the real reality that is 'out there', it is doubtful whether we can ever get a grip on the latter unless we have the means of constructing the former. It is this 'made-of-signs' version of reality that semiotics is mainly interested in. It is a moot point whether there can be a '*not*-made-of-signs' version of reality because even if there were, how, if we were deprived of the necessary signs required to do so, would we be able to describe it? What kind of thing is the 'reality' that exists outside or beyond our capacity to develop sign-system accounts of it?

Form and substance

This imposing question gives rise, in the work of Barthes and others working in the semiotic tradition in social theory, to a key distinction between 'form' and 'substance'. *Substance* is the actual stuff, the raw material, out of which social actors are trying to make some kind of sense, and *form* is the temporary manifestation of that understanding as it comes to rest in particular linguistic or other sign-system manifestations. We can detect a broad consistency here with Saussure's use of the distinction between linguistic **signs** (the **signifier–signified** combination) and the *objects* to which they refer (their **referents**). What language provides is a means of labelling and thus of dividing up what is otherwise an undifferentiated mass of potential referents into identifiable groups and categories. Ahead of being given a linguistic label of some kind, that which is yet to become a referent remains an indistinguishable part of general undifferentiated matter.

In the world of experimental physics, for example, as scientists have theorised and in some cases demonstrated the existence of subatomic particles, they have invented new names for them. Having given them names, these particles now exist in a way that they did not before; they are now included within the ordering language and concepts of particle physics. The codes that social actors use to impose order on the random and unknown stuff around them acquire an authority of their own because, temporarily or otherwise, they appear to be the best way *of ordering* the unknown. Scientists engaged in experimental physics today are in important ways governed and controlled in their experiments by the ideas and theories, the words and signs, of the physicists who came before them.

Barthes takes this key insight of first-wave structuralist theorising and applies it not so much to the relation between signs and objects, as to the *ideas* we form about them and the *meanings* we attach to them. In this scenario the undifferentiated substance that semiotics tries to make sense of is not the mass of actual physical objects waiting to be given signs (the realm of actual referents), but the realm of undifferentiated consciousness that is the raw material of organised thinking (thoughts that social actors might have, but have not yet had). Meaning is no longer seen as a kind of go-between between physical matter and the in-signs version of it we call knowledge, but as having a reality in its own right. This is a difficult concept to grasp but it is possible to conceive of a realm of organised knowledge that has no direct relation with anything physical at all. An approximate example of this is the fictitious world created as science fiction. We have no concrete evidence that life exists on other planets but this does not stop us imagining that there might be. Awareness of our own consciousness is enough to justify the idea that other consciousnesses might exist.

ILLUSTRATION – COLOURS, CODES AND MEANINGS

To give a relatively simple illustration, linguistically speaking, the colour charts produced by paint companies constitute a sign-system that gives form to what would otherwise be an unspecified range of colours that we see around us. Paint charts, and the names they give to particular colours, thus give specific (if temporary, and certainly arbitrary) *form* to the otherwise undifferentiated *substance* of colour. We can be reasonably sure that we know what 'red' is because there is a colour called 'red' on the paint chart.

Moving from the realm of labels to the realm of meanings and connotations, which semiotics is interested in, the connotation that red is a 'hot' colour and blue is a 'cold' one, that yellow and green connote the organic in a way that grey and black do not, brings us into a realm of altogether much more abstract senses of meaning. This raises the interesting question of whether 'meaning' in this more abstract semiotic sense is, like referents waiting to be given linguistic signs, always somehow already there just waiting for us to make it real by placing it inside a code. Is there an undifferentiated substance of meaning in the same way that there is an undifferentiated substance of colour?

Linguistics makes objects *real* by giving them names; semiotics makes referents *meaningful* by giving them places in codes of meaning.

'A man's gotta know his limitations'

We should also note, however, that even if there is an undifferentiated substance of meaning 'out there', we have a very strong predisposition to emphasise the bits that we have been able to incorporate within codes of meaning. Indeed we are so proud of doing so that we give this the very special label 'knowledge'. On this semiotic definition of knowledge, the limits of (coded) knowledge are very much the limits of our ability to apply coding systems to the stuff around us. Much of the emotional realm, for example, might be largely un-codable, since we lack suitable or sensible signs for translating it into a sign-system at all. Consciousness of un-coded or yet-to-be-coded stuff could loosely be called 'knowledge', but it is not the particular form we are most familiar with, which is coded knowledge.

Once bits and pieces of meaning have been given particular form through codes of meaning, both they and the code-systems of which they form a part, tend to impose a certain control over the substance and consequently over the sense of reality social actors have. The substance of colour does not change in itself just because a new paint chart has been produced, just as the astral bodies labelled 'stars' do not actually change just because we have given them names, but, for those who observe them, their meaning and significance almost certainly do change. If social actors can only make sense of substance by using signs and semiotic systems, then it could be argued that form does come to dominate substance, signifiers take precedence over signifieds. There can be no substance without the forms through which to express it.

This is similar to Lacan's argument, explored in Chapter Nine, that the real essence or substance of personality can only show itself at the surface *within the limits* of surface forms that are available for doing so. It is not possible to be/have the substance of a medieval prince or Korean-war pilot today, because the surface forms of this type of personality are no longer available. It is a personality type that is no longer expressible (the signified cannot be expressed if there is no signifier available for doing so). We could certainly say that one of the main characteristics of modern or **Enlightenment** thought is not only to strongly emphasise the stuff that has been codified into knowledge over that which has not (the physical over the metaphysical), but also to place great emphasis on the codes that use **empirical** scientific methods to do so. One of the reasons why it is so difficult to conceive of a realm of yet-to-be-codified 'knowledge' is that from a very young age social actors are trained to give much more significance to the things that they do think they know than to those that they have yet to find out.

Semiotics and culture

Given its close association with structural linguistics and its emphasis on meaning and interpretation, semiotics concentrates especially on the sign-systems that circulate within the realm of *culture*. We will have more to say about 'the cultural turn' in social theory in Chapters Thirteen and Fourteen, where we will see that one of the basic premises of **postmodernist** social theory is its belief that social life has become increasingly dominated by goings-on in the cultural realm. For now we can briefly define the cultural realm as the realm of institutions and practices in society, such as educational and religious practice, the mass-media, key aspects of domestic living and 'civil society', and the recreational domains of leisure, pleasure and entertainment, which are especially concerned with propagating ideas and beliefs. All realms in society are saturated with meaning and interpretation but there is a particular concentration of intellectual energy in the cultural realm that is devoted to exploring ideas, beliefs and values.

Working in semiotic mode it is reasonable to suppose that since society is made up of a number of fairly distinct realms or domains, there will also be a number of different codes of meaning operating in society at the same time. One of the tasks of social theory is to understand the processes by which the inferred meanings and interpretations associated with one system of codes, for example those that generate religious beliefs, do or do not converge with those associated with another sign–system, for example ideas about education. If a serious disjuncture were to occur between the codes of meaning in these two realms, then obviously this might have some fairly serious consequences for social cohesion and order. In order to understand the connections between different codes of meaning at a more abstract level we first of all have to think about the contents of different codes at a more grounded level of analysis.

ILLUSTRATION – BODY-TYPE CODES

We can illustrate the way in which different codes converge by thinking about different body-shapes. The sign-system of the fashion industry promotes particular kinds of body-shape as 'ideal'. Fashion-house models are very often tall and slender. This coding of tall and slender coincides with another, which is that tall, slender people are more elegant and glamorous than short, plump people. These inferences circulate within the mass media where they are further embellished and reinforced by images of tall, slender, elegant, glamorous women who, as a direct consequence of these attributes, are styled as highly attractive. The slender body-shape connotes not only charisma and style, but also achievement and success. Short, round-faced people find a place in a different strand of the body-shape sign-system, which connotes the idea that fat people are jolly and fun to be with. If people who are coded in this way do turn out to be attractive or successful this will be regarded as being *despite* their body-shape and not because of it.

Interpretations of what constitutes success are also often closely linked with codes connoting sexual attractiveness. The tall, broad-shouldered, muscular male body-type registers as attractive and desirable in a way that the undeveloped physique does not. These visible characteristics (and body-shape codes rely heavily on surface appearance) and their association with sexual desirability, fuels the presumption that sexuality and success are closely linked. The whole point of being attractive is that it increases one's chances of being successful.

Myths

In addition to being interested in how individual signs come to connote particular meanings, Barthes was also interested in the way in which a similar structuring of representation and signification could also be applied when looking into the **narrative** accounts or stories that social actors tell to each other as a way of making sense of society. Referring to these narratives as a series of 'myths' (see his book *Mythologies*, 1973 [1957]), Barthes describes how once these mythical accounts have become established or 'naturalised', it becomes very difficult to challenge them and the apparently self-evident truths that they have created. Barthes argues that key individuals and organisations within the cultural sphere (e.g. owners of media corporations, makers of official opinion, intellectuals of the cultural elite) are inclined to create mythic accounts of social reality that may or may not be true. In a cultural realm awash with myths and stories it becomes increasingly difficult for social actors to distinguish essence from appearance; truth from deception.

Pushing social theory very much in the direction of critical cultural studies, Barthes suggests that one way of showing that these official stories are in fact myths, is to challenge whether individual authors really do have control over, or are creators of, the texts/myths they produce. Like Saussure and Wittgenstein, who argue that the rules of the language game limit the number of meaningful utterances that can be made (see Chapter Nine), Barthes argues that semiotic systems, including those that create popular myths, also impose clear limitations on what the storyteller can say.

In his influential essay 'Death of the Author' (1977 [1968]), Barthes challenges the traditional Enlightenment view that it is only human beings that can attach meaning and significance to things (the idea of the **transcendental subject**). He argues instead that meaning is actually a property of the sign–system. Taking the process of creative writing as an example, Barthes suggests (somewhat controversially) that it is not the author who creates the text, but the text that **overdetermines** what that author is able to write. He suggests that the idea of the independent creative author *is itself* a myth. Even if the author has some freedom or control over the composition in terms of the actual words they use (and they still have to abide by the rules of the language they are using), *the sense or meaning* of what they have written is something that they cannot really control. Authors have art and influence in their writing as a creative act, but they do not create and control meaning. What they write gives temporary form to the undifferentiated, but nonetheless already-existing, mass or substance of meaning, from which, like everyone else, they borrow their thoughts.

Barthes thus takes the basic idea in structuralist thinking that structures below create the spaces above into which social actors are drawn, and extends it to argue that, having become occupants of those roles, the meanings social actors produce are also controlled by 'the power of the meaning'. It is not possible to write a genuinely new fairy story, for example, because the terrain of fairy storytelling is already overcrowded with all the fairly stories and their various permutations that have already been written. The best the author can hope for is to produce a copy of the themes and codes generally associated with this genre of creative writing, but using a new form of expression (idiom), some new character variations and perhaps different historical settings and social contexts. The very idea that there are a number of distinct genres of narrative writing (science fiction, romance, western, fantasy and so on) confirms the logic of Barthes' suggestion that novelty is seriously constrained by that which already exists.

Michel Foucault and the power of discourse

The story so far

The classical modernist approach in social theory (discussed in Chapters Three to Six) sees institutions and **social practices** as the product of historical processes. It treats social change over time **diachronically** as a continual and linear movement from one state or condition of development to the next. This idea of 'history' is modelled on the notion of physiological development, which is usually applied to biological organisms. It is also reminiscent of the notion of history as biography, which is used to describe the development of individuals. The structuralist and post-structuralist approaches in contrast, which are discussed in this and the previous chapter, concentrate much more on the **synchronic** or present-time dimension of social institutions and practices. They do not claim that society has no 'history' (and certainly there is plenty of it in social theory itself), but emphasise that lived experience is an immediate, spontaneous, real-time phenomenon that coincides entirely with the moment in which it occurs.

A major consequence of this move in social theory is to develop explanations of social phenomena, not as the outcome of past events, but very much at the level of immediate present-time experiences. Consciousness coincides exactly with the instant it is being experienced and so although society has history just like social actors have biography, neither social actors nor society have their experiences *in* the past. Both are hostages of 'the now'. It is generally recognised, for example, that although we can remember instances when we were in pain, and as a result try to avoid situations that might be painful for us, the real experience of pain only lasts as long as we actually are in pain. Our memory of this sensation is not the same as the real-time experience of pain, or hunger, or elation, or love.

Discourses of history

The theorist who has had the most to say about the issue of history from a post-structuralist perspective is the French historian and philosopher Michel Foucault (1926–84). In his early work Foucault sees history in terms of a series of 'intellectual paradigms', or **épistèmes** as he calls them (from the Greek word for 'knowledge', as in the more familiar term 'epistemology' – the theory of knowledge), which can be defined as distinct and identifiable patterns in how social actors from a particular historical period tend to think about the world around them:

KEY QUOTE – Michel Foucault, *The Archaeology of Knowledge* (1969).
Épistèmes can be defined as ...

The total set of relations that unite, at a given period, the discursive practices that give rise to epistemological figures, sciences, and possibly formalized systems [of knowledge], the totality of relations that can be discovered, for a given period between the sciences when one analyses them at the level of discursive regularities. (Foucault, 1972 [1969], p 39)

At this point in his career Foucault's analysis bears more than a family resemblance to the basic structuralist approach for at least two clear reasons. First, Foucault introduces the idea of *épistèmes* to capture the sense in which each historical period can be identified as having a particular intellectual style or approach that tends to be shared across the different branches of knowledge. Each intellectual approach and the various **discourses** in which they are made manifest at the surface can be regarded as paradigmatic for the way social actors interpreted the world around them at that particular time. Discourse can be defined as the prevailing mode and manner of accounts and conversations that go on in society and that make one historical period distinguishable from another. The idea of *épistèmes* is close to the semiotic concept of codes of meaning that we discussed earlier in this chapter. The *épistèmes* described by Foucault are a slightly grander and more elaborate term for describing how particular codes of meaning, and techniques actors use for encoding the stuff around them (e.g. the technique of empirical method in scientific research), accumulate and blend together to form an overall frame of reference for making sense of things at a particular point in time.

The fact that this style or approach does seem to recur across a number of fields of scientific and artistic enquiry at the same time would seem to indicate the presence of an underlying structuring process. Philosophers, scientists, intellectuals and ordinary social actors living in the same time period tend to see reality and to organise their thoughts about it in a generally similar way. The linguistic and semiotic frames of reference they use are common to all those living in that particular time and place. As far as Foucault is concerned, different *épistèmes* play a major role in accounting for the differences between one historical period and another. Today, for example, one would expect there to be a family resemblance between what a theologian, a politician, a business leader and a bricklayer might have to say about global warming. There would be differences in detail between their opinions and beliefs, but their general orientation, and the terminology, concepts and values they use in their discussions, would be quite similar. Epistemologically speaking, they are all 'talking the same language'. If they were not talking the same language and using the same conceptual frameworks conversation would be impossible.

Foucault identifies four *épistèmes* from his own historical research (see *Madness and Civilization*, 1967 [1961] and *The Order of Things*, 1970 [1966]). These are:

- the 16th century;
- the *âge classique* represented by the intellectual and scientific progress of the 18th century (i.e. the period of the European Enlightenment and the Age of Reason);
- the 19th century (the height of the first Industrial Revolution);
- the period from the mid-20th century onwards.

He believes that, at least at its high point, the intellectual motif of a particular period is largely invisible to the social actors who are using it. Where it does become visible is during the transition from one such period or intellectual epoch to another.

Expressing a view that has resulted in his being labelled a **postmodernist** thinker (postmodernism is discussed in Chapter Thirteen), Foucault argues that his own work, and possibly the post-structuralist movement he has been associated with, represents just such a moment of transition from one *épistème* to the next. The last gasp of the 'old' modernist Enlightenment *épistème*, which was the dominant frame of reference from the late 1700s until the start of the 20th century, was a recognition of the difference between the surface of things and the power of underlying structuring forces (e.g. the difference Marx identifies between 'appearance' and 'essence' or between 'base' and 'superstructure'). The 'new' thinking that emerged at the start of the

20th century, including most significantly the psychoanalytic theory of Freud and the linguistic turn initiated by Saussure, provided a radically new foundation for conceptions of knowledge. The emergence at this time of the new academic discourses (or disciplines) in anthropology, sociology, linguistics and psychology provide evidence of the new *épistème* that emerged in the universities at this time.

The second sense in which Foucault's ideas express a structuralist orientation is by giving priority to the synchronic rather than to the diachronic dimension. Rather than following the intellectual historian's usual method of researching academic disciplines separately and as they change over time, Foucault prefers instead to make comparisons *across* disciplines at the same moment in time. In his book *The Order of Things* (1970 [1966]), for example, he looks at developments in the 19th century across the disciplines of language, natural history and economics. Foucault is also challenging the **teleological** view of knowledge (also typical of Enlightenment thought), which assumes that each new idea is better than the one that came before it and will probably turn out to be inferior to those that follow. The ideas of today must be better than the ideas of yesterday, or one hundred or one thousand years ago, because they are more recent. Although this assumption could be regarded as acceptable in fields of technical knowledge such as science, medicine and engineering, where practical outcomes can be used as evidence for the best ideas and of 'progress', Foucault suggests that forms of knowledge in the fields of philosophy, social theory, political science and culture have to be seen differently. There is no logical way of showing that values and beliefs found in 20th-century culture are necessarily better than those of some earlier historical period. If Foucault's thoughts on this matter are reliable, then before long we can expect another change in the *épistème*, which will overturn current frames of reference and definitions of knowledge, including perhaps those proposed by Foucault.

History and historiography

Continuing to grapple with the structuralist dilemma of how to incorporate 'history' (the archetypal diachronic dimension) into 'the present' (the archetypal synchronic dimension), Foucault makes use of the important distinction between 'history' as the word used to refer to actual past events (things that really did happen) and 'historiography', which refers to the various records (literally 'writings about history') that social actors have produced to record it. This is equivalent to the difference between the birthday party I went to yesterday and the account of the party that I wrote in my diary. Using one of the basic structuralist concepts we discussed in the previous section on Roland

Barthes, historiography could be seen as the *form* that the real *substance* of past events takes on. Historiography is the *signified/signifier* and actual past events are the *referent*. Historiography is of the *synchronic* dimension, and actual history is the *diachronic* dimension.

Foucault accepts that it is impossible ever to really know how things were in the past because it is the very nature of consciousness that experience can only occur in the present. Although, rather confusingly, social actors refer confidently to 'history' and to 'the past', their consciousness of past events is always a present-time event. The best we can hope for, then, as Foucault recognises, is to infer what real past history was like by examining the various historical artefacts that provide a historiographic record of those events. It is by looking at these artefacts that Foucault claims to have worked out the various 'discursive formations' that underpin the *épistèmes* of past historical periods. If, in a structuralist manner of speaking, the present is a surface form of the past, then the historiographic artefacts we have accumulated (the currently-existing historical record) give us clues as to the nature of the structuring processes of previous periods of history.

Again there are some obvious difficulties here. First, even if the artefact is genuinely historic it can still only be read and interpreted using the linguistic and semiotic frames of reference of *today*. The artefact itself might be genuinely ancient but the frame of reference through which it is being read cannot be anything other than entirely contemporary. Nobody knows for certain what sounds dinosaurs made or what colours they were because 'the fossil record' does not retain this information.

Second, authenticity does not guarantee the accuracy of the artefact. We cannot know for sure if an artefact was, at the time it was produced, giving a genuine and reliable account or a false and misleading one. The further back in time we go, the fewer the number of surviving artefacts and so the more authority they seem to command. Rarity, however, establishes the durability of the artefact not its reliability. The question of authenticity raises a series of further questions since it is a moot point whether increasing sophistication in the means of recording events will make it easier or more difficult to disguise what was really going on. The postmodernist theorist Jean Baudrillard, for example, has argued that digitalised media make it possible to produce an entirely synthetic version of **hyper-reality** where 'reality' and 'fiction' become indistinguishable (these ideas are discussed in Chapter Thirteen).

Third, and despite his otherwise strong emphasis on the synchronic, present-time dimension, Foucault's social theory encounters a problem faced by all social theories that are based around the idea of distinct stages in social history, which is how to explain the *transition* from one to the next. Even if the stages are not seen in linear evolutionary terms, in which each stage is a precondition for the next, it would be useful to have some idea about how, when and why the next code of meaning, frame of reference or *épistème* emerges. In this respect at least, Foucault's social theory is much stronger in terms of working out the constitution of the *épistème*, and of describing *the discourses* it is made of, than it is in explaining movement from one frame of reference to the next.

Discourse and power

Perhaps the most influential suggestion made by Foucault, and certainly the one that he is most closely associated with, is about the nature or character of the various **discourses** that *épistèmes* are made of. Given that historiography is all about the interpretation of texts and artefacts that provide a record of the past, we are bound to ask who is it that gets to make the historical record? Just like my diary entry about yesterday's birthday party, the recording of current events might be a quite haphazard affair. How will my biographer in years to come be able to tell whether my diary account is accurate? Maybe I imagined a birthday party when none actually took place.

In his early work (e.g. *Madness and Civilization*, 1967 [1961] and to a lesser extent *The Order of Things*, 1970 [1966]) Foucault first approaches this dilemma by recognising that those in power in society usually have more control over the recording of events than those who have little or no power. Indeed he begins to define power as the ability a group or individual social actor has for controlling the recording of events: history is written by the winners, not by the losers. In this respect Foucault stays fairly close to the basic structuralist prognosis that power is a property of the sign-system, which shows itself when sign-systems, and the texts and discourses in which they are embedded, exercise control over the social actors who are exposed to them. In order for discourse to have any of the controlling properties that Foucault attributes to it, both as something that really does affect social actors in the real world and as a concept within social theory, he also has to retain the idea that discourses, and the *épistèmes* that are based upon them, exhibit quite a high level of internal consistency. They provide a unified, if sometimes rather oppressive, way of looking at reality and of reaching some conclusions about it.

In his later work, however (e.g. *The Archaeology of Knowledge*, 1972 [1969], *Discipline and Punish*, 1977 [1975], and the first volume of *The History of Sexuality*, 1979 [1976]), Foucault confronts the question of power more directly and especially the difficulty of separating the discursive realm of meaning from the material world of objects, practices and institutions. He now envisages discourses as facilitating forms of power that originate from within the wider political, social and economic realms of society and are thus outside the sign-system itself. Power is still focused through the structuring processes of the sign-system, but is nonetheless not an exclusive property of the sign-system. This new perspective on power allows him to retain the idea that there is similarity between one discourse and another in terms of how discourses do what they do (they are mechanically or functionally the same), but at the same time to emphasise the variety that is found among different discourses in terms of their content and how they are enmeshed with exterior power struggles of the day.

This marks the beginning of quite a shift in Foucault's thinking from some of the structuralist principles he started out with. His original concept of discourse as a kind of verbal or spoken text that imposes a particular intellectual code or mental frame of reference for looking at reality, is recast into the concept of 'discursive practice' to show that discourse is not just a verbal/textual representation of exterior social reality and of the power-play that this involves, but becomes *constitutive of* that reality. Discursive practice is much more than an intellectual framework that powerful groups make use of to express control and authority, but is itself a principal *mode of power* in society. The making and using of particular ways of seeing the world actually constitutes the power of dominant groups.

ILLUSTRATION – ANYONE FOR TENNIS?

We can illustrate some of the properties of 'discourse' and of 'discursive practice' developed by Foucault by thinking about watching a game of tennis on television. We already know from Saussure and others working in linguistic/structuralist mode that the players are governed in their actions by the rules of the game. Some actions are permissible and others not and the players do not get to choose. The 'rules of tennis' form a closed system in which one rule is constructed and enacted by reference to other rules in that system.

If we think now about the kinds of *discourses* that are involved in a game of tennis, there would be conversations between players, among the crowd and discourse *about* the game provided by the media commentator. Although in one sense the game itself is separate from the various discourses that it contains, and which go on around it, we can see that in some key respects these discourses are very much part of the event. When the umpire calls out the score or declares whether a ball was 'in' or 'out', her discursive intervention is actually *part of* the game; it is not just discourse but *discursive practice*.

Thinking about the commentator's discourse, to the extent that our understanding and enjoyment of the tennis match is affected by the commentary, that discourse also becomes part of the event for us. This would be the case even more obviously if one were listening to the commentary on the radio. The commentary is not just *about* the game but becomes an integral part of it. It is because commentaries are a form not just of exterior reporting, but of *discursive practice*, that different commentaries really do produce different events even if they are of the same match.

By replacing the concept of discourse with the concept of discursive practice, Foucault sets the concept of power free from the constraints of the sign-systems of language and semiotics altogether. In his new perspective power and control are released from the bondage of the sign-system first established in the work of Saussure. In terms of his own status as a social theorist we can also say that, at this point, Foucault moves decisively away from being a theorist of intellectual, ideational phenomena and towards developing a general social theory that also tries to account for material practices and institutions as well.

Power-knowledge

If we accept that discursive practice (and not just discourse) *is itself* a manifestation of power, we are still left with the problem of explaining what it is that social actors want when they exercise power. What, in other words, is power *for*? In trying to answer this question, Foucault makes the next and, as it turned out, final leap in his thinking (see, for example, the second and third volumes of *The History of Sexuality* published shortly after his death in 1984). The solution he arrives at relies heavily on one of the main ideas of the 19th-century German philosopher Friedrich Nietzsche known as 'the will to power'. Advocates of this perspective argue that 'power' expresses an underlying urge or desire, which they believe is part of the basic mental and psychological make-up of human beings everywhere, to exert power over others. In this perspective power and desire do not have to be *for* anything in the sense that economic power gives control over the economy, or military power gives control through physical force; the expression of 'pure' power and of 'pure' desire is an end in itself. For Foucault, the kind of power that social actors most desire is the kind of power that comes with knowledge or, as he calls it, 'power-knowledge'. Understood in its simplest sense, power-knowledge means control over the construction and operation of the codes of meaning or frames of reference that define objects, ideas and meanings *as* knowledge.

In terms of how the concepts of discourse, discursive practice and power-knowledge help us reach a better understanding of society, Foucault's social theory turns out to be mostly about the quest for

power. Discourses, and the intellectual paradigms or *épistèmes* of particular historical periods that they make up, represent one such manifestation of power. They exercise power not just on the intellectual plain of thoughts, ideas and meanings (what we might call the mental or cognitive terrain of power), but also in a much more concrete and physical sense because these ideas become inscribed into the material practices and institutions of society. The orthodox majority of the population seeks control over the deviant minority not just because it controls the discourse through which these individuals and groups become defined *as* deviant, but because the same attitude of mind becomes embedded in the political, cultural and legal institutions of society. Homosexuality, for example, is never in and of itself 'wrong' or 'bad', but in some cultures and at some particular historical moments it is *made* bad or wrong because of the presence within the cultural milieu of a dominant discourse that makes it so. This dominance, moreover, is not just a matter of cultural style or intellect, but is rigorously backed-up by the legal system.

In seeking out the kinds and sources of power in society social theorists should, if they accept Foucault's perspective, look for the 'apparatus' (or *dispositif* in French) through which power-knowledge operates. This apparatus is made up of 'a thoroughly **heterogeneous** ensemble consisting of discourses, institutions, architectural forms, regulatory decisions, laws, administrative measures, scientific statements, philosophical, moral and philanthropic propositions' (Foucault, 1980, p 194). The key point to note here is that the concept of 'apparatus' moves beyond Foucault's earlier idea of the *épistème* so that he can now include both discourse-based and non-discourse-based practices as feeding into the construction of power-knowledge: 'the épistème is a specifically discursive apparatus, whereas the *dispositif* [apparatus] in its general form is both discursive and non-discursive, its elements being much more heterogeneous' (Foucault, 1980, p 196). The apparatus of social control includes both structures of meaning and material structures in the form of social practices and institutions.

The act of recognising discourses for what they really are (i.e. mechanisms for the exercise of power-knowledge) places the researcher in the position of critical observer, who thus attempts to draw attention to the stories that the discourse *does not tell*. A bit like the critical intellectuals in Althusser's social theory, or the myth-builders in Barthes' account, archaeologists of knowledge, like Foucault, gradually tease away the layers of deception and misdirection that make up the dominant discourse, to the extent eventually of undermining the credibility of the *épistème* altogether.

This is as close as Foucault gets to developing an account of how one frame of reference is displaced by another. Although at an earlier stage in his thinking it is implied that the prevailing frame of reference remains largely invisible to the social actors who are dominated by it (they have yet to discover its mythic and ideological status), we can suggest that a point must arrive when some actors are able to peep around the edge of that frame of reference and catch a glimpse of possible alternatives. If Foucault were still operating in idealist mode, which is to say if he was still emphasising the distinctiveness of a separate realm of meanings expressed through discourse alone, he would at this point have come quite close to the Hegelian idea of dialectical change. As one world view reaches maturity (thesis), alternative views develop (antithesis) and, following a period of conflict between ideas, a new consensus (synthesis) will emerge (see Chapter Four). Using the concept of discursive practice Foucault is able to develop a general social theory in which social transition is seen as taking place in the realm of social practices as well as in the realm of ideas.

The subjective individual

The final key aspect of Foucault's social theory we need to look at here is what he has to say about the subjective individual. As we saw in the ideas of Barthes discussed in the previous section, second-wave or post-structuralist thinking carries on where the first wave left off in developing a view of individual social actors as not having much in the way of biography or autonomy. Foucault continues this trend and argues that individual actors are produced not just by the structures or discourses that create spaces for them, but by the discursive practices of power-knowledge. Power-knowledge has important structuring properties and one of the principal objects of its structuring activity is the social actor:

KEY QUOTE – Foucault, *Power-Knowledge* (1980), on individuals as an effect of power.
It is already one of the prime effects of power that certain bodies, certain gestures, certain discourses, certain desires come to be identified and constituted as individuals. The individual, that is, is not the *vis-à-vis* of power; it is, I believe, one of its prime effects. The individual is an effect of power, and at the same time, or precisely to the extent to which it is that effect, it is the element of its articulation. The individual which power has constituted is at the same time its vehicle. (Foucault, 1980, p 98)

What Foucault is saying in his rather complicated language is that power-knowledge creates social actors rather than being created by them. Although they have the interesting and unusual property of subjective consciousness, social actors are, like all other kinds of objects, given an identifiable form within the field of knowledge and by the same process of power-knowledge that makes all phenomena real. There certainly is something quite special about human consciousness, but it is not so special that it can be regarded as the origin of everything else. There is an intellectual echo here with George Herbert Mead's concept of the self as being made up of the personal 'I' and the social 'me' (see Chapter Seven). Foucault is suggesting that the self is very much dominated by how it appears to other social actors (the 'me'), rather than by how it is experienced self-referentially by the social actor itself (the 'I'). For Foucault it is not reasonable to regard human beings as a special and unique category of objects just because they happen to have a capacity for self-reflection.

Moreover, social actors cannot claim to be separate from, or to have an existence independent of, power-knowledge because without it they would not have any means of expressing themselves as real. If, for example, I am a cricketer and wanted to play 'in goal' this would not be possible because there is no such position in that game. The rules of cricket and the discursive practices, professional organisations and clubs that make the game what it is give 'cricketers' a way of expressing themselves as such while also disallowing deviant variations. The capacity social actors have for consciousness and self-reflection makes them especially sensitive to the conditions under which they can express themselves but they are still unable actually to do so without the facilities offered by power-knowledge.

Foucault does acknowledge, however, that the relationship between human being-objects and power-knowledge tends to work in both directions because without the existence of conscious social agents upon whom power-knowledge can work its magic, power-knowledge itself would remain a property without form. Without the presence of social agents power-knowledge would remain entirely abstract. Foucault defends his argument on this point by suggesting that the strong concept social actors in modern society have of individual uniqueness is actually one of the effects (rather than a cause) of the power-knowledge of the Enlightenment frame of reference. Before Enlightenment thinking popularised the myth of individual uniqueness, of rational self-sufficiency and political independence, quite different ideas about individuality, subjectivity and all the rest were in play. Part of the reason why the post-structuralist perspective sometimes seems so alarming and radical is because it forces us, both as individuals and as social theorists, to think again about many of the practices and meanings we have been taking for granted. Just because ideas are unsettling does not make them wrong.

Jacques Derrida on logocentrism, différance, decentring and deconstruction

Of those producing the largest number of new terms, or new ways of using old ones, in social theory, a prize must surely go to the French social theorist Jacques Derrida (1930–2004). Like Barthes and Foucault, Derrida uses basic structuralist concepts but attempts to move beyond them, often by following them through to even more radical conclusions than Saussure, Lévi-Strauss and other first-wave structuralist thinkers had managed to do. This effort required the use of several new terms, many of which have now become part of the jargon of post-structuralism. A number of these appear in Derrida's early writings, for example *Of Grammatology* (1976 [1967]) and *Writing and Difference* (1978 [1968]).

Logocentrism

The unfamiliar term 'logocentric' is taken from the Greek word *logos* meaning 'speech' and 'reason' and Derrida uses it to highlight the Enlightenment modernist belief in the existence of an essential something that exists beyond or outside human consciousness, but which at the same time requires human consciousness so that it can be revealed. Derrida argues in his early texts that although first-wave structuralists had highlighted a crucial distinction between the surface of things and the structuring processes that lie beneath, their perspective remained closely tied to some of the basic assumptions of the old modernist frame of reference. Developing a line of argument that became a dominant and occasionally a unifying theme in post-structuralist and later postmodernist thinking, Derrida, like Foucault, also traces the modernist perspective back to the period of the European Enlightenment. The particular idea he takes issue with is the core assumption in the Enlightenment world view (which it had in fact borrowed from the earlier classical period) that 'truth' and 'meaning' exist in a pure state 'out there', and that the human quest for knowledge is largely a matter of identifying, coding and recording these essences.

This is a **metaphysical** conception of stuff (ontology) and an **idealist** theory of knowledge (**epistemology**) in the sense that, although social actors come to know things at the level of the particular forms they temporarily take on, beneath these surface forms there is a deeper or inner essence that exists independently of the surface manifestation. In this perspective, 'truth' and 'meaning' are conceived as universal and timeless entities that exist despite, rather than because of, the particular forms they are given by conscious social actors at any particular time and place. Recalling our discussion of Barthes' ideas in the first section of this chapter, this frame of reference conceives of an abstract realm of yet-to-be-coded stuff that, although in some sense is waiting to be given form or brought to order by the conscious observer, remains indifferent to any particular form that it might be given. To take a frequently used example, a physical 'truth' like the presence of gravity on planet Earth does what it does *irrespective of* the particular theory of gravity that the scientific community might happen to have about it. If we had no theory of gravity, we would not all suddenly start floating off into space.

This belief in the essential or pure nature of things provided strong support throughout the 18th, 19th and 20th centuries for the notion of empirical, scientific investigation as the most modern and most rational way of bringing these essential forces within the range of human understanding. The conquest of nature and of God by **reason** is the central motif of the modern imagination. In the terms Foucault uses, these core assumptions and the various philosophical, scientific, religious, political and cultural discursive practices that make them up, constitute the *épistème* of the modern outlook.

Derrida's complaint against the traditional structuralist method first developed by Saussure, is that the distinction between signifier and signified (surface and depth, langue and parole) preserves the modernist presumption of an inner abstract or 'pure' form of something that can only be known once linguistic labels have been applied to it. Much like Lacan, Barthes and the early Foucault (the Foucault of discourse rather than of discursive practice), Derrida wishes to dispel what he sees as the myth that all phenomena possess a unique essence, by insisting that the only reality that social actors can really know is that which shows itself in the form of actually existing texts, that is, as surface forms. His logic here is that it cannot be known if there is anything below the surface because, until linguistic labels have been applied to it, it has no means of being expressed (it is inexpressible). Its existence is therefore entirely coincidental with and not separable from its surface form. Notions of underlying or deep-structural forces are in fact already part of the surface. Derrida felt sure enough of himself to declare that 'there is nothing outside the text' (Derrida, 1976 [1967], p 160). Texts are not representations of something else; they are all that there is and all that social actors can ever hope to find.

Différance

Derrida's reassertion of the signifier (form) over the signified (substance) combined with his energetic insistence that all that we can know is contained within texts of various kinds inevitably leads him towards a close examination of texts in order to discover more about reality. As part of this effort he introduces another new term *différance*. This is a deliberate misspelling of the French verb *deférer*, which means both to 'differ from' and to 'defer to' (i.e. to give way to). Derrida uses it to focus attention on the idea that texts are by no means random or accidental, but are obliged to take the forms they do because of a central characteristic of linguistic structuring, which is that things are constructed very much in terms of their opposites. Despite challenging Saussure's assumption that substance is more important than surface forms, Derrida uses a very basic structuralist method for examining or 'deconstructing' texts by looking at some of the underlying structuring processes that give rise to them. Concentrating on texts as purveyors of meaning, for example, he pushes the structuralist method to its limits by suggesting that if texts are indeed structured in terms of opposites and *différance*, then it becomes impossible ever to arrive at a final understanding or reading of the text. Each phase or moment of deconstruction simply pushes the reader of the text towards another pair or opposites or series of differences or deferrals. There can be no 'final meaning' in a text because meaning is perpetually elusive. The best social actors can hope for, when searching for meaning by way of texts, is that sufficient of them will agree at a particular moment that a particular reading is, albeit provisionally, good enough to be going on with. Texts only ever provide a temporary sense of permanence.

In this respect at least, we can identify a family resemblance among the post-structuralist fold between Derrida's deconstruction of the text, Barthes' focus on mythologies and Foucault's preoccupation with discourses. In their different ways each is trying to work out the mechanisms by which particular combinations of difference, myth and discourse become acceptable to social actors as a fair representation of what is going on in the social world around them. Although they follow slightly different paths, these theorists arrive at the same general conclusion, which is that nothing can be comprehensible outside or beyond the sign-systems, texts and discourses in which it is inscribed. The core belief within the Enlightenment *épistème* of an abstract realm of stuff having the potential to be brought within human knowledge is rejected. Far better to limit the definition of knowledge, truth, meaning and reality to things that have been inscribed in texts. Texts are the limit of what can be revealed to the inquisitive human mind.

Decentring the subject

The final aspect of Derrida's social theory we need to look at is that other old chestnut of the post-structuralist agenda, the subjective individual. As we might anticipate (given his criticisms of the metaphysical and idealist tone of the Enlightenment frame of reference), Derrida agrees with his post-structuralist fellows that it is a mistake to conceive of the social actor as expressing any kind of universal essence, spirit or soul. Human beings might be 'of a kind' in terms of their physiological make-up but this feature alone does not provide much of a foundation for the idea of an inner and universal **human nature** that transcends particular corporeal editions of *homo sapiens*. If knowledge, truth and meaning do not have a universal essence, then, as long as we are, as Foucault strongly suggests, prepared to see social actors as objects rather than as subjects (the social 'me' rather than the personal 'I'), social actors do not have a universal essence either. The strengths and weaknesses of arguments about the existence or otherwise of the 'transcendental human subject' have already come up a number of times in this chapter. What is slightly different about Derrida's approach is that he tackles the question by developing yet another new term – 'the decentring of the subject'.

The core of this idea follows on from the concepts of *différance* and distinction we have just been looking at. To understand his argument, social actors have to be thought of as a kind of objective text. If we add to this Derrida's conclusion that no matter how hard we try to find one, texts can never have a final meaning because all we have is a constant state of referral from one set of differences to the next, then the search for human essence is likewise futile. For Derrida, the search for human essence through the analysis of humans-as-texts is equivalent to the search for truth and meaning through the analysis of other non-human kinds of texts. Derrida thus uses an orthodox structuralist method in arriving at the idea that like other kinds of texts, social actors also turn out to be products of underlying structuring processes.

 ## ILLUSTRATION – A NETWORK OF SPACES

A simple way of imagining the notion of structuring used by Derrida and others working in post-structuralist mode is to think about the properties of the spaces in a piece of netting. Although the spaces between the strings appear to have a concrete form as identifiable squares, they only take this form as a result of the strings that make up the netting. The spaces are actually just empty air, which have temporarily been given an identifiable form as spaces within the structure of the net. Without the net the spaces are indistinguishable from all the rest of empty space. The precise form the spaces take is determined entirely by the size, shape and design of the netting. The temporarily identifiable spaces in the net are thus produced directly by a structuring process, in this example, of net making. The structuring processes that surround human experience are obviously much more complicated than those required for making nets, but, from a post-structuralist perspective, the basic principle that it is the structuring process that shapes and creates that experience is the same.

We can grasp the point about *decentring* by emphasising that the spaces created between the strings of a net *are not the same* as the spaces created between the threads of a spider's web. In the case of the web there is an identifiable centre; in the case of the net there is none. No particular space has greater significance, nor is it closer to 'the centre', than any of the other spaces.

In common with all other objects-as-texts, social actors can never find their source or centre because no matter how hard they search, all they will find is another space created by the structures around it. Running along much the same lines as Foucault's idea that it is the peculiar capacity for conscious self-reflection that leads actors to believe that there must be something unique about human beings, Derrida implies that the assumption that things have a particular centre or point of origin is largely an effect of the mind of the observer. It is the way in which the mind of the social actor *does its observing* that implies a focal centre, a transcendent and separate viewpoint; it does not follow that there actually is such a thing.

Overview and chapter summary

The post-structuralist perspectives we have looked at in this chapter bring into question a key assumption of modernist social theory. This is the core Enlightenment idea that whether we are looking at the nature of knowledge (epistemology) or at the nature of the stuff that reality is made of (ontology), whether we are interested in the development and impact on the present of past events (history), or whether we are interested in the nature of individuals as conscious subjects (biography), reality has properties that remain permanent despite or irrespective of the forces that act upon them.

According to this Enlightenment view, knowledge, history and subjective consciousness have 'transcendent properties' that go beyond and outlast the particular manifestations that they take on at any actual moment. Consciousness is undoubtedly a synchronic present-time phenomenon, but this does not mean that consciousness is born anew each time one thought turns into another. There is no compelling reason why we should doubt that consciousness itself, the basic capacity human beings have for self-awareness and thought, has essential properties that remain fairly constant both from one social actor to another and across time and place. Physiologically, one human brain works pretty much like another in its mechanical operations.

Even accepting the vast complexity of surface forms, there is within reality an inner or irreducible core of 'stuff' that social actors can find out about. The search for knowledge, and the increases in civilisation and advancement that are assumed to go with it, can be seen as the search for this irreducible stuff.

At the level of questions about *individuals*, modernist social theory presumes that social actors can be described accurately as biographical subjects who really do exist over and above, even beyond, the structures and experiences they have. Human beings do possess some kind of essential inner nature. At the level of questions about *society* and its development, this key modernist assumption takes it as self-evident that the institutions and practices that actors live with in their present are attached in significant ways with what went before. Progressing in a generally linear way, 'the present' is seen as a product of 'the past'. At the level of questions about the nature of *knowledge*, it is likewise assumed that 'knowledge' also has a certain permanency, that it accumulates or builds-up over time, and that it is sufficiently tangible to be grasped by conscious biographical human beings.

Barthes, Foucault and Derrida challenge these core assumptions by arguing that knowledge is not absolute or permanent, but is perpetually self-referential. The search for knowledge cannot progress in a linear fashion from a state of complete ignorance to a state of full enlightenment because the very concept of knowledge is caught up in a never-ending circuit of competing discourses. If knowledge is essentially elusive, then it follows that in significant respects the object of knowledge, that is, 'reality' or 'matter' itself, must remain unknowable.

The major contribution of structuralist and later of post-structuralist social theory has been to point out that social theory should be much more concerned with the frames of reference out of which different versions of what counts as knowledge have been created, than with the quest for knowledge itself. A failure to agree a definition of 'true' knowledge stems directly from the inability to resolve conflict between one frame of reference and another (for example between the Enlightenment and the post-Enlightenment view or between the natural sciences and the social sciences). The systematic organising of matter into particular codes or orders of meaning is a relatively straightforward task compared with the extremely demanding philosophical challenge of ordering one frame of reference in respect of its alternatives.

From a post-structuralist perspective both history and individual social actors are 'decentred' in the sense that both are constituted very much as present-time phenomena, and in the context of discursive rather than historical or biographical practices. Individual subjects do experience things, they do act, just as societies really do have cultural, economic and political practices and institutions. To understand these experiences and practices, however, it is misleading always to refer back to previous practices and experiences, because the proper reference point is the forces that exert pressure at the same moment as those events are actually occurring. The (synchronic) dimension of simultaneous happening matters much more than the (diachronic) dimension of things past. To the extent that we cannot know anything at all outside the various sign-systems, semiotic codes and discourses that we use to impose some kind of order on reality, these are the things that deserve closest attention. The transient nature of the meanings that are constructed and communicated by these structuring processes reinforces the post-structuralist view that knowledge is itself perpetually transient and elusive.

Key points box – in this chapter we have looked at how:

- ☑ Post-structuralist social theory explores the construction of *meaning*.
- ☑ Roland Barthes took the ideas of first-wave structuralism and extended these to analyse sign-systems as *codes of meaning* (semiotics), particularly in the realm of *culture*.
- ☑ Barthes also introduced the idea that some of these codes produce *mythical accounts* of society and its development.
- ☑ Michel Foucault started with a theory of how particular historical periods are characterised by a world view or intellectual paradigm (*épistèmes*), which are made up of a number of *discourses*.
- ☑ Foucault refines the concept of discourse into the concept of *discursive practice* to show how power operates through *institutional control* as well as through control over the intellectual paradigm (the realm of practices as well as the realm of ideas).
- ☑ Foucault uses Nietzsche's notion of 'the will to power' to develop his concept of *power-knowledge*, which is the capacity dominant groups have to control definitions of *knowledge* itself.
- ☑ Derrida introduced the idea of *différance* to emphasise that if knowledge is seen as a sign-system, then knowledge can never reach a final state; knowledge is in a perpetual state of being referred on to other knowledge claims.
- ☑ Derrida applies the same principle of perpetual deferment to human subjects arguing that they also are perpetually decentred.

☑ There is no universal truth or human essence because knowledge never reaches a certain enough state to be able to justify such claims.

☑ The Enlightenment ideas that reason will lead to the discovery of 'truth' and 'fact', and that human beings are uniquely placed to carry out this quest, are strongly challenged by post-structuralist ideas.

Practice box

⮕ Give an example of what a sign *stands for* and of what it *connotes*.

⮕ List three similarities between the sign-system of *words*, and the sign-system of semiotic *codes*.

⮕ Why does Barthes use the idea of 'myths' to describe the way societies construct ideas about their past?

⮕ What did Barthes mean when he said that the text creates the author?

⮕ How does Foucault develop the idea of *intellectual paradigms*?

⮕ What is the difference between Foucault's concept of *discourse* and his concept of *discursive practice*?

⮕ Give an example of how a dominant group might use *power-knowledge* to control social action.

⮕ Why does Derrida think that knowledge is in a state of perpetual uncertainty?

⮕ Can you give an example of a piece of knowledge that you are absolutely certain about?

⮕ Using Derrida's ideas, in what sense might individuals be described as *decentred*?

⮕ Which of the core assumptions in Enlightenment thinking does post-structuralist social theory challenge most consistently?

Further reading

Roland Barthes, *Mythologies* (Paladin books, 1973 [1957]).

Catherine Belsey, *Poststructuralism: A Very Short Introduction* (Oxford University Press, 2002).

Jonathan Culler, *Barthes* (Fontana, 1983).

Peggy Kamuf, *A Derrida Reader* (Harvester, 1991).

Lois McNay, *Foucault: A Critical Introduction* (Polity Press, 1994).

Christopher Norris, *Derrida* (Fontana, 1987).

Paul Rabinow (ed) *The Foucault Reader* (Penguin, 1984).

Websites
For specific material on Roland Barthes try: www.marxists.org/reference/subject/philosophy/index.htm

For specific material on Michel Foucault try: www.marxists.org/reference/subject/philosophy/index.htm

A useful gateway for further information about Jacques Derrida can be found at: http://prelectur.stanford.edu/lecturers/derrida/index.html

CHAPTER ELEVEN

FEMINIST SOCIAL THEORY

One of the most important shifts to have taken place in social theory during the latter decades of the 20th century is the recognition that even though the kinds of institutions and practices that social theorists are interested in affect all social actors, the way they are affected and the kinds of experiences they might have can differ significantly because of the intervening influence of sex and gender. The basic point of departure for feminist social theory is that this possibility needs to be taken seriously and that when prejudicial gender-related effects become evident, the theorist has a responsibility to uncover their causes. In its more overtly political aspect, and once such underlying causes have been identified, feminist social theory advocates social and political intervention to actively remove the causes of disadvantage faced by female social actors.

In this chapter we will be looking at:

The **social construction** of gender

Judith Butler's concept of performative discourse

The **gender regime** and practical effects on gender relations

Patriarchy theory and the gender regime

Feminist-Marxist accounts of social reproduction

Discussion

The social construction of gender

The basic point of departure for feminist accounts of relations between female and male social actors is a recognition that relations between them cannot be reduced to differences in biological function. The obvious physiological differences between women and men, that is, differences in hormones, chromosomes and sex organs, certainly provide a basis for certain key aspects of relations between the two sexes, but gender is much more than sex. Beyond this biological core, and in some instances quite independent of it, gender encompasses a range of other practices, assumptions and expectations about what it means to be male and what it means to be female. These aspects of gender are sociological (rather than biological) because they are part of culture not nature. Important aspects of culture depend directly on how society defines gender and the gender-roles of women and men. Although nature lurks within culture (in the same way that sex lurks within gender), both culture and gender are **socially constructed** in the sense that they are actively and knowingly produced by social actors. To the extent that the meaning and significance of sex and gender are mediated through language, even the basic biological categories 'male' and 'female' bear the marks of social construction.

The notion that much of what constitutes human culture is socially constructed is familiar territory to social theorists. It is also essential to the feminist approach, which is premised on the intellectual and political assumption that issues of equality and equity can be resolved by direct social intervention. If relations between the sexes were truly predetermined by nature there would be little more to discuss. There are three influential accounts of gender that draw on the basic idea of social construction: social embodiment, discourse and performative discourse. We will look at each in turn.

Bodies and social embodiment

In shifting the analysis of gender relations right away from biological causes and towards social ones, the pressure is on for feminist social theorists to explore what the social effects and purposes of gender might be. One influential approach sees gender as something that emerges from the attempts social actors make to incorporate their physical bodies into **social practices** of various kinds. However much gender is regarded as a cultural or ideological phenomenon that is 'all in the mind', social actors do interact with others very much as physical beings with real bodies; and a fundamental feature of those bodies is that they are either male or female. (The exception here is intersex bodies having rare chromosomal or sex-organ configurations that cannot be categorised unambiguously as male or as female. Perhaps ironically the very peculiarity of intersexuality tends to reinforce the orthodox sexual classifications 'male' *or* 'female'.)

The Australian social theorist R.W. Connell, for example, has described gender as a process of 'social embodiment' or 'body reflexive practice' or 'human social conduct in which bodies are both agents and objects' (Connell, 2002, p 47). The basic idea here is that 'there is a loop, a circuit, linking bodily processes and social structures … [these circuits] occur in historical time and change over time. They add up to the historical process in which society is embodied, and bodies are drawn into history' (Connell, 2002, p 47). The emphasis is on embodiment in the sense that social actors do have physical bodies and must therefore relate to each other as embodied beings. The kind of body an actor has and how embodiment is defined and constructed, is part-and-parcel of what gender is. Gender is intimately connected with the processes and structures within and through which actors arrange themselves and their social actions as embodied beings.

This notion of social embodiment is especially useful because although it stresses the importance of the social context for understanding gender, it does so without denying or disregarding the physical, sexual bodies that social actors are trying to come to terms with. As Connell puts it: 'Gender practice involves bodies but is not biologically determined' (Connell, 2002, p 79). Another way of putting this is to say that 'gender' is the name given to the various techniques and strategies social actors have for interacting with each other as beings who have sexual bodies. If there were no 'male' or 'female' in nature, such strategies would never have developed; there would be no need for a concept of gender (or sex) at all.

Discourse

The idea that gender is embodied, and that embodiment is a profoundly social process, has also been used in accounts that see gender as a form of text or **discourse**. Borrowing ideas from **post-structuralist** social theory, especially the idea of discourse and **discursive practice** developed by Michel Foucault (see Chapter Ten), gender has been conceived as a body-canvas onto which are inscribed social conceptions of gender-difference. In this account, as Connell puts it, gender becomes 'a discursive or symbolic system'; a kind of language game for gender. Notions of biological sexual difference, of sexual behaviour (sexuality) and of gendered social norms and social roles are conceived in terms of different layers or strands of meaning and interpretation that combine to form the prevailing discourses on sexuality and gender in that society.

In the discourse scenario, the understandings social actors have of reality are seen as existing entirely within the various overlapping fields of discourse where meaning and interpretation are developed. Therefore, what biological sex, sexuality and gender actually are, what they mean to social actors struggling to get along in a highly complex social environment, depends on how they are represented and articulated within the discourse. Even the apparently concrete elements in the puzzle, such as physical sexual bodies and a strong desire for sexual reproduction, are at the mercy of the discourse because the discourse supplies actors with the intellectual means of knowing 'what it means' to have a physical sexual body.

Judith Butler and the performative discourse of gender

A third approach within the social constructionist camp in feminist social theory, and again one that concentrates on how gender plays out in actual situations, treats gender as a particular kind of discourse called **performative discourse**. One of the most original descriptions of gender in these terms has been put forward by Judith Butler in her influential text *Bodies that Matter: On the Discursive Limits of Sex* (1993). Butler's basic idea is that gender (and in fact biological sex) is **instantiated** or made real, through 'performativity'. Maleness and femaleness are quite literally performed through action. Social actors can only discover and experience gender and, linking up with ideas about embodiment, their sexual bodies when they act them out. There is nothing hypothetical about sex and gender because unless it is made real through performance it can hardly be said to exist at all.

ILLUSTRATION – PLAYING THE GENDER GAME

Although performativity is quite a difficult technical term in social theory, which tries to capture the elusive moment when the virtual becomes real, or when the potential for something to become real is achieved, we can grasp the general idea by thinking about the difference between the written version of a play and the version that is played out by actors on the stage. However 'real' the images in our heads might be when reading the play there is a significant difference between this and the actual performance. The actors literally 'bring the play to life'. The written script for the play is the basic discourse; the live action turns this into a performative discourse.

In broadly similar fashion, when social actors interact in real life, they have a basic script or template in their heads of how gendered interaction should be played out. They soon move beyond this, however, as they become increasingly skilled at interacting in gendered ways. These experiences or performances of 'doing gender' soon build up into a complex repertoire of behaviour that can be applied in all situations.

Once social actors have got into the habit of interacting with each other using the repertoire of gendered behaviour it becomes very difficult if not impossible for them to interact *without* using it. The chance of behaving in a non-gendered way is lost. Depending on how gender-sensitive or gender-charged social interaction in a particular society has become, successful interaction might become heavily dependent on playing a particular version of the gender game. Gender becomes an essential part of social interaction whatever the situation. Gender, so to speak, cannot be 'turned off'.

Heterosexual hegemony

There are a number of important points that can be developed from Butler's idea of gender as performative discourse. First is the idea that although there might be variations within the gender discourse and even a number of different discourses in play at the same time, a particular version of it is likely to be dominant in society at a particular time and place. In this respect the prevailing gender discourse is **paradigmatic** or all-enveloping and thus potentially very difficult to shift. In the terms that Foucault uses, this is an important part of 'the power of the discourse'; it has the power to control how actors behave, what they think about their behaviour and what their behaviour means to them. Even if a particular individual or group chooses not to fall in with these performances of gender, or wants to suggest new variations, they are likely to find this very difficult at least while the majority continue to work from the established or orthodox version of the script.

The gender regime

In the jargon of social theory the overall **gender regime** of society is made up partly of the various **ideas** and discourses of and about gender and partly by gendered social practices. The practice of not allowing social actors of one gender or the other to become members of some private clubs and organisations, for example, is an example of the institutionalised form of the idea of gender separation, an idea that is also found in the gender discourse. Within the gender regime, the ideational and practical elements circulate in and out of one another thus giving the impression that the paradigm is legitimate. The gender regime can be seen as an example of power-knowledge discussed by Foucault.

As noted earlier, successful social interaction requires actors to act in accordance with what Butler calls the dominant 'gender matrix'. A defining feature of the gender regime or gender matrix of modern Western cultures, for example, is that it assumes that heterosexuality, or sexual relations with persons of the opposite sex, is normal, while homosexual relationships are interpreted as non-normal or deviant. The 'heterosexual hegemony', as Butler calls it in her later work, involves much more than specifying the rules of sexual behaviour and extends to include many other presumptions about how male and female social actors 'should' interact. An important motif in the discourse, for example, is that since men do the penetrating during the sexual act, they assume a dominant orientation in all their other relations with women, while women assume a receptive and thus subordinate position. (We will return to this important topic in the next section.)

On the surface

A second important aspect of Butler's notion of gender as performance encourages us to think about gender very much as a phenomenon of the surface of things. The background issue she is trying to resolve here is whether women and men can be thought of as essentially 'the same' despite the obvious physical differences between the two types (and possibly three, four or five types if we accept the full range of intersex variations alluded to earlier). This is an especially important issue for feminist social theorists who, as we have seen, are keen to stress that women and men should be treated absolutely equally. Even the possibility that there might be fundamental differences between men and women that cannot be adequately accounted for as effects of the discourse is potentially very disruptive.

Butler's approach to what is often referred to as the **essentialist** or **constructivist** dilemma is to argue that since 'gender' only becomes meaningful when it is performed, that is, when it enters the tangible observable world of real things and can thus be made meaningful by the discourse of gender, there is no need to look for any deeper or underlying basis for what gender is or what we think about it. Even if there were some deeper underlying basis, for example that gender takes its meaning from the underlying physical differences and biological priorities of the species or that gender is determined by Divine Will, these ideas also only become real in the surface world of the discourse. The discourse is not the secondary effect of some deeper process of 'real meaning' *it is* the place where meaning is created. Performance is what it is, it does not have to be interpreted as expressing something else.

The implications of this approach to studying gender are quite radical because if a majority of social actors regard those performances of gender as reliable and consistent, then, in principle at least, every kind of social interaction is just as authentic, genuine, meaningful and legitimate as any other. It provides a very democratic and liberal approach to theorising gender relations. For example, once the assumption is taken away that heterosexuality represents at the surface an underlying unity of male and female in nature, the grounds on which homosexuality appears abnormal and deviant are removed. Homosexual activity and heterosexual activity thus become equalised; each is as legitimate a way of expressing love and affection for another social actor as is the other. To the extent that the current gender matrix draws its legitimacy from the presumption that heterosexual relations really do provide the most sensible template for all other social relations between women and men, its removal implies that the current gender regime could be completely overhauled.

▸▸   This attempt to try to get rid of the idea of fundamental difference between men and women by rejecting the idea that human beings have an essential inner core, finds support in Derrida's ideas about deconstruction and the decentring of the subject (see Chapter Ten). If, as Derrida suggests, there is no such thing as an inner human nature, and that meaning and interpretation are indefinitely deferred because there is no such thing as final knowledge, then 'gender' can be seen clearly for what it is, namely a socially-constructed surface phenomenon. Gender no longer has to be explained as an outer cultural shell deriving from an inner biological core because there is no core.

Reality check

Although Butler's approach opens up many interesting possibilities for studying gender and offers feminist theorists an alternative way of theorising the nature of male domination and female subordination, we are still left with the enduring problem that no matter how enthusiastically we embrace the idea that gender is a socially constructed surface phenomenon, important material restraints remain. The literal physical experience of pregnancy, for example, is utterly inaccessible to men as is the physical experience of ejaculation to women. There are also many social, cultural and legal constraints that although they are evidently socially constructed, nonetheless have real effects in restraining the development of alternative discourses and performances of gender.

   Butler's solution to this difficulty is to propose a new way of defining 'reality' or matter 'not as surface or site' but rather 'as a process of materialization that stabilizes over time to produce the effect of boundary, fixity, and surface we call matter' (Butler, 1993, p 9, quoted in Fraser, 2002, p 611). Her approach is to try to expand the period of uncertainty that social actors encounter when they try to pin gender relations down; to postpone the moment when they think that gender relations have become **instantiated**. Biological sex cannot be made to disappear just by changing the discourse about sex, but the chances of thinking differently about it can be increased if social actors are in less of a hurry to see sex and gender only in terms of the established paradigm. As with all discourse approaches in social theory, the feminist strategy is to understand more about how gender relations are formulated in and through the discourse and to challenge the presuppositions upon which much of it is based.

A second and potentially much more serious difficulty is that having demonstrated categorically that gender is a socially constructed discourse, feminist social theorists are still faced with the problem of *explaining why* the discourse takes the form that it does. Why is it that the prevailing gender discourse appears to sanction gender inequality? In searching for an answer to this question we have to move away from the conceptual aspects of gender and into the realm of explanation. The point of departure for feminist theorists seeking to explain gender inequality is that, for most social actors most of the time, gender is very much about the practical impact of ideas about gender on actual **social relations** between women and men. Knowing what the mechanism is and how it works is merely a preamble to considering its practical effects.

The gender regime and practical effects on gender relations

A popular strategy among feminist theorists who want to study gender in terms of its real or substantive effects, rather than as a form of ideology, is to see gender as a multilayered or stratified phenomenon often referred to as the **gender regime** or gender order of society. The gender regime is made up of a range of social practices, each of which has elements of ideology built into it (i.e. the dominant gender regime casts its shadow across all forms of social practice), but which are most obvious as material practices and **structures** that constrain and enable social interaction on the basis of the sex and gender of the social actors.

The gender-regime approach is to identify which areas of family and social life are affected by gender, to provide some analysis of the practical effects of the gender regime in those domains and then to explore how these different levels are linked together through practice. It is the role of the gender regime *in linking together* different realms of actual social practice around a central core of ideas and practices that might help explain why the gender discourse takes the form that it does. The gender regime thus regulates actual social action in the manner described by Durkheim (see Chapter Three), first by bringing social actors into line with a dominant view of how women and men 'should' or 'ought' to relate to one another and, second, by choreographing their actual performances of gendered social relations.

Looking at some more recent examples of the effects of social regulation by gender, Catherine MacKinnon's model (*Towards a Feminist Theory of the State*, 1989) has four main domains in which such practical effects might be felt. These are: production, reproduction, socialisation and sexuality. Sylvia Walby (*Theorizing Patriarchy*, 1990) identifies six domains: paid work, housework, culture, sexuality, violence and the state. Connell (*Gender*, 2002), whose ideas about social embodiment we looked at earlier in the chapter, has a model comprising four types of social relations, which describe 'four main structures in the modern system of gender relations'. These are power relations, production relations (primarily defined as the sexual/gender division of labour), 'the structure of emotional relations, attachments and commitments', and symbolic relations in 'the dichotomous gender structuring of culture' (Connell, 2002, pp 58, 62, 65). We will look in more detail at the potential practical effects in three of these domains: gender relations and culture, sexuality, and production and reproduction.

Gender relations and culture

Connell and Walby both include in their models the realms of **culture** and 'symbolic relations'. This reflects aspects of the discourse approach to studying gender we have already touched on. If we define culture is a realm through which social actors express their ideas, beliefs and values, and experiment with new ones, it is inevitable that cultural practice is deeply affected by ideas about gender. Ideas about masculinity and femininity are very often created, rehearsed or played out through education, the mass media, religious beliefs and so on, all of which are important cultural practices.

The cultural realm also includes symbolic artefacts and practices that actors use to make sense of things and to develop a collective view of 'how things are' and this includes ideas about gender. The figure of the Virgin Mary in Christian religious belief, for example, portrays the mothering/caring/caregiving role as something that is not only decisively female/feminine, but also one that is right at the centre of, and provides an anchor for, the whole of society. Other cultures draw heavily on events in the natural world in search of ways to make sense of reality through symbolic imagery. Pagan images of the fertile, life-giving Mother Earth, combined with phallic symbols of manhood, bravery and physical strength, for example, provide another naturalistic template for making sense of gender relations.

Sexuality

A second core aspect of the social practice of gender in these models of a stratified gender regime is to do with the learning and expression of sexuality. We have already noted that the dominant gender regime that operates in many modern Western societies assumes a close association between the only-two-types approach (a social actor can only be male *or* female) and heterosexuality. Intimate sexual relations with social actors of the opposite sex are presented as normal, natural and socially productive; those with actors of the same sex are presented as abnormal, unnatural and socially destructive. To the extent that social actors are socialised into accepting heterosexuality as normal, that the dominant gender regime is a heterosexual paradigm (or, as Butler puts it, that we are living under pressure to conform to the 'heterosexual **hegemony**'), this presumption will affect every aspect of practical social relations between women and men and in all realms or strata of society.

One of the most interesting but challenging areas to think about is how the discourse *of* gender (dominant gender regime, heterosexual hegemony) and the discourse *about* gender (cultural artefacts, films, books, music), which are critical of that paradigm, come together in the cultural realm. Examples might include D.H. Lawrence's novel *Lady Chatterley's Lover* (published in Italy in 1928 but not in the UK until 1960), or the film *My Beautiful Laundrette* (1985), both of which caused a major stir when they first appeared by presenting alternative views, respectively, of heterosexual and homosexual love, lust and desire. Cultural representations of sexuality, especially through visual images of women and men in television, film and advertising, play a crucial role not just in shaping our ideas about how social actors should interact sexually, but in demonstrating the practical techniques required for doing so. They also provide ideas about what constitutes a successful sexual encounter. In a promiscuous culture, 'sex' might be represented as more separate from 'love' than in a culture that associates sex with long-term partnerships like marriage. Having sex in a lesbian or gay community might carry very different meanings than in a straight one depending, for example, and what the significance of sex was perceived to be in terms of commitment or other aspects of relationship-building.

Production (paid work) and reproduction (unpaid domestic labour)

Most prominent among all three gender-regime approaches in our selection are the relations of production and reproduction. These are the practical tasks required to ensure the economic viability of the household (usually taking the form of paid employment) and the tasks of 'reproducing' the family through bearing and raising children. An important component of the 'power relations' listed by Connell play themselves out in the ways that adult household partners negotiate how to divide up responsibility for obtaining income, and for maintaining the household through unpaid necessary domestic activity.

Gender is intimately connected with how the division of labour develops in society because, as we have already been discussing, perceptions of who should be, or is best suited to, doing particular kinds of tasks tap into some fairly basic social and cultural expectations about differences between the social roles of women and men; differences that seem to be justified if one also buys into a dominant gender regime of the 'only-two-types' variety. If the division of labour does follow established ideas about women staying at home to raise children and men going out to bring home the bacon then inevitably this reinforces both the apparent legitimacy of the dominant gender regime and the reasonableness of the idea that women do one kind of thing and men another.

We can illustrate these points by looking at the debate about work–life balance, which is a contemporary way of describing how adults try to balance their commitments to performing the paid and unpaid tasks that are necessary for maintaining the integrity of the households in which they live. Work–life balance also has to make space for activities in the realms of leisure, pleasure and enjoyment; activities that are necessary for the personal and psychological well-being of household members. The way in which adult household members divide up what we can call their 'total responsibility burden' tells us quite a lot about their attitudes, beliefs and expectations about the social roles of men and women in general.

ILLUSTRATION – BALANCING WORK, LIFE AND LEISURE

Until relatively recently the most typical kind of balance was the 'male-breadwinner model' in which the male partner took on the 'work' side of things through paid employment, while the female partner took on the 'life' or 'home' side by looking after the house and, in the case of households falling into this category, dependent children. More recently, and as more adult women with husbands/partners and dependent children have taken up paid work, the balance has shifted more towards a 'dual-earner model'. In this scenario, both partners have jobs although the male partner usually works longer hours and earns more. The mother/female partner, despite the fact that she is also working, still tends to do a high proportion of household chores and childcare.

The dual-earner scenario shows clearly that there has been a shift in the broad assumption that women do the caring and men the earning since both are involved in paid work. Paid work is no longer a predominantly 'male' domain. On the 'life' or 'home' side of things, however, things have been much slower to change, which implies that, especially in respect of childcare and other core household activities such as shopping, cooking, washing and cleaning, responsibility for caring-type activities is still marked up as a largely 'female' domain.

Some theorists have argued the 'dual-earner/single-carer' scenario, which has become fairly typical of many family households in more affluent Western societies, might continue to evolve into a 'dual-earner/dual-carer' type. This would embrace the idea of balance not only when it comes to working, but also to domestic/caring activities. The feminisation of the worker role would be matched by a corresponding masculinisation of the carer role. The social theorist Nancy Fraser (born 1947), for example, has suggested the idea of a 'universal caregiver' model, which not only shifts the emphasis in society away from paid work and towards caring activities (i.e. it gives priority to caring for people rather than to earning money), but also makes caring activities the universal or equal responsibility of men and women. Fraser is quite explicit that the gender regime that still operates in many affluent Western societies is intimately tied up with how social actors divide and balance their paid work and care work:

> The construction of breadwinning and caregiving as separate roles, coded masculine and feminine respectively, is a principal undergirding of the current gender order. To dismantle those roles and their cultural coding is in effect to overturn that order. It means subverting the existing gender division of labour and reducing the salience of gender as a structural principle of social organization. (Fraser, 1997, p 61)

In the latter part of the discussion we have moved away from the analysis of the socially-constructed gender discourse and towards a more direct consideration of the domains of social life over which it is likely to have a controlling influence. Much discussion of gender in social theory does, however, adopt a more critical feminist stance in asserting that the current gender regime has a harmful and politically unacceptable impact on practical social relations, and especially for women. It is at this point that we move decisively towards the effects of the gender regime on equality of opportunity. Unless one is prepared to accept that explanations can be traced back to essential or natural differences between women and men (which as we have already seen is highly problematic), the answer must lie in an account of how society has developed. Two kinds of explanation have been popular: patriarchy theory and feminist–Marxist accounts of social reproduction.

Patriarchy theory and the gender regime

As previously noted, the basis of all feminist discourses is to expose the fact that women suffer from various manifestations of gender inequality because men seek to reserve for themselves a leading role in those activities that attract the highest levels of economic power and social prestige. One highly influential approach to trying to explain how this situation has come about draws on the concept of **patriarchy**, which has been defined by Sylvia Walby as 'a system of social structures and practices in which men dominate, oppress and exploit women' (Walby, 1990, p 20; see also Walby, 1997). In this perspective it is men who construct and apply different levels of worth and value to different types of activity in order to ensure that the activities that they typically spend most of their time doing are categorised in the first division, while the activities of women are relegated to the second division. For as long as men are able to control this agenda, the attributions they make tend to become self-sustaining; the activities of men are more important and prestigious than those of women because it is men that do them.

In terms of questions about the practical means through which men are able to do this, patriarchy theory suggests that during the period of industrialisation in the 19th century, men consistently took practical steps to exclude women from formal paid employment. For Hartmann, this was done in order that men could maintain control over women's 'labour power' meaning their ability to be economically self-reliant, and thus to occupy positions within society independently of men:

> The material base upon which patriarchy rests lies most fundamentally in men's control over women's labour power. Men maintain this control by excluding women from access to some essential productive resources (in capitalist societies, for example, jobs that pay living wages) and by restricting women's sexuality. (Hartmann, 1981, p 15)

This reference to women's sexuality draws attention to the fact that there is a strong correspondence within the strategy of exclusion operated by men between the world of work and the domestic realm. In restricting women to monogamous relationships, and in enforcing strong legal and moral deterrents against having children outside of marriage, men simultaneously protect their property (the accumulate of economic power) under the law, fill their wives' time with childbearing and child-rearing responsibilities, and thus reinforce their own advantage over paid employment:

> For most men, then, the development of family wages, secured the material base of male domination in two ways. First, men have the better jobs in the labour market and earn higher wages than women. The lower pay women receive in the labour market, both perpetuates men's material advantage over women and encourages women to choose wifery as a career. Second, then, women do housework, childcare, and perform other services at home which benefit men directly. Women's home responsibilities in turn reinforce their inferior labour market position. (Hartmann, 1981, p 22)

Referring historically to developments in the UK, this strategy of excluding women from the paid workforce was sanctioned by the political and legislative institutions of the state within which men had established a monopoly of power and authority (Hartmann, 1981; Walby, 1986). This had the effect of reinforcing the apparently higher status of paid employment (and thus the personal status of those who do it, i.e. men), and conversely of undermining the status of unpaid domestic work within the home and those who do it, that is, women. Because they were so thoroughly excluded from the public world of paid work at this time, the argument runs that women inevitably became responsible for 'reproductive' activities within the household; activities that cannot be left undone since the welfare of the household depends on their successful completion. Worse still, because the state within capitalist society is unwilling to provide the resources necessary for meeting the additional social needs that social actors living in such a society have to cope with, households have no choice but to generate these labour resources for themselves. The state's effective denial that such needs exist, or, if they do exist, that they have a low priority (compared, for example, to the 'need' for national defence), implies that those social actors who are providing for these needs, that is, women, are not engaged in anything that matters very much; the greater the state's default, the more dismissive it becomes, and thus the lower is the social prestige that is attached to such tasks: 'The denigration of these activities obscures capital's inability to meet socially determined need at the same time that it degrades women in the eyes of men, providing a rationale for male dominance' (Hartmann, 1981, p 29).

Conscious of the need to theorise patriarchy as dynamic rather than static (it is after all a historical social construct not a force of nature), Walby (1990) offers a complex typology of patriarchy. At the most abstract level patriarchy 'exists as a system of social relations', which is in articulation with 'the major systems of capitalism and racism'. At an intermediate level 'patriarchy is composed of six structures' (production, paid work, the state, sexuality, male violence and culture), which we briefly discussed earlier. At the most grounded level of day-to-day experience each of these structures is associated with a number of 'patriarchal practices'. The relationships between these structures and practices, and between one set of structures/practices and another, is dynamic in the sense that although each is partly autonomous and can be conceptualised and analysed as such, they have 'causal effects upon each other, both reinforcing and blocking' (Walby, 1990, p 20). Applying these concepts, for example, to the incidence of sexual harassment at work, we can see that this practice makes manifest, and cuts across, aspects of 'the more deeply sedimented' patriarchal structures of gender relations in paid work, of male violence towards women and of gendered relations of sexuality. More abstractly, this practice is also a manifestation of the articulation of the even more deeply sedimented systems of patriarchy with systems of capitalism and racism.

In her historical analysis of patriarchy, Walby further suggests that 'there have been changes in both the degree [intensity] and form of patriarchy in Britain over the last century' (Walby, 1990, p 23). Reductions in degree or intensity might include greater equality of pay and access to higher education, while increases in intensity might include growing instances of male violence towards women. Most importantly, however, Walby argues that during the 20th century there has been a shift in the balance between the public and private forms of patriarchy:

> Private patriarchy is based upon household production as the main site of women's oppression. Public patriarchy is based principally in public sites such as employment and the state. The household does not cease to be a patriarchal structure in the public form [i.e. once the public form holds sway] but it is no longer the chief site. In private patriarchy the expropriation of women's labour takes place primarily by individual patriarchs within the household [its institutional form is individualistic], while in the public form it is a more collective appropriation [its institutional form is collectivistic]. In private patriarchy the principle patriarchal strategy is exclusionary; in the public it is segregationist and subordinating. (Walby, 1990, p 24)

Relating this to the notions of patriarchal structure and practice already identified, Walby argues that although both private and public forms of patriarchy are present in society at any given time, there has been a gradual but marked shift from the private to the public form within each of the structures during the 20th century; the public form with its segregationist/subordinationist strategy thus becomes the dominant form of patriarchy in modern society. For Walby, women's access to political citizenship through the right to vote, access to higher education and the professions, and legally sanctioned rights to property and divorce, together with the entry of women into paid employment, constitute respectively the first and second 'moments' of the change from private to public patriarchy: 'It is only with women's access both to waged labour and state welfare payments in the post-war period that the possibility of full economic as well as political citizenship is realized ... the increasing entry of women into waged labour ... could not have occurred without first-wave feminism' (Walby, 1990, p 191).

Feminist-Marxist accounts of social reproduction

Although perspectives that use the concept of patriarchy as the chief explanatory device for understanding the gendered nature of relationships between women and men are very influential, other feminist theorists have struck a different balance between the various causes of women's relative disadvantage within the home and at work. While all agree that it is men who generally get a better deal in both family and working life, they argue that this situation cannot be explained in terms of the operation of various structures and practices of patriarchy since these structures and practices *are themselves* a product of the prevailing social and economic contexts in which they are situated. It is not simply a matter of describing how or whether one form of patriarchy has superseded another but of looking much more closely at how the social and economic systems of capitalism affect all aspects of social relationships within society. Some of these effects may have specific implications for gender relationships, but they also have implications for the relationships between the economy of the household and the formal economy of paid employment, between women and men in different social and economic classes, and between the economy and the form of the state.

To take one example, while the state has certainly moved towards giving positive support for equal opportunities for employment, its motivation for doing so, and the precise manner in which it has done this, has a great deal to do with developments within the capitalist division of labour. In this sense, the suggestion that first-wave feminism played an important role in this process during the earlier part of the century is certainly true but it is not the whole explanation. One might ask why it is that the state has not gone further by, for example, providing nursery facilities for all or by actively enforcing equal opportunities legislation at work. As the feminist-Marxist theorist Michèle Barrett (born 1949) has put it (1980), we are dealing here not just with 'a state' or 'an industrial division of labour', but with a concrete and historically specific form of the *capitalist* state and the *capitalist* division of labour. For feminist-Marxists it is this specific form of economic organisation that sets the limits within which gender relationships are formed and re-formed.

An account that draws particularly on a Marxist-inspired characterisation of the modern industrial capitalist labour process deploys the idea of social reproduction in trying to explain inequality and exploitation. There are two aspects to the concept of social reproduction. First, the capitalist **division of labour** requires a continuously renewed supply of workers to meet its demand for labour power. Labour power is a renewable resource in the sense that currently active workers need to be 'renewed' on a daily basis in order to render them fit for work the next day and in the sense that new recruits are required periodically to replace them. Second, the household itself needs to be reproduced since clearly it cannot exist unless its members remain healthy and increase in number. Further, although biological reproduction and the specifically female type of childbearing labour that it involves overwhelmingly takes place within the household, many of the resources necessary for social reproduction are produced by men and by women in the public sphere of employment.

Up to a point, and adopting a **functionalist** or **utilitarian** mode of explanation, the interests of employees within private households and of employers within the public economy coincide; households need to generate resources in the form of income, and employers need to attract resources in the form of their employees' labour. The crucial point to recognise, however, is that despite appearances these two sets of interests do not coincide since the employment opportunities and choices that are available to household members are not chosen by them but are imposed in various degrees by employers. This lack of correspondence inevitably gives rise to conflict within the capitalist division of labour, conflict that is bound to have a significant bearing on relationships between men and women. In the **public sphere**, for example, conflicts between men and women within the labour movement are caught up in the fallout from the struggle that all employees face in trying to gain a living wage. To the extent that these internal conflicts may undermine a more concerted effort to challenge the basic advantages that employers have over their employees, it is clearly in the interests of employers, and arguably of the state, to allow them to continue. Within the private realm of the **lifeworld** the pressure of maintaining the well-being of family members gives rise to conflicts over who should be responsible for which tasks. The working activities of men and women thus circulate within both a public division of labour in paid employment *and* within a private or domestic division of labour in unpaid work. Although unpaid domestic labour is less visible than paid labour, both are essential for maintaining the integrity of the household.

Rather than attributing tensions between women and men in society to the presence of the gender regime or to various structures of patriarchy, the Marxist-inspired alternative suggest that conflict is an inevitable consequence of the structural inequalities inherent in the capitalist system of economic production. The gendering of social relations between women and men, a gendering that might be described as patriarchal, is overlaid (some might say **overdetermined**) by the structural conditions of capitalism.

Discussion

In this final section we consider briefly some of the implications of the concepts and modes of explanation we have been looking at in this chapter. First, and recalling our discussion of the central concept of gender, it is sometimes difficult not to fall into the mental habit of always seeing gender negatively as a mechanism of social division and social exclusion. As we have seen, gender is a property of all social actors and is thus universal rather than particular in its effects. Clearly it is relations between women and men that have been the focus of attention in the discourse of social theory, but gender also affects relations *between* men, *between* women and *between* social actors in different age groups. It is also implicated in notions of power and authority whatever the biological sex of the actors exercising it. To the extent that gender provides the foundation for ideas and expectations about intimate sexual relations, gender is also heavily implicated in discussions about sexuality. It may be that the prevailing gender regime currently presupposes the normality of heterosexuality and thus contributes to a context of comparative disadvantage for homosexual social relations, but this need not always be the case. A changing social construct of gender could become an enabling and liberating force for groups who are currently marginalised in society.

Second, a related difficulty shows itself in respect of the very specific concept of power associated with patriarchy theory. The difficulty here is that having developed a highly imaginative and sophisticated account of social relations between women and men, and having asserted most vigorously that all the advantages are on the side of men, the concept has little relevance to *other kinds* of social relations. At a very general and aggregated level of analysis it might be the case that 'all men' tend to relate to 'all women' in broadly the same way, but at a more grounded disaggregated level differences in the way that women relate to *other women*, or men to *other men*, might exhibit more formidable differences. Another way of expressing this is to say that although the concept of power (or 'power-knowledge' in Foucault's terms) in patriarchy theory as male-power-over-women might be a useful way of analysing relations between women and men, it is not a concept of power that can be applied to social relations more generally.

This observation leads to a third, which is that if critical theories of gender relations and of patriarchal power can be seen as paradigmatic of social relations in general (and it would be very foolhardy to try to take 'gender' out of the equation of social relations), then it becomes especially important to promote the a 'gender-neutral' notion of gender. Rather than using the concept of gender exclusively as a weapon in the battle of the sexes, in other words, it could be used more positively as a tool for engineering a more forthright awareness of that category of social activity that is not seen as the property of persons of one gender or the other. As long as the concept of gender continues to be premised on the notion of a strict binary opposition between men and women, this precludes the possibility of seeing gender as anything other than a divisive force in society.

Finally, and without underestimating the capacity of the gender regime to influence how social actors (and social theorists) think about gender and how they behave in gendered ways, it is important not to underestimate the influence of structural forces in shaping the choices that social actors make. For example, some critical accounts of the social situation of women tend to imply that historically men have found it relatively easy to control the choices available to women. Since it is ridiculous to suggest that women are simply unaware of their relative social disadvantage, that they somehow lack critical capacity for discovering its causes or for raising their voices against it, the explanation must lie in the fact that such controls are not ideological and psychological, but are profoundly material and practical. Critical explanations that emphasise the practical and material constraints faced by women have something of an advantage here since they are more easily able to resist the temptation of lifting one particular category of social relations, that is, relations between women and men, out of the contexts in which they are embedded in order to try to analyse them separately.

Key points box – in this chapter we have looked at:

☑ Gender as a social construction.

☑ Theories of gender as embodiment, discourse and performative discourse.

☑ Critical accounts of the gender regime put forward by patriarchy theorists and feminist-Marxists.

☑ The continuing importance of feminist approaches in social theory.

Practice box

⮑ What does it mean to say that gender is socially constructed?

⮑ Give an example of how social actors use gender as a way of understanding themselves as *embodied* beings.

⮑ In what ways can gender be seen as a *performance*.

⮑ What are the main domains in which the *gender regime* operates?

⮑ What does patriarchy theory have to say about relations between women?

⮑ What are the advantages and disadvantages of feminist-Marxist approaches to gender?

Further reading

Michèle Barrett, *Women's Oppression Today: Problems in Marxist-Feminist Analysis* (Verso, 1980).

Michèle Barrett and Anne Phillips (eds) *Destabilizing Theory: Contemporary Feminist Debates* (Polity Press, 1992).

Judith Butler, *Gender Trouble: Feminism and the Subversion of Identity* (Routeldge, 1990); and *Bodies that Matter: On the Discursive Limits of Sex* (Routledge, 1993).

Raewyn (Bob) Connell, *Gender* (Polity Press, 2002).

Sara Delamont, *Feminist Sociology* (Sage, 2003).

Nancy Fraser, *Justice Interrupts: Critical Reflections on the 'Postsocialist' Condition* (Routledge, 1997).

Catherine Hakim, *Work-Lifestyle Choices in the 21st Century* (Oxford University Press, 2000).

Barbara Marshall and Anne Witz (eds) *Engendering the Social: Feminist Encounters with Sociological Theory* (Open University Press, 2004).

Sylvia Walby, *Theorizing Patriarchy* (Blackwell, 1990); and *Gender Transformations* (Routledge, 1997).

Websites

For a very useful gateway to a wide range of material on feminism, feminist theory and feminist politics start with: www.cddc.vt.edu/feminism/enin.html

Also useful is: http://feminism.eserver.org/theory/feminist/

Other useful links can be found by using the key words 'feminism' and 'women's movement' in the search engines.

CHAPTER TWELVE

REVIVING THEORIES OF MODERNITY: HABERMAS, GIDDENS AND BOURDIEU

The purpose of this chapter is to provide an introduction to the work of three **contemporary modernist** social theorists who, in their various ways and while working quite independently of each other, have offered solutions to some of the established problems of social theory and largely without recourse to postmodernist concepts. The three thinkers we will be concentrating on in this chapter are the German philosopher and theorist Jürgen Habermas (born in Dusseldorf in 1929), the British social theorist Anthony Giddens (born in 1939) and the French anthropologist and theorist Pierre Bourdieu (1931–2002). Although they do not form any kind of school and do not have identical interests and objectives, there is nonetheless a degree of overlapping in their social theories that is helpful to us in getting to grips with some of the more recent developments in European social theory. The social-theoretical terrain that Habermas, Giddens and Bourdieu mapped out during the 1980s has certainly provided stepping-off points for other contemporary social theorists and sociologists doing empirical work. We will describe them as 'contemporary modernists' to emphasise that although they are critical of it, they still rely in some key conceptual and methodological respects on the classical modernism of Marx, Weber and Durkheim.

As a way of organising the discussion in this chapter we will look in some detail at the work of Habermas first and then, more briefly, and using this to provide a suitable theoretical and contextual background, look comparatively at aspects of the work of Giddens and Bourdieu. Each of these theorists has also contributed to debates on **modernity**, and on cultural aspects of social change, and so we will save discussing this particular aspect of their work until the next chapter, which is all about modernity and **postmodernity**.

The key ideas we will be looking at in this chapter are:

Habermas's theory of communicative action (Key text: *The Theory of Communicative Action volume 1*, first published in German in 1981; English translation, 1984)

Habermas's social theory: **system** and **lifeworld** (Key text: *The Theory of Communicative Action volume 2,* first published in German in 1981; English translation, 1987)

Giddens' theory of structuration (structuration theory) (Key text: *The Constitution of Society: Outline of the Theory of Structuration*, 1984)

Bourdieu's concept of **habitus** (Key text: *Outline of a Theory of Practice*, first published in French in 1972; English translation, 1977)

Some background

A persistent theme in the last few chapters has been the attempt by **post–structuralist** and **postmodernist social theorists** to overturn key presumptions of modernist social theory. One of the things that defines postmodernist perspectives as 'postmodernist' is precisely this urge to sever the link with **Enlightenment** thinking (which is assumed to be the foundation of modernist perspectives) and to rebuild social theory on entirely new conceptual foundations. In the terms that Foucault uses, to develop a new **épistème** or set of 'discursive practices' for trying to understand the contemporary social world. A list of core elements in the Enlightenment perspective is given in Figure 12.1.

A list of core elements in the anti–Enlightenment or postmodernist alternative is given in Figure 12.2.

Although the popular trend in social theory during the latter decades of the 20th century has been towards postmodernist thinking, attempts at demolishing the Enlightenment model have had mixed results. Part of the evidence for saying this is that other social theorists like Habermas, Giddens and Bourdieu, while also finding it useful to recast some of the original modernist concepts, have continued to develop social theory without relying that heavily on postmodernist ideas. The widespread influence of these contemporary modernist theorists would seem to indicate that modern varieties of Enlightenment thinking have survived the postmodernist holocaust. Continuing interest in Enlightenment themes and frames of reference mean either that the postmodernist claim of the need for a radical transformation of social theory is too strong or that the process of reformulation still has a long way to go. Postmodernist social theory has certainly been very influential, but this does not necessarily make it 'better than' all previous varieties of social theory. One of the paradoxes of postmodernism is that, despite its radical posture, *post*modern theory (i.e. theory that comes after 'modern' theory) has been largely unable to shake off its links with the modernist perspective that came before it.

Figure 12.1: Core elements in the Enlightenment perspective

Core elements in the Enlightenment perspective which are rejected by postmodernists are:

- An assumption that there is a clear distinction between human beings and all other kinds of objects in the world because human beings are unique in their capacity for conscious and reflexive self-awareness.
- The idea that there is a clear distinction between the interior world of the human consciousness, and the exterior world of objects (**subject–object dualism**) such that human beings can develop objective knowledge about the exterior world and the processes it is made of.
- The assumption that there are universal truths, meanings and values which can be discovered but which remain unaffected by the process of their discovery.
- The associated presumption that human beings have a subjective inner core, spirit or soul (sometimes labelled **human nature**), which is universal in the sense that it transcends or goes beyond any particular individual self (the **transcendental subject**).

Figure 12.2: Core elements in the anti-Enlightenment or postmodernist perspective

Core elements developed by postmodernists as a foundation for new social theory

- A willingness to accept that the idea of a separation between human beings and other objects is a myth generated by another key Enlightenment myth, which is that human subjectivity gives social actors a unique perspective on the world.
- Despite their capacity for reflexive self-awareness human beings are constituted as objects in the same way that everything else is constituted, which is as a result of occupying a space in a sign-system.
- All knowledge and meaning is relativistic in the sense that there are no universal or transcendental phenomena, and especially none that could be described as human nature, which provide social actors with a sense of destiny.

Habermas's theory of communicative action

What Habermas has to say most specifically about social theory (and not forgetting that he also has a lot to say about many other kinds of theory, for example in philosophy, politics, ethics and legal studies) can be found in his key work *The Theory of Communicative Action* (1981a, 1981b). As the title suggests, his intention is to build a new concept of social action that places the process of communication between social actors right at the centre of that theory. In Habermas's theory, communication is not seen as a by-product or incidental feature of some other kind of action, as a means to some other kind of end, but as a distinct form of action in its own right.

The different theories of social action

To emphasise the novelty of this conception of action (and demonstrating his own reconstructive approach, which is very much to draw together elements of theory from elsewhere), he begins by describing four models of social action that are already widely used by social theorists.

The first, which he associates with philosophers in the Classical tradition beginning with Aristotle, is *teleological* action. This is the basic kind of goal-oriented action where the actor has (or at least thinks they have) a clear idea of what they want to achieve and makes choices between one action and another in order to achieve it. The rationale or purpose for acting in a particular way is thus determined by the goals the actor wants to achieve; this kind of action is essentially a decision-making process.

The second kind of social action described by Habermas is *strategic* action. This is similar to the first type but this time the actor's decision to act in a particular way has to take into account the actions, or possible actions, of one or more other social actors. Teleological action refers particularly to simple situations whereas strategic action applies to more complex situations where other actors are involved. Habermas explains that this model of social action underpins **utilitarian** ideas about how social actors weigh up the costs and benefits of acting in particular ways in order to achieve maximum utility for themselves. The word 'strategic' emphasises that actors have a plan in mind when they act. Action is judged beneficial if it produces utility or positive outcomes for the actor.

The third type or model of social action identified by Habermas, and this time one that is associated with important social theorists like Émile Durkheim (see Chapter Three) and Talcott Parsons (see Chapter Six), is *normatively regulated action*. Although this sounds more complicated that the previous two types, the point Habermas is trying to get across is that social actors make choices about how to act in accordance with the kinds of action that might ordinarily be *expected* in a particular society. Following a fairly standard Durkheimian model of society, Habermas agrees that action is regulated by the norms and values found in that society. One could turn this around and say that one society can be distinguished from another because of the ways in which action is regulated or modified by the norms and values that actors apply when deciding how to act.

An important feature of the way that actions are regulated by social norms is that both the content of the norm itself (for example that it is rude to interrupt) and the pressure to comply with that norm (waiting for others to stop speaking before speaking oneself), and the sanctions that might be applied if the norm is broken (being told off for interrupting), are properties of social groups and not of individuals. In this context, Habermas defines norm-compliant social action as action that fulfils a generalised expectation of behaviour. Whatever the relative virtues of any particular social norm (in some cultures interrupting might be regarded as a good thing to do), it is the *general expectation* that social actors *will* comply with it that is really significant.

The fourth type of action is *dramaturgical action*. We have already encountered this variety of social action in the work of the social-interactionist theorist Erving Goffman (see Chapter Seven). The key feature of this type is that social actors select one form of action in preference to another in order to create a particular impression in the mind of an audience. As Habermas puts it: 'The actor evokes in his public a certain image, an impression of himself, by more or less purposefully disclosing his subjectivity', by presenting him or herself to other social actors in particular ways, the actor 'stylizes the expression of one's own experiences with a view to the audience' (Habermas, 1981a, p 90). As is the case with strategic and especially with normatively regulated action, the emphasis here is very much on social action in the context and presence of other social actors. In a limited sense a social actor can perform or reveal aspects of his inner self or personality to himself (by posing in front of a mirror for example), but the essence of dramaturgical social action is that it is performed for and among other social actors. It is a form of social action that depends almost entirely on the presence of other social actors for its effects. As Habermas puts it, 'encounter' and 'performance' are the key concepts of dramaturgical social action. In line with the **phenomenological** orientation of the Chicago School of micro social theory that Goffman's ideas grew out of, the meaning and significance of dramaturgical social action are seen as dynamic properties that are embedded within the moment of action itself. It is a **holistic** and circular, rather than linear or means–ends, conception of social action.

Having outlined these types of social action Habermas finally arrives at *communicative action*, which is his own special interest:

KEY QUOTE – Habermas, *The Theory of Communicative Action*, volume 1 (1981a), 'communicative action'.
The concept of communicative action refers to the interaction of at least two subjects capable of speech and action who establish interpersonal relations (whether by verbal or extra-verbal means). The actors seek to reach an understanding about the action situation and their plans of action in order to coordinate their actions by way of agreement. The central concept of *interpretation* refers in the first instance to negotiating definitions of the situation which admit of consensus. As we shall see, language is given a prominent place in this model. (Habermas, 1981a, p xx, original emphasis)

Drawing on the dynamic and interactive properties of social action developed in the dramaturgical model, Habermas's definition of communicative action emphasises that dialogue between social actors is fundamentally shaped by their mutual desire to reach understanding and agreement. Developing his own version of the idea of **universal pragmatics**, Habermas believes that the very logic of communication is that agreement *can* be reached. Social actors simply do not take part in dialogue *unless* they feel agreement is possible. Furthermore, and as we shall see, the possibility of successful negotiation depends on participants already being in agreement over the terms and concepts, the background assumptions, they are using (putting this the other way around, dialogue often fails because participants have different ideas about what is being discussed and even of how 'agreement' is being defined).

Habermas's optimism that mutually beneficial outcomes can be reached through negotiation and dialogue makes his social theory attractive to those who want to revive Enlightenment-type ideas about progress and human development and who want to challenge the highly relativistic and some would say nihilistic tone of much postmodernist social theory. If post-structuralists like Derrida and Foucault are correct in thinking that human knowledge and experience has no substance beyond or outside the discourses and narratives of various sign-systems or texts, then we are also compelled to abandon the idea that there are universal issues that social actors are able to agree about (or even that the concept of 'agreement' is stable). We can list several key features of Habermas's concept of communicative action.

Reconsidering barriers between objects and subjects

Looking again at the two lists of key features of Enlightenment and postmodernist thinking given in Figures 12.1 and 12.2, Habermas puts a lot of effort into developing a perspective that criticises and rejects aspects of the Enlightenment view but without going over to the postmodernist side either. His ideas are difficult to grasp at the first and even second or third attempt, but there are two essential elements in Habermas's argument on this point. The *first* is that the distinction between the exterior objective world 'out there' and the interior subjective world 'in here' (the subject–object distinction) is itself misleading. As far as Habermas is concerned, theorists should go beyond this dualistic view of two distinct categories of stuff in the universe (physical objects and human consciousness) and try to move towards the idea that the two are much more interchangeable. Social actors do witness the exterior world around them and often treat events 'out there' as separate from themselves, but they are also and quite fundamentally *part of* those events.

It would not be quite right to say that the objective and subjective dimensions are two different aspects of the same world, more that the two types of entity can be conceived of as interchangeable, or that, depending on circumstances and one's angle of view, one can be substituted for another. We already know that the forms that objects take on (and remembering that human beings are also objects despite their capacity for subjective awareness) are only temporary depending on which frames of reference or which types of knowledge claims we are making about them. Habermas's argument simply pushes this idea on a bit further to the point of saying that this temporariness also explains why at one moment an entity can be treated as an exterior object and at another moment as a subjective experience.

ILLUSTRATION – SUBJECTS AND OBJECTS

Imagine, for example, two players in a game of football who occupy the same position but on opposite teams. When the two central defenders are standing looking at each other, they are, at one and the same time, subjectively aware of themselves but also conscious of how they appear as objects in the perception of their opposite number. In looking at the player opposite, each catches a glimpse of the sense in which he or she has meaning for the other but without having to settle the question of whether this meaning is as a subject or as an object. The mirroring process allows actors to switch between being a subject to themselves *and* an object to others without ever really having to settle for one manifestation or the other. We can also note that the way in which the players relate to each other in this context is regulated by the social practice called 'football'. The temporary construction of 'self' and 'other', of subject and object, takes place in accordance with the rules and conventions of 'football'.

Individuals and society

The *second* main idea about the subject–object problem put forward by Habermas, and one that hopes to achieve the same kind of conceptual benefits as the first, is that the relations between individual social actors and society are also perpetually fluctuating between the subjective and objective states. **Society** should not be conceived (in the way that Durkheim and Marx did), as Habermas puts it, as a 'macrosubject' – an all-seeing and all-knowing other or organic whole – nor, as Weber tended to, as a kind of statistical aggregate of many individuals acting, but rather as a domain that is created by and within interactions taking place between social actors. Like 'football', 'society' exists in its most real sense at the point when social actors interact as they play the game. Subjectively, until the moment of action 'society' is little more than a hypothesis. Simultaneously, and in the objective dimension, 'society' provides a concrete context that regulates the forms of social action that can take place. Society has rules that permit some actions and inhibit others. Society provides the essential resources without which communicative action could not take place at all.

Pragmatic communication

We have already noted that Habermas is more interested in the *role* that language plays in communicative action and in the capacity social actors have *for* communication than he is in the heuristic or meaning-laden aspect of language. This is another important respect in which he differs from post-structuralist theorists such as Roland Barthes, Jacques Derrida and the early Michel Foucault who are preoccupied with myths and **discourses**, and with deciphering the underlying codes of **meaning** and **ideology** that they support.

This emphasis on the pragmatic significance of language as a tool of communication takes us neatly back to Habermas's conception of communicative action being mostly concerned with negotiation and agreement. The key point to grasp here is that Habermas thinks that meaning itself (his theory of **meaning**) is also something that arises out of communicative action. Meaning is not a separate something that social actors try to agree about by making various formal propositions about external objects in the world (propositions that can be judged to be true or false), but is arrived at while actors are engaged in communicative action. Meaning cannot be separated from the practical understanding actors try to reach through communicative action.

Again this is a rather tricky concept to get hold of but it is consistent with one of Habermas's key ideas we looked at earlier, which is that it is a mistake to see phenomena only as objects or only as subjective impressions. If we are able to move beyond the idea that all phenomena have to be placed in one category or the other we can also move away from the assumption that 'meaning' is mainly to do with making the right kinds if subjective statements or propositions about exterior objects. Instead, 'meaning' (like the subject–object and individual–society distinctions) can also be seen as something that arises between actors (intersubjectively) during the course of their communicative action. Standards of meaning and rightness are determined by participants within the communicative situation and in light of the circumstances and contexts where it takes place. They are therefore always negotiable rather than fixed.

Habermas thus envisages a very close connection between communicative action and meaning, both of which are grounded in, and profoundly shaped by, the practical outcomes the various parties involved wish to achieve. All three kinds of relations (subject–object, individual–society, meaning–practical outcomes) are embedded within the contexts where they occur and tend to have a temporary quality. Although there might be no universal standards of 'truth' or 'value', and human endeavour might not be geared towards achieving some kind of 'universal spirit' of the kind envisaged by Hegel (as discussed in Chapter Four), there are reasonable grounds for agreeing with Habermas that all social actors do at least share the capacity for communicative action. To the extent that the practical problems social actors seek to resolve through communicative action are evident in all kinds of society (for example the need to cooperate in order to survive) some of the outcomes they reach do acquire a recurrent if not perpetual character.

The process of communication

As far as the actual content of the communicative process is concerned, Habermas argues that social actors engaged in communicative action will accept that a particular proposition, claim or statement is 'valid' or 'true' if they are able to construct in their minds a feasible support for that proposition. Negotiation is not necessarily a confrontational thing in which the most assertive statements will be accepted over the quieter ones, but draws on the actor's capacity to recognise a valid statement when they hear one. This is another aspect of Habermas's theory that can be rather difficult to follow, but the idea he wants to get across is that as social actors engage in communicative action with each other they progress towards negotiated agreement by drawing on the accumulated experience they already have of making and using valid statements. Like meaning itself, validity is not something that every social actor has to make up from scratch every time she enters into communicative negotiations, but is developed and refined as part of her practical experience of reaching reasonable conclusions.

Ideal speech situation

For Habermas much depends on creating the right conditions for communicative action to take place. It is in fact the setting up of the situation through discourse that is more important than the content of what might subsequently be discussed and agreed. In effect Habermas is arguing that the outcome of the negotiation between participants is profoundly affected by the quality of the speech situation. An ideal speech situation creates the perfect conditions in which actors are most likely to reach fruitful agreement. In setting up an ideal speech situation, much of the hard work of negotiation has in fact already been done. Although Habermas deploys the idea of the ideal speech situation as a kind of Weberian **ideal type**, he sees it as being an open and non-coercive situation in which participants must treat each other as equals, and in which any kind of validity claim can be made and freely challenged. If all extenuating, restraining and inhibiting conditions can be removed (which is of course a rather tall order!), then the agreement that emerges at the end must, quite logically, arise from the strength of the better argument than from some other characteristic of the participants or their situation.

Discourse

Habermas uses the term 'discourse' to refer to the kinds of conversations that take place if the negotiating process breaks down. Recalling the notion of universal pragmatics mentioned earlier, Habermas sees discourse as the process through which social actors try to restore agreement over the basic terms of the communicative process. He identifies three kinds of breakdown: theoretical discourse, moral-practical discourse and aesthetic discourse. Habermas sees these three types of discourse as corresponding with the three main types of validity claims that social actors draw upon when engaged in communicative action. These are claims about the *truthfulness* of the statement (the factual or empirical accuracy of the statement); the *rightness* of a statement (which refers to agreement with an underlying social norm); and the sincerity of the validity claim (the assumption that the person making the claim does so in good faith). For example, if the government says to the people 'smoking is bad for your health', those hearing the message might reasonably expect (a) that there is some factual evidence that smoking is harmful, (b) that they should follow government advice because this is the normal thing to do, and (c) that the government is well intentioned in advising people to stop smoking.

Habermas elaborates even further on these three types of discourse (see Figure 12.3 for a summary). He suggests that the 'truth'–theoretical discourse combination is also aligned with the *cognitive* use of language and describes the objective world of *material objects*; the 'rightness'–moral-practical discourse combination is aligned with the *interactive* use of language and figures mostly in *interpersonal relations* of the social world; and finally the 'sincerity'–aesthetic discourse combination is aligned with the *expressive* use of language and refers to *subjective* states of mind and feelings. Recalling our earlier discussion of the subject–object dilemma, the point Habermas is moving towards here is that communicative action is the moment when the objective, the subjective, the individual and the social states of reality come together. Speech acts thus enable social actors to transcend the separateness of the different domains of reality in the instant when communication takes place.

Figure 12.3: Habermas's types of discourse, validity claims and types of phenomena

Type of discourse	Validity claim	Types of language use (or communicative function)
Theoretical discourse	Truthfulness (factual accuracy) of the statement	*Cognitive* use of language to describe material world objects
Moral-practical discourse	The 'rightness' of the statement as fitting in with social norms	*Interactive* use of language particularly in interpersonal relations
Aesthetic discourse	The sincerity of the validity claim (the claim is made in good faith)	*Expressive* use of language used in subjective states of mind

Source: Habermas, 1981a, p 23

Social order

The second of these types of discourse (moral-practical–rightness–interactive/interpersonal) is particularly important for Habermas's general social theory as he wants to persuade us that in drawing upon and consolidating agreement about underlying social norms, values and beliefs, communicative action plays a major role in establishing **social order**. The notion of 'normatively regulated action' (social action that is regulated by prevailing norms and values) described earlier, establishes a clear link from Émile Durkheim to Talcott Parsons to Jürgen Habermas. All three are strongly of the belief that social action is geared in important ways to agreement about underlying norms, values and beliefs. These beliefs do not exist in a pure, perpetual or abstract form (in the sense that social actors go in search of them like a quest for the Holy Grail), but rather are evident as regulatory forces that shape social action. In a reciprocal way, social action serves to reinforce underlying norms, values and beliefs to the extent that it provides practical justification for the sense that these beliefs are in fact 'true' or 'right'.

Again it is important to note here that Habermas places more emphasis on *the idea* that social actors are motivated to reach agreement than he does on *the content* of what they find agreeable. (Differences about content point to differences between one society and another, whereas the principle of seeking agreement is a characteristic of all human societies wherever they occur.) The same can be said of his account of underlying social norms where the actual content of the norm or value is less important than the willingness of social actors to treat norms and values as a basis on which agreement could be reached. All successful communication presupposes that agreement can, in principle, be reached, and *the principles of* making such agreements are embedded in the norms, values and beliefs of society. Habermas's theory of communicative action is therefore a theory of the architecture of the means by which social action takes place and of the design features that link individuals together through society.

Habermas's social theory: system and lifeworld

Communicative rationality versus instrumental rationality

The role that communicative action plays in creating and maintaining social order brings us on to the central point of Habermas's general social theory. Important parts of this can be traced back to Habermas's own analysis of the work of Max Weber. Weber argued (see Chapter Five) that modern industrial capitalist society took the form it did because modern social actors adopted a particularly vigorous form of **instrumental–rational action** geared to the idea of success. During the 17th and 18th centuries in Northern Europe, and drawing on the twin influences of an energetic new capitalist business ethic and the psychological energy of the Christian Protestant belief system, the business and entrepreneurial classes became the driving force in modern society. Unlike Marx (see Chapter Four), who had argued a few years before Weber that these developments originated with technological developments and changes in the **relations of production** within the economic sphere, Weber argued that the new form of instrumental-rational action could be observed right across society, not just in the economy. For him, the most pervasive force of modern society was the drive towards instrumental rationality in all aspects of human social endeavour. Modern capitalism was 'rational', not so much because of historic battles between social classes, but because it also aligned itself with this new kind of instrumental rationality. The enthusiastic and unswerving application of instrumental rationality to economic production is the very stuff of modern industrial capitalism.

Although Habermas agrees with Weber that instrumental rationality had indeed become a driving force in modern society, he also wanted to preserve aspects of Marx's social theory that, reflecting elements of the German **idealist** tradition, which could be traced back to Hegel and Kant, contained the idea that the collective human effort was also organised around the desire for higher levels of emancipation and equality. Just because this more **idealist** and **humanist** motivation for social action had an aspirational and ideological dimension to it, and was not easy to define in simple **utilitarian** terms, it did not mean that the desire for social improvement was not in its own way 'rational'. Habermas suggests, therefore, that alongside instrumental rationality there is another variety, which he calls, unsurprisingly, **communicative rationality**.

The basic structure of Habermas's theory on this point is that instrumental rationality is the appropriate form of rationality to use when making decisions about how to develop and organise the **social system**. In the terms used by Talcott Parsons (see Chapter Six), instrumental rationality is concerned with managing and integrating the various functions that maintain the social system itself. Instrumental rationality is very much a functional form of rationality aimed at solving fairly specific operational and practical difficulties. Instrumental rationality is strongly oriented around 'formal' (i.e. procedural) questions, rather than around 'substantive' questions that are to do with the much more general objectives and intentions social actors hope to achieve. No matter how well the central-heating system operates it cannot resolve debates about how people's homes *ought* to be.

In Weber's analysis of modern society, it is the application of instrumental rationality to the problem of how to organise large and increasing amounts of information that gives rise to **bureaucratic** systems of administration. At the beginning of the 20th century rational bureaucracy becomes a basic feature of all organisations, whether in government, the legal system, or business and economic affairs. Even military and religious organisations, which already contain strong traditions of internal discipline and order, adopted the modern bureaucratic model at this time.

Efficiency and effectiveness

The problem with instrumental rationality, however, is that it tends to treat all kinds of problem-solving as if they were problems of formal rationality. It leaves out of the account the more substantive, value-laden aspects of social practice. Based on his own analysis of what was happening in German society during the 1890s, Weber feared that as more and more aspects of the decision-making process became gathered into fewer and fewer hands, bureaucracies and the bureaucrats who ran them, would smother personal freedoms resulting in the emergence of what he famously called 'a new iron cage of serfdom' (Weber, 1978 [1921] p 300). The crucial difference here is between the most *efficient* way of organising something and the most *effective* way of doing it.

ILLUSTRATION – EFFICIENCY AND EFFECTIVENESS

A recent study of healthcare services carried out for the UK government showed that despite the many millions of pounds that had been spent on premises and equipment to improve facilities, on rationalising administrative procedures to shorten waiting times and on introducing best practice in clinical procedures to raise care standards, what hospital patients really wanted was for medical staff in hospitals to smile more. In terms of formal rationality, the drive for modernising state healthcare facilities was entirely reasonable and practical improvements could indeed be measured. What the instrumental approach completely failed to register, however, was just how sensitive service users are to the attitude, disposition and friendliness of staff. These aspects of substantial rationality, it turns out, are the crucial ones for making people's experience of hospital healthcare better.

For Habermas, and given what he had already said about the key role of communicative action in providing social actors with a means for reaching agreement through negotiation and discourse, instrumental rationality poses a major challenge to communicative action. Whereas instrumental rationality is reasonably well suited to dealing with practical problems of **systems integration**, it is much less well suited to facilitating debates about issues of **social integration**. Habermas draws here partly on the work of the British sociologist David Lockwood (who was himself dissatisfied with the American functionalist theorist Robert Merton's assertions about **latent** and **manifest functions**), who was among the first theorists to identify that just because the systems of society appeared to work efficiently, it did not follow that society would be an equitable and harmonious place. In agreeing with this conclusion, Habermas suggests that *social* *integration* takes place in a different part of society altogether and he calls this the **lifeworld**. The lifeworld is the proper domain of communicative rationality and not of instrumental rationality. The formal rationality that underpins ways of finding solutions to the practical problem of running organisations is simply not an appropriate way of organising debates over substantive issues in the lifeworld. Instrumental rationality is not transferable from system to lifeworld.

System

Looking at little more closely at the key terms **system** and **lifeworld** used by Habermas, **system** refers to the kinds of issues addressed by the **functionalist** school in social theory. The system includes not only organisations and institutions themselves (for example the institutions of government, education and national security), but also patterns of behaviour and functional routines, which institutions require for systems to operate in the ways that they do. A little more abstractly, and referring to the work of Talcott Parsons (see Chapter Six), system also includes knowledge of systems functionality in respect of how the various components of the social system are integrated one with another. In some accounts systems maintenance and system integration become more important than whether any individual system actually performs the function as intended. Of the various parts of the social system that have received closest attention, the economy and the systems of production it contains are certainly at the top of the list. For Marxist social theorists in particular, the economy is literally the engine room of society and the way it is organised, and how it is linked into other social and political institutions, provides the foundation for the social system as a whole. The system, as Marx might have said, is mainly concerned with 'the production of material life itself'.

Lifeworld

The lifeworld in contrast is, for Habermas, the domain in which society reproduces itself at the level of everyday practices. It is the realm of social integration. The routine conversations and common-sense understandings that social actors share in going about their business is the crucial stuff of social life. The pathways and patterns social actors develop between themselves through communicative action provide the informal structures of social reproduction and integration. If production and labour provide central motifs of the system, communication and interaction are the organising priorities of the lifeworld. Habermas describes the lifeworld more formally as follows:

KEY QUOTE – Habermas, *The Theory of Communicative Action*, volume 1 (1981a), 'lifeworld'.

I would like to replace the ontological concept of 'world' with one derived from the phenomenological tradition and to adopt the pair of concepts 'world' and 'lifeworld'. Sociated subjects, when participating in cooperative processes of interpretation, themselves employ the concept of the world in an implicit way.... The cultural tradition shared by a community is constitutive of the lifeworld which the individual member finds already interpreted. This intersubjectively shared *lifeworld* forms the background for communicative action.... When individual elements of the cultural tradition [are themselves made the topic of intellectual endeavour] participants must thereby adopt a reflective attitude toward cultural patterns of interpretation that ordinarily *make possible* their interpretative accomplishments. This change in attitude means that the validity of the thematized interpretive pattern is suspended and the corresponding knowledge made problematic. (Habermas, 1981a, p xx)

Integration between system and lifeworld

Consistent with what he has previously argued about the transitive and intersubjective nature of phenomena (as distinct from the dualistic subject–object and individual–society constructions that many other varieties of social theory have relied upon), Habermas wants to emphasise the interplay between system and lifeworld. A full explanation takes us too far from our introductory account but the thrust of his social theory on this point is, as we have just seen, that social development and individual development are interdependent and that much depends on the kind of balance that is struck between the two realms. For Habermas, maintaining a productive balance *between* system and lifeworld, *between* individual interests and social interests, is a prerequisite for social order.

Referring to what he calls the 'colonisation of the lifeworld' by instrumental-rational action, Habermas raises very similar concerns at the end of the 20th century to those raised by Marx, Weber and Durkheim at the end of the 19th century. Under the forces of capitalism, Marx envisaged a society where the majority of individuals had become fundamentally estranged from their real human essence by an economic system that treated them and their capacity for labour as nothing more than commodities. On the ethical-moral plain, Durkheim expressed similar concerns about how individuation and the specialisation of tasks across society tended to leave people in a state of **anomie**; fundamentally part of the wider society and yet apparently rejected by it. In the political realm, Weber had clear concerns about the loss of legitimacy of the decision-making processes, a loss that was an unintended consequence of the disenchantment of the world brought about by the spread of instrumental-rational action.

At the level of the individual social actor (the **micro** level), the implication of such a process of colonisation described by Habermas is that it takes away from social actors the autonomy they need if they are to feel that their lives are their own. At the broad or **macro** social level, it represents a compression of the range and depth of communicative action, and along with it a contraction of the means social actors have of debating and negotiating their agreements about the substantive questions that face them. In his first major work, *The Structural Transformation of the Public Sphere* (1989 [1962]), and providing historical background for the theoretical propositions made by Horkheimer and Adorno, Habermas explores how a contraction of the possibilities for communication and discourse in modern society is associated with the contraction of the public sphere. Situated between civil society and the state, the public sphere is an intellectual, political and cultural domain of public opinion in which established ideas can be challenged and new ones explored. Habermas regards the public sphere as a key forum for communicative action and argues that its reinvigoration is a necessary prerequisite for the continuing self-transformation of modern capitalist society.

Critical reflexivity

Referring back to the second part of the key quotation just given, we should note, finally, that the claim that a point is always reached where the taken-for-granted assumptions of a cultural tradition or paradigm *are themselves* subjected to fresh scrutiny, relates to another recurrent theme in Habermas's method, which is to see the forces of social change as coming *from within* the already-existing institutions and practices of society. We will have more to say about this when we discuss Anthony Giddens' concept of **reflexivity** later in this chapter, but at this point we should note how Habermas highlights the importance in social development of the principle of **immanent critique**. This is the idea that criticisms emerging from within a particular paradigm or cultural tradition demonstrate the capacity of the paradigm to turn its own critical and exploratory power *against itself*. It is this capacity for *self-criticism* that makes Habermas's social theory a **critical social theory**.

This aspect of Habermas's social theory places him firmly in the tradition of the Frankfurt School, which we discussed in Chapter Eight. Habermas was a student of Max Horkheimer and Theodor Adorno and was Director of the Frankfurt Institute for Social Research from 1983 to 1993. Although in his later work (particularly his *Theory of Communicative Action*, 1981), Habermas moves deliberately away from the overtly pessimistic outlook of the early Frankfurt School in order to recapture the idea of emancipation through discourse and communication, the idea of immanent critique retains key elements of classical critical theory. In this respect his method differs very significantly from the post-structuralist approach, which claims that it is necessary to get entirely *outside* the existing paradigm or set of discursive practices as a precondition of being able to make criticisms of it. From a postmodernist perspective, the tools of self-criticism and self-reflection contained within the Enlightenment perspective are regarded as wholly inadequate to the task of undermining the self-same paradigm that has given rise to them. Drawing on the principles of communicative rationality and the optimism inherent within his concept of universal pragmatics, Habermas argues the opposite, which is that the most valid kind of criticism emerges from within that which is in the process of transforming itself. For Habermas the intellectual and developmental project of the Enlightenment has simply entered another period of self-transformation: it remains an unfinished project.

Evaluating Habermas's social theory

Although we have only touched upon a few of the main themes in Habermas's critical social theory it should be clear already that his work is very much in the tradition of general theory. As such, and to the extent that one agrees with his arguments, it poses a considerable challenge to other contemporary social theorists who inevitably have to engage with his work when developing their own ideas. The importance of Habermas in the development of social theory during the latter part of the 20th century is that he has managed to defend many of the underlying themes of Enlightenment theory and philosophy, and continued to use the methods of the classical social theorists, very much in the teeth of the criticisms raised against them by post-structuralist and postmodernist thinkers (see Chapters Ten and Thirteen). Habermas is, however, difficult to follow because he embraces so many of the most basic, and thus most complicated, themes in modern social theory. One has to put a lot of effort into understanding the preliminary stages of his thinking. He assumes a high level of previous knowledge on the part of his readers.

Before proceeding to use Habermas's theory as a theoretical and contextual backdrop for exploring the work of Pierre Bourdieu and Anthony Giddens, we should consider briefly some criticisms of Habermas's work. At the very end of this chapter we will attempt a more general evaluation of the work of all three theorists.

A first possible weakness in Habermas's theory of communicative action is that it is developed against a background of utopian, some might say **ideological**, optimism about the human capacity always to be looking for knowledge, 'truth', emancipation and equality. It is certainly possible to argue strongly in support of these Enlightenment values, but, in doing so, the theorist can be accused of assuming things about human nature, culture and society that social theory really ought to be trying to *prove* and not *assume* from the outset.

A second and related difficulty is that in arguing that truth and meaning are always determined within the context of communicative action (truth and meaning are seen exclusively as emergent properties of the communicative procedure), communicants in Habermas's system have no exterior means, no independent criteria, for evaluating the statements and propositions that their communicative action produces. A group of people locked in a room until they reach consensual agreement might be quite unaware of some vital additional factor or circumstance outside the room that, no matter how convinced they themselves are about their negotiated outcomes, renders their conclusions false and meaningless to those outside the room. The 'force of the better argument' cannot make up for lack of crucial information.

Third, and rather like other grand theories such as the functionalist theory of Talcott Parsons, which we looked at in Chapter Six, Habermas works at a very high level of generality and thus abstraction. There is no question that social theory needs to be quite 'theoretical', but this does leave it vulnerable to questions about what concrete empirical evidence there is in support of the theory. This worry is further increased for theorists like Habermas (and also Giddens) who base their theories on a critical reconstruction of the work of other theorists whose own work might also lack clear empirical foundations.

This concern raises a fourth, which is that aspects of the theory are allowed to develop with what can sometimes appear to be a quite simplistic if not naive awareness of how things actually are in the 'real world'. While it is important to challenge social theory on its own terms rather than accusing it of lacking a deep sociological awareness that it might never have claimed for itself in the first place, it remains the case that lack of awareness of 'how things really are' can undermine the integrity of theoretical propositions. The ideal speech situation, for example, which plays an important part in the theory of communicative action, is difficult to reconcile with the generally much more confused and fragmentary way in which most social actors seem to do their communicating.

Although Habermas presents the idea as an ideal type, he seems quite confident in imagining that participants in communicative action do in fact possess highly developed capacities for well-informed, intelligent and coherent discourse, and all of this grounded in an optimistic belief in the prospect of arriving regularly at negotiated consensus. It may be that Habermas has this kind of communicative experience among his own academic colleagues, but it is surely rather far-fetched to believe that this is how most people communicate. One could reasonably conclude that the whole theory of communicative action is in fact an ideal type that never actually occurs as specified in the theory.

Finally, Habermas's theory seems to rely upon a rather depersonalised notion of individuality. Maintaining the integrity of the conceptual categories he develops sometimes seems to be at the expense of a truly multidimensional theory of the individual. Something has to give and it often seems to be the category of the individual subject. Indeed there is a logical progression towards this conclusion in his own argument because he relies so heavily on the notion of intersubjectivity. This is helpful as a way of emphasising the mutual nature of social action, but in focusing on what is shared, it does rather obscure elements that are unique to particular individuals.

Anthony Giddens and the agency–structure dilemma

Some shared concerns

As we suggested at the start of this chapter, there are a number of similarities between the techniques and interests of Habermas and Anthony Giddens (and Pierre Bourdieu who we will discuss in the next section). In their approach to developing social theory, for example, they both adopt a *reconstructive approach* in that they build new ideas and concepts often on the basis of a critical evaluation of the work of previous theorists. Although this is a common procedure in social theory, their approach is novel in the sense that they draw, sometimes quite eclectically, from a spectrum of previous work rather than working within one or other of the major traditions in social theory. Indeed they both argue that in order to move beyond the limitations, as they see them, of established schools of thought (for example of Marxism or functionalism or structuralism), it is essential that the theorist is prepared to risk making novel connections not only between alternative theories, but also between different academic disciplines. Both Habermas and Giddens draw equally confidently on European and American social theory and philosophy, and on social-psychological as well as on sociological research and concepts.

The interactive school of sociology

The most obvious example in this context is that they both make extensive use of the **social interactionist** perspective developed at Chicago University in America during the mid-part of the 20th century. The micro-level and phenomenological mode of analysis developed by Alfred Schutz and Howard Garfinkel, for example, and certainly the dramaturgical approach developed by Erving Goffman, figure prominently in the work of both Giddens and Habermas. One of the major consequences for social theory of the micro-level interactionist approach was that it tried to point out the limitations of the macro-level, and **general systems theory**, approach of Talcott Parsons. Functionalist social theory concentrates almost exclusively on the rather abstract analysis of social systems at the level of society as a whole, and tends to see 'the social actor' as secondary to 'structure'. As we saw in Chapters Six and Seven, this leaves it poorly equipped for accounting for everyday goings-on in the social world; it simply does not have the conceptual equipment and methodology for doing this kind of research. Habermas and Giddens have both tried to develop social theory that is grounded in the analysis of everyday life and to the decisions social actors make, which are driven by common sense or **practical consciousness**, rather than giving so much priority to 'the social structure'. The social theory they develop attempts to find a new accommodation between the macro and the micro, between social structure and individual **agency**.

Evolutionism and kinds of knowledge

We should also note in passing that, as part of his concern about the functionalist/**positivist** account of social phenomena, Giddens is dead against the assumption of a basic or inevitable continuity between the natural and social sciences. On this point he is in the same camp as Max Weber and Peter Winch (see Chapter Nine), arguing that the subject matter of the social sciences is so fundamentally different from that of the natural sciences that it not only needs very different methods of investigation, but also produces a *different kind* of knowledge. He rejects, for example, any notion of an evolutionary relationship between phenomena (which is quite common in the physical sciences) in the sense that what happens in one society, time and place, provides a reliable indication of what will happen elsewhere and at other times. The highly *contingent* nature of social life (meaning that much depends on a sometimes quite unexpected coming-together of circumstances), together with the fact that it is saturated with *meaning* that simply has no physical presence in itself, means that it is wholly unrealistic to suggest that social phenomena simply evolve from other social phenomena.

Structure and agency

Perhaps the most general overlap between Habermas and Giddens is that both want to look again at how social actors are restricted in what they can do by the **social institutions** and **social practices** that surround them. Neither is happy with the structuralist conception of **structure** as a fixed mesh or cage that entirely eliminates individual autonomy, and yet they also want to accept that society does restrict the range of possible actions. In this respect they concur both with each other and with Durkheim's insight that society exists as a set of organised restraints, in the form of social practices, which are beyond the capacity of any particular individual to control. One of the central problems of social theory is to raise awareness of these supra-individual societal practices, to describe them and to identify any wider patterns or trajectories that they might contain.

Changing structures

In looking again at how to conceive of structures and the influence they have over individual actors, Giddens and Habermas both concentrate on the problem (which remains particularly challenging in structuralist conceptions) of how structures or structural forces can *change*. If the structure forms a totality that really does restrict action, then it is difficult to see how anything ever changes. The forces of change must come either from inside the existing structures, in which case structures appear somewhat less stable than previously thought, or they come from outside the structure, which suggests the presence of supra-structural or 'outside-the-structure' forces. The latter then require explanation in their own right. There is also the closely associated problem of how to include actual people in the processes of social change. Unless one simply accepts the structuralist view that social actors are the recipients of change rather than the instigators of it, then there has to be some kind of provision within the theory for allowing social actors to influence the development of the social structure and social systems.

Both Habermas and Giddens develop solutions to these perpetual dilemmas in social theory in three main ways:

- First, they reconsider what constitutes 'structure'.
- Second, they accept that the *forces of change* must come from within what we might call the domain of actually existing institutions and practices rather than from some hypothetical domain that exists outside of it.

■ Third, they try to reconfigure relations between social actors and social structures so that the two domains are conceived as much more interconnected and mutually reinforcing.

We will organise the next part of our discussion around these three headings.

Redefining 'structure'

Habermas begins by challenging the idea in social theory that we need to organise our knowledge of the social world into distinct and **dualistic** categories, such as subject and object, individual and society. For him, it is the intersubjective realm (the between–subjects realm of genuinely *social* action), a realm that is made manifest through communicative action, that allows social theorists to dissolve away the need to see things as being in one category or the other. The intersubjective realm now appears as an enlarged border country that transcends the fixed boundaries between the territories of subject and object, individual or society, which were formerly seen as lying decisively and quite separately on one side or the other. Moving beyond the category of dramaturgical action, which already presupposes that action takes place in the presence and at the behest of other actors, communicative action emphasises how the most essential properties of meaning and purpose are expressed at the moment when social actors are engaged in honest dialogue with each other.

There is a clear similarity here with Giddens' strategy, which is also to displace the dualistic separation of categories, but this time with the notion of **duality**. 'Duality' describes how phenomena emerge as a combined effect of interaction between forces; the offspring as it were of sometimes opposed forces coming together. Giddens' main ideas about the duality of structure or **structuration** theory are set out in his book *The Constitution of Society* (1984).

Rules-and-resources

A first important step in Giddens' argument is to define structures as 'rules–and–resources' and to suggest that rules–and–resources enable rather than restrain action. He wants to move away from the wholly negative connotation of the idea of 'structure' used by some interactionist theorists as restraining action entirely, and towards a position where the limiting tendency of structures are seen as necessary and helpful. Taking ideas from Goffman and Garfinkel, Giddens argues that although structures do restrain social action, these restraints should in fact be seen as positive in the sense that the rules of conduct of everyday encounters prevent actors making fools of themselves. Without such rules social action would be barely possible. To take a relatively mundane example, the UK highway code, which sets out some very specific rules and regulations about driving motor vehicles on the public highway, could be seen as restraining individual freedom, but the kind of driving anarchy that might ensue if there were no rules might be even more painful to live with. And the same principle applies to the very many more subtle kinds of rules-and-resources, the conventions and etiquette of social action, social actors habitually use 'to get along' in the social world.

In Giddens' theory, structures (rules-and-resources) are **instantiated** at the moment when action takes place. Using language as an example (and drawing on Wittgenstein's ideas about language games), Giddens argues that when social actors make utterances the structure of language is, at least for the duration of the vocal interaction, instantiated or made real. Language always has a hypothetical form in the sense that you and I and all members of our language community have the potential to draw down our capacity to use language, but language only becomes really real when in use. In this scenario, structures only have a binding effect on action at the moment when they, as it were, allow them to do so. If I switched writing from English to Hebrew, for example, I would be instantiating a different kind of linguistic structure and thus a different linguistic paradigm for trying to get to grips with social theory. If nobody ever used English or Hebrew again, then both forms of language would no longer be instantiated and thus would cease to exist (or have any meaningful existence other than as linguistic artefacts).

Duality

By using rules-and-resources social actors also reproduce *the conditions* in which rules-and-resources are useful to them and thus also reproduce those rules-and-resources *themselves*. Although social actors are not generally aware of how their actions serve to reproduce rules-and-resources, the very existence of rules-and-resources depends entirely upon their being enacted. Structuration theory, therefore, has important consequences for how social theorists think about processes of social change, as it implies that any change in the rules-and-resources of society must begin from those very same rules-and-resources. Both the ingredients of social change, and the means by which social change actually takes place, must already be present in the rules-and-resources as they currently exist. This is reminiscent of the notion of immanent critique, of change from within, in Habermas's social theory. It stands against the general structuralist view that significant change comes from without.

Power

This configuration illustrates Giddens' preferred definition of 'power', which in this context is the capacity social actors have for drawing upon the rule-and-resources around them. There is reciprocity here, however, in the sense that even though a dominant partner or group has influence over a subordinate one, the two are still bound together by the various rules-and-resources at their disposal. A good illustration of this is Marx's observation that although the capitalist bourgeoisie dominates the industrial proletariat, neither class can do without the other; the two exist in a dynamic relationship with each other. Ultimately, for Marx at least, it is the very fact that the bourgeoisie depends so heavily on the proletariat that gives the latter its best chance of taking power away from the bourgeoisie through revolution. Social actors can be seen as having power 'over' social structures in the sense that they already have at their disposal a very extensive body of knowledge about how to act and behave in the social world. This gives social actors the capacity or 'power' not only to act (a capacity that Giddens calls **agency**), but to do so deliberately and intentionally and in ways that can seriously alter the world around them; they have what he calls 'transformative capacity'. If, as Giddens recommends, social theorists come to see the relationship between social actors and social structures in terms of dualism (rather than duality), it becomes possible to see power as an intrinsic property of social action rather than as an independent force or quantum that 'the social structure' draws upon to control individual freedoms.

'Structure' and 'system'

By defining structures as rules-and-resources Giddens also moves away from the functionalist method, which is to see 'structure' and 'system' as pretty much the same thing. Giddens argues instead that while **social systems** have a material existence and are embedded in time and space (we can actually see and describe social systems objectively), **social structures** are, like the example of language just discussed, largely hypothetical until they are made real at the moment when social actors make use of them. The habitual and routinised use of rules-and-resources (structures) is heavily implicated in the development of social systems in the same way that the habitual use of a particular language in actual speech is closely associated with the development of what we could call 'language systems' or simply language communities. Such communities/systems are identifiable as communities because of the linguistic structures (rules–and–resources) they use. The idea of 'language' and the idea of 'community' are thus entirely co–dependent.

Social integration

In terms that are very close to Habermas's use of Lockwood's distinction between system integration and social integration, Giddens also criticises the functionalist approach for failing to distinguish between social phenomena that are instantaneous or 'of the moment' (the social) and those that have built up over time (the system). Methodologically, this brings us back to the distinction between **diachronic** and **synchronic** modes of investigation developed by structuralist and post-structuralist social theorists. We looked at this issue in Chapters Nine and Ten where we noted that structuralist social theorists operate very much in synchronic mode by taking a snapshot of some aspect of society and analysing that as if it were entirely isolated in time and space. It makes little difference to Saussure or Lévi-Strauss, for example, whether the particular slice of language or segment of ritual practice they are looking at happens on a Tuesday or Thursday, in Pakistan or Peru. This method inevitably tends to treat phenomena rather abstractly and as if they really are devoid of context. The diachronic approach in contrast is much more historical and grounded in orientation and tries to explain how social phenomena develop in the dimensions of time and space.

Taking up these issues in his own theory, Giddens argues that functionalism is essentially blind when it comes to diachronic investigation and thus fails to recognise that some phenomena (for example *system* integration) have historical presence and take time to become established, while other phenomena (for example *social* integration) are very much 'of the present'. Like Habermas's concept of intersubjectivity, social integration only exists by virtue of the fact, and only for the duration, of actual goings-on between social actors.

Applying these rules-and-resources of structuration theory to kinds of phenomena that social theorists are interested in, we can now make some useful distinctions between one society and another in terms of the historically embedded structural principles that give them their particular form. Modern capitalist society, for example, is distinguishable from feudal and ancient society because it expresses historical structural principles, such as the separation of the state from the Church and the presence of particular economic and social classes, that are not found in the other types. It also has key structural properties such as the division of labour, the legitimacy of private property and the dominance of instrumental-rational action. Its leading social institutions include such things as monogamous marriage, representative democracy and compulsory education of the young. Each of these phenomena is, however, dependent on the continuing enactment of the many and various rules-and-resources (functionalists might be tempted to call these the subroutines of society) in real time. Social actors actually do kiss their partners goodbye and turn up to work, even on a Sunday. They do what the boss says, cooperate to produce things and enjoy spending the money they have legitimately earned. They take information from the mass media, debate the issues of the day and vote in elections. They habitually socialise with, live among and share the same value system as other actors who occupy the same kind of social space as themselves.

Summary

For both Giddens and Habermas, then, the answer to the mighty question in social theory of how social order is maintained is that the cooperative acting together of social actors at the same moment produces social integration in the present-time or synchronic dimension. Because these interactions presuppose the prior existence of, and at the same time serve to reproduce, rules-and-resources (especially for Habermas, the capacity for communicative action), the habitual use of these rules-and-resources produces system integration along the historical or diachronic dimension. Using an analogy, one could equate social integration with the present-time *act* of making stitches with yarn and needles while the knitted *fabric* that emerges from the constant repetition of that action equates with the emergence of system integration in historical time. Functionalist theory is well equipped for looking at the act of knitting but has little to say about that which has been knitted.

Forces of change

The second line of attack we identified in our list above, which Habermas and Giddens develop in their investigation of the nature and causes of social change, is to see change as a property that comes from *within* that which already exists rather than from a hypothetical realm, which, other than being conceived as 'outside that which already exists', has yet to be defined. Rejecting the idea of outside forces of change also reinforces the need to see structures themselves as being essentially fluid rather than fixed; structures are not *so fixed* that they cannot change.

Working within the tradition of European critical theory Habermas sees change as an **immanent** property of social action, and that currently-existing institutions and practices already contain within themselves the potential for change. Revolutionary change of the kind implied by Karl Marx, for example, is thus both im*man*ent in the sense that 'capitalism contains the seeds of its own destruction' and im*min*ent in the sense that in 1848, when *The Communist Manifesto* was first published, Marx and Engels literally believed that the revolution was just about to happen. Habermas thinks of the work of the social theorist as developing criticisms from within the current intellectual and discursive paradigm and, in order for the prospect of negotiated agreement to be possible, often in the same terms as that paradigm. For his part, and bearing in mind that he is less sympathetic to the Marxist tradition than Habermas, Giddens sees the forces of social change a little less in terms of 'the structural forces of change' (i.e. changes in the social infrastructure, the physical fabric and make-up of institutions and organisations) and more in terms of how social actors change their ideas, values and beliefs. It is the level of **meaning** that attracts his attention rather than the level of institutions. Giddens finds support for his approach in the German **hermeneutic** tradition of Hans–Georg Gadamer, and his view that social actors routinely make sense of reality for themselves; they do not have to rely on 'society' or 'culture' (and institutions like the mass media) to do this for them. While Giddens certainly accepts that norms and values play a crucial role in explaining the nature of social order, this should not be taken to mean that social actors are unable to challenge the norms and values that surround them.

Actors and structures

This brings us conveniently to the third strand of argument used by Habermas and Giddens to develop new notions of structure, which is how social actors *affect* social structure. As already noted, both theorists try to reconfigure relations between social actors and social structures so that the two domains are conceived as much more interconnected and mutually reinforcing.

Looking back to how Habermas defines the lifeworld in the quotation given in the second section of this chapter, we saw how he argues that the cultural assumptions of society (which are a collectivised representation of the norms and values of society) sometimes provide social actors with a template or guide for making sense of the world around them, and sometimes become themselves the main topic of conversation and debate. For Habermas, the intimate and more private realm of the lifeworld is where these debates (or perhaps 'renegotiations') tend to originate. In this respect, the social structure/ social system is seen as a delivery system that provides the means for articulating or operationalising the values that have been developed previously in the lifeworld. The basis of Habermas's and of Weber's concern about maintaining balance between system and lifeworld is that 'the system' can get above itself by mistakenly thinking that the operational or strategic logic of formal or instrumental rationality is an adequate substitute for the substantive rationality found in the lifeworld.

Drawing on this more interactive and dualistic conception of the relations between action and structure, Giddens develops the notion of **reflexivity** to propose a double-sided or twin process by which social actors are affected by the conditions in which they act and yet are also able to bring about changes in those conditions. The concept of reflexivity or reflexively organised practice explains how by constantly monitoring their own behaviour social actors are always altering the boundaries between structure and action:

KEY QUOTE – Anthony Giddens, *The Consequences of Modernity* (1990), on reflexivity.
The reflexivity of modern social life consists in the fact that social practices are constantly examined and reformed in the light of incoming information about those very practices, thus constitutively altering their character.... Modernity is constituted in and through reflexively applied knowledge, but the equation of knowledge with certitude has turned out to be misconceived. We are abroad in a world which is thoroughly constituted through reflexively applied knowledge, but where at the same time we can never be sure that any given element of that knowledge will not be revised.... The discourse of sociology and the concepts, theories, and findings of the other social sciences continually 'circulate in an out' of what it is that they are about. In so doing they reflexively restructure their subject matter, which itself has learned to think sociologically. *Modernity is itself deeply and intrinsically sociological.* (Giddens, 1990, pp 38, 39, 43, original emphasis)

This definition describes how, at the level both of day-to-day living and of the accounts put forward by social theorists, the objects and contexts of social action are constantly being changed by the knowledge actors have of those objects and contexts.

ILLUSTRATION – SMOKING TOBACCO IN PUBLIC

As people became more and more aware of the physical hazards of smoking tobacco the social context of smoking has changed quite dramatically. Smoking tobacco has changed from being a socially accepted habit of pleasure and relaxation, connoting adventure and excitement, and has become instead a socially unacceptable form of risk-taking behaviour. The fact that in practice fewer and fewer people smoke in public feeds into perceptions of the non-desirability of smoking tobacco. One kind of fact about smoking tobacco has thus been replaced by another, and directly as a result of new information about its medical consequences. It is not inconceivable (although in this particular example perhaps not very likely) that new medical 'facts' might one day emerge that will result in the revival of smoking as an acceptable social activity.

Giddens argues that reflexivity is an obvious property of knowledge developed by social theorists because the phenomena they focus on, that is, social phenomena, are bound to be affected in quite direct ways by the emergence of new knowledge about them. Although social theorists have always been interested in the ways social actors adapt their behaviour in light of new knowledge and circumstances, the concept of reflexivity developed by Giddens does have some novelty in that it involves the idea that in late-modern society these processes have speeded up. It is not just that social actors are surrounded by change, but that they are able to respond to it much more quickly than was the case in the past (Giddens' theory of modernity is discussed in Chapter Thirteen). The massively speeded-up rate of response feeds back into the processes of change and so provides it with even more energy and momentum. It is a characteristic of the modern consciousness that as social actors become increasingly aware of their capacity for generating change, the principle of 'change' itself becomes a focus of activity. The concept of reflexivity applies particularly at the level of what social actors think and believe about the social world around them. The more durable structural aspects of the organisations and practices also change over time as actors become more knowledgeable about them, but they do so much more gradually than those dimensions of social life that are to do with interpretation and meaning.

Real individuals

One further point we should make here in comparing the work of Habermas and Giddens on the interrelations of social actors with society is that when applied to the more intimate level of personal development, the concept of reflexivity helps to revive a more robust and multidimensional perception of the social actor. Especially in his later work, and possibly in view of the criticisms that Habermas has faced on this point, Giddens puts quite a lot of effort into exploring reflexivity as a mechanism for the development of personal and social identity. The quest for identity is a profoundly reflexive process since it is our own identities, as individuals and as members of different families and other groups, that are 'constantly examined and reformed in the light of incoming information' about who we are and how we should behave (Giddens, 1990, p 38).

Criticising structuration theory

The most elementary criticism made of Giddens' structuration theory is that, despite their being absolutely central to it, the theory does not contain a very clear definition of 'rules' and of 'resources' (see Thompson and Held, 1989). Here Giddens encounters a theorist's dilemma, which is that the coherence of his theory depends on the robustness of the concepts it contains but they in turn depend on the integrity of the theory. Descriptively, it seems fair enough to say that social life is governed by various rules or conventions of conduct and that these constitute resources necessary for 'going on' in the world, and Giddens relies heavily on the work of Erving Goffman to illustrate this point. We know how to be polite or how to buy things in shops. Analytically, however, we need to develop some basic principles of what constitutes 'a rule' or 'a convention'. The closest Giddens gets to doing this is to make a fairly basic distinction between rules that are to do with the meaning of things, and rules that are to do with the ways in which behaviour is positively or negatively sanctioned. His proof that there are such things as rules–and–resources relies on an intuitive recognition that, because social behaviour is affected by them, they must exist.

Second, and closely related to this, is the question of whether Giddens uses the notion of 'structure' in a way that other social theorists, and certainly most structural*ists*, would not recognise. Giddens needs a term to indicate that regularities in behaviour can be traced back to less visible but yet organising and systematising forces beneath, and feels that these structuring processes are reminiscent of linguistic structurings. He thus adopts the notion of 'structure' because this was a handy term to use, rather than starting out with the notion as traditionally used by structural*ist* social theorists before developing its meaning in a new direction. Giving the appearance of a theorist of structure, Giddens infers from regularities in social conduct at the surface the presence of underlying organising processes, but he does not offer much explanation about these beneath-the-surface structuring processes.

Theorists working in traditional structuralist mode, in contrast, have spent a great deal of time trying to work out the underlying rules of grammar and syntax by which the linguistic structure actually does its structuring. They do not just infer that language and meaning are produced from underlying structuring processes, they have worked out in some detail what the linguistic structure *is*. Similarly, post-structuralists have spent a lot of time working out the structuring of discourse and meaning. Without specifying some features that can be put to the test empirically, and especially in respect of what we can call its technical aspects, structuration theory leaves itself open to the challenge that it lacks empirical testability.

A key difference here is between 'structuration' used as a term for referring to the 'structuring of underlying forces' or the 'underlying structure-producing process' itself (i.e. the rule-forming mechanisms that social actors are unaware of but habitually use), and 'structuration' used as a term for describing the relations between surface elements once they have been (structurally) produced. The first use of the term is problematic for Giddens since this is the terrain on which structural*ist* social theory generally operates. Structural*ists* are experts in trying to work out the underlying structuring processes, and, to the extent that Giddens is using a key term from their conceptual vocabulary, they are bound to criticise him for not providing very much detail at this level of his analysis. Again Giddens uses inference as his preferred method of theory-building in that he infers what these underlying structure-producing processes consist of through reference to the work of Goffman and Garfinkel.

Giddens uses the term in the second sense (relations between surface items) as the basis of his idea of the duality of structure and his key definition of structure as rules-and-resources. Unfortunately for him this way of using the concept of structure has also been strongly challenged and by his own contemporary social theorists. Leading this challenge is the British social theorist Margaret Archer (born 1943) (the other leading players in this part of the social-theory game are Nicos Mouzelis [born 1939] and Roy Bhaskar [born 1944]). In an influential academic article, 'Morphogenesis versus structuration: on combining structure and agency' (*British Journal of Sociology*, 1982), Archer argues that by trying to combine (or 'conflate') the otherwise separate categories of clearly distinguishable types of matter called 'structure' and 'agency', structuration theory unhelpfully eliminates any possibility of understanding the various kinds of relationships *between* these two distinct types of social phenomena. Conceptually speaking, this is equivalent to saying that 'seahorses' and 'bricks' are no longer separate and distinct phenomena, but can be combined into a new entity called seahorse-brick. The new combination eliminates any possibility of ever making comparisons between these two types of matter and of any relationship that might hold between them. By 'collapsing', as Archer sees it, structure into agency, structuration theory effectively puts some of the most powerful analytical weapons of social theory 'beyond use'. Worse still, for Archer, Bhaskar and Mouzelis, this collapsing is very much in favour of the agency side of the earlier duality. Macro-level social structures (the social system Giddens refers to in structuration theory), the forces that provide the context in which social action takes place, and in many cases without which it could not take place, tend to be faded out of consideration altogether.

The price that Giddens has to pay for trying to find a new kind of solution to the age-old problem of how social agents and social systems interact, how the former shape the latter but always within the conditions created by systems that already exist, is to upset all those other social theorists who are quite happy to think again about the nature of the relationship between the two (how systems and agents interact), and indeed to consider some modification to the categories, but are not willing to do without the categories entirely. The viability of structuration theory *as a theory* depends on altering the categories of what the theory is about (agents and systems) to such an extent that these categories are required not just to accept modification, but to disappear altogether.

Working from within the perspective of **critical realism** (discussed in Chapter Fifteen), Archer's **morphogenic approach** (meaning that things perpetually, even if only gradually, undergo changes in form) treats structure and agency as intimately tied up with each other, but yet as analytically distinct. As Parker puts it: 'Morphogenesis is therefore about change in *the form of the relation and its consequences, not whether or not a relation exists*. Ontologically, structure and agency are necessarily related; analytically they must be distinguished to establish what the relation is' (Parker, 2000, p 72, original emphasis). Morphogenesis assumes that agent–structure interactions continuously change the contexts of action, and so, for as long as action takes place, there is a continuous unfolding of this relationship. The task of the social theorist is to understand how new structures emerge and how these condition social action: 'Analytically speaking, the relation between agency and structure is one of historical alternation between the conditioning of agents by structure and the elaboration of structure by interacting agents. Given time, systems can be both cause and caused, as can agency. Analytical dualism depends on temporality' (Archer, 1995, p 694; Parker, 2000, pp 74–5).

Third, and turning away from how structuration theory does its theorising and more towards the ideas and conclusions that structuration theory has produced, we can note first that structuration theory is rather conservative and actually not very well equipped for looking at processes of social transformation over time in the diachronic dimension. It helps us make useful distinctions between phenomena in terms of the kind of timescale they inhabit (i.e. in present time or historical time), but has less to say about what we could call the mechanism of historical change. Indeed the notion of **instantiation**, which Giddens uses to refer to the moment when action and system come together and thus reveal their truly dualistic constitution, does make it rather difficult to think of events as they unfold over longer periods of time. The idea of 'the instant' is largely incompatible with the idea of 'historical time', and yet it is in this latter dimension that social systems develop. As Archer has pointed out, structuration theory appears to offer novel ways of theorising how the present and past are interconnected but it certainly struggles to reconcile this with the highly compressed notion of time implied by the notion of instantiation. This weakness in structuration theory is rather ironic since one of Giddens' original intentions was to reject the synchronic or snapshot approach in functionalist theory on the grounds that it made it unable to develop an adequate theory of social change. As it turns out, structuration theory also tends to concentrate much more on the recursive aspects of social action, on how social systems and social institutions are reproduced, than on how they can be transformed.

Fourth, part of the problem here, for structuration theory, stems from the distinction it makes between practical and **discursive consciousness**. Between, that is, the kind of common-sense reasoning that allows routine daily action, and the more complex forms of reasoning required for the abstract consideration of things on an altogether more intellectual plain. Practical consciousness brings to mind Weber's realm of operational or formal rationality, while discursive consciousness implies the higher-level realm of substantive rationality. If, as structuration theory often implies, most of the time social actors get on with their lives at the level of everyday practical consciousness, this leaves precious little room for the more abstract kinds of discussions that go on at the level of discursive consciousness; the level at which, one might reasonably assume, ideas that foster social change (rather than social reproduction) are most likely to develop.

In this respect structuration theory comes up against the same difficulties as does Habermas's theory of communicative action, but from the opposite direction. Habermas tends to assume a world of social actors who spend most of their time engaged in high-level negotiation and so neglects the more mundane condition of practical day-to-day consciousness. Giddens gives so much space to the latter that high-level negotiation is virtually absent. To the extent that practical consciousness equates with the reproduction of social order (structure/social integration) and discursive consciousness with social transformation (system/system integration), structuration is mainly a theory of social reproduction. It does not have a very well-developed account of how discursive consciousness produces social change. One could reasonably conclude that the theory of communicative action and the theory of structuration tend to reiterate the nature of the social order–social change paradox in social theory but without taking social theory very far beyond it.

Finally, and relatedly, structuration theory lacks the kind of critical dimension that Habermas includes in his theory of communicative action. It could be argued that Giddens' theory is all the more useful because it concentrates on the process and mechanism by which social practices are reproduced, rather than containing within itself the implication that some outcomes are 'more desirable' or 'better than' others. Habermas's theory, in contrast, has a fairly obvious subplot, which is that communicative action is the best route to greater social emancipation and justice. The problems Habermas envisages of the colonisation of the lifeworld by instrumental-rational action, is part of the design specification of the theory itself. While it is by no means a condition of social theory that it contains a notion of what 'the good society' is or could be, it is useful if it provides some assistance about where social change is most likely to come from. Marx's theory of alienation, Weber's concerns about bureaucratisation, Durkheim's concept of anomie and Foucault's ideas on critical discursive practice all indicate possible points of weakness in the social fabric. In this respect, and although structuration theory works from the premise that the forces of social change come from within, it lacks its own sense of values or moral perspective.

Pierre Bourdieu's concept of habitus

In the third part of this chapter we turn to look briefly at part of the contribution to social theory of the French anthropologist and social theorist Pierre Bourdieu. Politically, Bourdieu has been a strong critic of Giddens, arguing that in his most recent publications on the 'Third Way' (Giddens, 1999), which Giddens (and, allegedly, the then British Prime Minister Tony Blair) envisage as a progressive combination of a liberal free-market economy and modernised state-oriented social democracy, Giddens betrays a latent conservatism and lack of critical edge, which also characterises his theoretical work. Bourdieu also has a dislike for what he calls the 'scholastic' mode of theory-building that has only minimal contact with empirical investigation. For his part, Giddens seems to have done his best to disregard Bourdieu and has made remarkably few references to the work of one of his leading contemporaries. Despite this lack of warmth, there are, at the level of their theoretical interests, some clear connections.

Agency and structure

Working in the context of French social theory during the 1960s and 1970s, Bourdieu was influenced by the French structuralist approach to defining 'structure', particularly that of the anthropologist Claude Lévi-Strauss (see Chapter Nine), and the existentialist notion of human agency developed by the philosopher Jean-Paul Sartre (1905–80). Like phenomenological approaches, **existentialism** argues strongly that meaning and purpose are features that come from within human consciousness, and that the essence of human existence coincides more or less completely with the moment of self-awareness, the moment of action itself.

Like Giddens, Bourdieu was not satisfied with these two apparently quite separate and opposed approaches to analysing the nature and contexts of human social action. Clearly reflecting his initial career in **anthropological** fieldwork in Kabylia and Béarn (Algeria), which at that time was still a French colony, Bourdieu felt that although social actors certainly make sense of the world around them by drawing on various structures of meaning that are embedded in culture, social actors have to be given credit for working some things out for themselves in a more spontaneous and autonomous way. The structuring context of traditional wisdom has to be balanced against the creativity of the human agent. He thus wants to resist the implication, contained in much analytical structural anthropology, that the 'rules of the game' are purely abstract and invariant, and to replace this with a sense in which social actors are regarded very much (as Giddens might put it) as 'knowledgeable agents' who are really very skilled at knowing 'how to go on' in the world.

In terms that are very similar to those used by Habermas in his notion of communicative action, Bourdieu goes further and describes how, in the case of how 'honour' operates in Kabylian society, these daily goings-on include a process of negotiation among members of the community. In this sense, and again like Habermas's idea that knowledge and a sense of certainty about how to act emerge through democratic negotiation, Bourdieu also develops a procedural notion of social competence and knowledge.

Habitus

The framework Bourdieu uses to explore these ideas is the concept of habitus. Although this is not a very familiar term, Bourdieu is trying to provide a suitable label for the generally quite localised day-to-day world of average stuff, and of the codes of meaning and signification associated with them, which constitute the immediate context of 'habitual' or 'lived' experiences. It is the fact that these activities and meanings are habitual, and what makes them so, that makes them interesting for social theorists. In terms that are similar to those used by Habermas in his distinction between system and lifeworld, Bourdieu distinguishes between the kinds of structurings that go on in the social system and those that guide actions in the habitus or lifeworld. There is a sense here that the dispassionate or inert character of the system needs to be treated as different from the more emotional domain of lived experience. Whereas systems function, social agents act.

Bearing in mind his continuing interest in structural–anthropological accounts of ritualised behaviours, the concept of habitus becomes a general term for describing the surface events that are generated from rules of conduct and practice that lie beneath. A guiding principle in this account is that habitus operates in terms of differences or distinctions between one set of practices (or simply social habits) and another set. Social actors fall into groups and groups become distinguishable from other groups because the actions of the individuals within them are shaped by the rituals and practices of the habitus whose rules they learn through socialisation and under the shadow of which they live their lives.

Combining this fairly orthodox structuralist perspective with his interest in existentialist and **phenomenological** philosophy (Edmund Husserl, Martin Heidegger and Alfred Schutz), Bourdieu argues that the basic motivation that drives social action, the underlying structuring principle of motivation, is the urge social actors have to experience their sense-of-self or simply to be. Social actors do have a sense of meaning, defined as the intellectual quest for knowledge, but meaning is primarily and overwhelmingly a practical (**rationalist**) rather than an abstract (**idealist**) thing. Perhaps because of his own training as a field-researcher, and certainly because of his conviction that meaning has to be understood very much at the level of practical consciousness, Bourdieu thus wants to make use of the structuralist method (i.e. looking for underlying structuring forces), but without cluttering his analysis of social phenomena as they appear at the surface with abstract notions and obscure relationships and causes. The grammar and syntax, if you like, of the underlying structuring processes are more in the realm of psychology than they are of sociology.

Subjects and objects

The concept of habitus also helps Bourdieu explain his ideas about the links between the subjective and the objective dimensions of social phenomena, and about the ways in which past events or 'history' continue to exert an influence over the present. A key distinction here is between what we can call the objective historical record of material artefacts, the concrete, tangible stuff that survives the persons who made it, and the forms and patterns of behaviour, the social mores of habits that, although not concretised in quite the same way, do nonetheless continue to be materialised when social actors behave in accordance with them. As Giddens might put it, the rules-and-resources of the habitus become instantiated or embedded in actual time at the moment when agents act. The practice, for example, of standing up when significant people enter a room, is just as tangible and observable as the chairs on which they were previously sitting.

Time

The concept of habitus also contributes to social theory in terms of how we can make sensible theoretical suggestions about how past events have a bearing on action in the present. Inferring David Lockwood's important distinction (which, as we have seen, both Habermas and Giddens have made use of in developing their own theories) between *system* integration (which builds up over longer periods of time) and *social* integration (which is much more a creature of the moment), the present becomes laced into the past because of the facilities offered by the habitus. The systemic or structural aspects of the contexts in which action takes place are themselves maintained by the constant re-enactment of the kinds of routine and sometimes ritualised practices that gave rise to them in the first place; a constant re-enactment that is operationalised by habitus-in-action. For something to become a tradition or a custom it obviously has to have been built up over time. Traditions and customs only have meaning, however, they only affect real lives in a practical way, if the practices of the tradition continue to be acted out. Christmas Day dinner, Thanksgiving dinner, Chinese New Year, Mardi Gras, can only become custom*ary* or tradition*al* if social actors continue to perform them as practices.

Cultural capital

The customary cultural practices of the habitus provide a basis for another of Bourdieu's key concepts, which is the idea of **cultural capital**. Bourdieu develops these ideas in his well-known study of

French social and cultural etiquette *Distinction* (1984 [1979]). For Bourdieu, the resources social actors make use of in trying to achieve their goals go well beyond economic resources and include resources in the social, cultural and symbolic fields as well. In this regard Bourdieu is taking a further step along a path first cleared by Max Weber (see Chapter Five), who had started to identify a range of cultural resources in the form of various kinds of social status or 'estimation of social honour' that can be mobilised in the strategic manoeuvrings between social groups. Developing beyond Weber's account of how life chances are affected by non-economic assets, Bourdieu argues that social actors learn how to go on by using the cultural practices appropriate to the classes and other culturally-determined groupings to which they belong. Over time there has been a shifting among the fields in which actors compete for resources (from economic to cultural, from material to non-material), and this is accompanied by a rearrangement of the hierarchy of resources themselves. In late-modern society cultural and symbolic resources have become progressively more and more valuable.

If we see cultural capital as one of the primary modes of operation of the habitus, then habitus can be defined as a set of attitudes or dispositions that actors acquire in early childhood, and which establish a kind of strategic framework for operating successfully in the social world. Habitus provides a template for how to behave as a member of a particular social group and cultural capital provides a form of currency for making these kinds of cultural exchanges. Habitus always emerges in practical contexts and so, unsurprisingly, social actors who tend to live under the same circumstances will tend to share the same habitus. Conversely, it is the fact that actors in particular groups or classes *do share* the same habitus that reinforces the notion of being 'the same as' others in that group and 'different from' those in other groups. Habitus is thus a form of 'generative structure' in the sense that it guides social action and so helps actors formulate how to act in particular situations. In very much the same way that Giddens sees social structures (rules-and-resources) as being instantiated through social action, Bourdieu sees habitus as being continually renewed through cultural practice.

Habitus and social change

The final main point of comparison to make between Bourdieu and Habermas is about the nature and origins of social change. Like Giddens' rules-and-resources, Bourdieu's habitus both enables and restrains social action. (As should have become clear, there is often only a slight conceptual difference between Giddens' and Bourdieu's ideas on this point. Where they are different is that habitus tends to emphasise historically sedimented cultural practices, whereas the rules-and-resources model tends to rely on a much more amorphous notion of social practices in general, derived from the more abstract notion of linguistic structuring.) To the extent that the ability to act successfully is endowed by the habitus/rules-and-resources where social action takes place, actors are likely to develop both a sense of vested interest in it and a desire to protect and preserve it against rival paradigms. Seen in this light, habitus/rules-and-resources become a recursive and often conservative force rather than a force for change. The rules-and-resources of the habitus are, just like social systems, sedimented in time. Habitus becomes a primary site of social reproduction rather than transformation.

We have also seen, however, that because he limits the notion of power to the capacity actors have to draw on the rather weakly defined category of rules-and-resources, Giddens' theory lacks a really robust concept of power. Bourdieu specifically links the notion of individuality to history, and thus to other social actors and to collective action. The logic of the habitus here is that customary practices must also be collectivising practices. Habitus assigns actors to groups, and creates boundaries between groups, and so inevitably it creates the conditions for solidaristic behaviours. If we add to this a concept of power defined in terms of the competitive exchanges between groups in search of different kinds of resources or types of capital in its various forms (Bourdieu lists the conventional 'big four' of economic, political, social and cultural capital), then we can see that Bourdieu's theory of structure and agency as habitus provides a very useful explanation of (a) the practical grounds on which the present links with history, (b) how practices link with resources, and (c) how in pursuing their own interests, individuals tend to consolidate links with other likewise-engaged social actors.

Although we must beware of the tautology in Bourdieu's argument, which is that it is unclear at what point in the passage of time the interactions between social actors become habituated as customary practice (as Althusser might have said, the 'first instance never arrives'), Bourdieu's theory does have a critical edge. Using a similar kind of procedural conception of knowledge as that developed by Habermas, social interaction is not limited to the more ritualised and customary practices of the habitus, and nor does it follow these blindly or always obediently. Embedded in common-sense or practical consciousness, social actors constantly monitor and re-evaluate the situation they find themselves in. The situation is not just 'read' in terms of pre-existing formulas and rules of behaviour and conduct, but is worked-out in the present and in terms of the new situations and contexts that are developing. It would not be pushing our comparisons too far to suggest that the elements of 'conditioning' and 'emergence' that Archer identifies (the contexts within which action takes place and the emergence of new courses of action resulting from them) could also find a place in Bourdieu's concept of habitus.

Chapter overview: modernism and postmodernism

We began this chapter by summarising a number of the basic contrasts that can be drawn between the Enlightenment frame of reference and the post-structuralist and postmodernist alternative. The basic difference between the two approaches is that the contemporary modernists we have been looking at in this chapter try to develop their alternatives largely within the conceptual and methodological parameters of the Enlightenment perspective while postmodernists reject the classical perspective altogether. In concluding our discussion in this chapter, it will be useful to reflect briefly on where Habermas, Giddens and Bourdieu can be fitted into this general modernist *versus* postmodernist picture.

Distinguishing the different realms of matter

First, and in terms of what kinds of differences there might be between the subjective world of human consciousness and the objective world in which they live, there is a fair degree of correspondence between the three theorists that, although they certainly are part of the world of physical stuff, humans do have a capacity for affecting the circumstances around them. For Habermas this comes in the form of negotiation through communicative action, for Giddens the human capacity for reflexivity is paramount, and similarly for Bourdieu humans have a unique propensity for critical self-awareness. Debates about the nature and limits of modernity should therefore include further detailed consideration of the human capacity for reflexive self-awareness; a capacity that, however you define it, sets humans apart from the rest of biological nature. And this capacity, too, does not remain unchanged, as both it, and the sense-of-self to which it is applied, can become the subject matter of change. In all three accounts there is a strong sense that human subjects are continuously learning how to interact with their physical and social environments.

Universal truth and value

A second core idea we listed in Figure 12.1 was the Enlightenment vision that social action is informed by universal truths and underlying values that not only guide the direction it takes, but indicate its ultimate objectives. Bourdieu, Giddens and Habermas again invoke a very practical or grounded idea of what constitutes knowledge and see meaning also as something that is very much tied up with practical decision making. We also noted, however, that whereas Giddens is almost silent on the topic of what kind of society might develop in the future, both Habermas and Bourdieu include in their theories a more critical element. Neither believes humanity is searching for ultimate truth, or that human activity is driven by metaphysical inner forces, and yet they do express the idea that human activity is oriented in a positive, rather than neutral or negative, way. Consistent with their ideas about the nature of meaning and knowledge just mentioned, Habermas's concept of communicative rationality and the practice-based and knowledge-giving properties of Bourdieu's habitus are procedural in the sense that outcomes emerge during the negotiating process rather than being external to it. They thus tend to reject the Enlightenment view of knowledge as the gathering-in of empirical facts about a separate realm of stuff that is 'out there'.

Practical consciousness

Third, and on the question of human nature and the transcendental subject, these theorists emphasise the highly practical and common-sense perspective that actors adopt in the lifeworld, and the complex and yet explicit patterns and routines that they rely upon in organising their lives. The logic of action that drives activities in the habitus is theorised very much in accordance with pragmatist conceptions of meaning and purpose; a perspective that also brings into the foreground a phenomenological conception of social action. Actors do certainly behave 'instrumentally' in the lifeworld in the sense that they act in accordance with outcomes they would like to achieve, but they also see their actions as having meaning in an experiential and intrinsic sense. For Habermas, as we have seen, an essential component of intrinsic meaning is the desire to find agreement with others through communicative action. We can certainly envisage human social life as also involving a quest for grand objectives and distant goals framed in terms of 'knowledge' or 'civilisation', but, according to this pragmatist conception, it is much more to do with making sense of the world in an immediate sense so that decisions can be taken.

This is a good example of Habermas's willingness to criticise aspects of Enlightenment thinking (in this instance the privileged position given to the biographical subject), but without adopting the more radical rejections of it offered by post-structuralist theory. He agrees with Foucault and Derrida that it is not reasonable to rely so heavily on the subject-oriented or subjectivistic conception of history, knowledge and reason, but rather than taking the subjective individual out of the equation altogether (which produces a rather pessimistic and largely dehumanised conception of social reality), he recommends instead developing an intersubjective conception of human social interaction. To the extent that 'other social actors' form an essential part of the context within which social actors express their practical consciousness, the concept of social action used by these three theorists already includes a recognition that although social actors are compelled to see themselves subjectively, they are nonetheless objects from the point of view of others. The subject–object distinction, in other words, is very much a question of where you are standing.

Social change

Finally, we looked at all three theorists in terms of what they have to say about social development and change. We noted that although there is methodological consistency in the way that all three see the problem of social change as closely tied in with the relationship between social structure and social agency (which is very much how Marx, Weber and Durkheim approached the matter), they come up with different solutions to the dilemma of where the structural and experiential realms divide. For Habermas it is necessary to maintain a *dualistic* conception, an analytical distinction, between system and lifeworld, but to see the relationship between the two as interactive and permeable, rather than separated and fixed. He deploys his concept of communicative action, and the dynamics of negotiation and intersubjectivity that this contains, in an attempt to find new ways of thinking about this basic problem in social theory.

For his part, Giddens moves decisively away from the **dualist** approach and tries not only to think again about the relation between structure and action (as duality rather than dualism), but in such a way as to require the removal of previous distinctions between the two categories. His theory redefines the relationship as one of structure-with-action, or structuration; structure is recast as rules-and-resources rather than as any kind of fixed entity that dominates human agency; and agency is defined in terms of the capacity to make use of rules-and-resources. Structure-action becomes real (instantiated) at the moment when actors act.

Like Giddens, Bourdieu wants to look again at both the nature of agency and structure *and* at how the two interact. Using the notion of 'genetic structuralism' (thus distinguishing his approach from first- and second-wave structura*lism* and from Giddens' structur*ation* theory), Bourdieu introduces the concept of habitus to describe the everyday terrain on which social actors mostly live their lives. Although habitus also includes a certain amount of concrete historical stuff, which can be seen as the established and apparently permanent systems and structures usually categorised as 'social structure', it is more important to see it as the product of the underlying rules and conventions of established cultural practices. Bourdieu thus stops short of requiring a complete redefinition of 'structure' and 'action', but he does provide what we could call a radicalised conception of them and how they are related.

Key points box – In this chapter we have looked at:

☑ A summary of the Enlightenment perspective and the postmodernist alternative (Figures 12.1 and 12.2).

☑ Habermas's concept of social action as *communicative action* and its key concepts of *pragmatic discourse* and *ideal speech situation*.

☑ Habermas's social theory and its key conceptual components of *system*, *lifeworld* and *communicative rationality*.

☑ Habermas's account of how communicative rationality provides a contemporary way of thinking about 'the problem of social order'.

☑ Giddens' concept of social action as *structuration*.

☑ His redefinition of 'structure' as 'rules-and-resources'.

☑ His key conceptual shift away from seeing agency and structure as a *dualism* (two distinct elements) and towards seeing it as a *duality* (two dimensions of the same phenomenon).

☑ His contemporary account of social order as created through the *instantiation* of social *systems* (physical institutions) and of social *structures* (structuring processes based on the language model) in historical time.

☑ Both Habermas and Giddens see the forces of social change as coming from within the social formation rather than from outside it.

☑ There can be no forces shaping society that are outside the social system (just like there cannot be cosmic forces affecting planet Earth that are outside the solar system).

☑ Bourdieu's concept of *habitus* as a cultural resource for helping people know how to 'go on' in the world.

☑ Habitus is also a mechanism of social order as it creates continuities of behaviour and expectations between social actors and over time.

Practice box

➲ What are the other four concepts of social action that Habermas uses as a basis for developing his own concept of social action as communicative action?

➲ What are the main differences between *system* and *lifeworld*?

➲ What does Habermas mean when he talks about the 'colonisation of the lifeworld'?

➲ List some of the limits of *instrumental rationality*.

➲ Why might instrumental rationality upset social order?

➲ Why does Giddens think it is necessary to stop thinking about structure and agency as two distinct things rather than as two aspects of the same thing?

➲ Briefly define Giddens' concept of *instantiation*.

➲ Structuration theory relies heavily on the idea of instantiation, does this mean that structuration has no historical dimension?

➲ Why does Giddens agree with Habermas that societies already contain within themselves the capacity for change?

➲ Give a brief definition of Bourdieu's concept of *habitus*.

➲ How do the concepts of habitus and *cultural capital* fit together?

➲ Is social and historical continuity in human society possible *without* habitus?

Further reading

Margaret Archer, 'Morphogenesis versus structuration: on combining structure and agency', *British Journal of Sociology*, 33(4): 456–83 (1982).

Pierre Bourdieu, *Distinction: A Social Critique of the Judgement of Taste* (Routledge and Kegan Paul, 1984 [1979]).

Christopher Bryant and David Jary (eds) *The Contemporary Giddens: Social Theory in a Globalising Age* (Palgrave, 2001).

Gerard Delanty, *Modernity and Postmodernity* (Sage, 2000).

Anthony Giddens, *The Consequences of Modernity* (Polity Press, 1990); and *Modernity and Self-Identity* (Polity Press, 1991).

David Held and John B. Thompson (eds) *Social Theory of Modern Societies: Anthony Giddens and His Critics* (Cambridge University Press, 1989).

Richard Jenkins, *Bourdieu* (Routledge, 1993).

Anthony King, *The Structure of Contemporary Social Theory* (Routledge, 2004).

Nicos Mouzelis, *Sociological Theory: What Went Wrong?* (Routledge, 1995).

William Outhwaite, *Habermas: A Critical Introduction*, 2nd edn (Polity Press, 2009); and (ed) *The Habermas Reader* (Polity Press, 1996)

John Parker, *Structuration* (Open University Press, 2000).
Kenneth Tucker, *Anthony Giddens and Modern Social Theory* (Sage, 1998).

Websites

For these contemporary theorists the most effective internet search strategy is to enter their names into the search engines. Further information about some authors can be found by visiting their home page at the institutions they are associated with. For example, Anthony Giddens can be found on the website of the London School of Economics: www.lse.ac.uk

For further information on Jürgen Habermas try: www.habermasforum.dk/ and: www.marxists.org/reference/archive/habermas/index.htm

For further information on Pierre Bourdieu try: www.marxists.org/ reference/subject/philosophy/works/fr/bourdieu.htm

CHAPTER THIRTEEN

THEORIES OF MODERNITY AND POSTMODERNITY

This chapter describes a distinct collection of recent approaches in social theory that promote what has be labelled a 'postmodernist perspective'. The narrative or storytelling approach that is typical of modernist social theory, where social phenomena and indeed theories about social phenomena are described as developing naturally from one another, is rejected by postmodernist theorists. We will therefore use a thematic rather than narrative approach in organising the material in this chapter.

The contents are summarised as follows:

Defining 'postmodernity'

Outline of the modernity versus postmodernity debate

Jean-François Lyotard on knowledge and meta-narratives

Stories that have been told – modernists and the unfinished project of modernity

Evaluating project-of-modernity approaches

Jean Baudrillard – telling stories the postmodernist way

Evaluating Baudrillard's story of simulation and hyper-reality

The impact of the modernity versus postmodernity debate on social theory

Defining postmodernity

Our first task is to think a little about how the three terms **postmodernity**, **postmodernist** and **postmodernism** are generally defined in social theory.

Postmodernity

Postmodernity is a name that social theorists use to describe a particular period, moment or state of human society. It is a periodising concept used to separate or bracket-off one state, moment or period, which is identifiable in social, historical and cultural time, from another one: 'Once there was a pre-modern period, then a modern period and now there is a postmodern one'. The term postmodernity or **postmodern society** is roughly equivalent to terms such as post-industrial society or post-Fordist society. Chronologically speaking, the modern period is from around 1750 to 1950 and the postmodern period from the 1950s onwards.

Part of the reason why debates about postmodernity are confusing is because the term postmodernism is rather ambiguous in its basic formulation. Postmodernists see themselves as describing something that comes after or later than modern society. At the same time they want to retain a sense of continuity with that very same modern society that they suggest has been superseded. Postmodernists resist the idea that postmodernity grew out of modernity and yet there can be little doubt that the two have followed each other in historical sequence. One cannot imagine postmodernity coming *before* modernity in historical time.

Postmodernist

The second variant of the term is postmodern*ist*, which is used to categorise groups of social actors rather than periods of time. It is thus a *categorising* concept rather than a periodising one. Although everyone living in the postmodern historical period can be categorised as postmodernist, postmodernist social theorists believe strongly that a state of postmodernity really has come into being. Postmodernist theorists adopt ways of doing theory that are characteristically postmodernist.

The emergence of the postmodernist style of developing social theory is taken as proof that advanced Westernised society has now reached a postmodern condition. Logically it is not possible to think in a postmodernist way, to express a postmodernist consciousness, until the postmodern period has actually come into being. It is possible to look at events that fall into the modern period (say 1750 to 1950) with a modernist or a postmodernist gaze, but it was impossible for pre-modern philosophers to think in modernist ways or for modernists to think postmodernistically. It is a moot point whether all theorists working today are bound to adopt a postmodernist perspective.

Equally clearly there must be periods of intellectual development where modernist and postmodernist perspectives overlap. In the terms developed by Foucault (see Chapter Ten), periods where one épistème gives way to another. The importance of **structuralist** and **post-structuralist** perspectives in the development of social theory is that, although they might not have described themselves as postmodernist, they instigated the movement away from the modernist and Enlightenment perspective and towards the postmodern. Second-wave post-structuralist theorists such as Roland Barthes, Michel Foucault and Jacques Derrida can be categorised as 'postmodernist' because in retrospect it can be seen that their ideas were an integral part of the emergence of the postmodernist perspective. Unambiguously postmodernist are theorists such as Jean-François Lyotard and Jean Baudrillard who are purveyors of a fully fledged postmodernist approach in social theory.

Postmodernism

The third variant of the term is **postmodernism** and is used to classify a particular creative style or aesthetic effect. Originally made popular as a term to distinguish the 'postmodernist' from the 'modernist' styles in architecture and building design, other kinds of artistic production can also be classified as constituting postmodernism. Although this term is essentially used descriptively (in the sense that 'cubist art' is classified as different to 'impressionist art' or 'surrealist art' because they look different), it also carries the idea that the artistic producer had particular intentions in mind when they produced the work. The modernist style in architecture, for example the 'international style' of Frank Lloyd Wright and Le Corbusier, expressed ideas about combining form with function in particular ways; the essence of modernism or postmodernism in architecture goes deeper than the appearance of the structures themselves.

Postmodernism is primarily associated with ideas, events and artefacts in the cultural realm rather than with happenings in the realms of economics or politics. The link between postmodernism as an artistic style or attitude enjoyed by an artistic or aesthetic elite and the lives of average citizens is often seen as lying within the realm of consumption, and so many theorists working in postmodernist mode focus attention on activities in this realm. The fairly dramatic turn towards the study of consumption can be attributed to the development of the postmodernist perspective in social theory. This 'cultural turn' has provided a theoretical framework that can be used to support investigations of identity, consumption, lifestyle and choice, which had not previously received very much attention. In this sense, postmodernism has created an academic/theoretical space where the more expressive and ephemeral domains of people's experiences can be investigated. Postmodernism operates in the metaphysical and ideological domains of meaning, signification and symbolism and not in the empirical and positivist domains of science, engineering and technology.

Outline of the modernity versus postmodernity debate

The most basic intellectual division that fuels the modernity versus postmodernity debate is essentially a continuation of the rivalry between social theorists who attempt to analyse late 20th- and early 21st-century society broadly within the parameters of the Enlightenment frame of reference and those who reject this perspective altogether. Contemporary modernists construct their social theory using concepts and methods developed by the classical modernists Marx, Weber and Durkheim during the late 19th century. Postmodernists generally take as their point of departure the battery of concepts and methods that developed from first- and then second-wave structuralist social theory during the mid-20th century.

The continuing project of modernity in the late-modern period

Looking at these differences in a little more detail, the basic assumptions and orientations of the two sides in the debate are listed in Figures 12.1 and 12.2 in Chapter Twelve. These summarise their contrasting positions in terms of ideas about the nature of stuff in the universe (the question of **ontology**), about what knowledge is and how we acquire it (the question of **epistemology**) and about whether human society is headed in any particular direction (the question of **teleology**). These differences inevitably produce different kinds of accounts of the nature of contemporary society. Contemporary modernists refer to 'the project of modernity' to convey the idea that the continued unfolding of the original forces of modernity can best be described in terms of a series of interrelated movements and developments, rather than as if there is a single identifiable end-point that everything is directed towards. The term 'project' also implies a capacity to generate and to cope with unexpected events and situations; it is a generative and dynamic way of describing social development.

Contemporary modernists prefer terms like 'late-modern' or 'high-modern' (rather than postmodern) to emphasise that, in their view, the current state of society is best regarded as the most elaborated or most advanced state of modern society that has yet been reached. From a modernist perspective, the economic, political and cultural forces that gave rise to modernity during the 19th century (industrialism, capitalism and rationalisation) are still in play. The challenge for social theorists today is to make more of an effort to understand those forces rather than getting distracted by the idea that entirely new forces have emerged to replace them. In his influential book *The Consequences of Modernity* (1990), for example, Anthony Giddens suggests that as they try to get a hold on the increasingly rapid pace and scope of change in late-modern societies, 'it is not sufficient merely to invent new terms like postmodernity and the rest. Rather than entering a period of postmodernity, we are moving into one in which the consequences of modernity are becoming more radicalized and universalized than ever before' (Giddens, 1990, p 2). For modernist social theorists there is still too much of 'the modern' in late-modern society to justify the postmodernist claim that a significantly different type of society has emerged.

A central idea in the contemporary modernist scenario is that the original forces that gave rise to modern society in the first place have started to speed up. Modern society is characterised by a much more rapid turnover of ideas and experiences than was the case in pre-modern society. Lives at the end of the 20th and the start of the 21st century are increasingly shaped by events and circumstances that are happening far away from where social actors live. Global travel and global communications, for example, have effectively changed the size and shape of the domains of social experience so that social action is now influenced in its immediate and local contexts by events that previously seemed distant and remote. Changes of these kinds often combine to create feelings of excitement and adventure, but also of insecurity and uncertainty as many of the things that were previously taken for granted seem less reliable and predictable than formerly. In a famous passage from *The Communist Manifesto*, which was published in 1848, but which seems just as relevant to events in the 21st century, Marx and Engels tried to sum up these new energies:

> All fixed, fast-frozen relations, with their train of venerable and ancient prejudices and opinions, are swept away, all new-formed ones become antiquated before they can ossify. All that is solid melts into air, all that is holy is profaned, and man is at last compelled to face with sober senses, his real conditions of, and his relations with his kind. (Marx and Engels, 1952 [1848] p 46)

Giddens has used the image of a juggernaut to try to capture the sense in which modern societies seem to be out of control as one kind of change piles in upon another, while the combined effects of these collisions produce yet more unintended and unexpected consequences. Modernity 'crushes those who resist it, and while it sometimes seems to have a steady path, there are times when it veers away erratically in directions we cannot foresee ... feelings of ontological security and existential anxiety will coexist in ambivalence' (Giddens, 1990, p 139).

New ideas for the new age of postmodernity

For postmodernist social theorists, however, this renewal of effort among modernist social theorists simply does not go far enough. Postmodernists would certainly agree that the postmodern world is characterised by an unnerving mixture of excitement and insecurity, vitality and paranoia, but they think it is futile to try to capture these dramatic developments, to try to understand how and why they are occurring, by using the same old conceptual tools, such as the interplay of social structure with human agency or Enlightenment-style assumptions about the transcendental quality of human subjectivity. Drawing on the kind of critical energy expressed by post-structuralist theorists like Foucault and Derrida, they argue that modernist accounts of these changes are reaching the point of failure because their underlying conceptual framework also needs to be thoroughly renovated. Reflexive identity, consumption-side activity and the **globalisation** of media and culture can be identified as new kinds of forces that are becoming more influential than the forces that dominated early modernity.

We can summarise these underlying intellectual divisions as follows:

- Modernists like using the classical concepts in social theory; postmodernists do not.
- Modernists continue with the Enlightenment project; postmodernists reject it.
- Modernists try to think about underlying forces in new ways; postmodernists think in terms of new forces.
- Postmodernists think that intellectual regime change is a precondition for social development itself.

Jean-François Lyotard on knowledge and grand narratives

The question of replacing one discourse in social theory with another features prominently in the work of the postmodernist French philosopher and social theorist Jean-François Lyotard. In his book

The Postmodern Condition (1984 [1979]), he argues that the shift from modernity to postmodernity has come about because the underlying **grand narratives** that give modernist accounts their sense of legitimacy have started to collapse. Lyotard is not only challenging the current state of knowledge in science and philosophy, but the modernist definition of what 'knowledge' is. Quite a number of the terms and ideas that Lyotard uses in *The Postmodern Condition* have been adopted by other postmodernist theorists as a basis for the new postmodernist discourse. It will be useful to look at the postmodernist framework he provides.

Two types of knowledge

Lyotard bases his survey of 'the current state of knowledge' on a distinction between scientific knowledge and narrative knowledge. Scientific knowledge is the kind of knowledge obtained by using objective, often empirical, techniques of investigation. It has its roots in the search for knowledge (or truth) through **reason** and implies a **positivist** conception that the underlying laws of social action and social structure can be identified. Narrative knowledge in contrast, which in some respects is also a child of the Age of Reason, is the kind of knowledge that is based on a reasoned explanation of how things are and how they came to be that way. Fairy stories, for example, or children's nursery rhymes, all seem essentially plausible (to young children at least) because they tend to reinforce common themes like happy outcomes, harmony and balance between people and nature, that goodness and justice always defeat wickedness.

Narrative accounts partly rely on factual information, but their main strategy of knowledge-building is to persuade an audience of the validity or reliability of the story by drawing on other taken-for-granted ideas. Much like Foucault's concept of discourse and Roland Barthes' concept of myths (see Chapter Ten), narrative knowledge tends to be built up from a number of other narratives or narrative fragments, all of which thus acquire a kind of group, or collective, legitimacy. If we imagine listening to evidence in a court of law, for example, the contrast between these two basic types of knowledge roughly equates with the difference between scientific forensic evidence, and the statements and accounts of witnesses. The defence will often use character witnesses to try to 'prove' that their client could not possibly be guilty as there are so many other good things they have done. The outcome of legal hearings often depends very directly on pitting scientific forensic evidence against such narrative and personalised accounts.

A first important twist in Lyotard's analysis of the state of knowledge, however, is that, paradoxically, scientific knowledge invariably also has to rely on narrative accounts of its own activity in order to be seen to be legitimate. Science has to use the very technique of explanation and legitimation that it otherwise rejects as being unscientific. 'It is not inconceivable', writes Lyotard, 'that the recourse to narrative is inevitable, at least to the extent that the language game of science desires its statements to be true but does not have the resources to legitimate their truth on its own' (Lyotard, 1984 [1979], p 28). Unless it is prepared to appear as an endless and pretty much disconnected mass of fragmentary statements about physical stuff in the universe, scientific knowledge also has to be organised into some kind of story. An obvious illustration of this is Charles Darwin's hugely influential analysis of the process of evolution through natural selection. It is virtually impossible to explain how particular species survive and others do not because they are better fitted to the environment where they live without putting this into some kind of narrative framework. The same could be said of the 'big bang' theory of how the universe came into being; the idea that there was an identifiable starting-point to everything in the universe where we now live is already a story.

Meta-narratives

In telling his own story of the current state of knowledge (even Lyotard cannot avoid using narrative), Lyotard needs to do more than point out the rather obvious paradox that science depends on storytelling. The more subtle and significant part of his argument is to look into the content of the current narratives of science and philosophy and to trace them back to the grand or meta-narratives from which they themselves are derived. The current state of knowledge in other words depends for its legitimacy on certain stories that are even more firmly embedded, more deeply rooted, in the Western consciousness. As Frederic Jameson helpfully points out in his critical Foreword to Lyotard's book (1984 [1979]), Lyotard distinguishes here between a German meta-narrative, which presupposes that humankind is perpetually separated from nature, and a French meta-narrative, which presupposes that ultimately humankind is part of a single universe of stuff. As Lyotard puts it: 'The alternative seems clear: it is a choice between the homogeneity and the intrinsic duality of the social, between functional and critical knowledge ... "positive knowledge" versus "the critical, reflexive or hermeneutic kind"' (Lyotard, 1984 [1979], pp 13–14). Again, a little confusingly, both these narratives draw much of their own legitimacy from association with the tradition of the European Enlightenment. We can think of these as two different paths that scientists and philosophers have followed, but which have some points of origin in common.

Meta–narratives: homogeneity versus duality

Looking into the content of the narratives themselves, Lyotard contrasts the basic society-as-unity model (which originated in the social theory of Auguste Comte) with the society-as-divided model expounded by Karl Marx. These two views define 'two major kinds of discourse on society'. For the French/**functionalist** side, knowledge is a means of ensuring the unity of the parts; knowledge is essentially integrative. Comte and Durkheim regard knowledge as positive because it is good for the running of society. For the German critical/**hermeneutic** tradition in contrast, knowledge is a means of discovering and overcoming the tension that emerges between, on the one side, the constraining influence of the social system and, on the other, the legitimate and emancipatory needs of social actors. Lyotard writes:

> The mode of legitimation we are discussing, which reintroduces narrative as the validity of knowledge, can take two routes, depending on whether it represents the subject of the narrative as cognitive or practical, as a hero of knowledge or hero of liberty [French/positivist model versus German hermeneutic model]. Because of this alternative, not only does the meaning of legitimation vary, but it is already apparent that narrative itself is incapable of describing that meaning adequately. (Lyotard, 1984 [1979], p 31)

The various narratives developed by the classical theorists of the modern period (Marx on **alienation**, Durkheim on **anomie** and Weber on disenchantment and bureaucratic domination) are essentially all about the same social phenomenon (the negative tendencies in modern society), but belong to different narrative traditions and thus produce different narrative discourses. The French/positivist/society-as-unity narrative sees anomie as dysfunctional to the harmony of the total social system, while the German/hermeneutic/society-as-divided narrative sees alienation/the iron-cage scenario as both confirming the fundamentally divided nature of matter, and as showing where its fault lines occur. The two dominant narratives work in the same way, which is by telling a plausible story of how things are and then using this to legitimise their suggestions about what needs doing to make sure things turn out alright in the end. The 'end' they have in mind (i.e. the kind of society they envisage humanity is progressing towards) is also a product of the legitimating narrative: systems integration versus emancipation.

Never forgetting that 'narrative wars' and 'discourse wars' are always also about how knowledge is defined, these two dominant traditions also hope to incorporate in their stories a sense that what they are saying must be true because they are using the most superior definition of knowledge. There is quite a strong process of mutual legitimation at play here, in the sense that a story seems true if it uses a robust definition of knowledge, and the robustness of that definition is itself reinforced by the strength of the story it supports. As we pointed out at the start of this chapter, much of the modernity–postmodernity debate is about one side trying to discredit the stories put forward by the other side by discrediting the definition of knowledge they make use of. The discursive underpinnings of the narrative become part of the narrative.

Telling stories

Drawing fairly directly on Wittgenstein's ideas about how language games are restrained by the rules imposed by linguistic structure (see Chapter Nine), Lyotard is also interested in how the *technique* of telling stories, and the structure of what is being told, impose certain constraints on the storyteller and their audience. These restraints in turn limit the kind of knowledge being constructed. He suggests: 'The narration usually obeys rules that define the pragmatics of their transmission' (Lyotard, 1984 [1979], p 20). The way stories are told thus follows a format and audiences are able to distinguish between one kind of narration and another because of differences in these formats. A classical Greek epic, for example, is distinguishable from a fairy tale or religious parable because they are told in different ways. Even if the content were largely the same, they would still become different depending on their mode of telling.

Showing quite a high degree of consistency with Roland Barthes' ideas about the telling of myths, and Michel Foucault's ideas about how discourses build into discursive practices (see Chapter Ten), Lyotard is suggesting here that the 'laws of knowledge' in modern society have in fact been reduced to the 'laws of the narrative form'. The listener, let us say an audience at a political event, knows the rules just as well as the speaker and so the audience is already preconditioned, already accepts knowledge as taking the form of, and as coming in the manner of, the dominant form of political narration in that society. The only qualification the narrator needs is to be able to get the story right and to tell it in the conventional way. The legitimacy of the speaker and of what is being said derives not from any personal quality or attribute of the speaker, but from the structural properties of the narrative form they are using: 'Narratives … determine criteria of competence and/or illustrate how they are to be applied. They thus define what has the right to be said and done in the culture in question, and since they are themselves a part of that culture, they are legitimated by the simple fact that they do what they do' (Lyotard, 1984 [1979], p 23).

This is quite an interesting argument because, if we take a step back, we can see that Lyotard is suggesting that a key reason why modernist scientists and philosophers are unable to step outside their own paradigm or discourse (which is a precondition for being able to see its weaknesses and limitations) is because they are perpetually trapped by the narrative form/content/technique that structures their entire conception of knowledge. The difficulty social actors have in imagining a non-narrative way of packaging knowledge is a restraint that is embedded within the very structure of their technique for looking at the world. Social actors cannot easily dismantle the intellectual apparatus they use for looking at things in order to look at the intellectual apparatus itself.

The postmodern condition

Combining his ideas about types of knowledge (scientific and narrative), his ideas about the underlying or background meta-narratives that modern post-Enlightenment science and philosophy are based on (society-as-unity, society-as-divided), and about the way the narrative form structures modernist ideas about what 'knowledge' is, Lyotard thus arrives at his definition of what makes a society postmodern:

KEY QUOTE – Lyotard, *The Postmodern Condition* (1979), on the modern and the postmodern.
I will use the term *modern* to designate any science that legitimates itself with reference to a metadiscourse … making an explicit appeal to some grand narrative, such as the dialectics of Spirit, the hermeneutics of meaning, the emancipation of the rational working subject, or the creation of wealth … I define *postmodern* as incredulity towards metanarratives. This incredulity is undoubtedly a product of progress in the sciences: but that progress in turn presupposes it. To the obsolescence of the metanarrative apparatus of legitimation corresponds, most notably, the crisis of metaphysical philosophy … the narrative function is losing its functors, its great hero, its great dangers, its great voyages, its great goal. (Lyotard, 1984 [1979], p 11)

His turns of phrase in this important quotation are sometimes a little bit obscure, but in essence Lyotard is saying that the postmodern consciousness has arisen at a point where social actors are becoming more and more sceptical about the stories they have been told about how and why society is the way that it is. This scepticism goes to the very root of society because the legitimacy of the various institutions that have been telling these stories (for example the Church, legal system, government, the scientific establishment, political parties, trade unions and academia) is itself dependent on those stories being believed. Both the story and the storyteller have to be seen as reliable, and in postmodern society neither of them are (or at least the threshold of believability is considerably raised). Peeling away the various layers of storytellers and their protective institutions we eventually trace the grand narrative all the way back to one of the great bogeymen of post-structuralism: the biographical subject of metaphysical philosophy.

Philosophical underpinnings of the narrative

The 'metaphysical philosophy' Lyotard refers to in this definition contains most of the ideas itemised in the list of pro-Enlightenment sentiments in Figure 12.1. Lyotard is suggesting that the failure of modern conceptions of knowledge stems from the fixation many post-Enlightenment philosophers have with the idea that there must be some inner unifying essence that runs through everything and that only the subjective human consciousness has access to. Building on a clear trend in post-structuralist thinking, the object of Lyotard's attack is the Enlightenment–humanist perspective, which claims that human beings have a unique and privileged perspective compared with all the other stuff in the universe: 'The humanist principle that humanity rises up in dignity and freedom through knowledge' (Lyotard, 1984 [1979], p 34). Worse still, and this time pointing towards an irresolvable paradox, which is where all the trouble begins, this search for pure essences (the Hegelian perspective) and for underlying causes (the Comtean perspective), drives the quest for meaning and purpose into the arms of the kind of empirical and positivist perspective that does its very best to keep the subjective dimension *out of* the analysis. What Jameson calls 'the two great legitimizing "myths" or narrative archetypes' (Lyotard, 1984 [1979] p ix) of modern thought, are, despite the best efforts of modernist philosophers and modernist scientists, fundamentally irreconcilable.

Postmodern philosophy and postmodern science

Having tried to expose the failure of modernist science and modernist philosophy to reconcile the basic schism in concepts of knowledge produced by the Enlightenment perspective (society-as-divided, society-as-unity), Lyotard now needs to make some suggestions about what might usefully fill the gap. Even the most radical of postmodernist philosophers cannot suggest that there are or can be no categories into which the stuff we call knowledge can be put. To get himself out of this rather tight corner (and remembering that he is also set against any notion of knowledge that relies on modernist narrative-type categories) Lyotard suggests that the new kinds of knowledge we can look forward to in postmodern society will be very different from those that went before. Most simply, postmodern science is not about empirical verification and the accumulation of facts, but about trying to look with fresh eyes and minds at the human capacity to go on creating new ideas. Postmodern science will concern itself with looking into the gaps between knowledge in order to reveal the spaces, the forbidden zones, the stories-not-yet-told about the essence of human creativity. The philosophical rationale of postmodern science is to try and rescue a really authentic and genuinely human humanism from the clutches of modernist philosophers and scientists who became so obsessed with technique that they forgot all about the more profound human purposes that they were supposed to serve. Lyotard describes postmodern science as follows:

KEY QUOTE – Lyotard, *The Postmodern Condition* (1979), on postmodern science.

Postmodern science – by concerning itself with such things as undecidables, the limits of precise control, conflicts characterized by incomplete information, 'fracta', catastrophes, and pragmatic paradoxes – is theorizing its own evolution as discontinuous, catastrophic, nonrectifiable, and paradoxical. It is changing the meaning of the word *knowledge*, while expressing how such a change can take place. It is producing not the known, but the unknown. And it suggests a model of legitimation that has nothing to do with maximized performance, but has as its basis difference understood as paralogy. (Lyotard, 1984 [1979], p 60)

Criticisms of Lyotard's narrative of modernism

Lyotard's account has been very influential and has provided several key definitions that now form part of the postmodernist vocabulary. Having looked at some of these we can certainly agree that ideas about narratives and meta-narratives, about how the narrative form enables, but at the same time imposes restrictions on, conceptions of knowledge, can be very helpful in developing a critique of modernist discourses and the Enlightenment perspective from which they derive. There are also some strong connections with other post-structuralist concepts such as **discourse** and discursive practice (Foucault), myths and language games (Barthes and Wittgenstein), the idea of decentring the biographical subject, and of différance and deconstruction (Derrida). In a sense, and perhaps to a greater extent than other explicitly postmodernist theorists like Jean Baudrillard, Lyotard has provided a means of linking the key concepts of postmodernist social theory into a kind of new paradigm. Inevitably there are a number of reasons why his account has so far failed to demolish the modernist paradigm he seeks to replace.

First, and although Lyotard tries to counter this point by saying that the modernist conception of knowledge is seriously hampered by the modernist narrative *technique*, he does not really offer a convincing alternative. Given that it is so very difficult to describe things without using the narrative form, maybe we should simply accept that narrative is actually the form of knowledge-description and knowledge-formation that *homo sapiens* intuitively uses. Indeed, it is difficult to see why postmodernist social theorists should object to the concept of narrative-knowledge because narrative is simply a useful refinement to the idea of language and it is they who have accepted most fervently that knowledge is determined by language. Discourse and narrative are two modes of linguistic structuring. To the extent that the real target of Lyotard's attack is the humanist/metaphysical *content* of the modernist narrative (what is told, rather than how it is being told), worrying about narrative technique might turn out to be something of a red herring.

Second, and looking this time at the content of the narrative, Lyotard suggests that although postmodernism is very much about developing critiques of the twin narratives that emerged from the Enlightenment perspective, he seems to suggest that a bright new postmodernist narrative-of-knowledge might in fact depend on a *revival* and *renewal* of the **humanist** principles that are characteristic of modernism. While it can be useful to think of modernist social theory as having a generally linear or sequential orientation compared with the more circular and disorderly orientation of postmodernist social theory, there does seem to be a lot more 'going back' than 'moving forward' in Lyotard's suppositions about what the philosophical underpinnings of postmodernism are.

Third, and again despite intending to put some clear water between modernism and the postmodernist critique of modernism, there are some striking similarities between Lyotard's analysis and that of some leading modernist theorists who are his rivals. The distinction he draws, for example, between two traditions of positive and critical knowledge is very reminiscent of the Weberian distinction between formal rationality and substantive rationality. Like Weber, Lyotard has suggested that the non- or anti-rational features of modernity often come down to the fact that the technical means of doing something obscure the reasons for wanting to do it in the first place. There are equally strong similarities with Habermas's diagnosis that what marks the modernist period or phase most clearly, and which is also the source of its major problems, is the tendency for the instrumental-rational mentality of social institutions and systems to displace the communicative-rational mentality of the **lifeworld**. The process of 'the colonisation of the lifeworld' identified by Habermas can easily be seen as a critical worked example of how and why the modernist discourse/paradigm/narrative is losing its legitimacy. There is novelty in the way Lyotard interrogates the modernist narrative but the contents of what he says remain pretty familiar. If he wants to offer a different kind of story, then one might expect him to introduce some genuinely new characters and a few original twists to the plot.

Fourth, and repeating the major weakness in Foucault's account of how new discourses emerge, Lyotard pays very little attention to the lesser or non-dominant narratives that exist alongside the dominant ones. In this respect, his description of narrative and of the techniques of narrative storytelling suggest a somewhat closed system. Either a narrative is dominant, in which case it matters a great deal, or it is subordinate and can be discounted entirely from the analysis. Although Lyotard is critical of Habermas's idea of communicative rationality and is sceptical about the possibility of the ideal speech situation (unlike Habermas Lyotard thinks the language game is inherently confrontational rather than consensual), his own account seems to disallow any possibility of new narrative fragments or of new techniques for storytelling entering the fray. He explores what we could call the negative side of narrative technique, which is that previously vibrant and challenging ideas become ossified and turn into **ideologies**, but he says little about the positive side, which is where new ideas emerge.

One could go so far as to suggest that Lyotard's unwillingness to offer any real detail about the new characters and plots we might expect to find in the exciting new non-narrative of knowledge produced by postmodernist science and philosophy reflects the fact that he has yet to work out a convincing account of where such new ideas come from. Like Foucault, his theory is strong in describing what happens when ideas become established and then stagnate, but is weak in accounting for the mechanisms by which such elements emerge in the first place and how they establish new narratives/discourses of their own.

Stories that have been told: modernists and the unfinished project of modernity

As should be clear from what we have said so far in this chapter, the kinds of stories that modernist and postmodernist social theorists can tell about how experience and context, action and structure, fit together are heavily determined by the concepts of history they are using. The issue here is one of causality in the sense of how events or experiences that happened in the past can affect what is happening in the present. As Giddens puts it: 'We have to grasp how history is made through the active involvements and struggles of human beings, and yet at the same time both forms those human beings and produces outcomes which they neither intend nor foresee' (Giddens, 1990, p 40).

Modernist theorists like Habermas, Giddens and Bourdieu are strongly inclined to argue that modern society is still being driven along by broadly the same forces that gave rise to modern society in the first place. If this is true, then it makes good sense to stick with the conceptual tools and strategies of analysis that were developed years ago specifically to look at the problems of modernity. This is not to say, however, that these three contemporary modernists have simply taken up the old tools and used them in the same old ways. Their various contributions to social theory are very much to do with how they have modified these tools and applied them differently. It is this ability to make necessary changes, and to have done so successfully, that should make us cautious about accepting postmodernist claims that everything in the modernist toolkit needs to be scrapped without further ado. As an example of 'project-of-modernity' storytelling, we can do worse than look again at the work of Anthony Giddens.

The consequences of modernity

Generally speaking, and as we have already noted a number of times in this chapter, modernist social theorists have persisted with the idea that modernity is not a spent force but is still, as Habermas puts it, an 'incomplete project'. In an extended essay based on a series of lectures given at Stanford University in 1988, and published as *The Consequences of Modernity* in 1990, Giddens begins by accepting the modernist view that societies are what they are because of the kinds of institutions they are made of. He acknowledges that the three most familiar stories told by modernist social theorists about how we came to have the kinds of social institutions we do in modern society are Marx's story of the capitalist enterprise, Weber's story of the rational control of information through bureaucracy, and Durkheim's story of the division of labour in industry (which need not necessarily be capitalist in nature). He immediately suggests, however, that although each makes a vital contribution, in his view we need a story that explains modern institutions as a product of all three of these storylines: 'Modernity, I propose, *is multidimensional on the level of institutions*, and each of the elements specified by these various traditions plays some part' (Giddens, 1990, p 12, original emphasis).

Developing a little beyond the storylines initiated by Marx, Weber and Durkheim, Giddens suggest that the modern period is constituted by four 'institutional dimensions' of modernity. The first two of these are capitalism and industrialism and are familiar enough (see Chapters Three, Four and Five). The third dimension, which builds upon the notion of the rational and bureaucratic organisation of information first told by Max Weber, is 'the development of surveillance capacities well beyond those characteristic of traditional civilisations'. Surveillance refers to 'the supervision of the activities of subject populations in the political sphere' and is often 'based upon the control of information' (Giddens, 1990, pp 57–8).

The fourth institutional dimension of modernity is 'control of the means of violence'. The difference between traditional and modern society here is that modern nation-states no longer have to rely on alliances in order to exercise military power but now have a complete monopoly over military power. Conducting warfare is no longer conditional upon the active willingness and participation of significant parts of the population. Defining society in terms of the institutions it is made of, modern society is thus constituted by and through the various linkages between, for example, the surveillance capacity of the state and its control over military power, the development of industrial technologies (which might of course be used by the military) under conditions of capitalism, business organisations and so on.

Having rearranged the leading tales about the capitalist enterprise, the industrial division of labour and rational administration into a single, but obviously more complex, narrative, Giddens goes on to suggest that social theorists also have to think again about the kinds of forces that these four institutions or 'institutional clusterings' exercise over or within society. In addition to the forces of capitalism, industrialism and instrumental rationalisation (**instrumental rationality**), he identifies three more driving forces: 'the separation of time and space' (time–space distanciation); the 'disembedding of social systems'; and 'the reflexive ordering and reordering of social relations in the light of continual inputs of knowledge affecting the actions of individuals and groups' (Giddens, 1990, pp 16–17). We will look at each in turn.

Time and space/place

The first of these driving forces, 'time–space distanciation', sounds complicated but actually refers to the ways in which notions of time and space (which for our purposes is more easily understood simply as 'place') are radically different in modern society compared with how they were in pre-modern society. Whereas experience was once tightly confined by the local contexts where social action takes place and was regulated by naturalistic notions of time determined by the seasons of the year and farming practice, in the modern world, time and place are recast in much more complex and abstract ways. Technologies like air travel, global media and the world wide web mean that the range of experience is much more varied than it used to be; time and place are no longer barriers standing in the way of experience.

Disembedding mechanisms

The second additional driving force that Giddens calls disembedding mechanisms refers to the new kinds of facilities the modern world offers that enable social actors to see time and place differently. Disembedding mechanisms are what make changes in time and place possible; 'they remove social relations from the immediacies of context' (Giddens, 1990, p 28) and thus enable social actions to be 'lifted out' of time and place. The leading contenders here, according to Giddens, are money and the various systems of 'expert knowledge' social actors rely upon to take advantage of the shifting of time and place.

Money

Giddens characterises money as disembedding because, following earlier analyses by Weber (1983) and Georg Simmel (1978 [1900]), it provides a means for conducting vital economic activities (especially the trading of materials, goods and services) without the various participants having to be in the same place and at the same time. Money, which is essentially a highly abstract medium for exchanging things, thus sets the whole process of economic exchange free from the confines of time and place. International finance, for example, no longer relies on the transportation of treasure and bullion across the oceans, and subject to the perpetual threat of piracy or natural disaster, but can now be achieved by the instantaneous transfer of funds electronically (threats from hackers and collapses in the currency markets notwithstanding).

Expert systems

Expert systems are also disembedding in the sense that whereas in pre-modern society social actors could pretty much see how things worked for themselves, they could understand the processes of farming, the social hierarchy, the Church, the legal system and so on, in modern society they increasingly have to rely on expert systems that they actually know very little about. The spread of industrial techniques for production, of capitalist business organisation, of legalistic and bureaucratic forms of administration and organisation, for example, all extend far beyond the comprehension and control of any individual social actor. Expert systems become much more complex in form, are often embedded in technological developments and increasingly involve abstract processes and relationships.

There are some fairly clear continuities here between Giddens' account and ideas we have encountered when looking at the accounts of the classical modernist social theorists. Weber's account of the dangers of bureaucracy, for example, or Durkheim's worries about what happens if technical developments in the division of labour remain incomplete or are misunderstood, can both be seen as failures in expert systems. The common feature in both cases is that experts and the expert systems they develop and operate are preoccupied with formal rationality and technique, rather than with qualitative or substantive judgements about the uses and implications of those systems. What the experts actually believe in, and this is also very much the basis of perceptions of their legitimacy among non-experts, is the fairly orthodox scientific technique that they apply in developing their expertise. The limited applicability of instrumental rationality to the more substantive and qualitative activities of the lifeworld, or in the worst case of instrumental-rational action taking over from communicative-rational action, is very much at the centre of Habermas's concerns about the 'incomplete project' of modernity. Completion, for Habermas, is very much about keeping expert systems in check.

Reflexivity

The third additional force identified by Giddens is **reflexivity** (see section three of Chapter Twelve) and this has two sides to it. At the level of specialist scientific or philosophical knowledge, Giddens is making a pitch for the importance of social theory and of the social-scientific research associated with it. He argues that the development of modernity is often conditional upon the development and incorporation of knowledge about the social world. The expertise we have developed for exploring the social world becomes *part of* the experience of living in that world; social-theoretical knowledge is *integral to* modernity. At a more personal or common-sense level, reflexivity refers to the ways in which social actors are increasingly able to monitor their own behaviour, and to change what they do, in light of their own experiences. Modern social actors are not creatures of routine who passively follow paths set out for them in advance by 'family', 'work', 'culture' and 'society', but are imaginative and creative beings always looking for novelty and challenge. The notion of reflexivity, especially as this relates to the formation of a unique sense-of-self, was an idea that first became established through the work of social interactionist social theorists such as George Herbert Mead (see Chapter Seven).

Globalisation

We have already used the example of how modern relations between time and place have radically reshaped the world so that there is global agreement about times, dates and geographical location. Towards the end of his story Giddens draws his tales of institutional clusterings and forces of modernity together, and suggests that social theorists should pay less attention to the notion of 'society' as their basic unit of analysis, and concentrate instead on the impact of shifts in perceptions and experiences of time and place at the global level: 'the undue reliance which sociologists have placed on the idea of "society", where this means a bounded system, should be replaced by a starting point that concentrates upon analysing how social life is organized across time and space' (Giddens, 1990, pp 63–4). For him, it is the way in which changes in configurations of time and place are changing experiences of near and far, of local and global and across the entire globe of human affairs that marks the really radical edge of the process of modernisation. The institutions or institutional clusterings of modern society, and the forces that drive modernity forward, can certainly still be analysed at the level of particular societies, but there is now an even more pressing perspective, which is how these institutions and forces are working themselves out at a global level:

KEY QUOTE – Giddens, *The Consequences of Modernity* (1990), on globalisation.
In the modern era, the level of time–space distanciation is much higher than in any previous period, and the relations between local and distant social forms and events become correspondingly 'stretched'. Globalisation refers essentially to that stretching process, in so far as the modes of connection between different social contexts or regions become networked across

the earth's surface as a whole. Globalisation can thus be defined as the intensification of worldwide social relations which link distant localities in such a way that local happenings are shaped by events many miles away and vice versa. (Giddens, 1990, p 64)

What Giddens is saying here is that one of the things that makes the modern period modern is that when social actors refer to 'the world' they are actually referring not just to a physical planet that orbits the sun, but to an economic/political/military entity, which is identifiable because it is bound together by agreed notions of time, place and geography. These temporal, spatial and geographical bindings are constitutive of what the world is as a social and cultural entity. Notwithstanding the physical stuff it is made of, the world is a social construction and the task of social theory is to understand how this construction has taken place.

For Giddens, then, the main focus of storytelling in the modern period ought to include the following essential elements:

- Seeing society in terms of the institutions it is made of.
- Seeing these institutions as being driven along by the forces of capitalism, industrialism, military power and surveillance.
- Understanding how systems of exchange using essentially abstract media like money and expert systems (disembedding mechanisms) are reshaping experiences of time and place.
- Understanding how knowledge has become reflexively organised and thus at best temporary and at worst utterly unreliable.
- Understanding how disembedding and reflexivity are forces that transcend the boundaries of 'society' and thus operate at the global level.

Evaluating project-of-modernity approaches to storytelling

The unstable nature of modernity

As should be clear, even from this brief résumé of Giddens' project-of-modernity-type story, it is not really the case, as is generally implied by postmodernists, that such accounts are simply an updating of stories told by the founding fathers. Especially useful is the fact that in identifying reflexively-organised behaviour and reflexively-oriented definitions of knowledge as core characteristics of modernity, Giddens' tale already contains a strong explanation of the feelings of uncertainty and change that postmodernists have also singled out as basic characteristics of the late-modern period. The idea of reflexivity, which Giddens relies on very heavily in the story he tells, is all about uncertainty and loss of confidence in what social actors thought they knew for sure. He writes:

> Modernity is constituted in and through reflexively applied knowledge, but the equation of knowledge with certitude has turned out to be misplaced. We are abroad in a world which is thoroughly constituted in and through reflexively applied knowledge, but where at the same time we can never be sure that any given elements of that knowledge will not be revised. (Giddens, 1990, p 39)

The new state of uncertainty obviously creates a potentially very unsettling and destabilising situation because the grounds for all kinds of decision making are thrown into doubt. Since, as Giddens also emphasises, the notion of reflexively-applied knowledge is itself also something that we reflect upon, even the sense of trust social actors might have had in their ability to define what knowledge is, is also undermined. The rate at which social actors re-evaluate what knowledge is, how to behave and so on is dramatically speeded up.

Moving beyond the idea of 'society'

Giddens' tale of globalisation is a second illustration of how contemporary modernist-type accounts of historical change are already well-placed in identifying some of the most radical transformative energies of the forces of modernity. To the extent that Lyotard and other postmodernists imply that modernist accounts have run out of steam when it comes to grasping the really big changes of the late- or postmodern experience, concepts like reflexivity and globalisation show that this is not really the case. Giddens' suggestion that social theory ought to raise its game by looking beyond society itself (bounded social systems/the nation-state) and towards the 'vastly increased transformative scope of human intervention' (1990, p 34) at the global level, is at least as radical as anything suggested by Lyotard. Although postmodernists emphasise the cultural rather than economic or political dimensions of society, they generally stick with the fairly traditional social-theoretical idea that experience takes place within the confines of something called 'society'.

Terminology

For Giddens, the basic reason why it is much more sensible to refer to late- or high-modernity rather than to postmodernity is because of the fundamental link between modernity and the institutions it is made of. Recalling the various ways of defining modernity we looked at at the start of this chapter (as a periodising concept, as a way of categorising social theorists and as a way of classifying objects according to artistic style), Giddens adds another, which is that modernity is what it is because of the kinds of institutions we find there. For as long as these remain largely unaltered we must still be in modern or *late*-modern rather than *post*modern society. On this society-as-institutions definition a real shift towards postmodern society would require the emergence of significantly different kinds of institutions. Although modern institutions have certainly changed during the modern period there is only weak evidence that they have been utterly transformed or that completely new institutions are emerging to take their place. Much more convincing is the contemporary modernist argument that the underlying forces of modernity are operating in changing ways: 'Rather than entering a period of postmodernity, we are moving into one in which the consequences of modernity are becoming more radicalized and universalized than before' (Giddens, 1990, p 3). It is by concentrating on these underlying forces and the impact they have on the institutional clustering that Giddens is able to deploy a 'discontinuist' method of storytelling. He thus preserves a notion that one set of events (for example the Industrial Revolution or the emergence of instrumental rationality) has dramatic implications for events that follow, but without seeing each such episode as linked in some kind of inevitable historical sequence.

Having used Giddens' account to illustrate the type of modernist story being told in social theory we can now look at an illustration from the postmodernist camp. The objective here is not to decide which might be true and which false, but to arrive at an informed appreciation of what contribution each style or type of storytelling can make to social theory, and thus to our understanding of the nature of contemporary social phenomena.

Jean Baudrillard telling stories the postmodernist way

Along with Jean-François Lyotard, Jean Baudrillard has provided some of the central concepts and terminology in the postmodernist's toolkit. Terms like **sign-value**, **simulacra** (simulacrum in the plural) and **hyper-reality** have enjoyed widespread circulation since Baudrillard started using them in his own social theory, which is widely read within postmodernist circles and beyond. In his early works (*The System of Objects*, 1996 [1968], *The Consumer Society*, 1998 [1970]) Baudrillard tells us a fairly orthodox, almost modernist, story about some important shifts in modern society and experience. Working initially from a Marxist point of view and against a background of what were then quite new ideas about the emergence of 'post-industrial society' or 'information society', Baudrillard's main argument is that a transformation is taking place away from a society dominated by work and production and towards one dominated by consumption. The main unit of society was no longer the worker, but the consumer. Although consumption is obviously an economic concept Baudrillard added some impetus to the trend of seeing consumption very much as a cultural phenomenon. As he puts it in *The System of Objects* (1996 [1968]): 'The system of consumption constitutes an authentic language, a new culture, when pure and simple consumption is transformed into a means of individual and collective expression.... From the outset we must clearly state that consumption is an active mode of relations (not only to objects, but to the collectivity and to the world), a systematic mode of activity and a global response on which our whole cultural system is founded' (Baudrillard, 1996 [1968], in Poster, 2001, p 15).

The shift towards consumption, and towards culture as the main site of consumption-type activity, he argues, is a necessary next stage in the development of capitalism because industry now has to put more and more effort into persuading its customers to spend their hard-earned cash on products that they choose to have rather than needing to have. Of particular importance has been the cultivation within capitalist culture of a link between consumption and identity. In the late- or postmodern phase of capitalism, consumption virtually becomes a prerequisite for having a sense of individual personality at all. The massive expansion of the advertising industry, of lifestyle magazines and other devices for stimulating consumer desire and consumer interest are taken as evidence of the cultural shift towards consumption.

Sign-values

The main analytical device Baudrillard uses here, and one that he discusses most directly in *For a Critique of the Political Economy of the Sign* (1981 [1972]), is the idea that along with the use values and exchange values of commodities identified by Marx (see Chapter Four), commodities and social actors also have **sign-values**. The currency of consumer capitalism or consumer society is no longer practical usefulness, or even the potential for profitable exchange, but symbolic value. To the extent that the meaning or significance that can be attached to actors, objects and actions is almost infinitely variable, capitalism has succeeded in opening up a whole new territory for consumer enjoyment: 'Today every desire, plan, need, every passion and relation is abstracted or materialized as sign and as object to be purchased and consumed', consumption 'is a systematic act of the manipulation of signs' (Baudrillard, 1996 [1968], in Poster, 2001, pp 26, 25).

The strong argument Baudrillard is making here is not just that signs 'stand for' things (the usual relation between signifiers and signifieds), but that *as a form of currency and exchange* sign–value dissolves away any significant distinctions *between* the real or original object and copies of it. Originality and authenticity are superseded by sign–value.

ILLUSTRATION – LEONARDO DA VINCI'S *MONA LISA* (1503)

To use an example from the world of fine art, in the economy of sign-values, reproductions of Leonardo da Vinci's masterpiece *Mona Lisa*, which visitors can buy from the gift shop at the Paris Louvre, have the same sign-value as the original. More than this, and again in the economy of sign-values, the actual fleshy human being who appears in the picture (thought to be Lisa Gherardini, wife of a wealthy silk merchant in Florence) is also reduced to the same sign-value as the original painting *and* all of its copies in the gift shop. The system of sign-values provides a universal melting pot into which all other distinctions of value are liquefied.

In his next book, *The Mirror of Production* (1975 [1973]), Baudrillard reaches the slightly unexpected conclusion that (although he uses it extensively in his own early work) Marxism no longer provides a useful platform from which to view and criticise the shift to consumption because the categories it uses are themselves products of the capitalist mode of production. As a theory about society and social development, Marxism cannot stand outside the object it is analysing (i.e. **capitalist society**), it cannot achieve sufficient critical distance because the conceptual categories it uses are *already* capitalist categories. As Baudrillard puts it:

> [It] is not enough to unmask what is hidden behind the concept of consumption: the anthropology of needs and of use value. We must also unmask everything hidden behind the concepts of production, mode of production, productive forces, relations of production, etc. All the fundamental concepts of Marxist analysis must be questioned starting from its own requirement of a radical critique and transcendence of political economy. (Baudrillard, 1975 [1973], in Poster, 2001, p 101)

For Baudrillard, this loss of critical capacity is symptomatic of the general situation in capitalist society where social actors continue to see such a system as legitimate or even natural because all attempts to be critical of it have so far remained within capitalist units of thought or modes of thinking. Although it is necessary and useful to have identified the notion of sign-value, even this concept has limited critical impact if it is only deployable within a Marxist framework. There is a clear similarity here with Lyotard's ideas that in order to challenge the conventional accounts of how society came to be as it is, the critical theorist has to step outside, or move beyond, the mindset of those conventions. If the narrative form of knowledge is guilty of providing falsely legitimising myths about the way society is, then something other than the narrative form will be required to demonstrate this.

Simulacra

Influenced by Marshall McLuhan's widely-read book *Understanding Media* (1964) and its telling suggestion that 'the medium is the message', Baudrillard was led towards developing an explicitly abstract-theoretical analysis of the form and content of the sign-system of consumer capitalism. Having dropped Marxism he went back to his own academic-cultural roots in the French structuralist tradition and started to build an alternative analytical framework for his work using concepts from de Saussure's structural linguistics (see Chapter Nine). His main conclusion in his book *Simulacra and Simulations*, published in French in 1981, is that the sign-system of consumer capitalism mediates between social actors and the actually existing reality that surrounds them to such an extent that the sign-system becomes *a substitute* for real experience. The sign-system can no longer be thought of as simply providing a convenient means of representing reality 'out there', a means of denoting objects and actions thus making them available for discussion and analysis by the human observer, but as constituting a distinct reality *in its own right*. Baudrillard adopted the ecclesiastical term 'simulacra' as a way of referring to signs, and the meanings and significances that they support, which, although in one sense are false, are becoming more real than the objects and actions to which they refer. It is a question not just of what constitutes the difference between the real thing and its graven image, but whether such differences actually matter.

The impact of these ideas on social theory was to show that the arbitrariness of the sign was not, as it had been for Saussure, a feature of the relations between one sign and another (nor, as for Barthes, of relations between one set of myths and another), but of the increasing arbitrariness of the sign-system *in relation to* the realty that everyone assumed was out there and that the sign-system helped actors to comprehend. In the new consumer society where the sign-system is being rapidly colonised by the electronic media of communication, and where social actors acquire their understanding through the mass media, it is, so Baudrillard argues, becoming impossible to tell the difference between (what used to be called) the 'real thing' and the synthesised alternative created within the sign-system. For Baudrillard, simulated reality created within the sign-system has become a legitimate substitute for real reality. Any residual distinction between the real and the simulation has become radically uncertain. The 'age of simulacra and simulation' is one in which 'there is no longer any God to recognize his own, nor any last judgement to separate truth from false, the real from its artificial resurrection, since everything is already dead and risen in advance' (Baudrillard, 1983 [1981], in Poster, 2001, pp 174–5).

ILLUSTRATION – BIG SHINY RED SPORTS CARS

One way of thinking about Baudrillard's ideas is to reflect on how advertisers try to present a particular image of the commodity they are promoting. While social actors are sufficiently media-wise that they can see through such attempts at manipulating how objects appear and what they connote, Baudrillard pushes this argument quite a lot further and claims that a point is being reached where the only real existence that objects *can have* is that which is already embedded within simulacrum form. For example, advertisers have created a reality that big shiny red sports cars connote power, authority, sexual prowess and success. Although it is still possible to have a sense of the residual components of metal, rubber and plastic, which big shiny red sports cars are made of, it is impossible to think of a 'sports car' in terms other than those that this object connotes. Big shiny red sports cars simply cannot connote other symbolic values such as environmental responsibility, impotence and modesty. The connotations applicable to any big shiny red sports car of the future are already embedded within the sign-system.

Hyper-reality

Any social theory that takes signs and sign-systems to be the basic unit of its analysis has to answer the question of what the signs are *of*? The classical structuralist answer is that signs stand for real objects (referents) that are 'out there'. There are thus two kinds or levels of reality: the real one of actual objects and the supplementary one made of signs that actors need in order to be able to make sense of it. In his discussion of the mediated sign-system of consumer society, however, Baudrillard challenges this view and suggests instead that signs can be seen as referring not passively and obediently to the separate, and by implication, superior or more valid reality of actual stuff, but as referring to a separate universe of *other signs*. Just as individual signs are replacing the objects and actions that we all thought they stood for, the sign–system as a whole has replaced the world of objects as a whole. Baudrillard calls this new reality, or sign–system reality, **hyper–reality**.

KEY QUOTE – Baudrillard, *Simulacra and Simulations* (1981), on hyper-reality.

Abstraction today is no longer that of the map, the double, the mirror or the concept. Simulation is no longer that of a territory, a referential being or a substance. It is the generation by models of a real without origin or reality: a hyperreal. The territory no longer precedes the map, nor survives it. Henceforth, it is the map that precedes the territory – *precession of simulacra* – it is the map that engenders the territory. (Baudrillard, 1983 [1981], in Poster, 2001, p 1, original emphasis)

To repeat this important point, Baudrillard is not simply reiterating the widely accepted position that there are two realities, one of real objects and another made of the various sign-systems social actors have invented for looking at it, but that in the media-saturated experience of consumer culture, the sign-system dissolves away any significant difference between (what used to be thought of as) two separate realities. Moreover, to the extent that it is possible to imagine a realm of raw material that exists outside any current version of 'the real' (for example a piece of territory for which no map exists), Baudrillard is arguing that any such material will only ever become real within the terms of the sign-systems that are currently being used. Its existence can only be confirmed using the terms, ideas and concepts of the already-existing sign-system. If no territory can really exist without there being a map of it, the virtual or hyper-real world of maps is more real than any chunk of land with rivers and mountains. Moreover, hyper-reality has generative properties of its own in the sense that new combinations of significances emerge from within the sign-system rather than new signs simply being generated in order to identify new kinds of actually existing phenomena. Hyper-reality is the condition in which the relatively stable and conventional relation between sign and referent (signifier and signified) is superseded by sign-systems acting autonomously.

Evaluating Baudrillard's story of simulation and hyper-reality

The challenge Baudrillard sets for himself is to persuade modernist social theorists that his notion of reality as hyper-reality is a fair substitute for the **rationalist/positivist** notion of reality as made up of real objects 'out there'. Even accepting the power of the sign and the sign-system as mediating between social actors and this actually existing and separate reality, can we reasonably conceive of a universe of social experiences in which all the real material stuff that surrounds social actors, even their experiences and emotional responses, are subordinated to an overarching hyper-reality created by and within the sign-system?

The core issue here is what level of credibility and reliability we are prepared to give to the mental representations that social actors make of what they assume to be exterior reality. In his Foreword to Lyotard's *The Postmodern Condition*, for example, Fredric Jameson refers to the 'crisis of representation' to emphasise that a key theme in the postmodernist perspective is a rejection of the assumption that rationalist/positivist knowledge presents the only true reflection of the world 'out there'. Against this view, anti-representationists, like Lyotard, argue that since reality can be represented in many different ways, there cannot be just one version of reality or of knowledge (defined as claims about reality). As we saw in the third section of this chapter, Lyotard believes that the ultimate 'representational accomplishment' of the modern period has been to convince so many actors for so long that the kinds of representations devised during the period of the Enlightenment are the best available. Both at the level of its representation of what knowledge is (i.e. the positivist, fact-gathering definition) and at the level of its contents (i.e. how it represents particular things like power and authority through grand narratives), this representation is losing its grip over the public imagination. It no longer enjoys the same levels of support and legitimacy as it once did.

Baudrillard's stab at answering the same question is that all such representations, narrative or otherwise, have been rendered utterly unreliable not just because the stories have worn a bit thin, but because hyper-reality has become even more real than real reality. Lyotard undermines the credibility of representations that rely for their credibility on underlying narratives, while Baudrillard undermines the credibility of representation altogether, by arguing that the only means of representation available to social actors, which is to say the various sign-systems they use for transposing reality into their heads, have become more real than the things that they (allegedly) stand for. In abstract terminology we could say that Baudrillard is adding the 'crisis of the referent' to match the 'crisis of representation' identified by Lyotard. There are a number of issues we need to reflect on here.

First, if real reality has been replaced by a wholly self-referential hyper-reality that has no need of any independent substance or entity outside of itself (there are no reliable means left for distinguishing the real from the virtual), then what are the anchoring points that Baudrillard himself is using to make his own arguments seem coherent and believable? How is it possible to make a coherent critique based on logical argument and illustration when it is these very same procedures of knowledge-building that are being questioned? Although it is an interesting and stimulating question as to how reliable our assumptions about certainty are, how confident we are that knowledge is even possible, it is *impossible* to break free from the paradox that raising such questions does rather reinforce the idea that, however difficult it is to explain what they are, some sources of certainty do seem to persist. Just like the fighter pilot who can continue to distinguish between simulation and real combat despite what all her physical and emotional senses might be telling her, so the philosopher, despite the logic of the claim, continues to distinguish between the argument that 'thought', 'knowledge' and 'reality' are impossible, and the real reality that makes it possible for her to have such thoughts in the first place. What the theorist is thinking might be fictional and illusory, but *the act of thinking*, the capacity to join things up in her head and to identify some sense of difference between these sensations and the view out of the window, is not.

Hyper-reality as universal reality

Second, Baudrillard tends to assume that hyper-reality completely envelopes *all* the experiences social actors have. While is it widely acknowledged in social theory that the proportion of such experiences that are mediated rather than direct has increased dramatically in the modern period, mediated experience is certainly not the only kind of experience social actors have. People do still actually touch and feel things at first hand where the only mediation involved is that between physical senses and the conscious mind. Although it can be argued that even basic physical sensations like hunger and pain are mediated by the cultural values in society (actors learn how to be in pain or how to feel hungry), a sense remains that there are experiences which are genuinely unmediated and others that either escape, or at least run alongside, the mediated experiences of hyper-reality described by Baudrillard. The question, then, is whether it is sensible to disregard such experiences entirely, whether to categorise them as 'inauthentic experiences', or whether they can be treated as sufficiently subordinate to the mediated variety as to be ineffective. Given the strong emphasis on actual and immediate felt experience in the postmodernist conception of action none of these solutions seems entirely satisfactory as they suggest the theorist is cherry-picking, or attributing different types and degrees of significance to, different kinds of experiences. Accepting, even if only minimally, that there is variation in the degree to which experience is mediated creates a space for looking back at the particular category of experiences called 'mediated experience' and thus establishes a vantage point from which to distinguish between the authentic and the simulation. It is still possible, in other words, to tell the difference between them.

The idea of simulation, for example, is potentially a powerful and useful concept for exploring how media-generated and media-circulated representations of actors, objects and actions are indeed becoming almost indistinguishable from 'the real thing'. It is also plausible to suggest that sometimes the simulations of the sign-system of consumer capitalism virtually provide a substitute for the real experience; they are acquiring a new kind of authenticity of their own. What we have to remember, however, is that even if the emotional response of the subject to the stimulus provokes thoughts and feelings that are *just as real* as those that might have arisen if the person really was having the experience at first hand, there is still a significant degree of difference between 'the real' and 'the simulated'. This difference persists despite the efforts of the postmodernist social theorist to close it down. Even if the fighter pilot becomes desensitised through simulation exercises to the actual death and destruction that his or her weapons will cause there is still a real difference between the simulation and actual combat.

Theory-building

This tendency of getting himself into difficulties by pushing things a little too far can be seen as symptomatic of Baudrillard's career as a theory-builder. In describing the development of contemporary modernist social theory we can note a contrast between Giddens' mode of theory-building, which is based around an exposition and then a synthesis of earlier currents of thought in social theory, and Bourdieu's more empirically-grounded approach (see Chapter Twelve). Bourdieu is in fact quite rude about Giddens' approach dismissing it as 'scholastic' because it lacks grounded or factual data. A similar kind of criticism can be made of Baudrillard in the sense that there is a notable shift away from the descriptive account of the development of consumer society and the increasing influence of the mass media in his early work, and towards a much more analytical and abstract approach in his later writings. As Baudrillard became increasingly concerned with developing an analysis of contemporary society that is as far removed as possible from the modernist narrative, he became increasingly cavalier about the illustrations he uses. His often bizarre descriptions of living in a postmodern consumer culture seem detached from reality because that is precisely what they are: detached. His descriptive and analytical work, in other words, certainly becomes a servant to the theoretical constructions that he is so keen to justify. Perhaps becoming rather self-conscious of this reversal in his own work he actually invents a new notion of 'fatal theory' to accommodate it. Fatal theory transcends critical theory (or any other kind of social theory for that matter) because just like the immanent loss of real reality caused by hyper-reality, fatal theory signifies the immanent loss of all traditional criteria of theory-building. The ultimate theoretical abstraction, one might say, the most determined leap from reality, is not only to go in search of random facts and examples to substantiate the theory, but to develop a new idea of what 'theory' is, in order to provide a kind of retrospective justification for such a procedure.

Culture and power

An associated difficulty with Baudrillard's approach is that he works with a largely cultural rather than economic or political conception of **power**. To the extent that postmodernists treat society and culture as if they are a kind of text (or in Baudrillard's case a hyper-text), this cultural concept of power is based largely on the idea that linguistic and discursive structures exercise power over social actors by controlling the way that they receive and interpret the world around them. This raises other important questions, however, because we might be interested to know *in whose interests* these interpretations are being controlled. Media organisations benefit commercially from attracting audiences in particular ways, and businesses certainly put a lot of resources into creating images and lifestyle templates that produce the kinds of customers they need for selling their commodities to. There is a strong sense, however, that postmodernists like Baudrillard see their claims about discourses, texts and hyper-reality as operating at a much more general level of signification than simply the idea that 'the media creates willing consumers' or that 'mediated discourses are ideological'. Unlike modernist social theorists, whose theoretical methods are very much designed to investigate the way that institutions and practices act as conduits for control over resources, Baudrillard's approach tends to blur the boundaries between the various institutional realms where different kinds of power are thought to operate. Texts are not bounded in the same way as economic and political structures are. One way of accommodating this situation is to accept that approaches in social theory that see society as a text are also making an assumption that the realms of *meaning* and *culture* really have become more important than the realms of politics and economics; that 'the cultural turn' is a genuinely social phenomenon, rather than just a change in the interests of academics. Seen in this light, the kind of postmodernism that

Baudrillard has imagined in his social theory is a largely philosophical, even literary–creative, process. It is not a theory of the social at all.

The impact of the modernity versus postmodernity debate on social theory

So where does Baudrillard's postmodernist account of experiential and chaotic hyper-reality leave our comparison of modernist and postmodernist approaches in social theory? In one sense we are not bound to look for common ground or synthesis between the two camps (although some social theorist somewhere is bound to make the attempt), but simply to accept that postmodernism constitutes an important new trajectory in social theory, which may or may not become the new orthodoxy, and leave it at that. In another sense, however, it is important to draw some conclusions about the impact of the postmodern turn on social theory itself. Postmodernists dislike being classified as such, and having their intellectual origins scrutinised, because the rather obvious point that their own thoughts have evolved from the theories and theorists that went before them, rather spoils one of their key claims, which is that notions of evolution and continuity, of living in a universe created out of the past actions and thoughts of others, should be set aside. One could suggest, for example, that Baudrillard abandons the analytical tools of Marxism, because he does not want his ideas to be seen in terms of any particular intellectual or academic heritage. There can be no doubt, however, that even despite the often idiosyncratic way that he presents it, Baudrillard's postmodernism remains connected in important ways to the social theory that went before it, just as it is already wired into the social theory that comes after it. Baudrillard's talk of signs and simulation, of simulacra and hyper-reality, certainly appears to offer a very different perspective on how we should be thinking about the nature of experience in late-modern society. Whether or not Baudrillard approves, his ideas are already part of the 'grand narrative' of 20th-century social theory.

On common ground

Mediated experience

Despite differences in approach between modernists and postmodernists, there are some clear overlaps in the features of modernity they identify as especially important. The emphasis on mediated experience, for example, is common to both and thus consolidates the idea in social theory that significant shifts in how social actors are getting information, and increases in information-intensive experiences made possible by electronic media, are having important impacts on how they interact with each other and with the social practices that surround them. In combination with the concept of reflexivity, Giddens uses the notion of mediated experience to develop his ideas about how individual lives are increasingly affected by global events. Whether we choose to define globalisation primarily as an economic, a political or a cultural phenomenon, its principal mechanism, the way it actually becomes a practical possibility, is through the global media of communication.

Working to a different scale of analysis, Baudrillard uses the idea of mediated experience to explore how reliable or otherwise the sign-systems and other devices are through which social actors interpret the world around them. Although neither theorist pauses to develop a specific theory of media technologies (this is the task of media theory and media studies), both use the concept of mediated experience to identify the impact of new technology as something that is unique to the late- or postmodern world. Neither hyper-reality as described by Baudrillard, nor globalisation as described by Giddens, could have emerged ahead of the development of appropriate technical means of communication.

Reflexivity

A second feature that modernist and postmodernist theorists tend to accept as unique to the late- or postmodern social experience is the way in which social actors seem to have become increasingly reflexive in how they respond to the actors, objects and actions that surround them. Although it has been widely accepted in sociological circles for some time that actors increasingly occupy social roles and positions on the basis of choices they have made rather than on the basis of circumstances they were born into, the notion of reflexivity in social theory goes further than this. Postmodernists like Baudrillard use it to explore how actors draw on a bewildering array of consumer and media resources to experiment with different kinds of selves, the different versions of identity, they can assume. Having recognised that signs and sign-systems are not fixed but essentially arbitrary, it is a relatively small step to suggest that the fixed, concrete and reliable idea of 'self' or 'personal identity' associated with the modern period is being displaced by one that is far less predictable. In the same way postmodernists argue that signs have been set free from their referents, reflexivity makes possible the liberation of the self from apparently class-, status- and gender-based assumptions.

In contemporary modernist hands, and again working to a different scale, it is widely recognised that the kinds of social structuring that have to be taken into account in deciding how to act, are not just at the level of grand social institutions and sweeping cultural prerequisites, but also at a much more intimate level of day-to-day living. Reflexivity, in other words, is not just a feature of personality formation and self-development (of looking inwards), it is also increasingly part of the strategy social actors use when trying to deal with social institutions and practices (of looking outwards). Both postmodernists and contemporary modernists tend to agree that actors are less compliant in respect of social structures, and more ambitious in respect of their sense-of-self, than they were at the midpoint of the 20th century.

Telling the same story?

Given these similarities it would not be surprising to find similarities in the broad-brush impressions Giddens and Baudrillard offer us about social conditions in the late-modern period. Giddens' image of society as a juggernaut running out of control is pretty much the same as one offered by Baudrillard:

> The simulated disorder of things has moved faster than we have. The reality effect that succumbed to acceleration – anamorphosis of speed. Events, in their being, are never behind themselves, are always out ahead of their meaning. Hence the delay of interpretation, which is now merely the retrospective form of the unforeseeable event. (Baudrillard, 1995, in Poster, 2001, p 272)

Giddens seeks to explain these developments in terms of the disembedding effects caused primarily by time–space distanciation, whereas for Baudrillard the key explanatory device is the destabilising reality shift caused by hyper-reality. In both cases their intention is to convey a sense of insecurity and change, of chronic uncertainty and even paranoia about the future.

Feeling the force

What is especially interesting is that even though they arrive at a similar destination by different theoretical and conceptual routes, they both emphasise the emotional and experiential dimensions of late-modernity, rather than, for example, the economic or political dimensions as perhaps Marx or Weber would have done. This focus on the emotional consequences of late-modernity leads them both to compress historical time into the actual moment of action. Although

Giddens spends some time writing about the 'institutional dimensions' and the 'driving forces' of modernity (capitalism, industrialism, surveillance and military power), forces that obviously have quite a long history and that provide the material and structural context in which social action takes place, what preoccupies him the most is the instant when all the hypotheticals of structure and action actually come together. Baudrillard's theory contains less historical baggage from the outset, but for him also it is how social actors react on the emotional level to the disruptions of hyper-reality that strikes him the most.

The contexts of social action

Finally, and looking again at the different perspectives modernists and postmodernists have developed about the balance between historical causes and immediate experience, we can note that although, on the face of it, postmodernists appear to be 'against' biography, history and structure, and 'for' culture, immediacy and openness, there is one crucial respect in which they do accept, and indeed attempt to make a virtue out of, the idea of structures that persist through time. Following Foucault's notion of discourse and Lyotard's critique of narrative storytelling, these structures are the frameworks of interpretation that social actors are obliged to use when having their experiences; frameworks that are obviously *structuring* in how they help people organise their experiences, and *structured* in the form that they take. Just as language is an integral part of the experience of speaking and listening, so the interpretive schemata actors use in having their experiences is also an integral part of that experience.

Moreover, these notions of myth, discourse, narrative and hyper-reality are based on the assumption that these structurings of experience are shared by members of the same culture. Culture is a factory for the manufacture of such frameworks and supplies a context where their associated discourses and narratives can be circulated. If 'the power of the discourse' or the 'reality-absorbing capacity of hyper-reality' are to be useful at all in describing social phenomena, then obviously they have to mean more or less the same thing, to carry the same meaning and significance, to everyone in the particular society where they are active. If the mode of communication is the same, and if the same message is received by all, then clearly there are structures in play. Human populations do not come to believe the same thing, to have the same view of reality, by accident. There is no such thing as a coincidental narrative. In both these respects, therefore, and however artfully the theorist tries to express it, 'structure' must have the property of persisting in time. We can argue about how far back it goes and where it gets its inspiration from, but in an important sense, and for both modernists *and* postmodernists, structures *are* the conduits of embedded experience or 'history'.

Permanent revolution

Just like previous revolutions in social theory, such as the 'linguistic turn' (see Chapter Nine) and the 'deconstructions' of post-structuralism (see Chapter Ten), the 'crisis of representation' identified by Lyotard and Baudrillard comes down to an argument about one conception of knowledge against an alternative conception. Postmodernist theorists like Baudrillard are in the luxurious position of being able to make highly challenging suggestions about the nature of reality and the current form of social experience because the legitimacy of modernist often Enlightenment-inspired notions of these things had already been softened up by the structural linguists and deconstructionists who went before them. It is still very much an open question whether postmodernist forms of theory making, and especially in the highly individualised form it takes in Baudrillard's work, are an inevitable consequence of those earlier ructions, or whether they will turn out to have been only individual trajectories. To suggest that there is a continuity or even a causal thread linking them together is of course to rely on the kind of narrative approach, and evolutionary conception of how social theory develops, that postmodernism wants to reject. The alternative is equally problematic because it seems silly to suggest that there are no such causal links. The work of Marx, Saussure, Foucault, Derrida and others is part of the lived intellectual experience of Baudrillard and so continuity seems inevitable. Baudrillard might have excommunicated himself from 'the Church of Marx', but Marx's concepts and methods are still very much part of his, and of our, social-theoretical background.

Definitions

As far as the problems of defining 'postmodernity' are concerned, it seems unlikely that any simple and agreeable definition will be reached. An underlying reason for this is that the various parties to the debate are working at different scales of analysis. Modernists work at the macro level of institutions and structures, of historical causes and consequences. The default setting of their analysis remains the integrity of society and 'the problem of social order'. Postmodernists, in contrast, tend to make sweeping comments about 'society' or, as they prefer to call it, 'culture', but actually their perspective on society/culture is more usually at the micro level and from the point of view of the individuals who live in it. This might be a reflection of the fact that modernists tend to be closer to sociology with its focus on structures and institutions, while postmodernists draw more from the anthropological tradition and its focus on how individual social actors interpret the world around them. Up to a point, the lack of clear definitions in the modernity versus postmodernity debate boils down to the difficulty social theorists often face not so much in seeing social phenomena from a different theoretical point of view, but of breaking the habit of seeing things at one scale rather than another. Is social theory really about society or is it about individuals? Is it about how actions are structured by context or is it about the actual experience of acting?

We have tried to organise the discussion in this chapter around a summary of the most obvious contrasts between the modernist and postmodernist positions that largely dominated social theory during the 1980s and early 1990s. It would be inaccurate to suggest that during this period there are no other games in town. In Chapter Fourteen we will look at the other trends in social theory that, together with the contemporary modernist and postmodernist accounts we have looked at here, underpin the current state of social theory at the start of the 21st century.

Key points box – In this chapter we have looked at:

- ☑ The different ways the terms 'postmodernity', 'postmodernist' and 'postmodernism' have been defined.
- ☑ The basic divisions between the modernist perspective, which draws on Enlightenment ideas and methods, and the postmodernist perspective, which rejects this approach.
- ☑ Lyotard's distinction between *narrative* and non-narrative types of knowledge and his argument that postmodernist conceptions of knowledge and science require a rejection of the narrative type.
- ☑ Within the narrative type of knowledge, Lyotard's distinction between the *meta-narratives* of the French/positivist/ society-as-unity model, and the German/philosophical/ society-as-divided model.
- ☑ Giddens' account of late-modernity as an example of a contemporary modernist story of society.
- ☑ The key concepts of *time–space distanciation*, *disembedding mechanisms* (money and expert systems) and *reflexivity*.
- ☑ Baudrillard's account as an example of postmodernist storytelling.

☑ The key postmodernist concepts of *sign-value, simulacra* and *hyper-reality*.
☑ The strengths and weaknesses of the modernist and postmodernist approaches.

Practice box

➲ What are the main differences between the terms 'late-modernity' and 'postmodernity'?
➲ Give an example of an Enlightenment idea that contemporary modernist social theorists continue to use.
➲ Is it true that although Lyotard rejects the idea of 'knowledge' as *meta-narrative* his own account is itself a narrative?
➲ In addition to the 'driving forces' of industrialism, capitalism and rationalism, Giddens adds *three* more. What are they?
➲ Give an example of an 'expert system'.
➲ Give an example of the concept of *sign-values* that Baudrillard used to develop his analysis of consumer society.
➲ What does Baudrillard mean when he argues that *simulacra* has taken over from real objects and experiences?
➲ Do you agree with Baudrillard's conclusion that postmodernity is the age of *hyper-reality*?

Further reading

Christopher Butler, *Postmodernism: A Very Short Introduction* (Oxford University Press, 2002).

Alex Callinicos, *Against Postmodernism: A Marxist Critique* (Polity Press, 1990).

Gerard Delanty, *Modernity and Postmodernity* (Sage, 2000).

Meenakishi Durham and Douglas Kellner (eds) *Media and Cultural Studies: Key Works* (Blackwell, 2001).

Anthony Giddens, *The Consequences of Modernity* (Polity Press, 1990).

David Harvey, *The Condition of Postmodernity* (Blackwell, 1990).

Douglas Kellner, *Jean Baudrillard: From Marxism to Post-Modernism and Beyond* (Polity Press, 1989).

Jean-François Lyotard, *The Postmodern Condition: A Report on Knowledge* (Manchester University Press, 1984 [1979]). (Note especially the Foreword by Frederic Jameson and the concluding essay 'An answer to the question: What is Postmodernism?')

Mark Poster (ed) *Jean Baudrillard: Selected Writings* (Polity Press, 1998).

Victor Taylor and Charles Winquist (eds) *Encyclopedia of Postmodernism* (Routledge, 2001).

Websites
For these contemporary theorists the most effective internet search strategy is to enter their names into the search engines. Also try entering the key terms 'postmodernism', 'postmodernist' and 'postmodernity'.

For Jean-François Lyotard also try the comprehensive Marxists website at: www.marxists.org/reference/subject/philosophy/works/fr/lyotard.htm

For further information on Jean Baudrillard and links to other useful resources try: http://plato.stanford.edu/entries/baudrillard/

CHAPTER FOURTEEN

REFLEXIVE MODERNISATION: THE GLOBAL DIMENSION AND CULTURAL THEORY

One of the key themes to emerge from the debates between contemporary modernists and **postmodernists** discussed in the previous chapter is whether modern society today continues to be driven forward by broadly the same forces that developed during the 19th century (**capitalism**, industrialism, instrumental rationalism). In arguing against this view postmodernists like Lyotard and Baudrillard describe other kinds of forces of change that are located in the realms of narrative discourse, culture and consumption. Baudrillard posits the emergence of an entirely different realm of social reality, called **hyper-reality**, in which the basis for making a reliable distinction between real reality and its mediated simulations has entirely collapsed. In this chapter we take these arguments and comparisons a little further by looking at a third contribution to debates about the character and direction of late-modern (postmodern) society that, while tending to reject some of the more literary and aesthetic versions of postmodernism, also think it necessary to renovate conventional ideas about the traditional forces of modernity.

In looking critically at the forces that are shaping modern society at the start of the 21st century these theorists characterise modern experience as one of chronic uncertainty about where **modernisation** is heading and where unexpected new trajectories, development and experience might be emerging. New concepts like **reflexive modernisation**, **globalisation**, **individualisation** and **de-traditionalisation** have been developed to try to describe aspects of social development that have only become evident during the more recent phases of the modernisation process. A further common feature of this approach is that although these contributions develop their accounts at quite an abstract level of analysis, often concentrating on the structural and institutional dimensions of contemporary modernisation at a society-wide level, they also try to see reflexive modernisation in terms of lived experience. The **hermeneutic** dimension in other words, the dimension where actions are invested with meaning and significance, occupies a prominent place in the social theory of reflexive modernisation.

> ### The theorists and themes we will be looking at in this chapter are:
>
> Ulrich Beck, Scott Lash and John Urry (reflexivity, de-traditionalisation, individualisation)
>
> Giddens, Beck, Urry, Manuel Castells (globalisation, network society, global complexity)
>
> Social theory and cultural theory (Margaret Archer, Frederic Jameson, Zygmunt Bauman)

Social theories of 'reflexive modernisation'

Defining reflexive modernisation

One of the dominating themes of social theory at the start of the 21st century is the theory of **reflexive modernisation**. Referring to the definition of **reflexivity** developed by the British social theorist Anthony Giddens (whose work has been discussed already in Chapters Twelve and Thirteen), Giddens argues that the process of modernisation (the process that produced modern society out of pre-modern society) has been driven along by **time–space distanciation**, disembedding mechanisms and **reflexivity**. What has been happening from the latter decades of the 20th century is that these forces and processes have become dramatically speeded up and more intense. There has been an acceleration in the rate and form of disembedding, and particularly of disembedding in time and space. Most important, the capacity for reflexivity has turned from being a relatively latent characteristic of the modernisation process (something that was always there but not yet fully realised) and into one of its driving forces. Simple modernisation has become *reflexive* modernisation because the 'institutional clusterings' of modern society (capitalism, industrialism, military power and surveillance) have become radically energised by reflexivity. The new energy and momentum caused by institutional reflexivity is unpredictable because there is no end to the amount of 'reflexing' that can be done or to the amount of reflexively-acquired knowledge that can be incorporated into subsequent action. The postmodernist notion of a radical break between modernity and late-modernity (between simple and reflexive forms of modernisation) is rejected in favour of stressing the continuities running through the various phases of modernisation. The forces of modernisation that operate today are already found, albeit in their pre-reflexive form, in the transition from traditional to modern society.

Ulrich Beck on reflexive modernisation and 'risk society'

A major contribution to the debate over reflexive modernisation, and one that although it was initially developed quite separately shares a number of similarities with Giddens' theory, has been put forward by the German theorist Ulrich Beck. The key text here is Beck's influential book *Risk Society: Towards a New Modernity* (1992 [1986]). The book was written during the early 1980s, published in German in 1986, and received very wide circulation following its publication in English in 1992.

The basic premise of reflexive modernisation for Beck is that it is no longer feasible to think about the processes of modernisation in the late 20th century as if they are an unproblematic continuation of the modernisation processes that produced modern society out of traditional society during the 18th and 19th centuries. He argues that 'modernization today is dissolving industrial society and another modernity is coming into being' (Beck, 1992 [1986], p 10, emphasis removed). Modernised society *is itself* being modernised. The key difference between 'old' modernity and 'new' modernity is that whereas the former developed from the processes of 'classical' or 'simple modernisation' new modernity is being developed from 'reflexive modernisation'. As Beck puts it 'we are witnessing not the end but the *beginning* of modernity – that is, of a modernity *beyond* its classical industrial design' (Beck, 1992 [1986], p 10, original emphasis).

The key implication of this for social theorists is that in order to grasp the transform*ing* and transform*ative* nature of reflexive modernisation it is essential to start thinking about social change without relying so heavily on the conceptual equipment developed by Marx, Weber and Durkheim. Beck argues that using the classical ways of thinking might in fact mean that social theory is conceptually deprived of the opportunity to grasp the novelty of contemporary changes. The radical character of reflexive modernisation stems from the fact that the modernising process itself becomes a primary object of reflexively-organised modernisation: 'Modernization *within* the paths of industrial society is being replaced by modernization *of the principles* of industrial society' (Beck, 1992 [1986], p 10, original emphasis). Modern experience is all about embracing the power of reflexivity.

Scarcity and risk

Applying this new and critical way of thinking about where reflexive modernisation might be leading, Beck develops what turned out to be the highly influential hypothesis of risk society. Whereas simple modernisation was designed specifically to solve the problems of scarcity by increasing production so that there would be survival and prosperity for all, reflexive modernisation turns its attention towards trying to solve some of the unintended **risks** that simple modernisation produced:

KEY QUOTE – Beck, *Risk Society* (1986), on the 'logic' of risk production.
While in classical industrial society the 'logic' of wealth production dominates the 'logic' of risk production, in the risk society this relationship is reversed. The productive forces have lost their innocence in the reflexivity of modernization processes. The gain in power from techno-economic 'progress' is being increasingly overshadowed by the production of risks. (Beck, 1992 [1986], pp 12-13)

Beck's original definition of risk is a largely environmental one referring specifically to risks that are a direct consequence of industrial processes and especially various forms of industrial hazard and pollution posing 'irreversible threats to the life of plants, animals and human beings' (Beck, 1992 [1986], p 13). Following its widespread adoption by social theorists the definition of 'risk' has been expanded to describe the negative potential of more or less any kind of social action or practice.

Expert knowledge and popular protest

In his analysis of risk society, Beck argues that it is a loss of popular faith in the scientific-technical elites of modern society, and of their capacity for making 'the right decisions' about scientific and technological progress, that will eventually result in the process of modernisation becoming more 'radicalised'. For him it is the increasingly contested nature of technical-scientific knowledge, the fact that the general and non-expert population is no longer prepared simply to accept what 'the experts' say, that is what distinguishes reflexive from simple modernisation. The forces of social change will thus be centred around **new social movements** and a more general awareness of scientific fallibility among the population. The mass media plays a very important role in this process not so much by setting the agenda for which risks and hazards are being highlighted, but by providing social actors with information about these phenomena. Awareness of risk is enough to get social actors thinking about which risks affect them.

Beck's description of the loss of faith suffered by the scientific-technical elite can be seen as one example of the issue of trust described by Giddens in his account of expert systems. To the extent that actors become increasingly sensitive to the question of risk (which is not the same as saying that late-modern society is *actually* any more risky than early or pre-modern society), this is likely to raise the threshold of trust that experts need in order to persuade social actors to carry on using the increasingly abstract and obscure expert systems the experts are developing. One might conclude that in late-modern society the value of expert systems is becoming defined in terms of levels of perceptible risk rather than in terms of technical efficiency. To the extent that 'risk' is itself being defined more generally as 'hazards with global consequences' (see later), trust in expert systems will also be defined as a globalising phenomenon.

From scientific rationality to social rationality

Writing from a liberal social-democratic perspective, and in the context of growing popular and electoral support for the Green Party in Germany in the 1980s, Beck argues that the **discourse** about risk, where these globe-affecting environmental hazards have come from and how to mitigate their effects, will be brought out of the laboratory and into the democratic political process. At the social and institutional levels, and in order to maintain their own credibility, the heavily defensive professional and academic bureaucracies of the scientific-technical elites will have to hand control over the discourse back to 'the people'. And one of the first things 'the people' will do is to make *lack of* globe-affecting environmental risk a primary criterion of technological and scientific progress. The old discourse in which the economic and military motivation for doing things was put ahead of a proper consideration of whether, and in what sense, something *should* be done, is being replaced by a new discourse of democratised risk assessment and risk awareness.

In explaining how risk awareness affects social action at a personal level, Beck relies on a notion of reflexivity that is largely the same as the one developed by Giddens. Self-assessment of risk implies a process of informed decision making in which social actors demand better-quality information about what affects them, and incorporate this knowledge into how they act. Although these decisions take place at a personal level, Beck is keen to emphasise that, as evidenced by the emergence of popular Green political parties, there is a strongly social and communal dimension to risk awareness as well. In an important sense what is truly significant about risk in late-modern society is precisely that it does affect the whole of the population and not just part of it.

Although Beck uses a modernist rather than postmodernist technique in forming his arguments, his description of the loss of legitimacy suffered by the scientific-technical paradigm of knowledge from the 1970s onwards in the West clearly echoes Lyotard's analysis of how different definitions of knowledge come and go. Although Lyotard distinguishes between **narrative** and non-narrative forms of knowledge and Beck's account tends to bridge both forms, the risk-society thesis relies heavily on the idea that whereas the scientific-technical elite used to have a monopoly over the narrative of what constitutes risk and thereby also retained authority over the science and technology debate, since the 1970s both its legitimacy and its authority have been radically undermined. A new environmentalist narrative premised on the rhetoric of climate change has risen to take its place.

We can also note that the distinction Beck relies on between **scientific-technical rationality** (which is heavily and negatively implicated in the emergence of risk society) and **social rationality** (which seeks to restore faith in a positive alternative form of progress) is close to Weber's distinction between **formal rationality** and **substantive rationality** (see Chapter Five). The former refers to the technical benefits of a particular course of action and the latter to the desirability of the ends that are being sought. There is also a parallel with Habermas's concern over the tendency for instrumental-rational action to overshadow the humanitarian priorities of 'communicative rationality' (see Chapter Twelve).

De-traditionalisation

Beck supplements his analysis of the transition from simple to reflexive modernisation (from scarcity society to risk society) by developing the notion of **de-traditionalisation**. In one sense this refers simply to the movement beyond or out of pre-modern society; modern society is no longer characterised by traditional institutions and traditional forms of social action. The more complex sense in which Beck develops the idea, however, is to show how despite the generally progressive forces of modernisation that are in play, some features of early-modern society, which are retained within late-modern society, have yet to become fully transformed by the modernisation process. The crucial effect of reflexive modernisation is to highlight which aspects of modern society have been left behind by, or have not reached their full developmental potential through, the modernising process. For Beck, in other words, modern society is not entirely 'modern' as it contains within itself remnants of the pre-modern, feudal or estate-society type that it grew out of:

> Components of a *traditionality inherent in industrialism* are inscribed in varied ways within the architecture of industrial society – in patterns of 'classes', 'nuclear family', 'professional work', 'democracy' – and their foundations begin to crumble and disintegrate in the reflexivity of modernization…. Reflexive modernization means not less but more modernity, a modernity radicalized against the paths and categories of the classical industrial setting. (Beck, 1992 [1986], p 14, original emphasis)

In the same way that risk society, as an extant social formation, is linked historically and developmentally to scarcity society because many of the risks that confront social actors in risk society arose directly out of attempts to solve the problems of scarcity (most importantly, industrial pollution and its associated hazards), so also reflexive modernity, conceived as an underlying force for social transformation, is linked with simple modernity because the yet-to-be-modernised institutions and practices of late-modern society arose directly out of the modernisation process. Forces of industrialism, capitalism and instrumentalism created the practices and institutions of modern society. The challenge posed by reflexive modernisation is to understand how, in late-modern society, these practices and institutions have themselves become limiting factors in the next stage of social development.

Defining risks as global phenomena

In addition to describing the general shift from early-modern society preoccupied with scarcity towards late-modern society preoccupied with the definition, perception and reaction to risk, the risk-society concept raises another set of questions that are to do with the extent to which modern society and modern social experience are globalised phenomena. Given that all of the most challenging forms of risk discussed by Beck operate at a global level (global environmental change, global pollution, global spread of disease), the risk-society scenario certainly implies that globalisation, 'globality' and 'globalism' are becoming important features of social experience in late-modern society. Neither risk itself nor the discourse about risk is constrained by national territorial boundaries and so the risk-society concept has to be theorised at a supranational level. It is not so much that social actors become aware of risks because of their knowledge of the global, but that they become aware of the global because of their increasing awareness of risk and of its often unbounded character. It is the changing nature of risks themselves from limited and localised worries to unlimited and globalised chronic uncertainty that makes risk globally significant.

Weaknesses of the risk-society scenario

Despite the major pull it has exercised on the sociological and social-theoretical imagination at the end of the 20th century there are a number of difficulties with the risk-society scenario. First, although it is fair enough to highlight the increasingly global impact of risk in the late-modern period, many of these risks arise from the actions of social actors, governments and businesses operating at a local level. The negative consequences of such activities might more often be felt at a global level, but their inception, strictly speaking, is not global, but local. Irrespective of the newer forms of globalised risk, social actors are still affected in their day-to-day lives by pre-modern kinds of risks associated, for example, with quality of local housing, healthcare and social amenities.

Second, account needs to be taken of perceptions of what constitutes *global* risk. Having seen pictures of planet Earth taken by Apollo astronauts, modern perceptions of 'the global' are based on a literal geographical awareness of what planet Earth looks like. Social actors in the late-modern world therefore have the capacity to scale-up their thoughts and ideas about risks to the level of the whole planet. The medieval peasant would not have been able to visualise the planet in this way, but they might still have felt that 'their whole world' was under threat from war, famine, pestilence and plague. In terms of their immediate impact on social action, in other words, modern-day perceptions of risk are no more all-encompassing or universal than were risks perceived within the villages and shires of pre-modern society.

Third, the relationship between *knowledge of risk* and *exposure to risk* is not straightforward. It may be that general society-wide faith in the capacity of the scientific-technical elite to 'solve risk problems' is in decline but even when detailed and relatively uncontroversial information is available (for example about the hazards of smoking tobacco or drinking alcohol), social actors may choose to ignore these risks and carry on drinking and smoking anyway. Just because social actors are better informed and potentially more risk aware it does not follow that they will invariably adopt risk-avoiding forms of behaviour. Knowledge that something is risky (for example riding a motorcycle) might add to its attractiveness, thus potentially increasing its popularity.

Fourth, and in terms of defining late-modern risk society as a place where social actors are confronted by a greater variety of risk, it is a moot point whether actors have learnt to protect themselves from 'old' risks at a faster rate than they have exposed themselves to 'new' risks. Even if new risks tend to circulate at the global level and to have more global impact, this does not mean that the balance between new and old risks has resulted in an overall increase in exposure to risk. Space junk is just the early 21st-century equivalent of dumping a dead pig in the local stream.

Finally, and looking at the hypothesis of risk society in social-theoretical terms, rather than becoming overly preoccupied with whether this or that situation is more or less risky than another it might be more useful to consider how *the definition of risk* has been shifted away from the local and towards the global. It is the strong tendency to define *as risks* those things that have negative consequences far beyond the locality where they originate that constitutes the link between the analytical concepts of 'risk' and 'global'. It is the range and scope of risks thus perceived at the global level that makes them global risks rather than a technical assessment of their geographical range of impact. Perhaps the most significant thing about the risk debate in social theory is that growing awareness of the global nature of *particular kinds* of hazards has contributed to current conceptions of what 'the global' *is*. The global becomes an analytical category within which a particular variety of risk and its likely social consequences becomes conceivable. We need the concept to make sense of particular kinds of late-modern social phenomena rather than these phenomena being deduced from the putative existence of 'the global'.

Reflexive modernisation according to Scott Lash and John Urry

Much of what we have been saying so far about reflexive modernisation as described by Giddens and by Beck is broadly reflected in the parallel thesis offered by the British cultural theorists Scott Lash and John Urry. Their key publications in this area are *The End of Organized Capitalism* (1987) and *Economies of Signs and Space* (1994) (Urry's ideas [2000, 2003] about new definitions of 'society' are discussed further later). Lash and Urry approach the topics of modernisation, individualisation and de-traditionalisation as much from the perspective of cultural studies as from economics and sociology. Like Giddens and Beck they are very interested in the ways that reflexive modernisation affects social institutions and social relations at a global level, but they tend to see these developments as being particularly concentrated with the global spread of cultural artefacts of various kinds. Unlike goods and services that take time to move from one physical location to another, cultural artefacts, and especially those that can be conveyed digitally, are in a sense 'set free' from these restrictions. The really significant step change caused by reflexive modernisation, as they see it, is not that goods and people move around, since this is already a well-established feature of simple modernisation (capitalism, industrialisation and rationalisation were already widely globalised early in the 20th century), but that information and communications technologies have dramatically accelerated this process. It is the uniquely modern form of 'mediatised' information, and of the various kinds of networks and flows by which this operates, that Lash and Urry see as the most significant outcome of reflexive modernisation. A key development, moreover, that was not foreseen by the classical social theorists.

Material goods and reflexive modernisation

Beginning with material phenomena, Lash and Urry follow the postmodernist and **culturalist** trend in social theory, which developed strongly during the 1980s, of attaching particular importance to signs or 'expressive symbols'. In this scenario objects are 'progressively emptied of material content. What is increasingly produced are not material objects, but *signs*' (Lash and Urry, 1994, p 4). Lash and Urry distinguish between signs that are 'informational goods' particularly those constituting the hardware of information and communication technologies, and signs that have 'primarily an aesthetic content and are what can be termed postmodern goods' such as popular cultural, leisure and entertainment goods like music, fashion and cinema. There is also an accentuation of the aesthetic or meaning-laden and meaning-forming content of more ordinary material goods 'the increasing component of sign-value or image embodied *in* material objects'. 'This aestheticization of material objects takes place in the production, the circulation or the composition of such goods' (Lash and Urry, 1994, p 4).

These arguments retain the same interest in processes of economic organisation and practice that featured in Lash and Urry's widely read thesis of *disorganised capitalism* (Lash and Urry, 1987). In contrast to the modern or Fordist industrial period, which was characterised by tightly controlled and synchronised methods of production held within national boundaries, the postmodern or reflexively modern economies are characterised by lack of sychronisation and an increasing disregard for the necessity of a distinctly national base. The post-Fordist regime, which developed from the 1980s onwards, is one of flexible specialisation, trans-national production and a kind of organised chaos. There is a shift away from the old 'heavy-industrial hub of the motor, chemicals, electrical and steel industries' and towards a new core 'clustered around information, communications, airlines and important parts of tourism and leisure' (Lash and Urry, 1994, p 17). Relations between core and periphery are also subject to transformation given the increasingly mobile nature of social actors. These processes constitute part of the economic-institutional dimensions of globalisation.

From cognitive reflexivity to aesthetic reflexivity

For Lash and Urry these defining characteristics of the structural and institutional dimensions of reflexive modernisation are accompanied by similarly significant developments in the nature and role of social actors; if there are signs and spaces there must be people to make sense of them. In fact, the momentum of Lash and Urry's argument takes us further than this to the point of strongly reinforcing the central role of the subjective individual in the constitution of reflexive modernisation. The **biographical subject** that was so strongly criticised in post-structuralist and postmodernist social theory (discussed in Chapter Thirteen), is reinstated by Lash and Urry in their social theory. Reflecting critically on what they regard as 'a universally pessimistic scenario' based on 'an overly structuralist conception of social process', which is typical both of critical (e.g. Habermas, Jameson) and non-critical perspectives in contemporary modernist social theory (Giddens, Bourdieu), and not infrequently of postmodernist approaches also (Foucault, Derrida), Lash and Urry explain that they want to focus instead on 'subjectivity and in particular on an increasingly significant *reflexive* human subjectivity' 'a subjectivity engaged in a process of "reflexive modernization"' (Lash and Urry, 1994, p 3). As they see it, reflexivity operates very significantly at *the individual level* as a positive force for social change, a source of optimism rather than despair.

The emphasis on subjects/subjectivities continues the long-standing interest in the nature of the human subject within contemporary social theory. Lash and Urry criticise Giddens' conception of reflexivity as being based too firmly on social-psychological models where the quest for well-being (**ontological security**) is very much a rational and cognitive process rather than an experiential and emotional one. Lash and Urry feel that this model is underdeveloped in terms of the creative/expressive dimensions of the self. In their version of the theory of reflexive modernisation, they want to see that part of the reflexivity process which is to do with the self-reflexivity of social actors as not being dominated by what they call 'the rationalist and Cartesian assumptions of the Enlightenment tradition of modernity', but with 'aesthetic reflexivity' or '**hermeneutic** reflexivity': 'If cognitive reflexivity is a matter of "monitoring" the self, and of social-structural roles and resources, then aesthetic reflexivity entails self-*interpretation* and the interpretation of social background practices' (Lash and Urry, 1994, p 5, original emphasis). Lash and Urry want to see reflexivity as a growing and positive capacity to develop new interpretations of self and society. For them, the cognitively reflexive self, identified by Giddens and others as characteristic of late-modernity, can be seen as an intermediate stage in the more full-developed, or at least develop*ing*, aesthetically reflexive personality of postmodern man. The emergence of what we could call the 'interpretive self'.

Consistent with their general approach (and with Giddens and Beck), which is to suggest that what is really radical about reflexive modernisation is its urge to reflect on the basic premises of its own existence, Lash and Urry argue that the emergence of the reflexive self is necessary for social actors to respond to the new economies of signs and spaces both as producers and as consumers. Selves who are preoccupied with the consumption of signs are the new consumers of **postmodernism**.

ILLUSTRATION – COMPLEX CONSUMPTION.

We can illustrate these developments by thinking about how forms of consumption have shifted with the advent of affluent society. In the 'age of production', where social actors were largely preoccupied with meeting their basic household needs (Beck's scarcity society), consumption was a relatively simple affair often involving little more than time away from the place of work. Work, Church and family provided the only bases for identity and self-expression. Today, widespread affluence has ushered in a whole new 'age of consumption'. Consumption is no longer about resting from work, but has involved an increasingly exotic range of leisure goods and leisure activities whose common feature is that they allow people to explore new forms of identity. Complex consumption in the 21st century is not just a release from work but provides new terrain for developing new selves, new identities, even new personalities (see Ransome, 2005).

New forms of community

Also consistent with Giddens' and Beck's characterisation of reflexive modernisation as helping to produce new kinds of communal and political activity, Lash and Urry see 'aesthetic reflexivity' as providing a basis for 'new communities' and **new social movements**. The notion of 'community' involved here, like the trend towards increased sign-content and sign-value of material goods in the new realms of 'reflexive production' and 'reflexive consumption', is weighted towards what social actors *imagine* these communities to be. The old-fashioned or 'ascribed' communities of class and place characteristic of modernity are displaced by the 'elective' communities of **postmodernity** that actors have chosen to belong to. For Lash and Urry, then, reflexive modernisation is characterised as a twin process marked by a shift in economic production towards sign–heavy material goods, and by the emergence of an increasingly self-assured and critically aware population who are equipped with the knowledge and appetites necessary for using them, but who are *also* prepared to be critical of them. The development of the creative-critical urge among social actors in post-organised society, and their willingness to form new groups and associations for expressing this, provides evidence that the liberating potential of reflexive modernisation is being realised.

Modernisation and individualisation

Looking a little more deeply into the special features of reflexive modernisation, in the same way that Beck argues that the newly emerging society characterised by reflexive modernisation (post-postmodern society perhaps?) actually *requires* the rooting out of 'traditional institutions', Lash and Urry argue that the emergence of reflexively-oriented producers, consumers and citizens is a precondition for the new flows of signs and spaces becoming a reality: 'This accelerating individualization process is a process in which agency is set free from structure, a process in which, further, it is structural change itself in modernization that so to speak forces agency to take on powers that heretofore lay in social structures themselves' (Lash and Urry, 1994, p 5).

Incorporating a much more phenomenological and present-time kind of orientation, one where rewards are not deferred but immediate, experiential rather than cognitive, Lash and Urry want to suggest that reflexive decision making is no longer guided by universal values and distant, often utopian, conceptions of the future, but by a strong sense of the present. One of the radicalising aspects of reflexive modernisation is that it sets social agents free from the authority of universal interests and the disciplines of self-restraint. This does not mean, however, that social action becomes entirely directionless and devoid of meaning. What happens instead, according to Lash and Urry, is that the space is taken up by a much more aesthetically charged and experiential appreciation of present-time events. In saving energy worrying about a doubtful and idealised future all the effort can be put into making the most of things now. The emergence of reflexive modernisation thus links with the **individualisation** thesis in the sense that it was consistency between decision making and universal values that is the very stuff of tradition. The process of de-traditionalisation, which Beck, Giddens, Lash and Urry all highlight, is very much to do with the shift away from action being guided by the quest for universal values and deferred gratification, and towards immediacy and pleasure in the here and now. Post-organised capitalist society, then:

- has a present-time orientation;
- focuses on emotion and experience rather than on values;
- gives priority to the domains of leisure, pleasure and enjoyment.

The de-traditionalisation of social theory

Applying the process of critical reflexivity to the conceptual tools and methods being used in social theory itself, Lash and Urry also want to identify a process of de-traditionalisation in terms of how social theorists envisage the transition from one type or stage of society to another. They do not want to go the whole way and argue that institutional structures as traditionally conceived in modernist social theory have been entirely swept away, but rather that, like the trend towards increasing sign-value in material goods, a similar and associated trend is taking place towards social forms based on 'information and communication structures':

KEY QUOTE – Lash and Urry, *Economies of Signs and Space* (1994). We propose that there is tendentially, the beginnings of the unfolding of a process in which social structures, national in scope, are being displaced by such global information and communication (I & C) structures. These information and communication structures *are* the very networked flows, *are* the very economies of signs and space which are [the main constituents of the process of reflexive modernisation].... Thus structured flows and accumulations of images, of expressive symbols are the condition of burgeoning aesthetic reflexivity. Thus the conditions of both cognitive and aesthetic reflexivity are economies of signs and spaces. (Lash and Urry, 1994, pp 6–7, original emphasis)

Lash and Urry support Giddens' and Beck's basic proposition that the processes of reflexive modernisation in late-modern industrial society (or 'post-organised capitalist order' as they sometimes call it) are taking on a new and even more radical trajectory, but want to stress that radicalisation *also involves* some fairly major rethinking about what new forms of social entity reflexive modernisation is likely to produce. A crucial starting point for the new kind of critically-reflexive social theory Lash and Urry have in mind is to try to move beyond modernist ideas about what 'society' is. Although this suggestion seems rather abstract and is certainly rather disconcerting for social theorists who might otherwise be quite happy to jog along with one or other of the classical conceptions of 'society', Lash and Urry have incorporated in their self-reflexive method one of the basis premises of postmodernist thinking, which is that the concept 'society', and the entity it is generally supposed to refer to, *is not something* that can be taken for granted (we will return to this important point later in this chapter and in Chapter Fifteen).

Social theory and the global dimensions of change

The second key concept that underpins contemporary debates in social theory is the widely-accepted notion that social processes need to be analysed not only at the local and national levels, but at a global level as well. Closely integrated with this re-scaling exercise is a third key theme, which we will be discussing briefly in the third part of this chapter, which is whether, and, if so, to what extent, this important new development also implies a change in focus in social theory away from economics and politics and towards culture. Considerations of 'the global' and of 'the cultural' are closely linked in recent social theory.

Defining globalisation for social theorists

At the risk of starting on a negative note we should emphasise straight away that when discussing the global dimensions of social change it is important not to drift into using the jargon of 'globalisation' if this implies that social life is shaped by economic, political and cultural forces that originate from a central global source or point of origin. Social theory has gone to a lot of trouble to develop awareness that social life is **socially constructed** and not **overdetermined** by nature or by God and the last thing we should do now is invent some mystical new source of all-encompassing global domination. In this negative sense 'globalisation' describes the drift *in social and cultural theory* towards imagining that all economic, political and cultural forces are being dragged together by the irresistible force of some kind of global magnet. We should not, as John Urry puts it, mistakenly think of globalisation as 'an overwhelming, singular causal force' (Urry, 2003, p 3); 'there is nothing approaching a single global economy or society' (Urry, 2000, p 13).

In referring to things as 'global' in social theory what we are really talking about are natural and social processes that, if we want to make sense of them, have to be thought of as operating at a global scale or across-the-globe level. Many aspects of climatic and environmental processes, for example, have to be analysed in this way and so can accurately be described as 'global processes'. Where social processes can be identified that have global reach and influence, which develop on a global scale and have a global dynamic, then they also can be described as global processes. Like the terms 'industrialisation' or 'bureaucratisation', the term 'globalisation' refers to the various means by which social practices and institutions begin to acquire a global presence or exert an across-the-globe influence. Globalisation is the process by which practices and institutions become global*ised*. The purpose of this part of the chapter is look in an introductory way at some of the social processes that can be described as global*ised* and to reflect on how they are being addressed by social theorists. Is it necessary and possible to develop a social theory of practices and institutions at the global level?

Reflexive modernisation and global social relations

As should be clear from the discussion in the previous section, reflexive modernisation (that is, the actual process not just the theory) opens up several possibilities for how institutions and practices might begin to develop and operate at a global rather than local level. In Giddens' account, the institutional clusterings of capitalism, industrialism, surveillance and military power are all already operating at a truly global scale. For Beck, the way risks have come to be defined as 'global hazards' presupposes that their negative consequences are similarly global:

KEY QUOTE – Beck, *Risk Society* (1986), on the global nature of risks in risk society.
Unlike the factory-related or occupational hazards of the nineteenth and the first half of the twentieth centuries, these can no longer be limited to certain localities or groups, but rather exhibit a tendency to globalization which spans production *and* reproduction as much as national borders, and in this sense brings into being *supra*-national and *non*-class-specific *global hazards* with a new type of social and political dynamism. (Beck, 1992 [1986], p 13, original emphasis)

Perhaps the most energetic account of the potentially global consequences of reflexive modernisation is given by Lash and Urry. For these theorists, the new forms of 'structures' and 'flows' associated with the spread of information and communication technologies are inherently globalised and globalising; it is difficult to envisage a situation where digitalised information can be prevented from spreading worldwide. The new 'global information and communication structures' described by Lash and Urry are globalising, first, because in a technical sense they operate at a global scale and, second, at the level of meaning and signification, because the information they carry has the potential for generating new kinds of global-cultural experiences.

What these theorists are envisaging here is not a simple media-studies-type account of the development of a homogenised global culture where all national cultures will be remodelled onto the template of Western and especially American culture, but a much more powerful and subtle process in which the increasing appetite social actors already have for signs, meanings and messages can begin to operate at a global level. Global media corporations certainly have a commercial interest in selling ideas and images around the world, there might even be a tendency for Western governments to try to influence these ideas and images for political and military reasons, but the really significant aspect of these developments for Lash and Urry is that signs or 'expressive symbols' carry meanings in *all* directions. Meanings and interpretations do not simply flow *out of* the West and towards the rest of the world, and neither do they just flow *back from* the exotic and unknown periphery and towards the centre. Meanings and interpretations circulate around the global networks potentially reshaping and re-imaging themselves as they go.

The new technologies combined with the growing reflexive attitude are establishing an informational-cultural domain where participants can move in or out as they please. Lash and Urry thus incorporate in their theory a strongly global-cultural dimension in the sense that they see reflexive modernisation as being driven by the increasing impact on experience of signs, ideas and meanings. And, now that digital technology has become available more or less worldwide, this cultural dimension, characterised by flows of information and by reflexively-active individuals, is a genuinely global phenomenon. Reflexivity in the global-cultural dimension is not an accompaniment to the modernisation process, but an integral part of it.

Redefining global 'society'

Working along the border country where social theory and cultural theory intermingle, Urry turns his attention in later publications (*Sociology Beyond Societies* [2000], *Global Complexity* [2003]) to what the implications might be for conceptions of global society under conditions of reflexive modernisation. He also considers how the analysis of globalising flows and networks of reflexively-organised information will affect some of the core concepts of social theory. There are three central elements in Urry's later theory of global-mobile complexity: the notion of *networks*, the notion of *social systems* and the notion of *complexity* including elements from chaos theory.

Networks

The first main point of departure for Urry is the concept of the network. Drawing on the influential analysis of 'network society' developed by Manual Castells (1996, 1997, 1998), Urry takes the idea of the network as a defining characteristic of globalised and of globalising social relations:

KEY QUOTE – John Urry, *Global Complexity* (2003), on network society.

A network is a set of interconnected nodes, the distance between social positions being shorter where such positions constitute nodes *within* a network as opposed to those lying outside that particular network. Networks are dynamic open structures as long as they continue to effect [bring about] communication with new nodes. (Urry, 2003, p 9, drawing on Castells, 1996, pp 470–1, original emphasis)

Urry is proposing that social theorists should replace the established notion of 'structure' as a way of envisaging how social relations are played out at a global level with a notion of 'network'. At the very least, network constitutes a different kind of structure. This suggestion produces some interesting possibilities.

Whereas the notion of structure tends to support the notion of national society as a separate, rigid, delineated and immobile entity having clear geographical and legal boundaries, the notion of network supports a different conception of global interaction as unrestrained by such borders and boundaries.

If flows of information moving across and between various networks come to be regarded as a distinct mode of social interaction in their own right (rather than being an accompaniment to social relations that were happening anyway), and if, as seems to be the case, such flows are only very minimally restricted by national boundaries or structures of whatever kind, then it makes less and less sense to see 'national society' as the basic unit of analysis in social interaction even at a global level.

Although the concepts used by social theorists are not necessarily the same as those used by sociologists, economists and political scientists, it would seem to be the case that if one theorises social power as something that originates within, or as being mapped onto, entities having identifiable geographical, territorial or legal boundaries (i.e. the conventional idea of society as nation–state), then a different concept of power will be required in light of the emergence of new kinds of global flows and networks (i.e. global interaction that no longer presupposes the nation–state concept).

Since networks have no centre (as distinct, for example, from the spokes of a wheel or spiders' webs that do), it is not necessary to try to account for their origins and foundations in the same way that we might want to find the foundations of the institutional structures. Global networking is much more interesting in terms of the effects it has than in how it works in a technical sense.

Networks and the processes of networking imply a horizontal rather than hierarchic form of organisation. There is no top and bottom, no base and superstructure as such, rather the various nodes in the network are seen as having the form they do as a result of the way material flows between them in the network. In principle at least, the power and influence of the national societies that form the nodes in the network of, for example, international diplomacy is subsumed within the network. Membership of the network is conditional upon the national-member being prepared to feed some of its authority into the network.

Global networks as systems

Despite the interesting analytical possibilities offered by Castells' notion of network, Urry has to exercise some caution because this model remains quite close to the much more familiar notion of a functionally-integrated system. It might be that nodes 'are not centres, but switches that follow a networking logic rather than a command network, in their function vis-à-vis the overall structure' (Urry, 2003, p 10), but this nuancing of the precise way that nodes do their stuff hardly detracts from the overall impression that nodes and their networks do what they do in order to maintain system functionality (**functionalist** social theory is discussed in Chapter Seven).

Using his innovative notion of structure as network, Urry then turns towards the second central idea in his theory, that of the social system: 'I will consider whether an emergent level of the "global" is developing that can be viewed as recursively self-producing, that is, its outputs constitute inputs into an **autopoietic** circular system of "global" objects, identities, institutions and social practices' (Urry, 2000, p 206). Unpacking this definition a little we begin with a very standard notion of 'system' commonly used in social theory. Systems (like a central-heating system for example) are 'closed' in the sense that they have an identifiable number of elements or, if the system is a network, an identifiable number of 'nodes' that are the identifiable and proximate elements being held together within the system. Systems are separate from the contexts or environments in which they function. Systems exist because they have an identifiable purpose or function. Being purposeless is not functional.

Urry then moves beyond this functionalist definition of system and towards the German theorist Niklas Luhmann's (1995 [1984]) influential account of *Social Systems* as modes of communication between subsystems. Working very much at the level of abstract **general theory**, Luhmann shifts the emphasis in **systems theory** away from a focus on the various elements or nodes in the system and towards *the process* that holds them together. Here Luhmann is using the generally familiar **structuralist** notion that elements in systems (or 'structures' as they would put it) are what they are because of the way the system holds them together. The concept of a particular number, for example, or of a particular colour, only makes sense because each can be located in a system of other numbers or colours. As Luhmann puts it: 'elements are elements only for the system that employs them as units and they are such only through this system' (quoted in Urry, 2003, pre-Preface list of quotes). Looking at systems in terms of this phenomenon of holding-together, Luhmann concludes that holding-together is essentially a mode of communication. What constitutes systems or networks in this scenario, and why they are of interest to Urry, is that they are constituted by and through flows of information.

The other attractive feature for Urry in Luhmann's approach is that for something to constitute a system or network it must be able to establish itself as *different from* other systems or networks. The system of numbers, for example, might be constituted in the same way as the system of colours, but obviously the two systems are different from each other. The number 'seven' has no place in the colour sequence 'red', 'white' and 'blue'. The existence of multiple systems/networks in the same time and place demonstrates not, as functionalist systems-theorists had argued, that all systems are mutually dependent on each other (system interdependence), but that the underlying principle of systemness must be one of differentiation rather than of convergence. Systems/networks should therefore be regarded as circular or autopoietic in the sense that they can regulate and renew themselves without requiring justification for so doing by reference to forces outside the system/network. If we imagine each independent system/network as if it were a single node in a larger system/network, then in the same way that each node has no centre, neither does any larger network it might form a part of. Essentially 'networks' have no tangible form at all, but are simply *modes of communication* between nodes. Smaller networks form nodes in larger networks and so one can begin to envisage 'the global' as a massively complex network of nodes, each of which is composed of many other distinctive and separate nodes/networks.

Global complexity

The third central element in Urry's thinking (in addition to network and system) is the idea of *complexity*. For him, the main deficiency in Castells' 'otherwise brilliant examination of intersecting global networks' is that it does not contain sufficient analysis of 'the materials, concepts and arguments within the science of complexity' (Urry, 2003, p 12). Urry sees the new cultural–informational networks and flows as an integral feature of what he calls 'global complexity'. As he puts it: 'People, money, capital, information, ideas and images are seen to "flow" along various "scapes" which are organised through complex interlocking networks located within and across different societies' (Urry, 2000, p 12). Global networking thus creates new 'travel-scapes', business-scapes, media-scapes and discourse-scapes in their various forms (Urry, 2003, p 5).

Building on the idea of replacing the concept of structure with the concept of network, Urry argues that the concept of 'society' should itself be reconceived as a coming-together of global networks made up of 'structured flows and accumulations of images [and] expressive symbols' (Lash and Urry, 1994, p 6). These networks have to be theorised from the outset as highly complex. Complexity theory, Urry says: '[W]ould lead one to see the global as neither omnipotent nor subject to control by society. Indeed it is not a single centre of power. It is an astonishingly complex system, or rather a series of dynamic complex systems ... there would be no presumption of moving towards a state of equilibrium' (Urry, 2003, Preface). It is not enough, in other words, simply to scale the analysis up from the local to the national and from the national to the global, but is also necessary to abandon some of the modernist-type assumptions that 'the global' is a total system having a core or centre in the same way that national societies are assumed to have. As the new unit of analysis, the global does not have an administrative head office, a centralised civic and military headquarters, a set of shared values or any unifying cultural icons like a global anthem or global flag. Urry recommends complexity because, among other things, it argues 'against reducing the whole to the parts' and that there is no 'central hierarchical structure that unambiguously "governs" and produces outcomes' (Urry, 2003, p 13).

Finally, complexity provides a highly innovative concept for moving beyond the modernist presumption that the unintended consequences of social action should primarily be interpreted as instances of system failure. For Urry, the highly fluid and dynamic character of communicative activity across and between networks strongly suggests that order and chaos are not only 'systemic features of the system in question', but are 'always connected within any such system' (Urry,

2003, p 14). Recalling Beck's narrative, the struggle in early modernity to break free from scarcity inevitably produced negative outcomes in the form of industrial pollution and associated dangers. These risks are not accidental but are inevitable products of the industrialisation process.

Limitations of the network model of global interaction

Urry's conception of global complexity in terms of networks and 'scapes' offers social theorists some interesting new ways of thinking about how or whether the standard equipment of social theory can be adapted for looking at social phenomena that have to be conceptualised as operating at the global level. A common theme in most of the following points is that inevitably, and not surprising given the complexity of the phenomena under analysis, Urry sometimes experiences the theorist's dilemma of slipping between the actual object being analysed and the concepts the theorist uses in attempting an analysis of it.

Power

First, the concept of global networks tends to have quite an ambiguous sense of **power**. Clearly there is plenty of power generated by the technological potential of the new information and communications technologies that produce massively more social output than the electrical input that makes them work. In terms of what we might call socio-political conceptions of power, however, and given the picture of highly dissipated and circulating kinds of energy that Lash and Urry envisage spiralling around the networks, it is less clear which social agents, if any, have control over networks and their products. One answer is probably that nobody is in power precisely because the new modes of communication are not aligned with institutional structures as these are usually thought of in social theory. In the old social-institutions scenario, structure implies hierarchy and those who control the structure are in power or have power while those who are subject to control by such structures do not. Power thus comes to be defined *in terms of* a capacity to keep particular kinds of structures in place. Although it is clear enough that in the new global-network scenario this particular definition of power is likely to be displaced, it is not yet clear what it will be replaced *by*. The shift away from structured organisational forms and towards network forms is important but tends to reinforce questions about hierarchy, authority and control rather than providing answers to them.

Not everything is a network

Although Urry is keen to emphasise that networks are different to structures because networks tend to have horizontal rather than vertical modes of connectedness, we should note that not all networks take this form, and neither is it possible to describe all kinds of organising behaviour in terms of, or as if they unambiguously do operate as, complex networks. A more reasonable position is that networks are a particular form of social organising; a form that has become more and more prevalent as the information and communications technologies they depend on have become universally available. The most promising procedure might be to supplement the analysis of modes of organising having structure form with those having network form. It is probable that hybrid forms of organising also exist where part of the activity can be described as network*esque* but still within the more familiar forms of structured organising. Urry's analysis is most applicable to networks in the cultural field where the 'goods' that are being conveyed most often take the form of signs and expressive symbols. It works less well in other contexts and as a way of describing social interaction that simply does not have the same properties of fluidity and reversibility. If the mode of operation of networks is not flexible and reversible, democratic and negotiable, then the metaphor of network might not always be appropriate.

Structure and agency revisited

Much of what we have been discussing so far has tended to concentrate on what used to be called the systems and structure of the structure-versus-agency debate. We know from Lash and Urry's version of the theory of reflexive modernisation discussed in the first part of this chapter that they feel that one of the main drawbacks of the classical modernist and of the postmodernist accounts is that they are unduly preoccupied with a particularly rigid notion of structure and thus pay insufficient attention to human agency. This is why they stress not only human agency as against social structure, but specifically the *aesthetic* aspects of reflexivity, the ways in which the unique human capacity for creative reflection and understanding must be regarded as a core feature of reflexive modernisation. One could easily interpret them as saying that the primary object, the thing that is most affected by reflexive modernisation, *is* the human subject.

Urry seems to reinforce this view in his later analysis of global complexity when he says that 'the global economy of signs is transforming the public sphere into an increasingly visual and emotional public space' (Urry, 2000, p 211). He also defines human agency in very experiential terms (rather than in terms of **rational choice** or cognitive equilibrium): 'Agency is not a question of humans acting independently of objects in terms of their unique capacities to attribute meaning or to follow rules. Rather what are crucial are the ways in which the physical world and artefacts are sensuously experienced by humans' (Urry, 2000, p 14). This would seem to place subjectively-aware and experientially-oriented social actors at the centre of the action; not render them obsolete particulars in the periphery of global action.

At the same time, however, and acknowledging that Urry (2000, pp 206–7) does identify this as a paradox, his prolonged and detailed discussion of new technologies, networks, flows and complex systems can easily be taken to imply that it is *the structural dimensions* of recent changes that tend to dominate human agency. He says for example: 'To describe [diverse mobilities, regions, networks and flows] as either "structure" or "agency" does injustice to the temporal and spatial complexity of such relations' (Urry, 2000, pp 15–16). Despite detailed descriptions of 'aesthetic reflexivity' and 'sensuous embodiment', however, there is a lingering impression that social actors are being pulled along by the processes of global complexity rather than being drivers of it.

Complexity and global disorder

A key dilemma Urry faces is that in order to capture the chaotic and unpredictable nature of networked global complexity, he opens his account up to the criticism that the global-complexity scenario implies that order and continuity can never be achieved: 'the emergent global order is one of constant disorder and disequilibrium' (Urry, 2000, p 208). If this is so, then even the notion of network, despite being defined very loosely in terms of flows and scapes, becomes chronically unstable. Network moves from being a kind of orderliness and towards being a kind of anarchy. Replacing the modernist concept of structure with the reflexivity theorists' concept of network is useful and informative because it encourages social theorists to try to see social interaction in a different perspective. If, however, the concept of network is defined in terms of almost total fluidity both between the nodes in a particular network and between one network and another, then it becomes very difficult to formulate an analysis at all. It is a bit like trying to find regularities and patterns in a bucket of water, and without a bucket to put the water in!

Network agency

The same concept of complex disordering undermines the capacity to analyse social action more directly. If, as Urry (2000, p 16) suggests, 'the ordering of social life is presumed to be contingent, unpredictable, patterned and irreducible to human subjects', then we are bound to ask whether this list of presumptions is *already* untenable; how can social life be 'ordered' and 'patterned' and at the same time 'contingent' and 'unpredictable'? Is it reasonable to propose a concept of global order that is inherently *disordering*? In this respect, Urry's attempt to move beyond ideas about structure and agency, to open up the border country between them as the new and de-traditionalised territory for social theory, seems to require a degree of lateral reflexivity that the analytical machinery of social theory will find difficult to achieve. As Urry puts it: 'The enormously open character of global systems might mean that they are currently beyond systematic analysis. One could hypothesize that current phenomena have outrun the capacity of the social sciences to investigate' (Urry, 2003, p 38). One could reply that the challenge for social theory, just as it is for other modes of systematic theorising, is to *impose* some kind of intelligent order on chaos; noting the existence of chaos is where we begin, not where we end.

Technological networks and social networks

In the same way that Herbert Spencer took biological evolution too literally as a metaphor for social evolution (see Chapter Two), Urry could be accused of taking technological developments in networking too literally as a model for envisaging social networking. To the extent that the material that flows in an electrical cable or fibre-optic string is not the same as the material that flows between social actors linked together in an interactive social network, the substance and behaviour of networking in a technical sense is *not the same* as the substance and behaviour of actors who are networking in a social sense. There always will be a difference between the hard networks of technology and the soft networks of human social interaction. Luhmann's concept of autopoietic systems, for example, which Urry incorporates into this own approach, has been criticised for using a cybernetic notion of information flow within systems/networks and of communication between systems that is modelled closely on the computer-like management of data in the form of binary codes. It is far from clear whether human beings process information and communicate in quite the same way.

Persistent systems theory

Although in some respects Urry wants to avoid linking the notion of 'social network' with the notion of 'social system', it is certainly possible to see much of his account of global networks, however fluid and complex they might be, as a version of systems theory. Reviving an idea from the functionalist version of system theory, which is that patterns or functional connections will always be found at some level of generality, one might conclude that theorising global complexity inevitably draws the theorist towards concepts like network and social system. It is difficult to see how this level of analysis can be made without using such concepts. Despite incorporating notions of non-linearity, fluidity and circularity into the concept of global complexity, Urry's notion of network-as-system is still vulnerable to many of the criticisms raised against systems theory (see Chapter Six). For example:

- Networks/systems eliminate individual autonomy.
- If networks/systems are self-reliant and self-contained, it is not clear how they change over time.
- Are the interactions between one system and another of the same order as interactions between the nodes within any particular system?
- What are the purposes of the network/system?

In terms of their impact on social theory more generally, the difference between Lash and Urry's account of reflexive modernisation, and to a greater extent still of Urry's later contributions in social/cultural theory, is that compared with the more traditionally modernist approaches of Beck and Giddens, the former certainly see the consequences of reflexive modernisation as having the potential for a much more radical reshaping of some of the conceptual equipment of social theory. Lash and Urry express ideas that are more de-traditionalised than those of many of their modernist contemporaries. In drawing on complexity theory and theories of chaos, which are much more commonly found in the natural sciences, Urry certainly follows his own advice, which is to incorporate into social science insights gained from the physical and biological sciences. These theorists do not just preach theoretical reflexivity, they try to practise it as well.

Social theory and the 'turn to culture'

The social theory-versus-cultural theory debate

The third key issue we are addressing in this chapter is the changing relationship between social theory and cultural theory. As should have become clear from our discussion of reflexive modernisation and of globalisation, much of the energy that drives social change at the start of the 21st century, and many of its consequences, are interpreted by social theorists as being firmly located in the realm of culture. Theories of globalisation, for example, did not really begin to invigorate the social-theoretical imagination until the focus shifted away from theories of global economic activity (theories that had been in vogue at least since Lenin's classic *Imperialism, the Highest Stage of Capitalism* [1917]), and towards the cultural dimensions of globalisation. An important first step here was Roland Robertson's (1992) *Globalization: Social Theory and Global Culture*, which contains a detailed plea for modernist social theorists to wise up to the central importance of 'cultural studies' even if *theories of* culture were still less clearly distinguishable. He is critical, for example, of Giddens' otherwise widely influential account of globalisation precisely because it lacks a properly worked out analysis of the cultural dimension: 'The whole idea that one can sensibly interpret the contemporary world without addressing the issues that arise from current debates about the politics of culture, cultural capital, cultural difference, cultural homogeneity and heterogeneity, ethnicity, nationalism, race, gender, and so on, is implausible' (Robertson, 1992, p 145).

Similar appeals in respect of the importance of the cultural domain have been made by other theorists working along the border country between social theory and cultural theory. The influential British theorist Mike Featherstone, for example, went further than Robertson in suggesting not only that the kinds of materials and processes that cultural theorists were interested in could make a major impact on social theory, but that the realm of culture *as a whole* needed to be taken more seriously:

> Culture was too often regarded as readily circumscribed, something derivative which was there to be explained. It was rarely conceived of as opening up a set of problems which, once tackled, could question and overturn such hierarchically constituted oppositions and separations [including economy–culture, production–consumption, work–leisure]. A set of problems which, when constituted in its most radical form, could

challenge the viability of our existing modes of conceptualisation. (Featherstone, 1992, p vii)

This quotation raises the stakes in the society–versus–culture debate because it suggests that social theory will never reach its potential unless it is prepared to reflect on whether its own basic formulation about how the various bits of society fit together, a formulation that has remained more or less unchallenged in modernist social theory since it was devised by Marx, Weber and Durkheim, is still up to the job. Although contemporary modernist social theorists like Habermas and Giddens have tended to regard postmodernism as a rather one-legged affair, being mainly a philosophical and epistemological discourse that is preoccupied with the aesthetic aspects of social existence, many leading cultural theorists do not see it quite like that. For theorists like Featherstone, Bryan S. Turner and Zygmunt Bauman, working along the new cultural theory axis developed through the influential academic journal *Theory, Culture and Society*, postmodernism has itself become a social/cultural phenomenon, the study of which gives rise to new kinds of cultural/social theory. As Turner puts it:

> I take the stand that postmodernism does reflect important changes, not so much in the structure of industrial capitalism, but in the place and nature of culture.... The weakness of traditional sociology has been its inability adequately to analyse culture. Postmodernism as a style of analysis can be seen as an attempt to provide an analysis of culture in late capitalism. (Turner, in Rojek and Turner, 1993, pp 73–4)

To culture or not to culture? That is the question

One of the especially difficult conceptual dilemmas that has to be overcome here, and one that is raised in a particularly acute form by the globalisation debate, is whether, if we are living in an era of global-cultural de-differentiation, it still makes sense to try to distinguish one actually existing national society from another on the basis of cultural difference. Cultural difference has generally been regarded as one of the key criteria for defining what societal boundedness is. Despite having so many economic and political institutions and attitudes in common, 'the British' are different from 'the Americans' because of cultural differences. If one of the emerging characteristics of a new global culture, possibly circulating by means of the fluid and mobile global networks described by Castells, Lash, Urry and others, is that it has no such boundedness, then does this not imply the redundancy of the concept of 'society' altogether? Might it be possible to theorise two dimensions of culture or cultural agency acting simultaneously; one based on residual notions of national-cultural differences and another based on an emerging sense of cosmopolitan global identity? If it turns out that the emergence of a homogenised global culture is improbable, then this might add considerable weight to the notion that 'society' really is a kind of bounded system. The null hypothesis of the globalisation scenario would confirm that actually existing national societies, and the associated concept of 'society' as a bounded system, have been the correct units of analysis for social theory all along!

Developments in society

In terms of the emergence of new kinds of social and cultural practices the latter certainly do now have a very sophisticated institutional and discursive infrastructure of their own. Lash and Urry's 'economy of signs and spaces' and Castells' 'network society' are attempts not only to characterise late-modern society as profoundly cultural, but to describe in some detail what the cultural realm consists of. It is not, in other words, just a question of being a bit more sensitive to the non-economic elements in the social mix, but of recognising that late-modern (postmodern) society is increasingly dominated by the hardware and software of expressive symbols, leisure, pleasure and enjoyment. If we accept Lash and Urry's version of the theory of reflexive modernisation, which identifies the communication and information infrastructure as a structural feature of reflexive modernisation, and an increasing preoccupation with signs and meanings as essential to the activities of reflexivity, then the quest for cultural goods might indeed have pulled ahead of the quest for economic and political goods. One of the conclusions that contemporary social theorists are facing up to is whether reflexive modernisation actively produces a much more cultural form of social practice. Many of the new skills associated with reflexive identity are precisely those needed for getting the most out of the new forms of mobile communications and complex consumption.

Developments in social theory

In terms of developments in social theory, the general sweep of European social theory during the second half of the 20th century has undoubtedly been strongly influenced by the post-structuralist and postmodernist preoccupation with questions about meaning and interpretation (modernist and postmodernist approaches are compared in detail in Chapter Thirteen). To the extent that the cultural realm is the realm of expressive symbols, the place where meanings and discourses are formed and circulated, 'culture' again asserts itself as a primary rather than supplementary domain of analysis for social theory.

This trend is further strengthened by accounts of globalised and globalising processes that, as we have seen, are theorised as being deeply infused with cultural practices. Social theorists who are interested in analysing the global dimensions of change need also to become cultural theorists. Certainly Urry is strongly of the opinion that the challenge of developing a general social theory of the global dimension is not helped by the fact that boundaries are still being maintained between social theory and cultural theory: 'mobilities rather than societies should be at the heart of a reconstituted social sciences' (Urry, 2000, p 210). A similar view has been put forward by Beck: 'The ageing sociology of modernization must ... liberate itself from its own intellectual blockades' (Beck, in Beck et al., 1994, p 24). Moving the old concept of 'society' as a bounded system from the centre-stage and replacing it with a concept of 'mobility' certainly also implies a major shift away from 'the social' and towards 'the cultural'.

The de-traditionalisation of social theory

We have noted a number of times in his chapter that theorists of reflexive modernisation are strongly of the view that social theory needs to apply a certain amount of reflexivity to its own activities. In this final section it will be useful to look at a number of different attempts to find ways of reconciling social theory with cultural theory. Rather than treating the territories of social theory and cultural theory as a kind of academic turf war, we could ask instead how, at the level of theory, the two realms might become more closely interrelated.

Delanty on culture as reflexive mediation

A first attempt at theoretical reconciliation has been proposed by the social and cultural theorist Gerard Delanty. Delanty sees culture as a reflexive realm that mediates between social actors and social structures: 'Viewing culture as a form of mediation between agency and structure, we can make the further claim that it is transformative. Mediation ... is a dialectical process of transformation' (Delanty, 1999, p 10). Drawing partly on Jeffrey Alexander's (1998) **neo-functionalist** analysis in which 'culture' is seen as being autonomous from 'structure', and thus as deserving full analysis in its own right, Delanty theorises culture, like Giddens theorises structure, as something that is **instantiated** at the moment when action takes place: 'Action is exercised through, not against, culture; it is inherently related to culture and is not a process standing outside it. But action is also autonomous in that it does not simply reproduce or internalize culture; it can also transform it' (Delanty, 1999, p 62). In this scenario social theory needs a strong concept of culture. It needs to see the cultural realm as having an integrative role in shaping and creating social experience because, without it, social theory finds it difficult to theorise the links between agents and structures under conditions of reflexive modernisation. Delanty's formulation encourages us to think of culture both as having the same kind of relationship with agency as does structure, and as making a significant contribution to the process by which social actors negotiate their way around and between those social structures.

Margaret Archer

A second solution to theory wars is the work of the leading social-cultural theorist Margaret Archer, who has taken a strong interest in developing a new formulation of the relationship between structure and culture. Archer is particularly well-known in social theory for her critique of Giddens' use of the concept of duality to reconcile the forces of structure and agency (see Chapter Twelve). For Archer, it is essential to retain a clear *analytical distinction* between structure and agency (even if ontologically speaking, as kinds of matter, they are intimately related), otherwise it becomes impossible to understand the social phenomena that arise out of, or are constituted by the coming-together of, structure and agency. For Archer the whole basis of the social-theoretical method is undermined if theorists simply 'conflate' or try to merge together its basic analytical categories; conflation is a cardinal sin that destroys attempts at theory making. There is in fact no great challenge in seeing things as part of an amorphous whole, since clearly at the highest level of generalisation everything is simply part of 'matter'. Archer has developed a strong version of the 'against duality' argument precisely because it conflates basic categories in this way. Archer holds a similarly firm line in asserting that 'the structural and cultural domains are substantively very different, as well as being relatively autonomous from one another' (Archer, 1988, p ix).

One of the clear advantages, as Archer sees it, of maintaining a clear analytical separation between the categories of the cultural realm and the social realm is that it offers an exciting new way of bringing social theory and cultural theory closer together. Highlighting the analytical usefulness to social theorists of the distinction the theorist David Lockwood (1964) made between **social integration** and **systems integration** (see Chapter Six), she proposes that Lockwood's technique of looking at how social structures and social agents fit together could be profitably applied in looking at 'the parts' and 'the people' in the analysis of culture: 'the problem of culture and agency directly [parallels] the much more familiar problem of structure and agency' (Archer, 1988, p xxv). She therefore proposes unification between social theory and cultural theory on the grounds that the relations between social agents and cultural practices and institutions are essentially of the same order as relations between social agents and social practices and institutions. Social theory and cultural theory are first-cousins in the sense that they are characterised by very similar kinds of relatedness.

Unification of the kind proposed by Archer would settle two problems. First it would prevent social theory from being entirely preoccupied with the structure–agency dilemma at the expense of the culture–agency dilemma. A preoccupation that, as noted in the quotations at the start of this part of the chapter, has resulted in the 'progressive subordination of culture until it becomes an epiphenomenon of structure' (Archer, 1990, p 98). Second, and accepting the principle of non-conflation that the two sets of social dynamics are analytically distinct, unification makes it possible to understand the connections *between* these two sets of dynamics. A bit like conceiving the rungs of a ladder that hold together *and* hold apart the two vertical parts of the framework, the relations of the social-cultural 'whole' can only be understood if the theoretical perspective that is looking at them has some unified concept of what the whole 'ladder' looks like.

Morphogenics

Unhappy as she is with Giddens' technique of conflating the categories of agency and structure, Archer develops an alternative account using the idea of 'morphogenesis'. **Morphogenics** is based on the relatively simple idea that social structures and social agents, cultural structures and cultural agents, are perpetually changing as a result of the mutual interaction between structure/culture and agency. In the same way that past experience (as a kind of structure) always affects action taking place in the present (agency), as soon as action has taken place the structure of past action has also changed: 'Analytically speaking, the relation between agency and structure is one of historical alternation between the conditioning of agents by structure and the elaboration of structure by interacting agents. Given time, systems can be both cause and caused, as can agency. Analytical dualism depends on temporality' (Archer, 1995, p 694; Parker, 2000, pp 74–5).

Taking a few moderate liberties, we can note that the theory of **structuration** and the theory of morphogenesis tend to converge in how the linkages between agency and structure and agency and culture are defined. Giddens defines 'structure' as the rules-and-resources that agents draw upon in order to act in a meaningful way, while Archer defines 'culture' quite similarly as a set of resources that agents use to negotiate their way through relations with other actors and as a way of coping with, and if necessary making changes in, social institutions. The difference between structuration theory and morphogenics might come down to a quite subtle variation in ideas about the time frame over which these processes of social change operate.

Structuration is closely aligned with Giddens' key concept of **instantiation**, which specifies that actions take on an identifiable form in the instant that they are enacted. Instantiation thus has a relatively short time frame that is virtually confined to the moment of experience itself (hence also the tendency for structuration/instantiation to be a force of social reproduction not social change). Although the 'morphs' or changes envisaged in Archer's theory of morphogenics can be either long term or short term, they are generally seen as having a *strategic* dimension and thus as operating over the at least medium term (hence the tendency for morphogenesis to be seen as a force of social change, not just of reproduction). As long as social theorists and cultural theorists are prepared to exercise a bit of reflexive imagination, it might be possible to agree that although 'culture' is not exactly the same thing as 'structure', both tend to operate in the same way in the sense that they provide *contextual resources* that social actors draw on and that shape and enable their actions in various ways. If we accept that agency is always 'of the present', both culture and structure might usefully be thought of as 'of the past' in the sense that they are a result of *previous* interactions. The terms 'structure' and 'culture' could almost be used interchangeably in that some structures could certainly be described as 'cultural', while culture could be regarded as providing part of the 'structural' context for action.

Frederic Jameson and the 'cultural logic' of capitalism

Another contribution to the debates about the relations between structure and culture has been made by the American social/cultural theorist Frederic Jameson. Unlike Lash and Urry, Delanty, Archer and others who are fairly determined to work out some of the analytical benefits of theorising structure and culture together, Jameson tends to rely on a more traditional construction in which culture is closely linked with (rather than autonomous from) other historical/structural features of modern society, especially economic ones. His highly influential argument, originally published in 1984 in the Marxist journal *New Left Review* as 'Postmodernism, or the cultural logic of late capitalism', is simply that postmodern cultural forms should not be seen as providing evidence of a radically new and distinct type of social formation (a formation that is dominated by cultural matters), but is actually more accurately understandable as 'the superstructural form' of late capitalism. Like Habermas and other contemporary modernists who have at various times followed a broadly Marxist approach, Jameson is a critical theorist in the sense that he maintains that there is a causal link between the cultural realm and the capitalist economy. As Jameson puts it: 'every position on postmodernism in culture ... is also at one and the same time, and *necessarily*, an implicitly or explicitly political stance on the nature of multinational capitalism today' (Jameson, 1991, p 3, original emphasis).

In his critical commentary on postmodernist cultural forms, Jameson draws a strong parallel between the particular historical/structural form of *Late Capitalism* developed by the Marxist economist Ernest Mandel (1975), and the particular cultural form of late- or **postmodernity**. Jameson suggests that mass production and commercialisation of artistic expression has reduced artistic creations to the level of ordinary commodities. Rather than providing a critical reflection upon the social world, which gave social actors time and space to think about stuff around them, art (or aesthetic reflexivity as Lash and Urry might call it) has become instead just another element of consumption: 'So, in postmodern culture, "culture" has become a product in its own right ... modernism was still minimally and tendentially the critique of the commodity and the effort to make it transcend itself. Postmodernism is the consumption of sheer commodification as a process' (Jameson, 1991, p x).

Artistic productions lose their own space and identity to such an extent that their emancipatory potential is lost. For Jameson, rather than representing a new threshold of liberation, as Lyotard had implied in his critique of the old modernist **grand narratives**, or new possibilities for critical reflexivity, as Lash and Urry have argued, postmodernism actually demonstrates the final collapse of any possibility that the cultural realm could remain independent from the structural/economic realm. Postmodernism signifies the final subordination of the cultural to the socio-economic.

Although Jameson is often interpreted as seeing the link between structure and culture as a linear one of cause and effect, he does, however, acknowledge a degree of reciprocity between the two. As he puts it: 'No satisfactory model of a given mode or production can exist without a theory of the historically and dialectically specific and unique role of "culture" within it' (Jameson, in Lyotard, 1984 [1979], p xv). Even if we take a hard-line traditionalist view in seeing culture as a product of structure we still have to pay close attention to culture because it shows us more clearly the current state of structural/economic relations: 'the interrelationship of culture and the economic is not a one-way street but a continuous reciprocal interaction and feedback loop' (Jameson, 1991, pp xiv–xv). To the extent that, like Mandel's analysis of late capitalism, events are examined at an across-the-globe level, postmodernism can also be understood as a global-cultural form. The fact that postmodernism *is* a global-cultural form thus confirms *the global nature* of late capitalism.

Concluding comments

One of the major challenges of developing an adequate theory of reflexive modernisation and of theorising the global is to trace *the connections* between all the fascinating changes that seem to be taking place among the social and cultural structures of late-modern society, and the social actors who give these changes a sense of meaning and significance. As Delanty puts it: 'If anything characterizes recent social theory it is the question of the possibilities for the autonomy of the subject under conditions of the fragmentation of the social and the increasing loss of unity in modern society' (Delanty, 1999, p 3). Current answers to the question 'What *does* happen to agency under conditions of reflexive modernization?' have so far been answered by social theorists using concepts of reflexivity, de-traditionalisation and individualisation. And all of these concepts in their turn raise further questions about experience and interpretation that cultural theorists would seem to be strongly placed to answer. Having said this, for theorists working from a postmodernist position, and this includes a large number of cultural theorists, this conclusion might seem rather depressing as it tends to restate, even if in slightly updated language, the age-old problem in social theory or how structure and agency fit together. Any notion of structure, even if it is remodelled on the template of networks, necessarily implies the presence of entities that have identifiable boundaries, and the strong notion of the bounded entity is one of the first things that postmodernists have tried to reject as an outmoded analytical category.

Perhaps the most certain conclusion we can reach on the basis of our discussion in this chapter is that any social theory of the global, of the global dimensions of social change and of globalisation has to begin with a reasonably clear idea of what its basic unit of analysis is going to be. Although the concept of society and its referent actually existing national societies are far from perfect, they have provided a reasonable degree of consensus about the subject matter of social theory. What the concept of globalisation has done is to challenge this consensus by suggesting that processes of change are now in play that are not the result of goings-on at the level of national society, their institutions and practices, but that local circumstances are *being shaped by* forces that arise at a uniquely modern level of global activity.

According to the theorists discussed in this chapter at any rate, 'the global' offers a genuinely new level at which social analysis has to be conducted. And in order to achieve this it will be necessary to devise new conceptual tools and new research perspectives in making this analysis possible. Although it might not be a condition of this process that the boundaries between social theory and cultural theory have to be brought down completely, analysing the global does seem to imply that insights gained from studying cultural phenomena have much to offer. To the extent that social agents really are increasingly preoccupied by expressive symbols, with meaning and interpretation, then as it attempts to devise strategies for understanding the global, social theory might be expected to become more culturally oriented in its own activities.

Key points box – In this chapter we have looked at:

☑ Giddens' and Beck's theory of reflexive modernisation, which emphasises that the original processes of modernisation became increasingly radicalised during the 20th century giving rise to new kinds of disembedding in time and space and to accelerated forms of reflexivity.

☑ Beck's characterisation of late 20th-century society as 'risk society' in which perceptions of risk, knowledge about risk and exposure to risk become simultaneously more acute and yet more difficult to identify and control.

☑ Lash and Urry's theory, which sees current social change as being driven by the transition towards a social culture dominated by expressive symbols or signs, and by the energetic quest for new meanings.

☑ Lash and Urry's reinstatement in social theory of the subjective, expressive and emotionally charged social actor. Increasing individualisation among social actors is a necessary accompaniment to de-traditionalisation at the institutional and structural level.

☑ How Urry adapts Manuel Castells' concept of network society to analyse a new mode of social connectedness based on complex global networks, a development closely associated with new information and communications technologies.

☑ Debates on globalisation in social theory, which centre on whether new social structures and practices are emerging that can *only* be theorised at the global rather than national or local level.

☑ How modernisation and globalisation both pose questions for social theorists that cultural theorists might already be well placed to answer.

☑ Social and cultural theorists who argue both for and against maintaining the separateness of these two realms of social institutions and social action.

☑ How Archer argues for convergence between social theory and cultural theory not by conflating their distinctive analytical constructs, but by looking at similarities in the way they do their theorising.

Practice box

⊃ What is 'reflexive' about *reflexive modernisation*?

⊃ What do Beck and Giddens mean when they say that the forces of modernisation have become 'radicalised'?

⊃ In what ways might the experience of 'time' and 'space' be different in traditional, modern and late-modern society?

⊃ Briefly define the notions of *de-traditionalisation* and *individualisation* used by Giddens and Beck, and by Lash and Urry.

⊃ What part do these concepts play in theories of reflexive modernisation?

⊃ How can you tell if modern society is a more or less risky place to live than pre-modern society?

⊃ What do Lash and Urry think are the main weaknesses of Giddens' and Beck's theory of reflexive modernisation?

⊃ Give an example of why theories about global processes tend to undermine the idea of social action taking place mainly within clearly defined legal and geographical boundaries.

⊃ What are the differences in social theory between the concept of 'structures' and the concept of 'networks'?

⊃ Do you think we are now living in 'network society'?

⊃ What does Jameson mean when he says that postmodernism is the 'superstructural form' of late capitalism?

⊃ Why do theories of globalisation and reflexive modernisation need to include a cultural dimension?

⊃ Describe one way in which social theory and cultural theory might be brought closer together.

Further reading

Margaret Archer, *Realist Social Theory: The Morphogenic Approach* (Cambridge University Press, 1995).

Jakob Arnoldi, *Risk: An Introduction* (Polity Press, 2009).

Ulrich Beck, *Risk Society: Towards a New Modernity* (Sage, 1992 [1986]); and *What is Globalization?* (Polity Press, 2000).

Ulrich Beck, Anthony Giddens and Scott Lash, *Reflexive Modernization: Politics, Tradition and Aesthetics in the Modern Social Order* (Stanford University Press, 1994).

Peter Beilharz, *A Bauman Reader* (Blackwell, 2001).

Alex Callinicos, *An Anti-Capitalist Manifesto* (Polity Press, 2003).

Manuel Castells, *The Information Age*, Vol. 1, *The Rise of Network Society* (Blackwell, 1996).

Gerard Delanty, *Modernity and Postmodernity* (Sage, 2000).

Anthony Giddens, *The Consequences of Modernity* (Polity Press, 1990); and *Runaway World: How Globalization is Reshaping Our Lives* (Routledge, 2000).

David Held and Anthony McGrew, *Globalization/Anti-Globalization* (Polity Press, 2002); and *The Global Transformations Reader: An Introduction to the Globalization Debate* (Polity Press, 2000).

Scott Lash and John Urry, *The End of Organized Capitalism* (Polity Press, 1987).

Roland Robertson, *Globalization: Social Theory and Global Culture* (Sage, 1992).

John Urry, *Global Complexity* (Polity Press, 2003).

Malcolm Waters, *Globalization* (Routledge, 1995).

Websites

For the contemporary authors discussed in this chapter the most effective internet search strategy is to enter their names into the search engines. Also try entering the key phrases 'risk', 'risk society', 'globalisation' and 'network society' and follow the links from there.

For a comprehensive list of links to worldwide organisations involved in the globalisation debate try Globalization101, which is situated in the Levin Institute at the State University of New York: www.globalization101.org/index.html

Also try the Global Policy Forum, which is an independent policy-monitoring organisation associated with the United Nations, in New York: www.globalpolicy.org/home.html

CHAPTER FIFTEEN

THE BOUNDARY PROBLEM IN CONTEMPORARY SOCIAL THEORY

In this short concluding chapter we take a step back from the descriptions of social phenomena that are being produced by social theory in order to take stock of what has been happening to social theory both as a body of knowledge and as a strategy or set of techniques for trying to understand social phenomena. If, to use a popular academic metaphor, social theory provides 'a toolkit for looking at society', then it is certainly worth pausing to look over the current state of those tools and at the main tasks that social theorists imagine they can be used for.

In this chapter we will look at:

The current constitution of social theory

The boundedness of social theory

The material in the first part of the chapter is presented in the form of a series of loose reflections on three of what we can call the dynamic couplets of social theory. The three dynamic couplets we will be looking at are:

- knowledge and strategy;
- theory and evidence;
- social theory as objective enquiry or as political practice.

In the second part of the chapter we will look at what is perhaps the most challenging question social theorists periodically encounter, which is the problem of **boundedness**. If, as recent accounts of globalisation have suggested, it is no longer feasible to see social processes as contained within local or even national boundaries, then can social theory carry on using 'society' as its basic unit of analysis?

The current constitution of social theory

Knowledge and strategy

The first dynamic couplet lies at the heart of social theory as a serious academic undertaking. Social theory is comprised of two main elements: a body of knowledge about social phenomena that it has built up over the years and a set of techniques for looking at social phenomena. These two elements exist in a state of dynamic tension, however, since it is not possible to ignore what is already known when making fresh analyses. One of the key properties of social theory is circularity in the way social theorists continuously refer back to the body of knowledge they already have before setting out new propositions.

Bodies of knowledge

One of the most important factors that limits the capacity for social theory to develop a complete knowledge of society, to accumulate a thorough inventory of social facts in quite the same way that the physical and biological sciences may be able to do, is that the object of social theory, which is to say the highly complex and fluid interactions between social actors and institutional contexts, is fundamentally variable. The limits of knowledge in social theory are thus set by the inconclusive and dynamic constitution of the phenomenon it is trying to analyse. Although certainly problematic this difficulty produces one of the great strengths of social theory, which is that the techniques it uses are also flexible and dynamic. Perhaps the main achievement of social theory, given the difficult task it sets for itself, is its capacity for generating a fairly constant stream of new concepts and ideas for looking at social action. As a set of intellectual and academic practices social theory deploys a rich body of knowledge or 'provisional understandings' that it has accumulated about the social world over the past century or so but in such a way that it is never closed to refining and adjusting its techniques of investigation. The other half of the dynamic duo of social theory as an academic undertaking sees social theory less as an accumulation of facts and more as a process of investigation. Social theory is able to shift its focus, to discontinue some lines of enquiry and open itself up to new ones in response to the social and political conditions that surround it. One could go so far as to say that social theory places particular emphasis on its strategic capacity rather than on the accumulation of facts because, in the end, facts are far less interesting than the process of investigation that may lead to their discovery.

Social theory as philosophical enquiry

The somewhat elusive and problematic nature of the subject matter of social theory also helps us understand why, as an academic undertaking in its own right, social theory often operates at a somewhat abstract level of analysis. Since both knowledge claims and the means of making them are under constant review any constancy they do have depends on social theorists being able to agree, even if only temporarily, that such-and-such a thing *can* be accepted as true or valid and that this-or-that analytical technique *does* work. These discussions and disputes form part of the **epistemological** core of social theory because they are about agreeing the limits of social-theoretical knowledge (what is knowable, what is known and what can become known). This is not to say that epistemological debates do not go on in the physical and biological sciences, but that in social theory they are an ever-present or chronic feature of the discipline. This also explains one of the recurrent features of social theory, which is that it is an inherently **reflexive** undertaking.

Critical realism

In recognising that there remains a substantial difference between theoretical constructs and the actually existing phenomena they seek to illuminate, social theory is perpetually confronted with how to manage the transition between real reality and its representation in the analytic-conceptual world of theory. One possible solution to this theorist's dilemma, and one that has become popular at least partly because it offers a kind of 'middle kingdom' between theory-world and real-world, is **critical realism**. Developed in its most influential form in the work of Roy Bhaskar (1979), critical realism uses the technique of thinking about the underlying causes of real-world happenings by developing analytical concepts whose mode of operating can be inferred from surface events. These analytical concepts can then be applied in looking for explanations of other kinds of social happenings. Critical realism envisages three levels or strata of reality; the 'actual' is the strata of events that really do happen; the 'empirical' is the strata of reality in which social actors become aware of and express knowledge about these really real events. The feelings and experiences that social actors have are also literally 'real' even though there might be some disjuncture or slippage between 'what really happened' and what participants *thought* had happened. The third level is the 'deep' level, which cannot be directly observed but is believed to consist of the mechanisms that produce effects at the other two levels.

There are obvious parallels here with the techniques of **psychoanalysis** and with the **structuralist** method. In the case of the former, there is no way of knowing for sure whether the unconscious mind is structured in the way that Freud imagined, nor that there are any real entities called Ego, Superego and Id. These constructs are, however, very useful heuristic devices for helping the therapist to resolve actual mental disturbances in the real world of the client. A similar analytical operation is used by structuralist social theorists who invented the idea of **deep structures** as a way of trying to explain how surface phenomena, like the syntactical organisation of words to form intelligible sentences, emerge from cognitive resources that cannot be observed directly. Whether or not we are prepared to agree with Bhaskar (or with Freud or Saussure for that matter) that these structuring or organising mechanisms do exist as some yet-to-be-confirmed physiological or cognitive entities, or whether we prefer to think of them as being purely analytical, they have certainly supplied social theorists with some useful and powerful explanatory devices.

The privileged position of the social theorist

Finally under the heading of knowledge and strategy we should note that the epistemological difficulties of social theory are associated with another dilemma, which is what kind of special status can social theorists claim for the provisional knowledge they are developing? One of the main criticisms raised by **post-structuralist** and **postmodernist** social theorists is that classical and modernist social theorists had fooled themselves into believing that, in the manner of a natural-scientific investigation, they really were developing some concrete and reliable conclusions about social phenomena. The main target of this accusation was the broader **Enlightenment** perspective, which included the core idea that positive scientific knowledge about the social world was achievable and that this knowledge and those who possessed it occupied a pretty important place in the hierarchy of knowledge. Following this challenge social theory has tried hard to move beyond the idea that one view of social phenomena, no matter how expert, is better than all the other views. **Functionalists** and **social interactionists** see the social world differently and deploy different concepts and techniques for examining it but ultimately it is very difficult to agree on some criteria for determining whether the accounts produced by one perspective are more accurate or worthwhile than those produced by another. The uneasy compromise has been to accept that different views of society are available and that none is inherently more truthful or meaningful than another. Social theory can also be strongly affected by intellectual trends, which means that the supremacy of one discourse over another will always partly be to do with levels of popularity.

Theory and evidence

Taking a slightly different tack, one of the criticisms most often made against social theory is precisely that it lacks **empirical** groundedness; that its linkages with actual reality are sometimes so tenuous that the worlds of theoretical speculation and of actual reality only ever meet by coincidence, never by appointment. One rather philosophical response to this accusation is to ask what grounds there are for assuming that *any* claims about the 'real' nature of 'actual' reality, whether they come from experts or from non-experts, are more empirically valid than any other. Realistically, we might have to accept that there are only ever *degrees of* groundedness. A little more constructively the theorist might reflect a little on the relationship between theory and empirical evidence. Fortunately, and although the question of where theory meets evidence is a perpetual one in social theory, this is one area of debate where reasonable agreement has been reached.

Following the recommendations of the functionalist theorist R.K. Merton (1949), a threefold distinction has been provisionally accepted. At one extreme we have full abstraction in which social theory produces its own resources and becomes an end in itself. Mid-range abstraction is the domain where social theory provides propositions of a more intermediate kind, which could in their turn be used for developing some specific questions about social phenomena. Third, and least abstract, are specific hypotheses that can be put to the test in the manner of a scientific experiment. In a more recent formulation, Nicos Mouzelis (1995, p 1) makes a similarly useful distinction between theory as 'conceptual framework, paradigm, metatheory or heuristic device' and theory as 'substantive theory', which is made up of actual detailed propositions about how the real world is. Social theorists have spent a good deal of time and energy reflecting on how the proving or disproving of substantive statements feeds back into either a confirmation or a revision of the conceptual framework that gave rise to the substantive proposition in the first place. Although there is continual discussion in social theory over how original ideas are taken up by social theorists, the emergence of novel statements of fact that cannot be easily accommodated within either the mid-range or within the abstract frameworks currently available, is certainly one of the ways in which new paradigms emerge. If a series of facts emerge that cannot be explained within the existing paradigms in social theory, then, once the initial furore has died down, the solution is to develop a new paradigm that *can* accommodate them.

The problem of interpretation

An associated manifestation of the problem of evidence for social theorists is the problem of interpretation. Although laboratory science also involves interpretation of data of various kinds, and certainly there are subjective choices when designing the research project in the first place, the kinds of evidence on which social theorists draw is almost always open to a variety of different interpretations. The link, in other words, between the evidence and the theorist's interpretation of it is always rather precarious. We can illustrate this difficulty by comparing social theory with cultural theory, which tends to adopt a more relaxed attitude towards drifting from theory to descriptive material and back again. The problem of evidence versus interpretation arises in a more acute form in cultural theory than it does in social theory for at least two reasons. First, and as objects of analysis, the various cultural artefacts and activities that form the core of cultural studies, for example a film, a visit to a gallery or a package holiday, have a degree of expressive content that makes them correspondingly difficult to analyse in an intellectually objective way. Second, and as a form of social/cultural action, the participation associated with the consumption and enjoyment of these artefacts is very much along the aesthetic dimension of reflection and appreciation. The mode of social activity associated with real cultural stuff, in other words, is already quite a long way up the subjective and interpretive end of the scale. To the extent that it is unavoidable for cultural theorists to engage in a fair amount of interpretation themselves when describing cultural artefacts and activities (interpretation being an integral part of what 'culture' is), it becomes more and more difficult to maintain an identifiable gap between what *the theorist thinks* about a particular phenomenon and the claims the theorist subsequently makes about how *other social actors* might be experiencing it.

Social theory as objective enquiry or as political practice

The third main aspect of social theory we need to reflect on is its critical dimension. There is a strong tradition among social theorists to regard social-theoretical knowledge not just as 'hard facts' associated with scientific undertakings, but as providing knowledge that has a direct bearing on social development. Given the rather intimate way in which social-theoretical knowledge is intertwined with its subject matter (which is to say neither it nor the theorists who produce it can be treated as separate or distinct from the social phenomena they are studying), the political interests of the theorist must be regarded as a matter of degree. Even very prominent social theorists who make a special effort not to become associated with any particular political objectives end up being criticised for showing a lack of moral commitment by theorists who are less cautious in this respect. In its more assertive form social-theoretical knowledge is regarded as providing legitimate support for arguments that society is not working as it should. Lengthy discussions then follow about what 'should' means and what 'the alternatives' are.

Maintaining critical distance

For many modernist social theorists the critical distance that can be achieved by careful training in the techniques of social theorising provides much of the **immanent** or 'from within' criticism of society as it currently is. The critical potential of social theory becomes one of the basic design features of the discipline on the grounds that informed criticism of society must come from within that body of specialist social-theoretical knowledge developed by social theorists. And the logical justification for *this* position is that it is difficult to argue persuasively that there are vantage points from which actually existing social reality can be observed that are not already located within society. There is no such thing as an extra-social vantage point. The essential continuity, for example, within all Marxist social theory is that followers of Marx are certain that, at the time he developed his ideas, Marx had achieved greater critical distance than almost any other social theorist in the insights that he gained. Distinguishing the appearance of things in capitalist society from how they really are in essence proved to be a key moment in the process of actual social change. The practical impact of Marx's critical social theory on the political and social development of Western society in the 20th century is proof that critical distance can be achieved, that this critical momentum comes from within the system as it currently exists, and that it can make a real and, some would say, necessary difference to the future shape and direction of society. Marxist social theorists differ in what they expect the outcome of such upheavals will be, but they all agree that immanent critique is a *necessary part* of social development. Although 19th-century classifications of social theory as occupying top position in the hierarchy of human knowledge would be expressed differently today, it is undeniable that the critical and reflexive instincts of social theory remain a powerful force within processes of social change.

The boundedness of social theory

The inception of social theory was marked by a strong insistence from its founding figures that 'sociology' could justly claim to constitute a field of serious academic research in its own right because it had successfully identified a distinct subject matter of its own. And one of the key elements in *this* original conception of the distinctiveness of social enquiry was the idea that the main object of study for social theory would be the entity called 'society'. One of the most interesting things that has been happening in social theory at the start of the 21st century is an increasing desire to look again at how social theorists might define society. As a name for envisaging the social contexts within which social action takes place, 'society' is one of the most basic units of analysis in social theory. Consequently, any serious review of that concept necessarily has major implications for the future of social theory.

The various arguments that have arisen over this point can all be seen as variations on the theme of the **boundedness** of social theory. Boundedness can be defined as a process in which the outer limits of one field of academic enquiry, or simply of knowledge, push up against the outer boundary of other such fields. Like the idea of 'difference', boundedness works in two directions at once: it gives theorists *within* boundaries a sense of sameness and continuity, but it also gives them a sense of positive distinction from theorists working within *other* boundaries. The relative solidity or fixity of boundaries between fields of knowledge will vary according to a number of factors not least the level of confidence that people have in the integrity of the bounded field where they do their thinking. Boundedness produces bound*aries*, which are essentially pliable in the sense that the relations between one field of knowledge and another are continuously shifting. If the notion of boundedness is to be useful at all, however, there must be *some limits* as to how porous these boundaries can be. The relative flexibility and permeability of the boundaries between social-theoretical knowledge and other fields of enquiry provides a useful means of assessing the current robustness of the social theory as a bounded field of knowledge.

Chaos out of order

The boundedness of 'society' and national society

The main challenge to the boundedness of social theory comes from theorists in neighbouring academic disciplines who argue that there has been a sufficient shifting in the subject matter of social enquiry, away from industry and institutions and towards consumption and expressive symbols, that social theory really does need to alter its own focus. This position is nicely summarised by the cultural theorist Mike Featherstone:

> The challenge for sociology [and social theory], still attempting to come to terms with the upsurge of interests in culture in the 1980s which has seen a lowering of the boundaries between it and the other social sciences and the humanities, is to both theorize and work out modes of systematic investigation which can clarify these globalizing processes and distinctive forms of social life which render problematic what has long been regarded as the basic subject matter for sociology: society, conceived almost exclusively as the bounded nation-state. (Featherstone, 1990, p 2)

The key phrase here is 'globalising processes' because it is claims about the emergence of new kinds of social processes that operate above or outside the level of the individual national society that has fuelled debates about the continuing usefulness of the concept of 'society'. To the extent that the social-theoretical concept of 'society' has been anchored to the idea of an actually existing geographical-territorial entity called 'national society', the emergence of processes that operate without apparent regard for such notions of boundedness imply that the concept has itself become detached from that to which it is assumed to refer. The actual and virtual notions of society no longer match up.

Several degrees of caution are necessary here. First, relatively little is known about the nature, extent and likely duration of beyond-society-type processes and so much of the debate so far tends to express quite high levels of speculative futurology. Second, the emergence of new kinds of beyond-society processes does not necessarily mean the total elimination of established social processes characteristic of the bounded national society. The really tricky bit will be to analyse the relations between 'old' processes and 'new' processes. Third, because beyond-society processes must have some kind of relationship with institutions and practices at the national and local levels, it might be sensible to regard such processes as hybrid forms of within-society processes (albeit processes that express high levels of boundary-breaking capability), rather than as signifying a genuinely new type.

The boundedness of disciplines

A further important boundary that is under threat here, and one that the above quotation from Featherstone refers to, is a possible shifting of boundaries between academic disciplines in the social and human sciences. This process has been usefully described by John Urry:

> [I]nnovation results from academic mobility across disciplinary borders, a mobility that generates what [Dogan and Pahre, 1990] call 'creative marginality'. It is this marginality, resulting from scholars moving from the centre to the periphery of their discipline and then crossing borders, which helps to produce new productive hybridities in the social sciences. (Urry, 2000, p 210)

Urry is drawn towards this recommendation because of his own strong interest in the emergence of new kinds of complex global networks that operate by means of global information and communications systems. He argues that these mobilities 'criss-crossing societal borders in strikingly new temporal-spatial patterns hold out the possibility of a major new agenda for sociology … mobilities rather than societies should be at the heart of a reconstituted social sciences' (Urry, 2000, pp 2, 210).

Recommendations like these are not, however, just about moving the furniture around between departments in academic institutions, they are also, and much more profoundly, about shifting boundaries between traditions of enquiry in social theory itself. Again we can usefully quote Urry on this point:

> Sociology thus appears to be cast adrift once we leave the relatively safe boundaries of a functionally integrated and bounded society, or of an autopoietic social system *à la* Luhmann (1995 [1984]). There is a theoretical and empirical whirlpool where most of the tentative certainties that sociology had endeavoured to erect are being washed away. (Urry, 2000, p 17)

Similarly revolutionary suggestions about whether the classical perspectives for imagining what 'society' is are still up to the task have been raised by other cultural theorists. For example, in wanting to address 'the structural conditions of reflexivity' (Lash is referring to the allegedly real processes of **reflexive modernisation** but we can also include the 'reflexivity' of social theory noted earlier), Lash concludes: 'What indeed underpins reflexivity is then neither the social (economic, political and ideological) structures of Marxism, nor the (normatively regulated and institutional) social structures of Parsonian functionalism, but instead an articulated web of global and local networks of *information and communication structures*' (Lash, in Beck et al., 1994, pp 120–1, original emphasis). A similar point is made by Delanty: 'What is collapsing is the organic image of the body as the metaphor of the social … the concept of the "net", which is diffuse and decentred … is more appropriate to characterize the changes which are occurring today' (Delanty, 1999, p 51). And it is not only boundaries between disciplines *within* the social sciences and humanities, but *between these* and the natural sciences that might also be subject to review: 'The obsolescence of positivism as a scientific methodology even in the natural sciences … opens up new possibilities for mediation between society and nature' (Delanty, 1999, p 48).

Order out of chaos

Against this challenging and stimulating hypothesis of collapsing boundaries, however, there is another, which starts from the premise that it is not so difficult to argue for complexity and chaos. Chaos is actually the default-setting of human understanding; it is what there is *before* understanding emerges, before bounded*ness* and boundar*ies* have taken shape. The challenge for social theorists is to find useful and reliable ways of getting past chaos and towards something on which to build a more orderly analysis. Obviously many arguments then ensue about what constitutes orderly knowledge, what the best techniques for developing it are and whether we have ulterior motives in doing so (issues that we addressed briefly in the first part of this chapter), but the common point of departure is the desire to move beyond *unboundedness*.

Accepting that in order to theorise at all we do need some kind of bounded entity to theorise *about*, and accepting that out of habit and for convenience we might as well call this bounded entity 'society', the next set of issues are whether we carry on defining 'society' as a kind of 'system'. This is a central question for social theorists because, despite the best efforts of postmodernist social theorists to argue otherwise, and in fact of more recent contributions whose concept of network also presumes quite high levels of systemness or 'systemicity', human social activity and the contexts where it takes place do have systemic properties. Similarly unavoidable is the fact that any notion of 'system', or just of systemness, also implies boundedness. Compelling evidence of the very ordinary nature of the idea of boundedness comes from other disciplines. Irrespective of the enormous diversity of thoughts that human beings can think, none can do so in non-human ways. The human brain thus constitutes the physiological foundation for the bounded system called human consciousness. There can be no human thought outside this bounded system. Applying the same albeit rather crude logic of boundedness to natural systems, we might reasonably conclude that, within any timescale that might reasonably be thought of as affecting *homo sapiens* in any future that can currently be imagined, planet Earth, the immediate gaseous envelope that surrounds it and at a stretch the gravitational effects of the Moon and the solar effects of 'our' Sun, also provide the bounded physical limits of human existence.

Assuming we can agree that systemness and boundedness provide some of the most basic building blocks of human understanding, the next question is how to theorise the linkages between the 'parts' of the system/society, and to determine the nature of the boundaries that give our chosen object of analysis sufficient shape to allow us to carry out some analysis of it. Clearly answers to these questions will reflect earlier decisions about what model of system and what kind of systemness the theorist envisages 'society' as having. Biological systems have provided one influential model; structuralist conceptions of relations between sign-systems another. Post-structuralism and postmodernism have offered yet other models, although in this case based on a notion of anti-system or disembodied systemness. The more recent idea of system as a kind of network comprising nodes linked together by flows of information adds a new and potentially valuable alternative to those that have already spent time on the social-theoretical test bench.

Enlightenment projects and boundary disputes

Debates about the original Enlightenment project can also be seen in this light in the sense that, from the point of view of social theory, what the Enlightenment thinkers tried to do was set up some basic parameters about the boundedness of social knowledge and the boundaries of social phenomena. This included simple ideas about the fact that this kind of knowledge could actually be developed, that society probably formed some kind of system and that since conscious human beings were the only creatures smart enough to develop this kind of knowledge, it was not unreasonable to imagine that they occupied a central position in the dominion of knowledge. The objections raised by post-structuralist and later by postmodernist social theorists against these first organising thoughts in social theory have caused a great deal of disturbance along the way, but perhaps their greatest achievement has been to carry out a necessary intellectual stocktaking exercise in the discipline. At first sight it appeared that they had managed to find a new and independent vantage point from which to criticise some of the basic assumptions of the Enlightenment/ classical/modernist perspective (the idea of boundedness, the idea of system, the centrality of subjective individuals), but now that the dust has settled it is more likely to turn out that the 'posts' have simply re-established social theory's *own capacity* for immanent critique.

It is an interesting and stimulating exercise to think imaginatively and constructively about how to challenge the paradigm of social theory, its boundaries and its sense of its own boundedness, but what makes social theory paradigmatic in the first place is its capacity to incorporate new ways of thinking as and when the need arises. It also tells us some interesting things about the difficulty of trying to establish new paradigms in social theory. Although we might be able to hazard a guess about some of the general contours of the 'new society' of the future or of 'the new paradigm' in theory-world that will be required to understand it, it is impossible to offer a ready-formed alternative. Logically, since there is no *non*-societal vantage point, no *non*-paradigm or *non*-bounded position, from which to explore social phenomena, then nor can there be a yet-to-be-discovered resource of alternative paradigm ingredients. These issues may represent both a renewal of debates about the boundedness of social theory as a serious undertaking in the development of human knowledge, and, a little more abstractly, a contribution to the debate about what boundedness *is*.

Further reading

Andrew Collier, *Critical Realism: An Introduction to Roy Bhaskar's Philosophy* (Verso, 1994).

Nichols Gane, *The Future of Social Theory* (Continuum, 2004).

John Urry, *Sociology Beyond Societies: Mobilities for the Twenty-First Century* (Routledge, 2000).

GLOSSARY

Abstract/abstraction A technique for looking at associations between things using concepts and ideas rather than simple description. A useful way of finding connections without claiming that they are literally true or to be found in exactly this form in reality. See *critical realism*.

Action What happens when people exercise their capacity for *agency*. Social theorists are especially interested in *social action*.

Agency The capacity to act. A property associated especially with human beings. A capacity to act does not presume that this capacity will be exercised.

Age of Reason Period of European intellectual development during the late 17th and 18th centuries dominated by the idea that social and scientific progress would be based on the systematic and rational analysis of facts. Reason is opposed to emotion and superstition. See European *Enlightenment*.

Alienation A term developed by Karl Marx to describe the loss of well-being experienced by workers in *capitalist* society. Alienation is associated with forms of working in which the products of work, working relationships and any sense of self-worth and self-esteem become debased. Marx argued that the compulsion to work in this way would eventually result in *revolution*.

Anomie A concept developed by Émile Durkheim to describe situations where *social actor*s lose their connection with society. Anomie means estrangement, separation, isolation, disjuncture. In his classical study *Suicide* (1968b [1897]) Durkheim uses the concept to describe the social causes of the suicide rate in modern society.

Anthropology/anthropologist/anthropological An applied discipline in the social sciences that conducts comparative investigations of patterns of economic, political, social and cultural activity. Originally developed during the late 19th and early 20th centuries to investigate traditional, non-industrial society. At various times strongly influenced by *structuralist* methodology and by *functionalism*.

Antithesis See *thesis/antithesis/synthesis*.

Asceticism/ascetic An attitude of self-restraint, abstemiousness or self-denial whose adherents impose strict limits on themselves in respect of the enjoyment they may take in the products of their work. The ascetic style is simple and minimalist rather than elaborate and indulgent.

Authoritarian As distinct from liberal, social regimes, which control *social actors* through coercion and sometimes direct force rather than by consensus and persuasion. See *hegemony*.

Autopoietic system A self-generating or self-creating system which operates with high levels of self-reliance. Often associated with the German systems theorist Niklas Luhmann. See *homeostatic system*.

Behaviourist psychology A school of thought that emphasises the instinctual, rather than the learned or cultural, basis of human action. Behaviourists believe that understanding human behaviour can best be achieved, not through abstract speculation, but by looking carefully at what people actually do.

Beliefs Ideas that are held to be true even if concrete evidence is lacking. Sometimes taking the form of aspirations or moral objectives that guide the choices *social actors* make. See also *ideas* and *values*.

Belief system Combinations of sets of beliefs that form a general outlook, perspective or world view. To constitute a *system* the various belief elements have to be reasonably consistent with other elements in the same system. Conflict might arise between different social, economic, political or cultural groups because of differences in their belief systems. See also *conscience collective, ideology, hegemony*.

Biographical subject An idea used by social theorists to emphasise the individual and personal nature of human experience. Even if *social actors* share elements of a common *human nature* and live similar lives in similar contexts with similar belief systems, their experiences and thus their biographies remain unique. More generally the idea of the biographical subject is associated with the *Enlightenment* perspective that human beings are subjectively-aware, conscious beings with the capacity for self-direction and independent action.

Biography Biography is the term used for describing the personal life history of an individual. The key ingredients of biography are personality and experience.

Boundedness Boundedness is the property of having boundaries. Bound*aries* are what are produced by different kinds of bounded*ness*. Often used in social theory to refer to the boundedness of particular fields of knowledge.

Bureaucracy/bureaucratic A highly instrumental administrative technique for organising large amounts of information in a systematic way. Bureaucracies are characterised by anonymity, lack of personality and subjective judgement, formal rules and regulations.

Bureaucratisation The process by which organisations and institutions take on bureaucracy as their main means of administration.

Capitalism A type of economic and social undertaking whose underlying organising principle is the cooperative production of commodities for profitable sale at market. Critics of modern capitalism like Karl Marx regard capitalism as a predatory undertaking based on the exploitation of workers and the manipulation of consumers.

Capitalist Literally a person who owns sufficient capital or financial resources to invest in business opportunities to generate more capital. In more informal terms, a person who broadly agrees with the principle of making profit for personal use.

Capitalist society A particular kind of social formation where capitalism has become the principal and dominant means of producing commodities and services. For Karl Marx, capitalist society is a particular historical form of society that comes after feudal society and before communist society.

Civil society Refers to the realm of private institutions and associations, including privately owned economic enterprises and businesses, which stand between the apparatuses of government and the private lives of *social actors* and their families. Distinct from the *state*, which is the public realm of social life together with the public institutions and practices it is made of.

Class A key term in social theory and sociology, used for distinguishing between different large groups or collectivities of *social actors*. Karl Marx defines class in terms of economic criteria, particularly ownership of the means of production. Max Weber defines class in terms of economic and social criteria. See *means of production, cultural capital.*

Common sense A pragmatic mode of thinking directed towards solving practical issues in an uncomplicated way and often based on previous experience or custom. Distinct from abstract forms of thinking involving reflection and contemplation. Sometimes referred to in social theory as *practical consciousness*, as distinct from *discursive consciousness*.

Communicative rationality A form of rationality associated especially with Jürgen Habermas, which emphasises that social actors enter discussions on the presumption that the potential for agreement always exists. Habermas argues that failure to reach agreement often arises because of misunderstandings over what constitutes agreement. See also *instrumental rationality*.

Conflict A social situation that arises often from lack of consensus over the acquisition and distribution of resources. Conflict can also arise between different *belief systems*.

Conflict theory A very broad distinction can be made in social theory between 'conflict theorists', like Karl Marx and Max Weber, who tend to presume that society is always fraught with conflict, and 'consensus theorists', like Émile Durkheim and Talcott Parsons, who tend to presume that the 'normal' state of society is one of equilibrium and harmony. See also *social order* and *ideology*.

Conscience collective A specialist term developed by Émile Durkheim, which translates both as 'collective conscience' and as 'collective consciousness', to describe the main source of social solidarity in pre-modern society, which is based on custom and faith rather than *reason*. See also *division of labour*.

Constructivist/constructivism See *social construction*.

Contemporary modernist A category of social theorists working from the 1970s onwards who retain the idea that the underlying forces that gave rise to modern society in the first place (*capitalism*, *industrialisation*, *rationalisation*) are still in play even though they have possibly been supplemented by new forces such as globalisation. The category includes theorists like Habermas, Giddens, Bourdieu. See *postmodernist social theorists*.

Cosmopolitan A term referring to a new kind of critically self-reflexive citizens who locate themselves in the world not on the basis of simple national identification and affiliation but on the basis of various forms of universal or international rights and expectations. It is a perspective that represents a value system and social orientation based on the experiences of 'the global' rather than 'the local'. Being cosmopolitan means being mobile.

Critical realism An influential perspective in social theory associated with the ideas of Roy Bhaskar (1979, 2002) and Margaret Archer (1988, 2000). The underlying *realist* premise of critical realism is that it is possible to explain key aspects of the surface forms of social phenomena by inferring the existence of underlying mechanisms that cannot themselves be observed. Its *critical* aspect is that it is not logically necessary to assume that particular outcomes must always occur. It embraces the possibility of alternative outcomes. See also *realism, realist* and *retroductive reasoning*.

Critical social theory Closely associated with members of the Frankfurt Institute of Social Research, which was established in Frankfurt in 1923 and was made up of philosophers, social and cultural theorists, literary theorists, musicologists and psychologists adopting a Marxist and *humanist* perspective. Its mode of analysis is heavily intellectual and analytical. In its early period in particular critical theorists including Theodor Adorno (1903–69), Max Horkheimer (1895–1973), Herbert Marcuse (1898–1979) and Eric Fromm (1900–80) developed a detailed and vigorous *ideology* critique of capitalist mass culture.

Critical social theorist An advocate or practitioner of *critical social theory*.

Cultural capital A concept developed by Pierre Bourdieu in *Distinction* (1984 [1979]) to describe the largely non-economic assets social actors draw on to establish their social status. Social attitudes and tastes, including such things as the appreciation of culture and the arts, or of popular television and sport, establish 'distinctions' between groups in society. Cultural capital supports Bourdieu's wider concept of *habitus*.

Culturalist Literally 'a lover of culture'; someone who embraces the importance of the cultural realm and who stresses the cultural origins of many social phenomena.

Cultural practices A subcategory of social practice in general, is concerned with the cultural dimensions and cultural products of social action.

Culture That realm of human social life that is primarily taken up with the circulation of ideas, values and beliefs. The realm of culture is generally regarded as distinguishable from the economic and political realms. Culture is essentially a product of *society* and not of nature.

Deductive reasoning A basic type of methodology where general propositions and hypotheses are tested by examining whether they are supported by specific instances. An analytical procedure that goes from the general and towards the particular. Contrasts with *inductive reasoning*. Most reasoning in the human and social sciences involves a combination of deductive and inductive reasoning. See also *critical realism*.

Deep structures An abstract term used by *structuralists* to refer to the underlying patterning and structuring forces that generate particular kinds of phenomena at the surface. Language performance is a specific and observable surface manifestation of the general underlying capacity for linguistic competence. Social actors do not have to be conscious of deep structures in order to be affected by them. Contrasts with *surface structure*.

De-traditionalisation A phenomenon associated with the process of *reflexive modernisation* in which social actors become increasingly detached from traditional markers of their social position and beliefs. A way of describing the extent to which the ascription of social position, social roles and beliefs has been displaced by individual choice.

Diachronic A specialist term for referring to the way that social phenomena are shaped by the passage of time. Contrasts strongly with the present-time or *synchronic* dimension.

Discourse A specialist term used by Michel Foucault to describe the prevailing modes of debate and conversation that go on in society and which tend to be shared across the different branches of knowledge. Discourses are the surface forms of what Foucault calls the *épistèmes* or dominant intellectual perspectives that blend together particular styles of analysis and types of knowledge to form an overall frame of reference for scientific, philosophical and political activity. Discourses can be regarded as paradigmatic for the way social actors interpret the world around them at a particular historical moment.

Discursive consciousness A term used in social theory to describe types of thinking directed at trying to understand the deeper causes or meanings of social phenomena. Contrasts with *practical consciousness*, which deals with things at a much more superficial level often without any obvious underlying process of analysis.

Discursive practice A term in *post-modernist* social theory associated particularly with Michel Foucault, referring to the way in which the discourses that characterise particular historical–cultural periods are not just 'in the mind' but provide practical frames of reference in which real action takes place.

Division of labour   Initially introduced by the economist Adam Smith (1723–90) in his highly influential treatise *The Wealth of Nations* (1970 [1776]) to describe the division of the individual elements in the production process between workers using the principle that one worker continuously doing a single ask is more efficient than having them do several tasks less frequently. Widely adopted as a way of describing how the industrial production process is organised within *capitalism*. Adopted by Émile Durkheim to describe *individuation* in modern society not just between technical tasks and occupations but between social roles more generally. See also *industrial society*.

Duality/dualist/dualistic   Terms used by *contemporary modernist* social theorists to distinguish between two kinds of analytical procedure. Seeing phenomena dualistically means seeing them, in an analytical sense, as distinct and separable. Regarding them as components of a duality means seeing them as two parts or aspects of the same phenomenon. Margaret Archer strongly advocates a dualistic approach and argues that in order to analyse key phenomena such as agency and structure it is essential to keep them analytically distinct. The relationships between them become invisible if agency and structure are 'conflated' or collapsed into each other. Anthony Giddens in contrast advocates the procedure of duality on the grounds that describing agency and structure dualistically means imposing a false sense of separation between what are for him two aspects of a single entity. See *structuration*.

Economic rationality   An attitude of mind in which choices are driven primarily by economic considerations. Success and failure are judged in terms of material and financial outcomes. See *rationalisation, instrumental rationality*.

Egoistic   From the Greek word 'ego' meaning 'I', is an attitude of self-interest and self-centredness. Distinct from altruistic meaning having regard for others over regard for oneself.

Empiricism/empiricist/empirical A philosophical attitude towards the nature of human knowledge that states that knowledge is based on experiencing phenomena through the physical senses. Following John Locke (1632–1704) it regards the human mind as a 'blank slate' that only becomes knowledgeable through experience. A scientific methodology that seeks to arrive at objective descriptions and measurements of phenomena as facts. The empiricist laboratory method involving detailed experimentation is the stereotype of 'hard' science as distinct from the 'soft' science used in the arts, humanities and social sciences. Opposed to *idealism* and some forms of *rationalism*.

Enlightenment The period from the late 17th and 18th centuries in Europe dominated by a series of new ideas in philosophy, politics, the arts and intellectual life generally, which promoted a progressive and liberal attitude based on reason rather than on tradition or religious faith alone. Advocates the idea that human beings do not occupy a special place in the universe ordained by God but that *homo sapiens* is part of nature and that knowledge of nature and of life can be gained through observation, experimentation and rational judgement. Growing awareness of individuality and the human capacity to affect the conditions of their own existence provided a foundation for modern ideas about social development and progress, political representation and social organisation.

Épistème Michel Foucault devised this term and defined it in the following way 'The total set of relations that unite, at a given period, the discursive practices that give rise to epistemological figures, sciences, and possibly formalized systems [of knowledge] the totality of relations that can be discovered, for a given period between the sciences when one analyses them at the level of discursive regularities', in *The Archaeology of Knowledge* (1972 [1969], p 42). See also *discourse*.

Epistemology/epistemological A branch of philosophy concerned with understanding what knowledge *is*. *Empiricists* argue that knowledge comes only through experience while *rationalists* argue that ideas and cognitive reasoning are the basis of knowledge. Distinct from *ontology*, which is concerned with the nature of matter, and *teleology*, which, in respect of human subjects, tackles the question of the nature and direction of development.

Essentialist Denotes theories that strongly emphasise the 'natural' rather than the socially-constructed constitution of various phenomena. Contrasts with constructivist. See *social construction*.

Ethnography A methodology often used by social scientists to describe social phenomena from the point of view of those affected by them and in the contexts where they occur.

Evolution A term used in the biological realm to describe the process whereby an organism develops by moving through a number of stages and where each stage is necessary for the next. Evolution implies processes of development that take place over a long period of time. See *social evolution*.

Exchange theory Similar to *rational choice theory*, first developed in the United States by G. Homans in 1958 in an influential article in the *American Journal of Sociology*, 'Social behaviour as exchange'. Homans sought to understand decision making not in terms of the pressure to conform altruistically to social norms and values but as a sequence of instrumental judgements or 'exchanges' about personal benefit versus expenditure of effort. The major weakness of exchange theory for social theorists is that it cannot explain individual action without constantly referring back to notions of values, interests and purposes, which are already normatively determined.

Exchange value The exchange value of a commodity is an expression of how many of one commodity can be exchanged for another commodity. One hammer, for example, might be exchanged for a thousand nails. See also *use value* and *surplus value*.

Existentialism Originating in the thought of the Danish theologian Søren Kierkegaard (1813–55) but developed by the French philosopher J.-P. Sartre (1905–80) during the 1940s and 1950s, existentialism is a philosophical position claiming that the personal experience of being is much more important than the orderly quest for objective knowledge. Since the experience of being is only accessible subjectively there is no point at all in trying to investigate it as if it were an external or exterior phenomenon. Knowledge of self is inaccessible to all but the self that is being experienced. Existentialism generally rejects the *rationalist* and *realist* perspectives that there is an independent world 'out there' that can be studied separately from the experiences of any particular individual. All knowledge is in fact experiential.

False consciousness Associated with the Hungarian Marxist theorist Georg Lukács (1885–1971), is the idea that social actors in capitalist society have an incomplete and possibly distorted awareness of the circumstances in which they live. It is the role of the political party or intellectual vanguard to bring them to a state of true consciousness, which is a precondition for *revolution*.

Formal rationality In relation especially to the work of Max Weber, refers to the decision-making process in respect of the best technical means of achieving particular ends. Distinct from *substantive rationality*, which refers to the desirability of the ends that social actors are trying to achieve. In relation to bureaucracy, for example, Weber suggests that although bureaucracy is highly administratively efficient the rationality of the ends that it is meant to serve become obscured.

Frankfurt School See *critical social theorists*.

Functionalism An abstract approach in social theory that describes the various institutions and practices of society in terms of how they function to the benefit of society or the *social system* as a whole. Notions of 'purpose' and 'function' are seen as largely identical. Leading functionalist social theorists are Talcott Parsons (1902–79) and R.K. Merton (1910–2003). See *neo-functionalism*.

Functionalist A social theorist who accepts *functionalism* as the most appropriate model for understanding society.

Game theory A variant of *rational choice* and *exchange theory* that tries to include in its analysis the fact that social actors take account of the actions of other actors or 'players' when making their decisions. It might help explain why some individual decisions appear wrong or counter-intuitive if it can be shown that, in the game as a whole, the actor is willing to make short-term sacrifices in order to achieve long-term success. Game theory tends to have the same limitations for social theorists as do *rational choice theory* and *exchange theory*.

Geist A difficult philosophical term associated with the German idealist philosopher G.W.F. Hegel, this German word translates literally as 'spirit' or 'mind'. Hegel uses it to describe the role of an all-pervasive moral and ethical force which unites all of humanity in its quest for enlightenment and civilisation. *Geist* emerges at the moment when people achieve full awareness of their relation with, or their place within, reality.

Gender In social theory, a social and cultural construct used to distinguish between women and men. Gender is often underpinned by the classification of persons according to their biological sex, but sex and gender are not the same thing. Gender is articulated in terms of possible or alleged differences in the behavioural characteristics of women and men.

Gender paradigm Alternative term for *gender regime*.

Gender regime A dominant set of social and cultural beliefs about the respective roles of men and women in society. Feminist social theorists tend to assume that the gender regime of contemporary Western society is largely determined by men and serves their interests rather than the interests of women. In this context the gender regime is seen as a core *discourse* in *patriarchy*. The gender regime also includes attitudes towards sexuality, sexual relations and expectations about expressions of maleness and femaleness.

General theory/general systems theory An attempt to analyse social phenomena as parts of an overall system. The properties of the social system as a whole are seen as having a determining influence over the parts and over the relations between the parts. General system theory operates at the *macro* level and often uses complex analytical descriptions as it attempts to deduce the nature of the social system. The notion of 'general system' and of system*ness* provides a core concept in *functionalism* and *neo-functionalism*.

Globalisation A contested term in sociology and cultural studies describing social phenomena that are seen as operating at the global rather than national or local levels. It is important to distinguish between phenomena that originate at a genuinely global level, have genuine across-the-globe impacts and are caused by global processes, like the world weather system, and processes that have an increasingly global aspect like international media or financial institutions but which are *not* the result of an imaginary global source of power.

Grand narratives A concept developed by J.-F. Lyotard in his influential discussion of *postmodernity* in *The Postmodern Condition* (1984 [1979]), where he argues that the grand narratives or general explanatory accounts of why society is the way it is, and which legitimise the world view of *modern society*, have collapsed. In *postmodernity* the whole idea of grand narratives has been discredited with the result that 'postmodern science' shifts endlessly from one temporary state of uncertainty to another.

Habitus A concept introduced by Pierre Bourdieu (1931–2002) (1977 [1972], 1984 [1979]) to describe the localised day-to-day realm of experiences and practices and the codes of meaning and signification associated with them, which constitute the immediate context of 'habitual' or 'lived' experience. Bourdieu uses the concept to distinguish between the kinds of structurings that go on in the anonymous realm of the social system, and those which guide people's actions in their immediate and more intimate and emotionally-charged living spaces. Broadly comparable with Habermas's concept of *lifeworld*.

Hegemony A concept used especially by the Marxist theorist Antonio Gramsci (1891–1937) to describe modern forms of economic and political *power* that are based less on physical force and more on consent. A hegemonic society is one where the general population agree to be governed in a particular way. Gramsci criticised some forms of political hegemony on the grounds that 'consent' might be based on a false and *ideological* understanding of the 'real' situation. Actors agree to be ruled under false pretences. See *authoritarian* and *conscience collective*.

Hermeneutics A field of knowledge that is interested in the formation of *meaning* and with meaning as a prime motivator of social action. Originally associated with the scholastic interpretation of religious texts, it is now used widely in social philosophy in the analysis of cultural processes and artefacts. Associated in social theory with the social interactionist and *interpretivist* traditions and with the deconstruction of *discourses* in *post-structuralism* and *postmodernism*.

Heterogeneous/heterogeneity From the Greek word 'hetero' meaning 'other', a term used widely in social theory to describe societies that contain diversity, difference and differentiation. Modern society is distinguishable from pre-modern society because it is more heterogeneous. Contrasts with *homogeneity*.

Heterotopia From the Greek word 'hetero' meaning 'other', a specialist term in recent social theory to describe an idealised interpretation of a new kind of social-cultural reality or society that makes a virtue out of otherness especially geographical and cultural differences. Newness, novelty, the unfamiliar are the kinds of emotions involved in heterotopia. Contrasts with *utopia* denoting the society of complete freedom and dystopia denoting complete lack of freedom.

Historical materialism A formal name for Karl Marx's (1818–83) theory of social change in which one form of society or 'mode of production' is superseded by another. The historical element emphasises that all social development is embedded within actual historical circumstances and contexts. The materialist element emphasises that the root of all forms of social organisation is the production of material necessities that are essential for maintaining physical life. For Marx, control over social resources, which in effect means control over the means of production, is the basic form of *power* in society. Each historical form of society contains within itself 'the seeds of its own destruction' in the sense that new forces of economic production and social organisation emerge out of those that developed in the previous historical stage. Thus feudalism gives way to capitalism and capitalism to socialism.

Holism Refers to phenomena in terms of the greater whole of which they are part. The whole might be regarded as having properties which are not found in its individual parts. The individual parts are significant and have meaning to the extent that they contribute to the greater whole.

Holistic Referring to a phenomenon as constituting a complete 'whole'. For example, the biological body of an animal, or the global weather system of planet Earth, could be described as 'holistic'. *Holism* implies that the phenomenon is a 'closed *system*' and that the purpose of the various parts is geared in some crucial respects to the *functioning* of the whole.

Homeostatic system A term used by the German *systems theorist* Niklas Luhmann (1921–98) to describe social systems that have the property of not relying on other parts of the same or some other system for their continued operation. Distinct from the conception of 'integrated system' in *functionalist* theory, which supposes the existence of an overarching social system into which all other subsystems can be fitted, and upon which the continuing functioning of both them and the overall system is wholly dependent. Homeostatic systems are thus largely self-regulating. Seeing systemness in terms of difference rather than convergence allowed Luhmann to pay particular attention to the ways in which systems communicate with each other. Systems can be seen largely in terms of their modes of communication. See *autopoietic system*.

Homogeneous/homogeneity From the Greek word 'homo' meaning 'the same', a term to describe a society that lacks variation and differentiation. Contrasts with *heterogeneous*.

Human agency See *agency*.

Humanism A philosophical and political perspective that explores reality from the point of view of the human subject. The humanist perspective, especially in its liberal and Marxist formulations, tends to assume that social actions are driven by a benign and sympathetic regard for the needs of others.

Humanist Adopting a humanist perspective.

Human nature The idea that despite superficial differences all human beings have certain common characteristics, needs and capacities. Human nature is therefore a universal rather than individual phenomenon. The capacity and desire to transform nature through creative cooperation with others is a key element in the *humanist* notion of human nature. Often aligned with the idea of the *transcendental subject*. See also *biographical subject*.

Hyper-reality Controversial concept developed by Jean Baudrillard to press his claim that in *postmodern society* real reality has become indistinguishable from the largely fictitious and illusory versions of it existing in the realm of *signs*. The sign system becomes detached from extant reality to such a degree that it becomes impossible to tell the real reality of actually existing stuff from an illusory and possibly false hyper-reality in the domain of free-floating signs.

Idealism   The philosophical position that the highest attainments of human activity are ideas rather than material objects. Material developments are seen as a means to a higher end usually conceived in terms of reaching advanced forms of consciousness or of intellectual/spiritual accomplishment. Idealist philosophers differ over whether there is a single point of ultimate attainment to which all human endeavour is converging, and which provides a measure of how far civilisation has progressed, or whether there are separate end-points in different fields of effort and between cultures. Distinct from *materialism*.

Idealist   A theorist who adopts the philosophical position of *idealism*. Less formally a theorist who accepts that speculative thinking is a genuine human activity that might help the development of alternative ideas about how things could be. An idealist is a person who aims to achieve things that they themselves recognise might never be achievable. In common-sense terms an idealist might be described as 'a dreamer'.

Ideal type   A widely used analytical concept developed by Max Weber to describe the 'ideal' or 'perfect' form of a particular phenomenon as a model against which to compare and analyse real instances of the phenomenon. Real instances are not expected to converge entirely with the ideal type.

Ideas   An intellectual and conceptual vocabulary for interpreting experience. The relationships between real objects or *referents* and the ideas and intellectual representations made about them are hotly disputed questions in philosophy.

Ideological critique   An attempt to undermine the credibility of the belief system of a dominant group by uncovering its negative ideological content. The 'battle of ideas' might be seen as a necessary part of the conflict between social groups in society.

Ideology/ideological   A coherent set of ideas and beliefs based on an incomplete understanding of actual reality. Ideologies are usually deployed by a dominant group to secure some form of advantage over a subordinate group. Some ideologies, such as racism, are negative while others, such as environmentalism, could be regarded as positive. See also *conscience collective* and *hegemony*.

Immanent/immanent critique   Referring to how social change comes from within a particular social phenomenon or situation rather than being imposed on it by forces from outside. The main distinction is with the idea of imm*inent*, which means things that are just about to happen. Karl Marx believed that radical social change was *immanent* since capitalism contained within itself 'the seeds of its own destruction' and that it was also *imminent* because around 1848 when the *Communist Manifesto* was published, actual capitalist society really had reached the moment of revolutionary upheaval.

Individualisation A phenomenon associated with the process of *reflexive modernisation* in which social actors become increasingly and willingly detached from each other in terms especially of their collective political *beliefs* and expectations. Traditional linkages are progressively weakened in the context of increasing personal choice and individual *reflexivity*. The possibility that human *agency* is no longer being controlled by social *structure*. See also *de-traditionalisation*.

Individualism A broad philosophical and political attitude that sees the quest for individuality, of acting independently of the collective will and of not being dominated by authority as positive expectations. Individual*ists* can be distinguished from collectivists on the grounds that the former see the benefits of acting separately from others as likely to be greater than the benefits of acting together. See also *voluntarism*.

Individuation Associated particularly with Émile Durkheim, refers to one of the principal effects of the *division of labour*, which is that as social roles become more and more specialised in a technical sense the social actors carrying them out also become more individually identifiable. Not to be confused with *individualism*.

Inductive reasoning A basic type of methodology where general propositions and suppositions are developed on the basis of one or two specific instances. An analytical procedure that goes from the particular and towards the general. Contrasts with *deductive reasoning*. Most reasoning in the human and social sciences involves a combination of deductive and inductive reasoning. See also *critical realism*.

Industrialisation The process by which society becomes industrial society. Beginning with the mechanisation of spinning and weaving tasks from around 1750 in Britain, industrialisation developed rapidly into factory production during the 19th and 20th centuries. A further period of industrialisation took place with the development of powerful and flexible computer-based technologies from the 1970s.

Industrial society Society in which commodities are produced with the assistance of machines. The wheels of industry are turned by mechanical sources of power. Often associated with modern *capitalism* and the industrial *division of labour*.

Instantiation/instantiated   Associated particularly with Anthony Giddens, a term referring to the way in which structures, defined as 'rules-and-resources', acquire a real material form at the moment when they are actively used. Until rules-and-resources are enacted they remain essentially abstract.

Instrumental rationality/instrumental–rational action   An intellectual framework or world view in which the main criteria for judging whether an action is or is not rational is the degree to which it enables specified objectives to be achieved in the most effective way possible. Actions come to be defined *as* rational as long as they are instrumental in achieving particular ends. Weber's critique of this form of rationality, subsequently taken up by *critical theorists*, is that in modern *capitalist* society there is a tendency to become obsessed with technique (*formal rationality*) at the expense of a proper awareness of the ends that society is trying to achieve (*substantive rationality*). See *rationalisation* and *bureaucracy*.

Interpellation   A specialist term developed by the French *structuralist* Marxist philosopher Louis Althusser (1918–90) to describe how social actors are drawn towards a false or *ideological* understanding of their situation. See also *false consciousness*.

Interpretivism   A methodology in the social sciences associated particularly with Max Weber and his method of *verstehen*, which means literally 'to interpret' social action in terms of what social action means to those performing it. See also *methodological individualism* and *hermeneutics*.

Labour theory of value   Associated particularly with Karl Marx but not exclusive to him, the theory that the value of commodities is directly related to the quantity of human labour power that has been expended in making them. It is the elastic nature of human labour power that enables the capitalist to extract surplus value from the worker over and above the necessary labour that workers must perform (recompensed in the form of wages) to keep themselves alive. See *use value*, *exchange value* and *surplus value*.

Latent functions   See *manifest functions*.

Liberal   An economic and political outlook based on the principles of universal representation and freedom of expression. A social perspective underpinned by a tolerant attitude towards diversity and difference and an open view of gender roles, of sexuality and of cultural and religious outlooks. Opposite of *authoritarian*.

Lifeworld/system Key terms used by Jürgen Habermas to distinguish between the private and intimate realm of everyday living and the distinctly public realm of the social system. 'System' includes not only organisations and institutions, such as those of government, education and security, but also the patterns of behaviour and functional routines upon which they depend. 'System' operates by means of *instrumental rationality*. Lifeworld is characterised as the realm of 'communicative rationality' where debates over substantive issues take place. Lifeworld is broadly comparable with Bourdieu's concept of *habitus*.

Logical positivism A rigorous system of philosophical thought premised on the idea that true knowledge is a direct product of and is strictly limited by the intelligibility and meaningfulness of the utterance a social actor can make. If it is not possible to verify by practical empirical means that a proposition is meaningful then it must be false. Drawing especially on mathematics it places great emphasis on the logical relation between the various terms used in trying to achieve verification.

Logocentrism/logocentric A term used by Jacques Derrida, taken from the Greek word *logos* meaning 'speech' and 'reason', to highlight a core element in *Enlightenment* and *modernist* thought, which is that the highest form of knowledge is that which comes from logical discourse and debate. Knowledge expressed in non-logical and non-discursive forms becomes secondary. Also reflects a view from first-wave *structuralist* social theory that the spoken form of language (logos) provides a more faithful representation of external reality.

Macro/micro An important distinction between the large-scale mode of theorising and analysis and the small-scale mode. Large-scale general theories such as *systems theory* and *functionalism* operate at a high level of abstraction looking for patterns that might only be identifiable when phenomena are examined in an aggregate way. *Phenomenologists* in contrast are interested in much smaller and more intimate types of social encounter and social experience. Methodologically, the choice of scale will determine the research design and the particular methods that will be used in researching and theorising particular social phenomena. See also *deductive reasoning* and *inductive reasoning*.

Manifest functions and **latent functions** Developed by the *functionalist* theorist R.K. Merton (1910–2003) to distinguish between functions where the observable practical outcome of an action is consciously intended and recognised by the actor, and functions where the outcome is not intended or recognised by them. Latent functions are partly hidden from view although their effects are often considerable.

Materialism An approach in social theory and philosophy that asserts the importance of actual material phenomena over metaphysical representations of them in the form of ideas. Distinct from *idealism*.

Materialist In social theory a person adopting the philosophy of *materialism*.

Meaning The sense of significance, defined in terms of the physical, intellectual or emotional sensations, that the social actor hopes to achieve through his or her actions. In social theory associated with *hermeneutics*, which defines meaning in terms of the intentions of the social actor.

Means of production Karl Marx introduced this term to describe the premises, tools, equipment and technical knowledge necessary for transforming raw materials into products for human consumption. He distinguishes these from the *relations of production*, which are the working relationships between workers and between workers and the owners of the means of production. Marx sometimes also refers to these as 'the social relations of production' to emphasise how relationships in society are deeply affected by patterns of ownership of necessary resources. Social classes can be defined *in terms of* the economic resources they own. A particular historical combination of means with relations becomes identifiable as a distinct mode of production.

Metaphysics/metaphysical A philosophical term referring to phenomena which do not have a concrete material form. Because they cannot be observed directly, the existence of such phenomena has to be deduced or inferred from the effects they are claimed to have on material phenomena. For example, the ideas a social actor has can be inferred from the actions she or he takes. Metaphysics tends to be a highly conceptual and abstract form of analysis investigating non-physical or non-material phenomena and the possible relationships between them.

Methodological individualism Associated particularly with Max Weber, a method in social research that attempts to explore social phenomena from the point of view of the individual social actor. Distinct from the collectivist approaches of Émile Durkheim and Karl Marx, Weber's approach is that the basic unit of analysis in social research is the individual social actor and not collectivised entities such as 'class' or 'society'.

Methodology General approach to studying something in a systematic way. Distinct from *methods*, which are the specific techniques used to put a particular kind of methodology into practice. The same technique (method) can be used by researchers who in other respects are using different methodologies.

Methods See *methodology*.

Micro/macro See *macro/micro*.

Mode of production See *means of production*.

Modernisation The process by which pre-modern societies become *modern societies*. See *industrialisation, rationalisation* and *reflexive modernisation*.

Modernist A social theory or theorist that/who tends to see phenomena using the terms of reference developed following the European *Enlightenment* or *Age of Reason*. Also often associated with the social-theoretical concepts of Karl Marx, Max Weber and Émile Durkheim. Distinct from *postmodernist*.

Modernity A short-hand term for describing the various social, cultural and institutional features associated with the historical period of *modern society*. Used with reference especially to cultural change, modernity also denotes the widespread acceptance of modern *ideas* and modern *values*. Modernity is not just something that can be described but is also constitutive of a set of *beliefs* and attitudes about what being modern is and what it means to live in a modern society. Contrasts with *postmodernity*.

Modern society In the social sciences, the term 'modern' is used chronologically to distinguish a form of society emerging in Northern Europe from around 1760. Modern society is identifiable as industrialised, urbanised and democratised. It generally also has a largely *Western world view*. See *postmodern society*.

Morphogenics Associated with the British cultural theorist Margaret Archer, *morphogenesis* refers to the way in which structure and agency are both continuously altered as action takes place. It is not possible for structure to remain untouched by action or to conceive of action as being unaffected by the structural conditions in which it takes place.

Narrative See *grand narratives*.

Natural sciences The natural, physical and biological sciences specialise in developing factual knowledge about physical and organic matter. Distinct from the Arts, Humanities and Social Sciences, which specialise in developing knowledge of human experience.

Neo-functionalism/neo-functionalist   A revival of *functionalist* social theory developed most energetically in the 1990s by Jeffrey Alexander (born 1947). A main argument is that, even if at quite high levels of generality, all systems are characterised by functional patternings, which can be described. Alexander (1998) also stresses the importance of theorising the cultural system as an autonomous realm that plays an important role in social integration in its own right rather than being a subsystem of the social system. In some formulations the cultural system is seen as mediating between individual actors and social institutions.

New social movements   Campaign groups in modern society that are not based wholly on shared class or economic interests. New social movements usually pursue a single issue often having a political dimension. Examples include the Women's Movement, the Civil Rights Movement and the Green Movement.

Nominalism/nominalist An approach to describing social phenomena in which the intellectual and analytical process of naming things is held separate from the assumption that phenomena so named really do exist. For example, Karl Marx refers confidently to 'class' as an actually existing social entity that has the power to affect historical development. As a nominalist Max Weber uses the term 'class' only in order to give a convenient name to collectivities of individual social actors exhibiting the same characteristics.

Objectivism/objective/objectivity The exterior form of phenomena. Looking at phenomena factually and dispassionately in terms of their external physical properties. Implies consistency and invariance. Distinct from *subjective*, which focuses on personal experience.

Ontological security A term used by Anthony Giddens, from the Greek word for 'being', which characterises human well-being as a feeling of continuity in the social actor's inner sense-of-self and confidence in his or her continuing process of physical and mental development. Giddens links ontological security to *reflexivity*.

Ontology   From the Greek word for 'being', a branch of philosophy concerned with understanding the nature of matter. The basic distinction is between matter, which has an observable material form, the stuff of the physical universe studied by the physical and natural sciences, and *non*-material *meta*physical matter like thoughts and ideas, which have no directly observable form and are studied by philosophers and social scientists. See *materialism* and *idealism*.

Organic Having the developmental characteristics of organisms in the realms of animal and plant life. Contrasts with 'mechanistic', which implies a non-natural, linear or automatic mode of development.

Overdetermination/overdetermined In social theory and psychoanalysis refers to the way in which a phenomenon might be determined in advance, or is overshadowed in its surface form, by some previously-occurring or underlying force. Louis Althusser uses the concept to explain that however independent the political sphere might appear to be, 'in the final instance' underlying economic forces will assert themselves.

Paradigmatic Belonging to and representative of a wider group or category or phenomena. A specialist term in structural linguistics referring to the set of *signifieds* from which a particular signified is drawn. The signified 'oak' denotes a particular type of tree within the larger set or paradigm of signifiers used for naming this category of *referent*. In choosing the particular word-sign 'oak' the speaker also invokes something of the wider category.

Patriarchy An authority system based on male dominance. A sociological theory developed by feminist social theorists (e.g. Walby, 1990) to support arguments that men dominate women by continuously manipulating social practices and institutions to their own advantage. Men dominate women because they have the power to do so. See also *gender regime*.

Performative discourse Drawing on Michel Foucault's ideas, a theory developed by the feminist writer Judith Butler (born 1956) that gender and biological sex are *instantiated* at the moment when social actors literally perform their maleness or femaleness. It is the performance of gender that makes the thoughts, ideas and beliefs that social actors have about it become part of real reality. Gender can only be discovered and experienced when acted out.

Phenomenology/phenomenological A school of thought first developed in philosophy by Edmund Husserl (1859–1938) and Martin Heidegger (1889–1976) and later in sociology by Alfred Schutz (1899–1959). The underlying premise is that objects are mainly of interest in terms of how they impact on consciousness in real-life situations. Phenomena might also have abstract or hidden properties but these are less significant than their more obvious and immediate material forms. Phenomena might be deemed significant to the extent that they have an impact on consciousness. See also *hermeneutics* and *interpretivist*.

Philosophical pragmatism Introduced by the US philosopher C.S. Peirce (1839–1914) and later developed by William James (1842–1910) and John Dewey (1859–1952) the assertion that *meaning* and knowledge are embedded in practical usefulness. Objects and actions that serve a useful practical purpose are more meaningful and more truthful than those that do not. Dewey argued that abstract or metaphysical propositions could be tested by considering what their practical implications might be. Also influenced the thinking of members of the Chicago School of *social interactionism* including G.H. Mead and Herbert Blumer. See also *common sense* and *practical consciousness*.

Pluralist/pluralistic A situation in which a number of separate elements are seen as operating in combination, with none having a dominant position. Typically used to describe the *liberal* economic and political composition of *social institutions* and *social practices* in modern Western industrialised society.

Political economy An earlier term for economics. The original term usefully reminds us that although economics now tends towards orthodoxy the discipline and theory of economics are not separable from the political context.

Positivism/positivistic Based on the *realist* presumption of an actual exterior reality existing separately from human knowledge of it, a term introduced by the French social philosopher Auguste Comte (1798–1857) to describe the most rigorous form of scientific investigation aimed at the discovery of 'facts' and 'laws'. Metaphysical speculation is rejected as incapable of producing factual knowledge. As a form of methodology, proceeds by way of systematic often *empirical* investigation of phenomena and attempts to describe the laws that govern them.

Positivist A social theorist who accepts the principles of positivism in studying social phenomena.

Post-industrial society A stage in *industrial society* in which the production process becomes dominated by microprocessor-based technologies, information systems and communications. Production shifts away from heavy industry and manufacture and towards personal, social and financial services.

Postmodernism/postmodernist A particular creative style or aesthetic effect associated with the postmodern period. Originally introduced during the 1960s as a term to distinguish postmodernist architectural design from the modernist or 'international style' of designers like Frank

Lloyd Wright and Le Corbusier. Now used much more loosely as a term in design and fashion.

Postmodernist social theorists A category of social theorists who adopt the position that a fundamental change has taken place, usually dated to the early 1970s, in the nature of modern society. A common theme is a rejection of key ideas in *Enlightenment* thought and a claim that, since all traditional reference points of meaning and interpretation have become chronically insecure, new forms of knowledge are required to understand postmodernity.

Postmodernity The cultural conditions, attitudes, *ideas*, *values* and *beliefs* associated with living in the historical period of *postmodern society*. Contrasts with *modernity*.

Postmodern society A term used to distinguish a new kind of society coming after modern society possibly beginning in the early 1970s. The definition of the term is disputed as are the characteristics that postmodern society is claimed to have. Some *contemporary modernist* social theorists prefer the terms late-modernity or high-modernity. See also *reflexive modernisation*.

Post-structuralism/post-structuralist A highly influential variety of social theories in the mid-20th century, which adapted key aspects of the model of linguistic structuring developed in first-wave structuralism and applied them in the analysis or 'deconstruction' (Jacques Derrida) of the struct*ural* and struct*uring* properties of texts (Roland Barthes) and discourses (Michel Foucault). Although post-structuralism has been criticised for saying quite a lot about ideas and meanings and relatively little about institutions and social structures it instigated a fresh appraisal of many of the core assumptions of the Western philosophical and intellectual tradition that began with the European *Enlightenment*.

Power The capacity to cause another actor to act, or to prevent him from acting, against his will. Social theorists see the different forms of power as manifestations of the desire to control different kinds of economic, political, intellectual, cultural and symbolic resources in society.

Practical consciousness See *common sense* and *discursive consciousness*.

Praxis A concept developed by G.W.F. Hegel and Karl Marx and refined by Georg Lukács, which refers to the realisation through action of the creative human essence. Praxis is the process whereby thought is transformed into action. Philosophically, it is the realisation that human-beingness and human action are inextricably linked.

Psychoanalysis A clinical analytical technique developed by the Austrian Jewish psychiatrist Sigmund Freud (1856–1939), which operates on the principle that mental disorder or neurosis in adults can be traced back to significant moments of personality development in early childhood. Freud sees personality as comprising three elements the Ego, which is the ordinary conscious sense-of-self; the Superego, which is partly conscious and exercises a monitoring or supervisory influence over the Ego, and the Id, which is unconscious and is made up of the basic instincts and drives especially those associated with sexual expression. Using hypnosis and other techniques the psychoanalyst attempts to lead the adult into his unconscious mind in order to uncover and thus alleviate features of his past that have become repressed.

Psychology A branch of knowledge in the behavioural sciences concerned with developing a scientific understanding of human cognitive development, mental processes and the behaviours associated with them. Social psychologists are interested especially in how these processes are played out in interactions between social actors. Contrasts with *sociology*, which tends to focus on the society-wide and institutional levels of social interaction rather than the level of individual cognition and personality.

Rational action See *instrumental rationality*.

Rational choice theory Attempts to analyse social action as a whole in terms of an economic model of self-interest. Actors are regarded as 'rational, autonomous, self-sufficient, wily, and clever' (Alexander, 1998 217). *Rationality* is defined in strictly *utilitarian* terms as that which produces maximum benefit for the individual actor. Rational choice theory has intuitive appeal because it relies on an apparently simple truth that actors tend to act in their own best interests. The difficulty is that notions of 'value' and 'utility' are socially constructed as are the contexts wherein action takes place. See also *exchange theory* and *game theory*.

Rationalisation A process described in its classical modern form by Max Weber in which all economic, legal, social and cultural practices and institutions become organised according to the principles of *instrumental rationality*. The clearest example is the strong tendency for all complex information-handling procedures to become *bureaucratised*.

Rationalism/rationality/rational The philosophical position that reality only becomes accessible to human consciousness because of the human capacity for intellectual reasoning. Resists the alternative empirical view that things can only be known as a result of having direct physical experience of them because these sensations still have to be interpreted or made sense of by the human mind. Some rationalists like Immanuel Kant (1724–1804) argue that even if knowledge is limited by experience, the capacity for intellectual reasoning presupposes the prior existence within the human mind of various capacities for rational thought, which exist independently of the sensations and experiences people have of the world around them. In order to make sense of the very first sense-experiences that it encounters the human mind must *already* be equipped with 'synthetic knowledge' or the capacity for processing sense-data. See *idealism* and *materialism*.

Rationalist   Somebody who adopts the philosophical position called *rationalism*. A belief that explanations of social phenomena derived from evidential reasoning must be stronger than those based on speculation, emotion, faith or custom. See also *rationality*.

Realism   The philosophical position that it is possible and reasonable to describe an actually existing reality that exists independently of anything we might have to say about it. Non-material phenomena such as ideas, values and beliefs might also be considered as part of reality. The method of description is usually *empirical*. See also *idealism* and *rationalism*.

Realist   A theorist who adopts the philosophical position of *realism*. A belief that social phenomena actually do exist in the form they appear to the observer. An assumption that appearance and essence are closely related and that essence has a relatively stable concrete form. In social theory somebody who resists *ideology* and *abstraction*. See *critical realism*.

Reason   See *Age of Reason*.

Referent   A philosophical term for the actually existing objects that social actors try to describe using sign-systems like language. The referent and the word-sign used to describe it are not the same thing. A major insight from structuralist linguistics is that the relationship between the actual object or referent (*signified*) and the word-sign attached to it (*signifier*) is an arbitrary relationship. Much of structuralist and post-structuralist social theory is preoccupied with working through the consequences of this insight.

Reflexive modernisation   A concept developed by contemporary modernists like Anthony Giddens and Ulrich Beck, and by the cultural theorists John Urry and Scott Lash, to capture the sense in which the processes of *modernisation* are increasingly characterised by *reflexivity*. Reflexive modernisation is essentially a variant of modernisation in which the original forces of social development (capitalism, industrialisation, rationalisation) are radicalised and speeded-up.

Reflexivity/reflexive An influential concept developed by Anthony Giddens to describe a leading characteristic of experience in late-modern society, which is that social actors continually monitor their own behaviour and adjust their future actions accordingly. As a characteristic of late-modern society more generally institutional practices are similarly monitored and revised. Continual monitoring of action can create a state of instability and uncertainty. See *reflexive modernisation*.

Reification A concept developed by Karl Marx and refined by Georg Lukács referring to the tendency within capitalism for all the subjective and qualitative states of human existence to be reduced to external objects or 'things'.

Relations of production See *means of production*.

Retroductive reasoning Developed by *critical realists* to describe an analytical technique that involves making inferences about underlying causative mechanisms, which are unfamiliar and cannot be observed directly, by using concepts that are already familiar. A technique for describing invisible forces and mechanisms using analogy. Differs from the *structuralist* notion of deep structure by resisting the idea that underlying forces are necessarily interconnected. Contrasts with *deductive reasoning* and *inductive reasoning*.

Revolutionary Refers to change that is rapid and which dramatically transforms the conditions that existed before the revolution takes place. Distinct from 'reformist', which refers to a more gradualist political strategy.

Risk Originally defined narrowly by the German theorist Ulrich Beck in his influential book *Risk Society* (1992 [1986]) as referring to threats to animal and plant life caused by industrial pollution, the term is now used much more generally to describe the unintended and negative effects of social action. It is important to distinguish between actual risk and perception of risk. Beck argues that risk has replaced scarcity as the major organising dynamic of social production in late-modern society.

Scientific-technical rationality A term used by Ulrich Beck as part of his analysis of *risk society* to describe activities that are judged to be rational against scientific and technical criteria of achievement, but which fail to give adequate consideration to their negative and unintended social consequences. Contrasts with *social rationality*.

Semiotics/semiotic Developed by Swiss linguist Ferdinand de Saussure (1857–1913), semiotics or the science of signs is a distinct aspect of the study of linguistics in which language is seen not just as a linguistic mirror for representing the world but as a system of *signs* having distinct patterns and structures that are independent of the *referents* that word-signs refer to.

Sign Any symbol used to stand for something else. Most often used in structural linguistics to identify the properties of word-signs, whether in their written or spoken form, which refer to specified *referents*. Following Ferdinand de Saussure (1857–1913) signs are seen as having two components the *signifier*, which is the written or acoustic component of the word-sign, and the *signified*, which is the mental image that the word-sign raises in the mind. The relationship between the sign and the referent it is associated with is arbitrary in the sense that it is only by convention that particular signs become associated with particular referents. Although Saussure implied that that which does the signifying is less important than that which is signified, much *post-structuralist* social theory is concerned with whether signifiers are more important because without them nothing can be signified at all. A preoccupation with the relation between signifiers is a basic feature of *post-structuralist* thought.

Signified In structural linguistics that component of the *sign* that is the mental image of the object or *referent* being referred to by the word-sign.

Signifier In structural linguistics that component of the *sign* which is the written or acoustic component of the word-sign.

Sign-value A term introduced by Jean Baudrillard to develop his argument that in postmodern society the concepts of *use value*, *exchange value* and *surplus value* developed by Karl Marx in his critique of capitalism have been superseded by a new kind of value based on the symbolic significance of signs. As Baudrillard pus it 'Today every desire, plan, need, every passion and relation is abstracted (or materialized as sign and as object to be purchased and consumed)' consumption 'is a systematic act of the manipulation of signs' (Baudrillard, *The System of Objects*, 1968, in Poster, 2001 26, 25).

Simulacra A specialist term used by the postmodernist theorist Jean Baudrillard to describe the emergence of signs that, although originally devised to articulate real objects or *referents*, have taken on an independent existence of their own. The chaos and loss of certainty that Baudrillard thinks is a defining characteristic of *postmodernity* is closely associated with the emergence of simulacra, which have taken the place not just of other kinds of signs but of real objects themselves. The simulation of reality or *hyper-reality* becomes indistinguishable from actual reality.

Social Phenomena that result from human action in *society* as distinct from phenomena that arise from natural processes in nature.

Social action Action that takes place in social contexts usually involving other social actors. Phenomena that are produced when social actors express their capacity for *agency*. Often associated in social theory with the presumption that social actors have control over their actions. Contrasts with *social structure*.

Social actor Somebody who acts. Somebody who instigates action. Somebody having the special capacity for expressing *agency*.

Social construction An influential school of thought in social theory that strongly emphasises the socially constructed rather than naturalistic nature of many social phenomena and especially of how they are perceived by social actors. Knowledge is treated as a matter of active interpretation rather than of detached description. For example, biological sex is an anatomical type whereas *gender* is a social construct.

Social contract An idea developed in the political theory of Thomas Hobbes (1588–1679), John Locke (1688–1774) and Jean-Jacques Rousseau (1712–78) to describe different kinds of social bargain in which social actors agree to exchange some of their individual freedoms for political control from the centre. The centre might be The Sovereign or Parliament. Mutual self-interest takes over from 'the war of all against all'.

Social Darwinism A generally derogatory term in social theory referring to attempts to describe social development as crudely operating according to the same mechanisms of the 'survival of the fittest' and 'natural selection' that Charles Darwin (1809–82) used to explain the development of biological species. Sometimes used to support ill-conceived notions of social engineering in which 'the weak' might be selected for extinction by 'the strong'. See *social evolution*.

Social evolution A term used in the sociological realm to describe the progress of society *as if it were developing* like a biological organism. This 'biological metaphor' is generally discredited in social theory as it cannot be assumed either that societies are a *holistic* entity and still less that they develop through the same mechanisms as biological organisms do. Often associated with Herbert Spencer (1820–1903). Sometimes inadequately referred to as *Social Darwinism*.

Social institutions Institutions and organisations in modern society concerned with the provision of economic and social well-being. Further distinctions can be made between public and private institutions. The former include the institutions of the *state* such as government offices, the civil service, the legal system, the military and security organisations, health, education and social welfare agencies. The latter include the institutions of *civil society* such as political parties, religious organisations, private firms, businesses and corporations. Social institutions provide much of the contextual infrastructure of *social action*.

Social integration/system integration Associated with the British sociologist David Lockwood (born 1929) (1964), is a way of distinguishing between the kind of technical or mechanical coordination associated with the functioning of the *social system* and forms of 'active consensus that might develop between social groups in society. Lockwood raises the distinction to show how the assumption in *functionalist* social theory that 'system integration' and 'social integration' are naturally related and always imply each other is misplaced. Even if the social system appears to be functioning at optimum efficiency it does not follow that a state of perfect *social order* will also be found.

Social interactionism/social interactionist An approach within the Chicago School of *micro* sociology developed during the 1940s and 1950s by G.H. Mead. Social interactionism is concerned with the exploration of social encounters in real-life situations. Adopting a *phenomenological* perspective social interactionists assume that the real substance and meaning of interaction is embedded within the interactive situation itself. Interaction produces effects and consequences that exceed the sum of its individual components. Distinct from the *macro* social theory developed by *functionalist* social theorists that attempts to develop abstract accounts of the whole social system.

Social order Originating with Émile Durkheim but taken up continuously during the 20th century by social theorists such as Talcott Parsons and Jürgen Habermas, the question of how social cohesion manages to survive under conditions of equally persistent social instability is one of the core preoccupations in social theory. 'The problem of order' takes different forms depending on which view the social theorist takes about what is *produced by* social cohesion. Systems theory sees social order *holistically* and in terms of the stability of the overall system. *Functionalist* theory (which is a variety of systems theory) sees social cohesion in terms of the generally long-term mutually beneficial functioning of the various parts of the social organism. Micro theory sees social cohesion in terms of the more transient moments in which successful social interaction takes place. Marxist theory tends to see social cohesion as a rather temporary and fragile period of momentary calm between periods of revolutionary social upheaval. A broad distinction can be made between social theorists who see consensus as the default setting of modern industrial society and those who see conflict as the default setting. Social order and social disorder coexist in a permanent state of dynamic tension.

Social practice Established ways of doing things in social life. The routines of behaviour that have become characteristic of a particular society. Social practices are inscribed in behaviour a bit like well-trodden footpaths in the countryside. Social practices become the normal or expected way of doing things and as such provide an important guide to *social action* and *social order*.

Social rationality A term used by Ulrich Beck to describe ideas and strategies based on agreement about social need and social benefit. The implication is that social rationality is altruistic and universalistic, that it serves the interests of the many rather than the few. Has some similarities with Habermas's concept of *communicative rationality*. Contrasts with *scientific-technical rationality*. See also *instrumental rationality*.

Social structure A disputed term in social theory but used approximately to refer to combinations of material and/or intellectual forces that have the *power* to shape *social action* beyond the control of individual social actors.

Social system See *general systems theory*.

Social theorists Academic specialists whose challenge is to develop coherent knowledge of human social action as it takes place in the context of other actors so acting and with the help or hindrance of the *social practices* and *social institutions* that surround them.

Social theory A body of knowledge about *society* and social life that emerges at the intersection between historical contexts (real events and circumstances) and intellectual contexts (key ideas, concepts and authors), between circumstances that *need* explaining and attempts *to* explain them. Social theory operates at a relatively high level of abstraction and takes the form of arguments and propositions about the essence of social interaction and experience.

Socialisation The process by which social actors, especially children, learn or acquire the norms, values and modes of behaviour that are characteristic of the society where they live. Successfully socialised social actors are those who have assimilated prevailing social norms and have accommodated their own actions accordingly.

Socialism A political doctrine based on the principle that social actors contribute equally to the production and maintenance of society. Notions of class especially those associated with ownership of private property and other forms of privilege are rejected. Summarised by Karl Marx in the slogan 'from each according to his ability and to each according to his needs'.

Society An abstract term devised by social and political theorists to refer to the bounded space in which social action takes place. A term for referring to actually existing geographical and territorial, legal, linguistic and culturally bounded entities that are often assumed to coincide with the various national states. There is much debate in social theory as to whether the abstract concept *society* is adequate for the task of analysing actually existing human communities *or societies*.

Sociology/sociologist An applied academic discipline concerned with gathering data about social phenomena in industrialised society using systematic, often *empirical*, methods. Emerging in European universities at the end of the 19th century along with *anthropology* and *psychology*, sociologists often use *social theory* to develop middle-range theories about such phenomena. Sociology has become increasingly interdisciplinary in its relations with other academic specialisms.

State The public realm of social life together with the public institutions and practices it is made of. The public bureaucracies of administration and governance are the most familiar forms of the state apparatus. Distinct from *civil society*.

Structuralism/structuralist A mode of systematic investigation into the structuring processes that control how phenomena are held together. Originated in the analytical linguistics of Ferdinand de Saussure in the first part of the 20th century but spread rapidly as a new methodology in anthropology, psychoanalysis, literature studies, developmental psychology, Marxism, media and cultural studies. See also *post-structuralism*.

Structuration A specialist term introduced by Anthony Giddens (1984) to describe *structure* not as a fixed entity that is part of the invariable context of *social action* but as a set of 'rules-and-resources' that allow the expression of *agency*. A common example is language, which, although having detailed rules that have to be followed, provides the principal means of communication.

Structure An entity, practice or phenomenon having an identifiable form that is regarded as remaining relatively stable over time. In social theory structure is generally regarded as providing the context for *action*. The exact nature and constitution of structure is a topic of much debate in social theory. See *social structure, structuration*.

Subjective/subjectivity Referring to the personal or interior thoughts and feelings of social actors. Acknowledges the emotional and personalised nature of social experience. Looking at meaning from the social actor's own point of view. Acknowledges variation and difference in perception. Distinct from *objective*.

Substantive rationality See *formal rationality*.

Surface structure Surface effects that are assumed to be controlled or produced by underlying deep structural forces such as the capacity for cognitive reasoning and language. Patterns and regularities at the surface that strongly imply the existence of underlying structuring processes. See also *deep structure, psychoanalysis*.

Surplus value An expression of how much the market price of a commodity exceeds the costs of producing it. For Karl Marx surplus value (or profit) is an expression of the amount of labour that has been put into making a commodity but which the labourer does not get paid for and is thus a measure of exploitation. See also *exchange value* and *use value*.

Symbolic interactionism An approach within the Chicago School of *micro* sociology developed during the 1940s and 1950s by Herbert Blumer. Similar to *social interactionism* developed by G.H. Mead, symbolic interactionism places great emphasis on the way social relations are largely constructed on the basis of symbolic exchanges and especially those using language and other means of meaning-formation.

Synchronic A specialist term for referring to the present-time dimension rather than the historical or *diachronic* dimension of phenomena. Often associated with the *structuralist* method in social theory in which the analysis of structures is treated abstractly without regard for when something happens. Structures may develop over time but time is not a necessary dimension *of* structure.

Syntagmatic A specialist technical term in structural linguistics referring to the rules and conventions of grammar and syntax that govern the linear or horizontal relations between language elements in a sentence. 'Mat the sat the on cat' breaks these rules and thus fails as an attempt at communication. Contrasts with *paradigmatic*.

Synthesis See *thesis/antithesis/synthesis*.

System integration/social integration See *social integration*.

System/lifeworld See *lifeworld/system*.

Systems theory See *general systems theory*.

Tautology A circular form of argument in which the validity of a proposition is assumed rather than challenged by subsequent propositions. For example, the statement 'tall people are successful because they are tall' tells us nothing about the qualities of tallness that bring success or about why success is related to tallness.

Teleology/teleological The capacity for, and nature of, development. In social theory an interest in how social actors are 'drawn forward' by the developmental trajectories they occupy rather than being 'pushed from behind' by past experiences. Human and social development might be described as 'teleological' rather than 'mechanical' to emphasise that there is a directionality and intentionality about it.

Thesis/antithesis/synthesis Associated particularly with G.W.F. Hegel and with Karl Marx, a form of reasoning in which an established set of ideas is challenged by a rival set until eventually a new set or synthesis emerges. The synthesis becomes the established view until it also is challenged. Marx suggests that actual historical change can be described in the same way. Feudal society is challenged by capitalist society and this conflict is resolved with the emergence of communist society.

Time–space distanciation A concept developed by Anthony Giddens (1990) to capture the ways in which one of the most evident differences between the pre-modern and modern society is that experiences of time and space have changed. 'Distanciation' describes these changes in terms of the shortening of geographical and temporal distances so that new relations emerge between things that are far away and those which are close at hand, between 'the local' and 'the global'. Similar to notions of time–space compression used by the geographer and cultural theorist David Harvey (1990), which refers to the shrinking of the planet as travel technologies have developed. See *globalisation*.

Transcendental subject Associated with *Enlightenment* thought, is the idea that human agents have inner properties of independence and autonomy that exist separately from or 'transcend' the immediate context. Also that such properties are universal in the sense that all human agents are affected by them. Implies that *agency* is not something that is shaped by social structure but which arises spontaneously as a property of the social *agent*. *Post-structuralist* social theorists in particular tend to reject the idea of the transcendental subject on the grounds that social existence is entirely constituted out of *discourses* of various kinds and that discourses have no permanent or time-escaping properties of their own. See also *biographical subject* and *human nature*.

Universal pragmatics A philosophical project which argues that misunderstanding and conflict often arise because one party misunderstands the terms of reference being used by the other party. The presumption that agreement can be reached is a universal characteristic of human communication.

Use value The use value of a commodity is a measure of how useful it is, in a very practical sense, in meeting a particular human need. See also *exchange value* and *surplus value*.

Utilitarianism/utilitarian A doctrine which holds that the main motivators of social action are the quest for pleasure and the avoidance of pain. Asserts that the purpose of society is to provide the greatest happiness for the greatest number. From a moral point of view, actions that produce pleasure are 'right' and those that produce pain are 'wrong'. This formulation was first put forward by the English philosophers Jeremy Bentham (1748–1832) and John Stuart Mill (1806–73).

Utopian An invented term made up from the Greek words 'ou' meaning 'no' and 'topos' meaning 'place' that was the name given to a fictional Atlantic island described by Thomas More in his book *Utopia* published in 1516. Utopian ideas and beliefs connote a highly *idealistic* conception of the perfect society characterised by freedom, equality, harmony and leisure.

Utopian socialism A term for distinguishing between pre-Marxist socialists and followers of 'scientific Marxism' developed by Karl Marx and Friedrich Engels. The word 'utopia' refers to an unattainable or non-existent state, and so the implication is that utopian socialists are idealists rather than realists. See *idealism* and *realism*.

Value-neutrality   Sometimes also referred to inaccurately as 'value-freedom', is a principle of method in social research highlighted by Max Weber, which is that although all research is infused with value-positions of various kinds (social research is very often precisely *about* the values social actors hold) researchers must strive not to allow their own values to invalidate the conclusions they express.

Values   *Ideas* that provide a source of motivation. Values might be based on religious beliefs or on ideas about desirable economic, political and ideological objectives and how to achieve them. For example, acting rationally in pursuit of individual economic advantage is part of the Western *capitalist value system*. Value has a different meaning in economics; see *use value*, *exchange value* and *surplus value*.

Value system   A combination of various ideas, values and beliefs that provide an intellectual and motivational template for action. Value systems are often referred to in order to justify or legitimise particular actions. The elements in the value system are likely to be consistent with one another hence 'system'.

Verstehen   Associated with Max Weber, is a German word meaning 'understanding'. Weber develops the term to describe the particular *methodology* of the social sciences, which is concerned with understanding and interpreting social action if possible from the point of view of the social actor. The *interpretive* approach and the style of *inductive reasoning* associated with it is a defining characteristic of the social-scientific technique. Distinguished from *deductive reasoning*, which is associated with the physical and biological sciences. See also *hermeneutics*.

Voluntarism/voluntaristic   The assumption that despite the influence of social structure social actors are not forced to act but choose to do so. Associated with the expression of autonomy and free will. See also *individualism*.

REFERENCES

Adorno, T.W. (1973 [1966]) *Negative Dialectics*. London: Routledge. Published in German.

Alexander, J. (1998) *Neofunctionalism and After*. Oxford: Blackwell.

Althusser, L. (1969) *For Marx*. London: Verso. Originally published in French.

Althusser, L. (1984 [1971]) 'Ideology and ideological state apparatuses', in *Essays in Ideology*. London: Verso.

Althusser, L. and Baliber, E. (1969 [1965]) *Reading Capital*. London: New Left Books. Originally published in French.

Andreski, S. (1983) *Max Weber on Capitalism, Bureaucracy and Religion: A Selection of Texts*. London: Allen & Unwin.

Archer, M. (1982) 'Morphogenesis versus structuration: On combining structure and agency', *British Journal of Sociology*, 33(4): 456–83.

Archer, M. (1988) *Culture and Agency: The place of culture in social theory*. Cambridge: Polity Press.

Archer, M. (1990) 'Theory, culture and post-industrial society', in Featherstone, M. (ed.) (1990), pp. 97–119.

Archer, M. (1995) *Realist Social Theory: The Morphogenic Approach*. Cambridge: Cambridge University Press.

Archer, M. (2000) *Being Human: The Problem of Agency*. Cambridge: Cambridge University Press.

Barrett, M. (1980) *Women's Oppression Today: Problems in Marxist-Feminist Analysis*. London: Verso.

Barthes, R. (1973 [1957]) *Mythologies*. London: Paladin Books. Originally published in French.

Barthes, R. (1977 [1968]) 'Death of the author', in *Image, Music, Text*. London: Fontana. Originally published in French.

Baudrillard, J. (1975 [1973]) *The Mirror of Production*. St Louis: Telos Press. Originally published in French.

Baudrillard, J. (1981 [1972]) *For a Critique of the Political Economy of the Sign*. St Louis: Telos Press. Originally published in French.

Baudrillard, J. (1983 [1981]) *Simulacra and Simulations*. New York: Semiotext(e).

Baudrillard, J. (1995) *The Perfect Crime*. London: Verso. Translated by Chris Turner, London: Verso.

Baudrillard, J. (1996 [1968]) *The System of Objects*. London: Verso. Originally published in French.

Baudrillard, J. (1998 [1970]) *The Consumer Society*. London: Sage. Originally published in French.

465

Beck, U. (1992 [1986]) *Risk Society: Towards a New Modernity*. Translated by M. Ritter. London: Sage. Originally published in German.

Beck, U., Giddens, A. and Lash, S. (1994) *Reflexive Modernization: Politics, Tradition and Aesthetics in the Modern Social Order*. Stanford: Stanford University Press.

Bhaskar, R. (1979) *The Possibility of Naturalism: A Philosophical Critique of the Contemporary Human Sciences*. London: Harvester Press.

Bhaskar, R. (2002) *Reflections on Meta-Reality: A Philosophy for the Present*. London: Sage.

Blumer, H. (1969) *Symbolic Interactionism: Perspective and method*. Berkeley: University of California Press.

Bourdieu, P. (1977 [1972]) *Outline of a Theory of Practice*. Translated by R. Nice. Cambridge: Cambridge University Press. Originally published in French.

Bourdieu, P. (1984 [1979]) *Distinction: A Social Critique of the Judgement of Taste*. Translated by R. Nice. London: Routledge and Kegan Paul. Originally published in French.

Brubaker, R. (1984) *The Limits of Rationality*. London: Allen & Unwin.

Butler, J. (1993) *Bodies that Matter: On the Discursive Limits of Sex*. London: Routledge.

Castells, M. (1996) *The Information Age*. Vol. 1, *The Rise of Network Society*. Oxford: Blackwell.

Castells, M. (1997) *The Information Age*. Vol. 2, *The Power of Identity*. Oxford: Blackwell.

Castells, M. (1998) *The Information Age*. Vol. 3, *End of Millennium*. Oxford: Blackwell.

Connell, R.W. (2002) *Gender*. Cambridge: Polity.

Delanty, G. (1999) *Social Theory in a Changing World: Conceptions of Modernity*. Cambridge: Polity Press.

Derrida, J. (1976 [1967]) *Of Grammatology*. Baltimore: Johns Hopkins University Press. Originally published in French.

Derrida, J. (1978 [1968]) *Writing and Difference*. London: Routledge.

Dogan, M. and Pahre, R. (1990) *Creative Marginality*. Boulder, CO: Westview Press.

Durkheim, É. (1933 [1893]) *The Division of Labour in Society*. Translated by George Simpson. New York: Free Press. This 2nd edn published in 1902, Paris: Alcan. Originally published in French.

Durkheim, É. (1964 [1895]) *The Rules of Sociological Method*. New York: Free Press. Published in French.

Durkheim, É. (1968a [1912]) *The Elementary Forms of Religious Life: The Totemic System in Australia*. London: George Allen & Unwin. Originally published in French.

Durkheim, É. (1968b [1897]) *Suicide*. London: Routledge. Originally published in French.

Durkheim, É. and Mauss, M. (1903) [Primitive Classification] 'De quelques formes primitives de classification: contribution à l'étude des representations collectives', *L'Année Sociologique*, Vol. vi, 1-72.

Engels, F. (1958 [1845]) *The Condition of the Working Class in England*, Oxford: Blackwell. Originally published in German.

Featherstone, M. (ed.) (1990) 'Introduction', in *Global Culture: Nationalism, Globalization and Modernity: A Theory, Culture and Society Special Issue*, pp. 1–14. London: Sage.

Featherstone, M. (ed.) (1992) *Cultural Theory and Cultural Change*. London: Sage.

Foucault, M. (1967 [1961]) *Madness and Civilization*. London: Tavistock. Originally published in French.

Foucault, M. (1970 [1966]) *The Order of Things*. London: Tavistock. Originally published in French.

Foucault, M. (1972 [1969]) *The Archaeology of Knowledge*. Translated by A. Sheridan. London: Tavistock. Originally published in French.

Foucault, M. (1977 [1975]) *Discipline and Punish*. London: Allen Lane. Originally published in French.

Foucault, M. (1979 [1976]) *The History of Sexuality, I: An Introduction*. London: Allen Lane. Originally published in French.

Foucault, M. (1980) *Power-Knowledge: Selected Interviews and Other Writings, 1972–1977*. Edited by C. Gordon. London: Harvester Wheatsheaf.

Foucault, M. (1985 [1984]) *The History of Sexuality, II: The Use of Pleasure*. New York: Pantheon Books. Originally published in French.

Foucault, M. (1986 [1984]) *The History of Sexuality, III: The Care of the Self*. New York Pantheon Books. Originally published in French.

Fraser, M. (2002) 'What is the matter of feminist criticism?', *Economy and Society* 31(4): 606–25.

Fraser, N. (1997) *Justice Interrupts: Critical Reflections on the 'Postsocialist' Condition*. London: Routledge.

Garfinkel, H. (1967) *Studies in Ethnomethodology*. Englewood Cliffs, NJ: Prentice Hall.

Giddens, A. (1984) *The Constitution of Society: Outline of the Theory of Structuration*. Malden, MA: Polity Press.

Giddens, A. (1990) *The Consequences of Modernity*. Cambridge: Polity Press.

Giddens, A. (1991) *Modernity and Self-Identity: The Self and Society in the Late Modern Period*. Cambridge: Polity Press.

Giddens, A (1999) *The Third Way: The renewal of Social Democracy*. Malden, Massachusettes: Polity Press.

Goffman, E. (1959) *The Presentation of Self in Everyday Life*. New York: Doubleday Anchor.

Goffman, E. (1961) *Asylums: Essays on the Social Situation of Mental Patients and Other Inmates*. Garden City NY: Anchor Books.

Goffman, E. (1964) *Stigma: Notes on the Management of Spoiled Identity.* Englewood Cliffs, NJ: Prentice-Hall.

Goffman, E. (1967) *Interaction Ritual: Essays in Face-To-Face Behavior.* New York: Pantheon.

Goffman, E. (1974) *Frame Analysis: An Essay on the Organization of Experience.* London: Harper and Row.

Goffman, E. (1981) *Forms of Talk.* Philadelphia: University of Pennsylvania Press.

Gramsci, A. (1971) *Selections from the Prison Notebooks.* Edited and translated by Q. Hoare and G. Nowell Smith. London: Lawrence and Wishart.

Habermas, J. (1981a) *The Theory of Communicative Action.* Vol. 1, *Reason and the Rationalization of Society.* Translated by T. McCarthy and published in English by Heinemann, London, in 1984. Originally published in German.

Habermas, J. (1981b) *The Theory of Communicative Action.* Vol. 2, *Lifeworld and System.* Translated by T. McCarthy and published in English by the Polity Press, Cambridge, in 1987. Originally published in German.

Habermas, J. (1989 [1962]) *The Structural Transformation of the Public Sphere.* Cambridge, MA: MIT Press. Originally published in German.

Hartmann, H. (1981) 'The unhappy marriage of Marxism and Feminism: Towards a more progressive union', in Sargent, L. (ed.) (1981). Originally published in *Capital and Class,* 1979, no 8: 1–33.

Harvey, D. (1990) *The Condition of Postmodernity: An Enquiry into the Origins of Cultural Change.* Oxford: Blackwell.

Hegel, G.W.F. (1910 [1807]) *The Phenomenology of Mind.* Translated by J.B. Baillie, New York: Macmillan. Originally published in German.

Hegel, G.W.F. (1991 [1821]) *Elements of the Philosophy of Right,* Edited by A.W. Wood. Translated by H.B. Nisbet, Cambridge: Cambridge University Press. Originally published in German.

Homans, G. (1958) 'Social behaviour as exchange', *American Journal of Sociology,* 62: 597–606.

Horkheimer, M. (1972 [1937]) 'Traditional and critical theory', in *Critical Theory.* New York: Herder and Herder. Originally published in German.

Horkheimer, M. and Adorno, T.W. (1972 [1947]) *The Dialectic of Enlightenment.* New York: Herder and Herder. Originally published in German.

Jameson, F. (1984) 'Postmodernism, or, the cultural logic of late capitalism', *New Left Review,* 146: 53–92.

Jameson, F. (1991) *Postmodernism, or, the Cultural Logic of Late Capitalism.* London: Verso.

Kumar, K. (1983 [1978]) *Prophecy and Progress: The Sociology of Industrial and Post-Industrial Society.* Harmondsworth: Penguin Books.

Lacan, Jacques. (1998 [1973]) *On Feminine Sexuality: The Limits of Love and Knowledge.* New York: Norton. Originally published in French.

Larrain, J. (1983) *Marxism and Ideology*. London: Macmillan.

Lash, S. and Urry, J. (1987) *The End of Organized Capitalism*. Cambridge: Polity Press.

Lash, S. and Urry, J. (1994) *Economies of Signs and Space*. London: Sage.

Lenin, V.I. (1917) *Imperialism, the Highest Stage of Capitalism*. Peking: Foreign Language Press (1964). English translation published in 1952 by Foreign Languages Publishing, Moscow.

Lenin, V.I. (1947) *What is to be Done?* Moscow: Progress Publishers.

Lévi-Strauss, C. (1963 [1958]) *Structural Anthropology*. New York: Basic Books. Originally published in French.

Lévi-Strauss, C. (1966) *The Savage Mind*. Chicago: Chicago University Press.

Lévi-Strauss, C. (1969 [1949]) *The Elementary Structures of Kinship.* Boston: Beacon Press. Originally published in French.

Lévi-Strauss, C. (1970 [1964]) *The Raw and the Cooked: Introduction to a Science of Mythology.* London: Jonathan Cape. Originally published in French.

Lévi-Strauss, C. (1973 [1955]) *Tristes Tropiques.* London: Jonathan Cape. Originally published in French.

Lockwood, D. (1964) 'System integration and social integration', in Zollschan, G. and Hirsch, W. (eds) *Explorations in Social Change.* London: Routledge and Kegan Paul, pp. 244–57.

Luhmann, N. (1995 [1984]) *Social Systems*. Stanford: Stanford University Press. Originally published in German.

Lukács, G. (1968) *History and Class Consciousness: Studies in Marxist Dialectics.* Translated by R. Livingstone. London: Merlin Press.

Lyotard, J.-F. (1984 [1979]) *The Postmodern Condition: A Report on Knowledge.* Translated by G. Bennington and B. Massumi, Foreword by Frederic Jameson. Manchester: Manchester University Press. Originally published in French.

MacKinnon, C. (1989) *Towards a Feminist Theory of the State*. Cambridge, MA: Harvard University Press.

McLellan, D. (1977) *Karl Marx: Selected Writings*. Oxford: Oxford University Press.

McLuhan, M. (1964) *Understanding Media*. Düsseldorf: ECON Velag.

Mandel, E. (1975) *Late Capitalism.* Translated by J. De Bres. London: NLB. Originally published in German in 1972.

Mannheim, K. (1936) *Ideology and Utopia*. London: Routledge. Originally published in German in 1929.

Marcuse, H., (1955) *Eros and Civilization: A Philosophical Inquiry into Freud*. Boston: Boston Beacon Press.

Marcuse, H. (1964) *One Dimensional Man: Studies in the Ideology of Advanced Industrial Society*. Boston: Beacon Press.

Marx, K. (1954 [1867]) *Capital*. Vol. 1. London: Lawrence and Wishart. Originally published in German.

Marx, K. (1973 [1953]) *Grundrisse: Foundations of the Critique of Political Economy*. London: Allen Lane in association with *New Left Review*. Written in German 1857-58.

Marx, K. (1975 [1844]) *Early Writings*. Introduction by L. Colletti, translated by R. Livingstone and G. Benton. Harmondsworth: Penguin.

Marx, K. (1977) *The Poverty of Philosophy*, in McLellan (1977).

Marx, K. and Engels, F. (1952 [1848]) *The Communist Manifesto*. Translated by S. Moore in 1888 from the 1st German edn of 1848. Moscow: Progress Publishers. First English translation by H. Macfarlane published in 1850.

Marx, K. and Engels, F. (1971 [1859]) *A Contribution to the Critique of Political Economy*. London: Lawrence and Wishart. Originally published in German.

Marx, K. and Engels, F. (1991) *The German Ideology*. Translated by C.J. Arthur. London: Lawrence and Wishart. This edition first published in 1970. First published in full in 1932. Originally Written in 1845.

Mead, G.H. (1932) *The Philosophy of the Present*. Edited by A.E. Murphy. New York: Prometheus Books.

Mead, G.H. (1934) *Mind, Self and Society from the Standpoint of a Social Behaviourist*. Edited by C.W. Morris. Chicago: University if Chicago Press.

Mead, G.H. (1938) *The Philosophy of the Act*. Edited by C.W. Morris. Chicago: University of Chicago Press.

Merton, R.K. (1949) *Social Theory and Social Structure*. New York: Free Press.

Mill, J. S. (1982 [1859]) *On Liberty*, London: Penguin.

Mills, C.W. (1953) *The Sociological Imagination*, London: Oxford University Press.

Mouzelis, N. (1995) *Sociological Theory: What Went Wrong?* London: Routledge.

Nisbet, R. (1967) *The Sociological Tradition*. London: Heinemann.

Parker, J. (2000) *Structuration*. Buckingham: Open University Press.

Parsons, T. (1937) *The Structure of Social Action*. New York: Free Press.

Parsons, T. (1951) *The Social System*. London: Routledge and Kegan Paul.

Parsons, T. and Shils, E. (1962) *Towards a General Theory of Action*. New York: Harper.

Poster, M. (2001) *Jean Baudrillard Selected Writings*. Edited and Introduced by M. Poster, 2nd edn (1st edn 1988). Cambridge: Polity Press.

Ransome, P.E. (1992) *Antonio Gramsci: A New Introduction*. Hemel Hempstead: Harvester Wheatsheaf.

Ransome, P.E. (2005) *Work, Consumption and Culture: Affluence and Social Change in the Twenty-First Century*. London: Sage.

Robertson, R. (1992) *Globalization: Social Theory and Global Culture.* London: Sage.

Rojek, C. and Turner, C. (eds) (1993) *Forget Baudrillard?* London: Routledge.

Saussure, F. de (1916 [1915]) *Course in General Linguistics.* London: Peter Owen. Originally published in French.

Simmel, G. (1978 [1900]) *The Philosophy of Money.* London: Routledge. Originally published in German.

Skinner, B.F. (1938) *The Behavior of Organisms: An Experimental Analysis,* New York: Appleton-Century-Crofts.

Smith, A. (1970 [1776]) *Inquiry into the Nature and Causes of the Wealth of Nations.* London: Routledge.

Spencer, H. (1876) *The Principles of Sociology,* 3 vols, New York: D. Appleton and Co.

Spencer, H. (1969 [1873]) *The Study of Sociology,* Ann Arbor: University of Michigan Press.

Spencer, H. (1970 [1851]) *Social Statics,* New York: Robert Schalkenbach Foundation.

Spencer, H. (1971 [1876-97]) *The Principles of Sociology,* in Thompson, K. and Tunstall, J. (eds).

Tawney, R.H. (1960 [1926]) *Religion and the Rise of Capitalism: An Historical Study,* (Holland Memorial Lectures, 1922). London: John Murray.

Thompson, J.B. and Held, D. (eds) (1989) *The Social Theory of Modern Societies: Anthony Giddens and his Critics.* Cambridge: Cambridge University Press.

Thompson, K. and Tunstall, J. (eds) (1971) *Sociological Perspectives: Selected Readings.* Harmondsworth: Penguin.

Tönnies, F. (1957 [1887]) *Community and Society.* New York: Harper & Row. Originally published in German.

Turner, B.S. (1993) 'Baudrillard for sociologists', in Rojek, C. and Turner, C. (eds), pp 70–87.

Urry, J. (2000) *Sociology Beyond Societies: Mobilities for the Twenty-First Century.* London: Routledge.

Urry, J. (2003) *Global Complexity.* Cambridge: Polity Press.

Walby, S. (1986) *Patriarchy at Work: Patriarchal and Capitalist Relations in Employment.* Cambridge: Polity Press.

Walby, S. (1990) *Theorizing Patriarchy.* Oxford: Basil Blackwell.

Walby, S. (1997) *Gender Transformations.* London: Routledge.

Watson, J.B. (1925) *Behaviorism.* New York: People's Institute Publishing Company.

Weber, M (1927 [1923]) *General Economic History.* Translated by F.H. Knight. London: Allen & Unwin. Originally published in German.

Weber, M. (1949 [1903-17]) *The Methodology of the Social Sciences.* Edited and translated by E.A. Shils and H.A. Finch. New York: Free Press.

Weber, M (1957 [1916]) *The Religion of China.* Translated by H.H. Gerth. New York: Free Press. Originally published in German.

Weber, M. (1958 [1916]) *The Religion of India.* Translated by H.H. Gerth and D Martindale. New York: Free Press. Originally published in German.

Weber, M. (1976 [1904-05]) *The Protestant Ethic and the Spirit of Capitalism.* Translated by T. Parsons. London: Allen & Unwin. This translation originally published in 1930. Weber's original text 1904–05.

Weber, M. (1978 [1921]) *Economy and Society.* Vols 1 and 2. Edited by G. Roth and C. Wittich. Berkeley, CA: University of California Press.

Weber, M. (1983) *Max Weber on Capitalism, Bureaucracy and Religion: A Selection of Texts.* Edited and in part newly translated by Stanislav Andreski. London: Allen & Unwin.

Winch, P. (1958) *The Idea of Social Science and its Relation to Philosophy.* London: Routledge.

Wittgenstein, L. (1961) *Tractatus Logico-Philosophicus.* London: Routledge and Kegan Paul. Originally published in German in 1921.

INDEX

A

abstract/abstraction 135, 153–4, 429
action 429
  and structure 11–12, 318–21
  see also social action
actor *see* agent
Adorno, Theodor 200, 201, 203–5, 206, 307
aesthetic reflexivity 387–8, 410
Age of Reason 23–5, 130, 223, 235, 260, 343, 429
agency 25, 429
  Archer 323, 407–8
  Giddens and Habermas 311, 312, 315
  Urry 399–400, 401
  unit act 145
AGIL system 147–9, 151
Alexander, Jeffrey 162, 406
alienation 66, 75–7, 192, 306, 325, 345, 429
  act of production 78
  and anomie 96
  common purpose 78
  impact on social theory 93–4
  loss of humanity 78
  praxis 204
  products 77
Althusser, Louis 57, 229–30, 233, 234, 330
  ideology 231–2, 241
  interpellation 233
  role of theory 232
  role of theory and of the intellectual 232
  social formation 230–1
anomie 57, 306, 325, 345, 429
  and alienation 96
  and the limits of the division of labour 57–8
  regulation, solidarity and the suicide rate 58–60
anthropology 223–4, 326, 429
anti-Enlightenment perspective 203–4, 292, 293
antithesis *see* thesis/antithesis/synthesis
apparatus 256
Archer, Margaret 322–3, 407–8
  morphogenics 408–9
Aristotle 22
ascetic, asceticism 114, 430
authoritarian 101, 430
autopoietic system 395, 430

B

Barrett, Michèle 285
Barthes, Roland 212, 240, 242, 339
  form and substance 243–4
  knowledge 244–5, 264
  myths 247–8, 343, 346, 349–50, 362
  semiotics and culture 245–6
Baudrillard, Jean 90–1, 206, 339, 359–60
  evaluation of 364–9
  hyper-reality 252, 363–4, 377
  impact on social theory 369–74
  sign-values 360–2
  simulacra 362–3
Bauman, Zygmunt 404
Beck, Ulrich 379
  cultural theory 406
  de-traditionalisation 382–3
  defining risks as global phenomena 383–4

expert knowledge and popular protest 380–1
from scientific rationality to social rationality 381–2
  globalisation 392
  risk society 380
  weakness of the risk-society scenario 384–5
behaviourist psychology 146, 430
belief system 10–11, 430
beliefs 9–11, 430
Benjamin, Walter 204
Bentham, Jeremy 32, 53
Bhaskar, Roy 322, 417–18
biographical subject 387, 430
biography 210, 235, 430
Blair, Tony 325
Blumer, Herbert 133, 170, 174, 211
bodies 270–1
boundedness 415–16, 422, 425–7, 431
  of disciplines 423–5
  of society and national society 422–3
Bourdieu, Pierre 84, 291, 325–6, 331
  agency and structure 326
  habitus 327–9, 332
  habitus and social change 329–31, 333–4
bourgeois 100
Brubaker, R. 119–20
bureaucracy 108, 117–18, 143, 345, 431
  and Giddens 352, 353, 355
  instrumental rationality 303–4
bureaucratisation 118, 325, 431
Butler, Judith 272–6

C

Calvin, John 114–15
capital 3
capitalism 431
  Baudrillard 361–2
  Frankfurt School 199–200, 201
  Giddens 353
  Jamieson 409–11
  Lash and Urry 386–7
  Marx 76–8, 79–80, 82, 84, 85–6, 90–3, 229–30, 352
  Marxism 192–3
  Weber 10, 99, 112–13, 115–17
capitalist 77, 84, 431
capitalist society 1, 3–4, 229, 431
Castells, Manuel 394, 397, 405
change *see* social change
charismatic leadership 128
Chicago School 165, 169, 209
  see also social interactionism
Chomsky, Noam 223, 228
civil consensus 127
civil society 32, 47–8, 69, 431
class 82–3, 87–8, 124, 431
class consciousness 193–5
class interests 85
coercion 198–9
collective approach 94–5
collective consciousness 110
common sense 176–7, 431
communicative action 295–302, 313, 324–5, 331, 332
  criticisms of 308–10
communicative rationality 303–5, 432

473